A

HISTORY OF EDUCATION

IN THE

STATE OF OHIO.

A CENTENNIAL VOLUME.

PUBLISHED BY AUTHORITY OF THE GENERAL ASSEMBLY.

COLUMBUS, OHIO.
1876.

THE GAZETTE PRINTING HOUSE.

PREFACE.

At the annual meeting of the Ohio Teachers' Association, in July, 1875, it was resolved that a complete historical record of educational effort and progress in Ohio should form a part of the representation of the educational interests of the State at the Centennial Exhibition in Philadelphia. This recommendation was approved by the State Board of Centennial Managers, and the Centennial Committee of the Ohio Teachers' Association was entrusted with the preparation and publication of the proposed volume.

At a meeting of this Committee, held in the office of the State Commissioner of Common Schools, October 1st and 2d, 1875, E. E. White, of Columbus, and Thos. W. Harvey, of Painesville, were appointed general editors. The preparation of the several chapters was subsequently assigned to different persons, as follows:

School Legislation—Eli T. Tappan, Professor of Mathematics in Kenyon College, Gambier.

Ungraded Schools—Alston Ellis, Superintendent of Public Schools, Hamilton.

Graded Schools—R. W. Stevenson, Superintendent of Public Schools, Columbus.

High Schools and Academies—D. F. DeWolf, Superintendent of Public Schools, Toledo.

Higher Education—Prof. E. B. Andrews, Lancaster.

Normal Schools—Delia A. Lathrop, Principal of the City Normal School, Cincinnati.

Teachers' Institutes—Thos. W. Harvey, Painesville.

SCHOOL SUPERVISION—John Hancock, Superintendent of Public Schools, Dayton.

TEACHERS' ASSOCIATIONS—E. E. White, Columbus.

PENAL, REFORMATORY, AND BENEVOLENT INSTITUTIONS—E. D. Mansfield, LL. D., Morrow.

BIOGRAPHICAL SKETCHES AND EDUCATIONAL PERIODICALS—W. D. Henkle, Editor of Ohio Educational Monthly, Salem.

The chapters have been written by the persons appointed, under the supervision of the general editors. Though prepared, in most instances, in such intervals of leisure as can be commanded by persons engaged in the exacting duties of professional life, it is believed that the leading facts in the history of education in Ohio have been stated with great accuracy. Much care has been taken to consult all known sources of information. School reports, educational journals, volumes of statutes, local historical sketches, etc., have been examined, and a free use made of the facts contained in them. It has not been deemed necessary or advisable to refer, except in a few cases, to the sources from which facts have been obtained.

The omission of special reference to the Female Seminaries in the State is not intentional on the part of the committee or editors. There is not a large number of these institutions in Ohio, but they rank among the best in the Union. They have received a generous patronage in the past, and are now enjoying a marked degree of prosperity.

The plan adopted for the preparation of this volume, has made some repetition necessary, but care has been taken to avoid, as far as possible, the repetition of details given in the appropriate chapter.

It has been the aim of the editors to secure a general uniformity in the use of capitals and in punctuation, but the taste of the several writers has been consulted.

E. E. WHITE.
THOS. W. HARVEY.

June, 1876.

TABLE OF CONTENTS.

CHAPTER I.

CHAPTER II.

CHAPTER III.

CHAPTER IV.

CHAPTER V.

CHAPTER VI.

CHAPTER VII.

CHAPTER VIII.

CHAPTER IX.

CHAPTER X.

CHAPTER XI.

CHAPTER XII.

EDUCATION IN OHIO.

CHAPTER I.

SCHOOL LEGISLATION.

The State of Ohio is situated centrally among the States of the Union. It extends from Lake Erie on the north to the Ohio river on the south, an average distance of nearly two hundred miles. From Pennsylvania on the east to Indiana on the west, the distance is about two hundred and twenty miles. The area is nearly forty thousand square miles, the State being nearly square.

The first immigrants came from the older states to the Ohio Valley in the year 1788. The population, in the year 1800, was 45,365. In 1840, the number reached 1,519,467. Ohio was then the third state in population, and has maintained the same rank at each succeeding decennial census. In 1870, the number was 2,665,260, and the increase during the last six years has been about 200,000.

ORGANIC LAWS.

Legislation concerning schools in the territory north-west of the Ohio river began in the Continental Congress, which was organized under the Articles of Confederation.

2

In the year 1787, Congress provided, by ordinance, a temporary government for this north-western territory, until the number of inhabitants should justify the formation of a state, to be admitted to the Union "on an equal footing with the original states."

The ordinance of 1787, after some general laws and the form of territorial government, set forth six articles of compact between the original states and the people and states of the territory, which articles shall "forever remain unalterable, unless by mutual consent." The following is part of Article III:

"Religion, morality and knowledge, being necessary to good government and the happiness of mankind, schools and the means of education shall forever be encouraged."

It was also inserted in one of these articles of compact, that no local legislature should ever interfere with the primary disposal of the soil by the United States. The land was to be the great source of endowment for schools.

The ordinance of 1787 was the organic law of all the territory lying north of the Ohio and east of the Mississippi, until Ohio, the first state formed within these limits, was admitted to the Union, with a constitution formed in November, 1802. The following is from Article VIII of this constitution:

"SEC. 3. Religion, morality and knowledge, being essentially necessary to good government and the happiness of mankind, schools and the means of education shall forever be encouraged by legislative provision, not inconsistant with the rights of conscience."

This is evidently copied from the ordinance, with an attempt to make it more precise and guarded. The following from the same article is also intended to guard against possible injustice:

"SEC. 25. No law shall be passed to prevent the poor in the several counties and townships within this State from an equal participation in the schools, academies, colleges, and universities within this State, which are endowed in whole or in part from the revenue arising from donations made by the United States for the support of schools and colleges; and the doors of said schools, academies and universities shall be open for the reception of scholars, students, and teachers of every grade, without any distinction or preference whatever, contrary to the intent for which said donations were made."

The above, with the following, is all that relates to education in the first constitution of Ohio:

"SEC. 27. Every association of persons, when regularly formed, within this State, and having given themselves a name, may, on application to the legislature, be entitled to receive letters of incorporation, to enable them to hold estates, real and personal, for the support of their schools, academies, colleges, universities, and for other purposes."

It seems doubtful whether the framers of this constitution contemplated any other legislation to encourage schools, than the granting of corporate power and the protection of rights of person and property. They seem to have believed that twelve hundred square miles of land, including the three college townships, would be adequate to the support of "schools, academies, colleges, and universities." It is very evident that they did not contemplate any gap between the several grades, but expected students to pass regularly from the school to the university.

The constitution of 1802 was superseded by that of 1851, which remains still in force. A sentence in the bill of rights again repeats the clause from Article III of the ordinance, with slight verbal changes, not amendments. There is also the following separate article on education:

"SEC. 1. The principal of all funds arising from the sale or other disposition of lands, or other property granted or entrusted to this State for educational and religious purposes, shall forever be preserved inviolate and undiminished, and the income arising therefrom shall be faithfully applied to the specific objects of the original grants or appropriations.

"SEC. 2. The General Assembly shall make such provisions, by taxation or otherwise, as, with the income arising from the school trust fund, will secure a thorough and efficient system of common schools throughout the State; but no religious or other sect or sects shall ever have any exclusive right to, or control of, any part of the school funds of this State."

The first section is simply a pledge of the honor of the State to the faithful execution of a trust. The second indicates, that in half a century the sentiment of Ohio had grown from encouragement of schools to the demand for a thorough and efficient system.

This constitution also recognizes and sanctions the permissive feature of the school legislation of Ohio. Among the restrictions upon the legislative power is the one that no act, "except such as relates to public schools," shall be passed, to take effect upon the approval of any other authority than the General Assembly.

SCHOOL LANDS.

Before the coming of the first settlers to the territory northwest of the Ohio, before any provision for their government, the Continental Congress, in 1785, made an ordinance for the survey and disposition of the land which they were to occupy. This law reserved from sale "lot number 16 of every township, for the maintenance of public schools within the said township." Each township was to be six miles square, thus containing thirty-six square miles or sections. The section or lot number 16 is one of the four at the center of the township. Several of the states made claims to the ownership of all or part of this western territory. The Continental Congress, before the formation of the present constitution of the national government, made compromises with those states which did not voluntarily yield their claims. Thus the State of Connecticut retained the ownership of the land between Lake Erie and the forty-first parallel of latitude, and extending westward one hundred and twenty miles from the western boundary of Pennsylvania. This was called the Connecticut Reserve, frequently the

Western Reserve. The State of Virginia retained as much of the land between the Scioto and the Little Miami as might suffice, with other lands which belonged to Virginia, to satisfy the bounties which had been promised by that state to her soldiers who had served in the war of the Revolution. Both states yielded all claim to territorial jurisdiction or powers of government.

It has been said, and the state of the public treasury in 1785 warrants the assertion, that the reservation of a section of land for the support of schools in every township, was a business operation on the part of Congress, in order "to induce purchasers." This only transfers the credit from the legislators to the people at large. The greatest inducement that could be offered to immigrants was the endowment of schools in every township. Congress was actuated by far-seeing wisdom; these legislators were laying the foundations of great states, and they knew that there could be no more solid basis for the structure than religion, morality, and knowledge.

During the existence of the territorial government, there was no legislation by the territorial authorities, upon the subject of schools or school lands, except a law passed in in 1799 to punish the offense of destroying trees on school lands, and an act passed in 1802 to incorporate the American Western University in the town of Athens. No organization was effected under this act, and it was superseded in 1804 by an act of the state legislature.

The ordinance of 1785 reserved for support of schools part of all lands belonging to Congress, but made no provision for maintenance of public schools in the Connecticut Reserve and the Virginia Reservation. These together are one-fourth of the present territory of the State of Ohio. In addition, Congress, in 1796, appropriated a tract of nearly four thousand square miles to satisfy land bounties granted to officers and soldiers of the army of the Revolution. This tract, nearly in the center of the present state, was surveyed into townships of five miles square, with no reservation for school purposes. These defects were remedied in the following manner.

In 1802, the Congress of the United States authorized the inhabitants of the territory to form a constitution and state government. The act provided for the election of a constitutional convention, to assemble in November, and Congress offered to the convention: 1st, section 16 in every township for the use of schools; 2nd, one township and two sections of salt lands; and 3d, one twentieth of the net proceeds of the sales of Congress lands within the State, to be applied to making public roads; *provided*, that the convention should make an ordinance that all lands to be sold by Congress should be exempt from taxation until five years from the day of sale.

The convention wisely proposed to accept the offer, if Congress would agree to make a donation equal to one thirty-sixth part of the lands of the United States Military District for the support of schools in that tract, and that a like provision should be made for the support of schools in the Virginia Reservation, so far as the unlocated lands in that tract would supply the proportions aforesaid; and also, that a donation of the same kind, or such provision as Congress should deem expedient, should be made to the inhabitants of the Connecticut Reserve; that one thirty-sixth of all lands afterwards to be purchased from the Indians, should likewise be given for the support of public schools; and that the title of all lands before mentioned should be vested in the legislature of the State for said purpose.

Congress assented, in a short time, to these modifications of the contract. Immediately, lands within the present counties of Guernsey, Coshocton, Muskingum, Licking, Delaware, and Morrow were given for school purposes in the United States Military District. These lands amounted to

112½ square miles, "being the one thirty-sixth part of the estimated whole amount of lands within that tract." In fact, it was two or three square miles in excess of that quantity. The land in the Virginia Reservation was still open to location with bounty warrants, and it seems that no school lands were located within that district; but in 1807 Congress appropriated land for schools for the inhabitants of the Virginia Military Reservation, within the limits of the present counties of Holmes, Wayne, Ashland, Richland, Crawford, and Morrow, amounting to 165 square miles. This was probably as much as one thirty-sixth part of the territory between the Scioto and Little Miami rivers.

Congress also gave 87½ square miles of land within the present counties of Tuscarawas and Holmes, for schools for the inhabitants of the Connecticut Western Reserve. This was not equal to one thirty-sixth of the Reserve; but a large part of that district was still in the occupation of the Indians. In 1805, the Indians by treaty ceded the lands to the United States. It was not until 1834 that Congress gave, from other public lands in the north-western part of the State, 59 square miles, making, with the former donation, an amount equal to one thirty-sixth of the area of the Connecticut Reserve.

Along the Ohio river every township was fractional—that is, it contained less than thirty-six square miles—and the same thing occurred in many parts of the State, at the boundaries of the land districts. The original grant of school lands to every township was generously executed in all these cases. Every fraction as large as three-fourths of a township was allowed a whole section; every fraction of more than half and less than three-fourths was allowed three quarter sections; every fraction of more than a fourth and less than a half township was allowed a half section; and every fraction of more than one square mile and less than a fourth part of a township was allowed a quarter section. These school lands were selected by the Secretary of the Treasury from public lands either in or near the fractional townships. Also, to several whole townships, in which section sixteen had been disposed of by the government agents, a section of land was allowed as in case of fractional townships. Thus, finally, eleven hundred square miles, one thirty-sixth part of all the land in the State of Ohio, was devoted to the maintenance of public schools.

In the ordinance of 1785, Congress reserved three Indian villages on the Upper Muskingum river, now called the Tuscarawas, for the use of the Christian Indians. This grant was enlarged to include 12,000 acres, and the title was vested in the Moravian Missionaries in trust for the Indians; but in 1824, Congress making other provision for the Indians, the land was reconveyed to the United States. Then, one thirty-sixth part of the land was set apart for the use of schools, the title being vested in the State of Ohio.

It has been claimed, with great reason, that Ohio paid in full for all her school lands by yielding her right to tax the land within her limits belonging to the general government, and by yielding the right to tax land sold for five years from date of purchase. However, the foundation of the public school system in the new states was the act of the Congress of the United States, the policy of Congress being that of a wise proprietor of an immense domain. Ohio was the first of the five states formed in the territory north of the Ohio river, the first state formed on land belonging to the nation. The spirit which we have seen gradually pervading the national legislation on this subject with reference to Ohio, has been the established rule with all the other new states. In those admitted since about the middle of this century, the portion has been doubled, so that they receive one eighteenth of the land for public school purposes. Every child educated in a public school in any of these new states, is in a peculiar manner a beneficiary of the Union.

In addition to the grants of lands for the public schools, three townships were secured for the establishment of schools of a higher rank. In 1787, the Ohio Company made a contract for the purchase from Congress of a million and a half of acres in the south-eastern part of the territory. One of the covenants in the bargain was, that two townships of land should be set apart for the endowment of a university under the management of the territorial or state legislature. Two townships were selected, being the one in which the town of Athens is situated, and the one next south of it. In the same year, Mr. John Cleves Symmes, encouraged by the success of the Ohio Company, proposed to purchase the land between the Great and Little Miami rivers. Instead of two townships for a university, he asked that "one only be assigned for the benefit of an academy." Mr. Symmes partially failed to fulfill his contracts, and no land was dedicated for this purpose within the bounds of his purchase; but in 1803, Congress gave to the State other lands west of the Great Miami river, equal in quantity to one township, "in lieu of the college township given to Symmes." In 1804, the General Assembly of Ohio passed an act to establish the Ohio University in the town of Athens; and in 1809, an act to establish the Miami University. The latter was, in 1810, located at Oxford, on the land last mentioned.

The care and management of these embryo universities and their land endowments was entrusted to the State. How this trust was executed is shown by the fact that the yearly income of the Ohio University from the forty-six thousand acres is only a little over four thousand dollars, and that the income of the Miami University from her twenty-three thousand acres is less than six thousand dollars. About the year 1843, the former institution was closed for several years on account of financial embarrassment; and the same cause has shut the doors of the Miami University since 1873. Yet some of the most distinguished men of the State and of the nation have been educated at these schools.

LEASES OF LANDS.

The first General Assembly of the State of Ohio convened in March, 1803. This body passed an act to provide for leasing the school lands in the several parts of the State, "for the purpose of improving the same, and thereby rendering them productive, that the profits arising therefrom may be applied to the support of schools." Accordingly, it was enacted that the school lands within the United States Military Tract should be leased for terms not exceeding fifteen years, and the "number sixteen" sections not exceeding seven years. The rent for every quarter section of one hundred and sixty acres was to consist in making the following improvements: fifteen acres cleared of all timber and other wood, and fenced in separate fields, one field of five acres to be sowed down in grass, and one of three acres to be planted with one hundred thrifty and growing apple trees, and the remaining seven acres to be arable land; these improvements to be made within the first twelve years in the fifteen year leases, and within the first five years in the seven year leases.

The Governor was authorized to appoint suitable agents in the several counties and districts, to make these leases. The agents were to give public notice, and were to receive bids and make leases to those bidders who should offer to make the improvements required for the .shorter term of lease. The agents were also to have the care of the lands, and might bring actions against persons wasting the timber, one-half of the sum recovered to belong to the agent and the remainder to be for the use of schools.

Two years after, in 1805, that part of the above act which relates to sections sixteen was so amended that the several boards of township trustees were authorized to grant leases of such lands for terms not exceeding fifteen years, "to those who make the most advantageous proposals." It was made the duty of the trustees "to see that the proceeds arising from the leases be duly and impartially applied to the education of youths, within the particular surveyed township, in such a manner that all the citizens resident therein may be equal partakers of the benefits thereof."

The first act looked only to the improvement of the property and its preservation from damage by trespassers. This act is the first contemplating revenue and providing for its application to the use of schools.

Before the adoption of the first state constitution, in 1802, Ohio had been divided into nine counties. The process of division was continued till the adoption of the second constitution, in 1851, when there were eighty-eight counties, the present number. Each county is divided into townships, and the boundaries of the townships may be changed by the county commissioners, under certain restrictions. These civil townships might not coincide with the "original surveyed" townships which had been marked off by the United States surveyors for the purposes of sale. Yet section sixteen had been given for the use of the citizens of the original township. This distinction applies only to those parts of the State which were originally laid out in square townships of thirty-six square miles, and to fractions of such townships. In these, however, the distinction is kept up to the present time, and a knowledge of it is necessary to an understanding of school laws.

Accordingly, in 1806, an act was passed to incorporate every original surveyed township, even when there was "a county line running through" it. This act provided for the election of three trustees and a treasurer. The power to grant leases was transferred to these boards, the act of 1805 being thus far amended. It was made their duty to take care of the lands, and to apply the rents paid in cash to the use of schools in the township. The rents paid in produce were to be disposed of in the "manner best calculated to promote the interest of the institution."

In 1809, an important change was made. Hitherto the leases were for limited periods, not exceeding fifteen years. In two or three instances, perpetual leases had been authorized by special laws—for instance, the lands belonging to the Ohio University. In this year, a law was enacted for the survey and disposition of the lands recently granted by Congress for the use of schools in the Virginia Military Reservation. These lands were now ordered to be surveyed in quarter sections, and after public notice, to be sold to the highest bidder, at not less than two dollars per acre in addition to the costs of survey and sale, these costs to be paid down; but on the remainder the purchaser was to pay yearly forever six per centum, "subject, however, to alteration by any succeeding legislature, so as to enable the purchaser or purchasers to make such commutation as said legislature may think expedient."

In effect, this was a perpetual lease with proviso for alterations in favor of the tenant, but with no provision for revaluation or any other change in favor of the schools. The next year, the legislature agreed to a cash payment of ten dollars per quarter section, as a commutation of the cash payment for cost of survey and *for five years of rent.* The rent on one hundred and sixty acres for five years would have been at least ninety-six dollars. It was also enacted that the tenant must make certain improvements and build a house within three years. In 1813, a further time of one year was allowed to make these improvements, many of the lessees having been "driven from their possession by the savage enemies." In 1814, a further time of one year was allowed. In 1816, the laws relating to leases of Virginia Military school lands were replaced by a new statute, the most important section requiring all subsequent leases of these lands to contain a proviso for the revaluation of the land in the year 1835, and every twenty years thereafter, without taking into consideration the improvements, the rent to be six per centum per annum on each valuation.

In the year 1817, a law was enacted to provide for leasing sections sixteen. This act was drawn up in a bungling manner. The trustees of original townships, and in case no such trustees had been elected in the township, the county commissioners, were authorized to lease the lands for terms of ninety-nine years, renewable forever, at an annual rental of six per centum of their value as appraised by disinterested freeholders, but the lands were to be subject to a revaluation every thirty-three years. If no applicant would pay so high a rent, then after twelve months the lands might be leased to the highest bidder. The same powers to lease the school lands in the United States Military District were given to the courts of common pleas in the several counties of that district. The framers of this act paid no attention to the law limiting the terms of leases of section sixteen to fifteen years, as provided in the act to incorporate the original surveyed townships. The last named act was again revised in 1824, the limitation of leases to fifteen years being re-enacted. It was again revised in 1831, the length of leases being reduced to seven years for improvement leases, and three years for leases of improved lands. But in 1823, a law had been enacted that no lease should thereafter be granted of any school lands in Ohio for a longer term than one year.

What was the actual income from sections sixteen, we have no means of knowing. From 1821 to 1828, the State borrowed the income of the Virginia Reservation school lands, paying annual interest and compounding the same every year. In 1825 and 1826, the income was about five thousand dollars, but it was less in previous years. In January, 1829, the fund amounted, with interest, to $54,000, which was then by law distributed among the several counties and parts of counties in that district, in proportion to the number of children in each, "except black and mulatto children;" and the law provided for the annual distribution of the income thereafter by the same rules. The income from the school lands in the settled portions of the State may be assumed to have been as much per acre as the above.

During the years of various and contradictory legislation for leasing the lands, those who made the laws were becoming convinced that any system of leases was bad. In 1821, Governor Brown, in his annual message to the General Assembly, said:

"So far as my information extends, the appropriation of the school lands in this state has produced hitherto (with few exceptions) no very material advantage in the dissemination of instruction—none commensurate with their presumable value."

SALE OF LANDS.

As a remedy, it was proposed that the lands should be sold absolutely; but there might be doubts as to the power of the State to sell without the consent of the Congress of the United States. Accordingly, in 1824, a memorial was addressed to Congress by the "State of Ohio in General Assembly." This memorial first gives a statement of the various grants of school lands in the State; then, in a few words, refers to the effort to render them productive, in particular by the method of leasing. Experience, however, had fully demonstrated that this fund would be wholly unavailing in its present shape.

By reason of the facilities which the State of Ohio afforded for acquiring a property in real estate, a necessity existed of leasing the lands in question to persons almost wholly destitute of pecuniary means, whereby the avails were rendered at least uncertain. The tenants were of the lowest class of the community, persons who possessed no permanent interest in the soil. They wasted the timber, and the loss was equal, perhaps, to the whole revenue which may have been derived. The fact that the State was compelled to offer upon lease so great a proportion of her soil as to invite and retain a population of a character not to be desired, also deserved consideration. In the language of the memorial, "The great body of those who constitute the strength and basis of every government, and who are to be considered as the friends of good order and public improvement, are among those who are the owners as well as occupiers of the soil."

The memorial might have added, that this tenant element of the population, having the right of suffrage, exerts a pernicious influence on legislation, and procures the enactment of laws in the interest of the renter rather than for the good of the school fund.

The memorial proceeds to assert that the State has the power of disposing of these lands in fee, and this is maintained by a convincing legal argument; yet an act of Congress declaring the authority of the State of Ohio to sell the school lands, would be productive of benefit by removing every doubt.

Congress took no action in reply to this memorial. After waiting three years, the General Assembly began to provide for the sale of the school lands in the State. In January, 1827, three acts were passed: 1. To provide for obtaining the consent of the inhabitants of the United States Military District to the sale of lands appropriated to the use of schools in said district, and to authorize the lessees of said lands to surrender their leases and receive certificates of purchase. 2. To provide for the sale of section sixteen, granted by Congress for the use of schools. 3. To enable the inhabitants of the Virginia Military District, to give their consent or dissent to the sale of lands, granted by Congress for the use of schools in said district.

It was made the duty of the county assessor, in all the counties of the United States Military District, to take a vote of all the white male inhabitants over 21 years of age. The name of each voter was to be entered in a book, in a column of those "in favor of a sale," or in a column of those "opposed to the sale." A similar duty was imposed upon the assessor of every county in which there was an original surveyed township or fractional township owning school lands. Several months were allowed for taking this vote. A simple method was taken for deciding the legality of any contested vote. In the United States Military District, the results were to be returned to the Secretary of State before the first of July following; and the results in the case of section sixteen were to be returned to the Auditor of State the next October. In the former case, the Governor was immediately to proclaim the result, if in favor of sale. The returns of votes on the sale of section sixteen were to be reported to the General Assembly; and when no vote was taken in any township owning such a section, or when a majority voted against a sale, another vote might be taken in any subsequent year. Whenever the vote was in favor of sale, the land should be "offered for sale in such year as the legislature may direct." The vote of the inhabitants of the Virginia Military District was to be taken at the ensuing October election of state officers. It was also viva voce. The act only provided for taking the vote and returning the result to the General Assembly at the next session. The vote was in favor of a sale, both in the United States Military District and the Virginia Reservation, also in some townships.

The act of 1827 contained full and careful details for the manner of selling a section sixteen. When the land was not leased, or the lease was to expire within a year, the land was to be re-appraised with all the improvements, and to be sold to the highest bidder at not less than the appraised value—one-fourth cash, the remainder in three annual payments without interest. If not sold for want of bidders, the county auditor might sell at private sale, but not at less than the appraised value. Early in 1828, laws were enacted for conducting the sales of both the Virginia Military and the United

States Military school lands, and the unleased portions were ordered to be sold during that year. These laws were similar to those for the sale of section sixteen; but in the sale of the Virginia Military school lands, the deferred payments were to bear interest, and in the sale of the United States Military school lands, the purchaser was to pay one-sixth down and the remainder in five annual payments without interest.

In all these acts for the sale of unleased lands, provision was made for the leased lands also. Every owner of a permanent lease might surrender his estate, and then, after paying all rents due, he was entitled to purchase the land at the last appraised value—one-eighth cash down, and the remainder in seven annual payments with interest. In the two military districts, the payment was in ten installments. These very generous enactments were amended several times within a few years, and generally the amendments were in favor of the lessees, and never against their interests.

The operation of these laws was thus described by Hon. Samuel Lewis, the first Superintendent of the Common Schools of the State, in his first annual report, in January, 1838.

> "The tenant may surrender his lease, and, on paying the former appraisement, take a deed in fee simple for the land sometimes worth six times as much as he pays. Cases have come to my knowledge where land has been taken at six dollars per acre, worth, at the time, fifty dollars. * * * The tenants, to be sure, make their fortunes, but the schools are sacrificed."

In March, 1838, the sections of the law authorizing surrenders by the tenants of section sixteen, were repealed, but similar laws for lands belonging to the two military districts remained in force. However, in 1839, the sections of the law of 1827 were revived with this modification—the holders of perpetual leases of school lands were allowed the further time of one year to surrender their leases and become entitled to certificates of purchase, on paying all the rent

3

due and the value as found by a new appraisement, to be made by three disinterested freeholders under oath, appointed by the court of common pleas. The appraisement was to be of the land alone without reference to improvements. The time was repeatedly extended by subsequent acts, and the manner of authorizing the sale was also amended. In 1843, a law was passed revising the whole subject, the provisions of which remain substantially still in force.

It was declared in the first section, that when any law shall authorize the sale of school lands, the proceedings should be regulated by this act. As the act of 1827 was not repealed, it was requisite that the legislature direct the time of sale of any section sixteen. In 1852, this law was re-enacted with slight change, the first section providing that all school lands known as section sixteen may be sold; the act of 1827 was repealed—so that since 1852 the whole business has been under the control of the township authorities and the courts, except so far as frequent special and local laws have interfered.

Since 1843, the vote of any original surveyed township upon the question of selling the school lands belonging to such township, is taken by ballot. If a majority vote against sale, at least one year must elapse before another vote. If the majority is for the sale, the court of common pleas appoints appraisers who must not be residents of the township. These, under oath, with the aid of the county surveyor, divide the land into such parcels as will be best for the sale, and appraise the value of each parcel. The court examines the proceedings, and if satisfied, decrees that all is just and fair. The auditor of the county, after publication, sells the land at public sale to the highest bidder, at not less than the appraisement, one-twelfth cash down and the balance in eleven equal annual payments, with interest. This was reduced to one-third down and two annual payments in 1873. If no person bids as high as the appraised value of the land or some parcel of it, the auditor may offer it again, after the required notice. If not sold within two years, the court may direct a new appraisement or authorize the auditor to offer it for sale again under the former appraisement. The proceedings in the case of permanent leases were not changed from the law of 1839, except that the lessee was only required to pay one-twelfth down, the same as other purchasers at public sale. The greatest amendment of this law was made in 1844. It was then enacted that when the holder of a permanent lease wishes to surrender his lease in order to acquire a more perfect estate in the land, a vote of the township must be taken, the same as in case of a sale. In the revision of this law in 1852, it was provided that the holder of a permanent lease, wishing to purchase the fee of the land, must obtain the consent of the township trustees; and this can only be given after submitting the question to the voters and receiving the approval of the majority. By the act of 1873, the lessee must pay one-third down, as is the case with other purchasers. All of these statutes are silent as to the time when the lessee is to make the deferred payments, though the intention was evident to put both classes of purchasers on the same footing.

The statute details the mode of collecting and accounting for the money, and paying the principal into the state treasury, and for deeds to be executed by the Governor. These details have remained from 1827 with scarcely any change.

The school lands of the Connecticut Reserve, lying in the counties of Tuscarawas and Holmes, had been leased only in accordance with the statute of 1803. No perpetual leases had been granted. In February, 1828, a law was passed for submitting to the inhabitants of the Reserve the question of the sale of these lands, the vote to be taken at the time of the presidential election, in November of that year, in the same manner as provided for in the previous laws. It seems that owing to neglect or for some other cause, the vote was not taken under this law.

In accordance with another act passed in December, 1829, the question was again submitted to the inhabitants of the Reserve. Their decision at the October election, in 1830, was in favor of sale, and in February, 1831, the lands were ordered to be appraised and sold, the details being similar to those of former laws. The payment was to be one-third in cash and the remainder in four equal annual installments, with interest. These lands were soon sold; the final payments were made in 1837.

The additional lands granted by Congress, in 1834, for the support of schools in the Connecticut Reserve, were located in the northern part of the State. In 1848, the General Assembly submitted to the inhabitants the question of their sale. The act stipulated that if consent were given, provision should be made by law for the appointment of three residents of the Reserve to appraise the lands, and the lands should not be sold for less than the appraised value. The vote was viva voce, as by former laws, and consent was given. In 1850, a law was passed for the appraisement and sale, and the lands were sold, the final payments into the state treasury being made in 1858.

The sale of the school lands belonging to the United States Military District, which began in 1828, was completed in 1849. The lands belonging to the Virginia Military Reservation have not all been sold. There remain between nine and ten thousand acres, which are under perpetual lease at an annual rent of twelve cents per acre. The lands which belonged to the Moravian towns have been sold.

The sales of section sixteen began in 1828, and have continued to the present time. The greater part are sold; very few whole sections remain. Only about one-eighth of the original surveyed townships and fractional townships now own any school lands. The records in the public offices in Columbus do not show the number of acres remaining unsold, but it is very much less than the eighth part of the original quantity. Nor have we the means of ascertaining what quantity is under perpetual and what under limited lease, these things being controlled by the local officers. The School Commissioner's Report for 1875 shows that the receipts from rents of the unsold school lands in Ohio for that year, and for interest on deferred payments due on sales, amounted to over twenty thousand dollars.

One township and two sections of salt lands were granted to the State at the time the state government was organized, with the stipulation that the lands should never be sold. In 1824, Congress released this condition, but stipulated that "the proceeds be applied to such literary purposes as the legislature may hereafter direct." The State accepted the condition, and the township in Jackson county, and the sections in Muskingum and Delaware counties, were accordingly sold, and the proceeds funded for the use of common schools.

The United States, in 1850, granted certain "swamp and overflowed lands" to the several states in which they were situated. In Ohio, there were 25,720 acres—that is, over 40 square miles. In 1853, a law was enacted to provide for draining and reclaiming these lands, under the direction of the county commissioners, the expense "to be paid in said lands lying in said county." The county auditors were to sell the remaining land, and after paying all expenses, the residue of the money was to be paid "into the state treasury for the use of common schools."

In the year 1862, Congress gave to each state a portion of land for the endowment of a college, whose leading object should be to teach "such branches of learning as are related to agriculture and the mechanic arts." Each state received land in proportion to its representation in Congress; viz., thirty thousand acres for each member. The portion of Ohio was 630,000 acres, equal to 984 square miles. The land was to be taken in the State, if the United States owned any surveyed land in the State; otherwise, certificates were issued, which could be located on any public lands. In Ohio, at that time, there remained only eighty acres of surveyed land belonging to the general government. Accordingly, the State received certificates, called land scrip, for the remaining 629,920 acres. The proceeds of the sales amounted to $342,450. This remained in the state treasury until, with interest, it amounted to half a million, which constitutes the endowment of the Ohio Agricultural and Mechanical College, at Columbus. The United States, in 1871, gave to the State all the unsurveyed and unsold land in the Virginia Military Reservation. The State gave these lands also to the Agricultural and Mechanical College. The quantity and value are not known.

IRREDUCIBLE FUNDS.

In January, 1827, when the first laws for the sale of school lands were enacted, the General Assembly also made a law to establish a fund for the support of common schools. The act contains six sections. All, except the last, have remained with scarcely a verbal change, and constitute the present law on this subject.

The Auditor of State is superintendent of the common school fund. Whenever any moneys are paid into the state treasury, from the sale of lands appropriated by Congress for the support of schools, the Auditor keeps an account, crediting each sum to the proper township (original surveyed) or the reserved district. The money constitutes an "irreducible fund for the support of common schools within the township or other district having credit for the same." All moneys so paid into the treasury bear an annual interest of six per centum, payable on the first day of January annually; "and the faith of the State of Ohio is hereby pledged for the annual payment." The fourth section details the mode of paying the money, by the state and county officers, to the proper person in each school district. Section five provides for receiving any gift to the State in trust for the common schools, and for appropriating the interest according to the intent of the giver.

In some of the western states, the entire proceeds of the the sale of common school lands have been consolidated in one fund. In Ohio, there are 823 distinct funds which the State holds in trust for the use of common schools. Three are large—the Connecticut Western Reserve, the Virginia Military Reservation, and the United States Military District. The rest are comparatively small, being one for each township and fractional township in about three-fifths of the State, and one for the Moravian towns.

The amount of these funds, on the 15th of November, 1875, was as follows:

Connecticut Western Reserve........................	$257,429 21
Virginia Military Reservation.......................	181,290 79
United States Military District........	120,272 12
Moravian Towns....................	3,160 58
Section Sixteen (819 distinct funds)..............	2,972,674 08
Total common school irreducible fund.......	$3,534,826 78

On a portion of the Connecticut Western Reserve Fund, arising from the sale of the first allotment of land, the interest was for several years added to the principal, which increased this fund a little over fifteen thousand dollars.

The last section of the act of 1827 to establish a fund for the support of common schools, constituted a fund "which shall belong in common to the people of this State, which shall consist of the net amount of money paid into the treasury from the sales of the salt lands, and such donations, legacies, and devises as may be made to the fund." The interest was to be funded annually till 1832, and afterwards paid to the several counties in proportion to the free male inhabitants, for the support of common schools. In 1831, this was amended by substituting the word "white" for "free," and by extending the period of accumulation of interest till 1835. It remained in this shape on the statute book until 1873, when it was repealed, and a pledge made in the law that the State will pay for the support of common schools the interest of the money paid into the treasury from the sales of the salt lands. The State is, in truth, bound to pay interest on the principal of the fund, which is some thousands of dollars more than the proceeds of the sales.

In 1851, a law expressly referring to the sixth section of the act of 1831, directed that the proceeds of the sales of the swamp lands should be "appropriated to the general fund for the support of common schools," and directed the interest thereon to be funded until 1855, and after that year the interest on the whole to be distributed as other school funds. Nothing was paid into the state treasury on account of these lands for many years. The receipts from sales during the last two years have been about seven hundred dollars.*

DISTRIBUTABLE FUNDS.

The distributable common school funds provided by the laws of Ohio have been derived from various sources. The annual interest on the irreducible funds, together with the rents on the unsold lands, amounts now to about two hundred and forty thousand dollars. Since 1821, taxes have been levied by various authorities, and some local revenues have been devoted to the annual support of common schools, of which we shall speak hereafter.

In 1838, a state common school fund was established, to consist of "the interest on the surplus revenue at five per centum; the interest on the proceeds of the salt lands; the revenue from banks, insurance, and bridge companies; and other funds to be provided by the State to the amount of two

*For some of the most important facts and dates in the last two sections of this chapter, the writer is indebted to Chas. J. Wetmore, Esq., of the State Auditor's Office.

hundred thousand dollars." This sum was to be distributed annually to the various counties, townships, and school districts, to be expended for the support of common schools. The sources of the fund named in the act did not usually suffice to make up the sum named, and the remainder was made up from the general revenue of the State, raised by direct taxation. The amount was reduced, in 1842, to $150,000, and was raised, in 1851, to $300,000.

The salt land fund has been explained. In 1838, the principal of this fund amounted to $27,868. In 1850, the fund was $41,024. The revenue from banks, and from insurance and bridge companies was five per centum of dividends declared. The amount varied very much from year to year. In 1838, it was $46,581. In 1839, it was $75,230, but it was not so large after that year.

The Congress of the United States, in 1836, directed the surplus revenue of the general government to be deposited with the several states, in proportion to the number of representatives and senators in Congress. The share of Ohio was a little over two million dollars. The General Assembly, in 1837, directed this money to be deposited with the several counties in proportion to population. Commissioners of the fund in each county were to make loans at from six to seven per centum annual interest. Five per centum of the principal was to be accounted for to the State Treasurer for school purposes. In the following year, by an amendatory act, the fund commissioners of each county were authorized to retain the income, except the five per centum just mentioned, and "to invest the same in profitable stocks and mortgages, and to fund annually the dividends and interests, to accumulate a permanent fund for the support of schools, or for the promotion of public improvements, or for the building of academies in their counties." Laws passed in 1847 and 1848, authorized the county commissioners to appropriate the avails of this county fund to the support of teachers' institutes. In what counties this fund now exists, or what is its amount, we have no means of ascertaining.

For several years the five per centum of the surplus revenue yielded to the common school fund a hundred thousand dollars annually. By the act of March, 1843, the surplus revenue fund was recalled from the counties, and devoted to the payment of a state debt, but the annual five per centum of the fund was continued to the use of the school fund.

In 1851, it was enacted that the balance of the fund, after payment of the particular debt for which it had been pledged, be added to the state common school fund; but in 1853, the "principal and proceeds" of the fund were made part of the sinking fund for the payment of the state debt.

In the year 1844, several special revenues from auctions, peddlers, lawyers, and physicians, were added to the fund, and for some years a special direct state tax had been levied in order to make up the required fund for yearly distribution. In 1853, a new system replaced the law of 1838 and its amendments, and also the so-called county tax.

In 1825, a law levying a tax in every county was passed, and such a school tax continued to be levied until 1853. At first, it was one-half mill on the dollar; increased, in 1829, to three-fourths of a mill. In 1831, the county commissioners were empowered to add one-fourth of a mill, if they deemed it expedient. So it was increased gradually, till, in 1838, it was made two mills; but in 1839, the county commissioners were authorized to reduce it to not less than one mill. Not one-fifth of the counties in Ohio took advantage of this permission in 1839. In 1847, the rate was reduced to two-fifths of a mill, but the proceeds were not reduced in this proportion, for under the new tax law of 1846 the total valuation of taxable property in the State had been increased more than one hundred and seventy per cent. It was again increased to one mill in 1851. In 1853, it was set aside entirely. This tax, from 1825 to 1853, was rather a township than a county tax, for the amount collected in each township was for the use of schools in that township. In 1836, the township officers were authorized to increase the rate, if a majority of the voters consented.

The law of 1853 entirely ignored all special sources of revenue, and enacted that "for the purpose of affording the advantages of a free education to all the youth of this State, the state common school fund" should consist of the sum produced by a tax of one mill and a half per dollar on all the taxable property in the State. The total value of taxable property in the State of Ohio, in 1853, was nearly six hundred million dollars, and this was increased the next year, by a revaluation, to nearly nine hundred millions. Thus, the distributable funds, under this law, very far exceeded the sums previously distributed from the state and county funds. The rate of the state tax has been several times diminished, and since 1871 it has been one mill on the dollar; but the amount of taxable property has increased in a greater ratio, and for several years past, about one and a half million dollars have been distributed every year, from this fund, for the free education of all the youth of the State.

In 1827, the legislature began the system of making offenders against the laws help to pay for public schools. It was enacted that "all fines imposed and collected by any justice of the peace, for any offence or immoral conduct done or committed in any school district, shall be, by such justice, paid over to the treasurer of such district, for the use and support of schools within the same."

In 1831, the "act for the prevention of certain immoral practices" provided that all fines collected under its provisions be "paid into the township treasury for the use of common schools in the township" in which the offence was committed. The offences named in the act are such as are punished generally by a fine only. In many other laws for the punishment of minor offences, it has been enacted that the pecuniary penalty shall be paid to either the county or township treasury for the use of schools. There seems to be no established principle to decide which treasury shall receive the penal sum.

Such moneys in either the county or township treasury were distributed, as other school funds, among the districts. Since 1853, this money in the township treasury is at the disposition of the board of education.

DISTRICT TAXES.

The first mention of a school tax, in the legislation of Ohio, was in the law of 1821, which was the first general school law enacted in the State. This act authorized the division of every township into school districts. The property of all persons residing in a school district, and which was situated therein and liable to taxation for state or county purposes, was liable to be taxed for school purposes; that is, to build a school-house, and to make up deficiencies that might accrue by schooling children whose parents were unable to pay their share of school expenses. The tax was limited to one-half the amount of state or county taxes. The omission of the property of non-residents was not made in subsequent laws; but in 1831, it was enacted that a district school-house tax should not be levied upon the property of a non-resident twice within three years, "by any alteration of districts;" nor should such tax be levied on non-residents' property lying more than three miles from the school-house. The act of 1825 authorized the district meeting to provide means for building a house; also to provide fuel and other things necessary for a school. In 1827, the power of the district meeting to levy a tax to erect or repair a school-house was limited to the sum of $300, and then only by a vote of three-fifths of the householders and tax-payers present. This was reduced to a simple majority in 1838. In 1830, the school-house tax was limited to $50 in any one year, unless at least one-third of the taxable property of the district was owned by residents; to $100 when from one-third to one-half, and to $200 when from one-half to two-thirds was so owned. The last of these items was diminished to $150 by the act of 1831. In no case was the tax to exceed $275 in any one year. In 1836, the maximum yearly tax was again placed at $300, and the law of 1838 made no limit. In 1834, the law required one-third of the householders as a quorum of a district meeting to levy a tax. This was changed to one-half in 1836.

Previous to 1838, the laws authorized the district to receive a gift of ground, not exceeding two acres, as a site for a school house; but the law of that year was the first to authorize a tax for "the purchase of a lot or lots on which to erect such house." Fuel and furniture were also added to the objects for which a tax might be raised. The act of 1821 uses the general expression "to make up deficiencies" as one object of the tax, and the act of 1825 authorizes the district meeting "to provide the necessary fuel," but seems not to intend any tax for that purpose. The act of 1829, which repeals that of 1825, says nothing about fuel. The act of 1834 makes it the duty of every person sending a child to school to provide his just proportion of fuel, in proportion to the number of children, but no child should be excluded from the school on account of the parent's delinquency in this respect. In 1849, it was enacted that whenever a parent or guardian should fail to furnish his quota of fuel as ordered by the district directors, the same might be furnished by the directors, and the price paid might be collected, in the same manner as district school taxes, from the parent or guardian—that is, "by distress and sale of personal property." The power of the directors to provide fuel and to levy a tax for this purpose also remained in force. The laws previous to 1838, and to a less extent after that year, contemplated that a large portion of the district school expenses should be paid by voluntary contributions. It was made the duty of the district treasurer or directors to keep an account of such moneys, and they were held responsible for their proper expenditure.

Previous to 1838, the district taxes were collected by a district collector or treasurer. The act of that year gave the directors power to choose whether the district tax should be collected by such officer or by the county treasurer. In 1839, the former method was restored, and remained in force until 1853; but in 1842, it was provided that at least thirty days notice should be given before taxes collected by the district collector were payable.

From 1827 to 1853, the directors had power to commute any tax for labor or materials expended in building or repairs. In 1827, each householder's tax was to be at least one dollar, which he might discharge by two days' labor at building the house. This minimum was reduced to fifty cents in 1831, when the rate of a day's labor was omitted, and to twenty-five cents in 1836. It was omitted entirely in 1838.

In the act of 1838, the township clerk, acting as township superintendent of common schools, was directed to make an estimate of the money required, in addition to the distributable funds, "to provide at least six months good schooling to all the white unmarried youth in the township, during the year ensuing." The question of levying a tax to raise this sum was to be submitted to the voters of the township, at the township election on the first Monday of April. A similar duty was imposed on the directors of districts consisting of incorporated towns or cities, such districts not being under the authority of the township superintendent. The object of this tax, as stated in the law, would in many cases necessarily preclude the distribution of the money to all the districts of a township, and the statutes did not expressly direct such money to be distributed as other school funds. In effect, whenever this tax was voted in any township, the township became to that extent a school district. In the act of 1839, the limit of two mills on the dollar of taxable property, was affixed to the special tax that might be voted to give good schooling to the youth of the township. In 1848, it was made the duty of the district clerk, in the several school districts of the State, to make such an estimate as was required of the township clerk by the act of 1838; the question of tax to be decided by the voters, at the annual school district meeting on the second Monday in April. An amendatory act of 1849, declared that this should not be construed to take away the power of the township to vote an additional school tax under the law of 1838. These acts were further amended in 1850, as to the details of collecting the money by the proper county officers. In 1851, this tax, when voted by the township, was limited to three mills on the dollar, and was made distributable among the districts. The act of 1838 made every incorporated town or city a separate district, with power to divide into subdistricts, and provided that in assessing taxes for building school houses, the property not before taxed for this purpose should be assessed at a rate equal to that which had been paid by property already taxed for such buildings, before a general assessment should be made.

In 1839, a vote was authorized to be taken, in any district, upon the question of borrowing money to purchase a lot and erect a school house, and if it was voted, the directors were to levy such a tax as would pay the principal and interest in not more than ten annual installments; but no loan should be made whose interest would exceed one mill on the dollar of the taxable property of the district. By the same act, the directors were authorized to levy a tax to pay rent, when the house or houses belonging to the district were not sufficient to accommodate the scholars.

The act of 1842 exempted from sale, on the execution of a judgment of a court, every lot appropriated for the use of a common school, not to exceed two acres, and if in a town one acre, on which there is a building occupied for the purpose, howsoever the legal title may be vested. In 1843, it was enacted that when a judgment is obtained against a school district for the payment of money for the land, or house, or labor, or materials used in building, repairing, or furnishing the house, it shall be the duty of the county auditor, on receiving a transcript of the judgment, to levy the amount on the property of the district, and that when the tax is collected, the county treasurer shall pay it over to the owner of the judgment.

In 1846, a district meeting was authorized to levy a tax of not over $30 the first year, and $10 each subsequent year, for the purchase of a school library and apparatus. In 1851, the district directors were authorized to levy a tax of not over $50 for necessary maps, apparatus, and repairs, and to provide fuel.

The act of 1853 attempted an entire reorganization of the district system, making each township a school district, and doing away with all the former districts which were parts of townships, except those districts which consisted in whole or in part of a city or village. The districts previously established in the townships were thenceforth to be sub-districts, with three directors as formerly, but neither the sub-district meeting nor the directors had any powers of taxation. A township board of education was organized, and it became the duty of this board to make every year an estimate of the money needed for all school purposes other than the payment of teachers; that is, for purchasing sites, for erecting, purchasing, and repairing houses, for fuel, etc. The board was authorized to certify their estimate to the county auditor, whose duty it was to assess the amount on the taxable property of the district; that is, the township. By the amendatory act of 1857, if the sum so estimated was less than two mills on the dollar of the taxable property of the district, the board had power to determine the tax; but if in their opinion more than the amount of a two mill tax was requisite, they must call a special meeting of the voters to decide whether such greater tax should be levied. By the act of 1853, if the board judged it necessary or desirable to establish one or more central or high schools, the question was to be decided by a meeting of the voters of the district, who should decide the amount of township tax which might be levied for the purpose. The board of education had power to order a tax of not over two mills on the dollar for the purpose of sustaining the teachers in such school, or for the purpose of prolonging, after the state funds were exhausted, the terms of the several sub-district schools in the township. Every city or village of three hundred inhabitants was made a distinct school district, with its own board of education, who had the same powers of taxation as the township boards.

In 1861, the local school tax was limited to three mills for all purposes, except purchase of sites, erection of houses, and payment of debts. In 1862, the local tax for school and school house purposes was limited to two mills and three-fourths. In 1864, the limit was three mills. In 1867, the limit was two mills for sites, houses, and repairs, and three mills for all other purposes, with authority, however, to add one mill for the years 1867 and 1868.

The act of 1873 authorizes every board of education in the State to determine the amount of tax to be levied as a contingent fund for all school expenses, not exceeding seven mills on the dollar. This act also authorizes a board of education to borrow money "to obtain or improve public school property." This phrase seems to include every expenditure except the payment of salaries. The board may issue bonds for the loan, but not to a greater amount in one year than would equal two mills on the dollar of the taxable property of the district. It is provided that the order of the board issuing bonds must be by a majority of the whole board, and the names of those voting for and against must be recorded on the journal.

Whenever the board of education deem it necessary to expend more money for purchase of sites or building houses than they are authorized to raise by taxation, they may submit the question of a loan and the tax necessary to repay it to the qualified voters of the district. The law as it now stands provides for no other tax question to be submitted to public vote, and cities of over one hundred and fifty thousand inhabitants are excepted from this. This exception applies now only to Cincinnati. The law details the mode of issuing bonds, limiting the rate of interest to eight per centum per annum.

It was not possible to reorganize the districts in 1853, without some provision to do justice to those districts which had already expended large sums in the erection of school houses, and which, being merged in a township district, became liable to assessment to build houses for their neighbors who were behindhand in that respect. Therefore, the board of education was authorized to estimate separately the expense of site and house for any particular sub-district where the inhabitants had borne less than their reasonable share of taxation for such purposes, as compared with the other sub-districts of the township. The design was to make a temporary arrangement, and the section was amended several times to carry out this intent. It is omitted entirely in the revised act of 1873.

Having now hastily sketched the legislation of a general character, from the origin of the State to this time, on the subject of providing money for the support of common schools in Ohio, it is proper to close this branch of our history with the following statement of the sums raised in the year 1875, for one year's expenditure:

State tax, 1 mill	$1,597,599
Interest on irreducible funds	209,856
Rents and interest on deferred payments for land (estimated)	20,000
District taxes	6,362,533
Fines and licences	270,161
Total	$8,460,149

SCHOOL DISTRICTS.

The school district is the simplest element of the common school system of Ohio. Its formation was the first thing in the legislation for the purpose of organizing the common schools. In 1806, fifteen years before any law for the regulation of common schools, trustees of original surveyed townships were authorized to lay off said townships into proper divisions for the purpose of establishing schools, in such manner as would best suit the convenience of the inhabitants. This was repeated in several subsequent enactments.

The law of 1821 authorized the trustees of any civil township to submit to a vote of the township the question of organizing into school districts. In laying off the districts, regard was to be paid to any incorporated school company, in order to include the members within one district. Provision was made for districts composed of parts of two townships. Without a township vote a district might be laid off on petition of the inhabitants of a neighborhood. No district was to be made with less than twelve resident householders. The householders in each district were to elect each year a committee of three, a collector who should be treasurer, and a clerk to make the tax bills and keep the accounts. The committee were authorized to cause the erection of a school house, and to receive for that purpose a lot not exceeding two acres, by donation or purchase, two-thirds of the householders having agreed thereto. No provision was made for tax to purchase a lot, and if school lots were purchased before 1838, the price was raised by voluntary donation. Except the collector, who was also district treasurer, no township or district officer was to receive any compensation for services performed under this act.

Governor Morrow, in his annual message, December, 1823, said that the provisions of this law were "rendered nugatory by the option given to the electors in the several townships, to give them effect or not." The act of 1825 had quite a different tone. It declared it the duty of the trustees of every incorporated township in the State, to lay off the township into one or more school districts, suitable and convenient, with due regard to school houses and districts already made, also to incorporated school companies and to schools in villages and towns. No township could receive any portion of the school tax until districted, and if it remained undistricted five years, it was the duty of the county auditor to divide the school tax collected in such a township among the organized districts in other townships of his county. The law imposing this duty upon the township trustees was re-enacted five times within the next thirteen years. The penalty for failure to obey within a limited number of years, was also repeated in several laws, but it was omitted in 1838, and has never been renewed since.

In the act of 1838, it was made the duty of the trustees of the townships not already districted, to lay off their townships into school districts on or before the next first day of June, in the manner most convenient for the population and different neighborhoods, paying due regard to any school house already erected, school districts already laid off, and all other circumstances proper to be considered, so as to promote the interest of the inhabitants and also to include all the territory of the township. The time for laying off districts was extended in 1839 and in 1841. In 1849, authority was given to the township trustees to district the township at any time thereafter. The duty of the township trustees to lay off districts was once more enacted, in 1851, to be done in the manner best calculated for the convenience of the inhabitants and to promote the interests of common schools.

In 1825, provision was made for districts composed of parts of several townships by the joint action of the several boards of trustees. In 1841, this was amended so that such a district could be made only on the petition of a majority of the citizens in the contemplated district. In 1843, districts composed of parts of several counties were authorized.

Power to alter the boundaries of school districts was given to the township trustees in 1825. This was amended in 1839, so as to forbid any alteration in a district, unless a majority of the householders of the district signified their assent in writing; but this amendment was repealed in 1842. In 1850, any future alteration of a district, so as to include in one district parts of several townships or counties, was forbidden. In 1851, the trustees were authorized, at the request of five freeholders and after twenty days public notice, to make, alter, or abolish a school district.

The act of 1825 required the township trustees to describe and number the districts. The description and numbering were recorded by the clerk of the township, and a copy of the record given to the county auditor. The same duty was devolved upon the clerk when the trustees made any changes in the districts. This was altered in 1838, by requiring a map as well as a description of the district; and, with verbal changes only, these requirements remained in force till 1853. In that year, it became the duty of the township board of education to have a map made of the township as often as they deem it necessary, and the board had entire control over the boundaries of the sub-districts.

The act of 1825 authorized any householder resident in a newly formed district to call a meeting for the purpose of electing three directors, and to "do all other things necessary for organizing a school." It was his duty to notify all the householders in the district of the time and place of meeting, and if one-third of them were present it was a legal meeting. This was amended in 1831, by making ten householders a quorum of a district meeting in a district having over thirty householders. In 1838, the voters present were authorized to transact the business, the rule as to a quorum being omitted.

Householders only could constitute the district meeting under the law of 1825. In 1827, tax-payers were admitted to vote when a tax question was to be voted upon, and in 1839, resident tax-payers as well as householders were entitled to vote in all elections. By the first constitution of Ohio, every white male adult inhabitant who paid or was charged with a state or county tax, was entitled to vote in all elections; and laws were so framed, long before any of these school laws, as practically to include as tax-payers all white male adults. In some of the laws for taking a vote upon the question of selling school lands, alien residents were expressly mentioned as entitled to vote. The state constitution of 1851 gives the right of suffrage to white male adult citizens, and the school laws since that time use the expression "qualified voters." Since the amendment to the national constitution in 1870, the right to vote cannot be denied on account of color.

Besides the general delegation of powers to the district meeting by the act of 1825, the meeting was specially authorized to designate the site of a school-house. In 1836, the consent of two-thirds of all the voters at a district meeting was made requisite to sanction the sale of a school house—changed to a simple majority in 1848. We have also noticed the laws requiring a direct appeal to the will of the voters on questions of taxation, sale of lands, and alteration of districts, and we see that action by the popular meeting was more frequent forty or fifty years ago than it is at present. By the law of 1838, it was the duty of the directors to make an annual written report to the district meeting, and to perform all lawful acts required by that meeting.

The act of 1825 provided for three directors to hold office for one year, who were the only district officers. In 1842, the term was made three years, one director to be elected each year. In 1827, the directors were authorized to appoint a treasurer, and in 1829, a day was fixed as the time of the annual district meeting—the third Tuesday in October—when three directors, a treasurer, and a clerk should be elected. In 1838, the time of the annual meeting was changed to the third Friday in September, and remained so for ten years. Since 1848, it has been the second Monday in April. In 1829, the directors were authorized to call special meetings to decide questions involving taxation, and this power remained with the directors till the districts became sub-districts in 1853. From 1831 to 1838, if the annual meeting failed for want of a quorum, or if the annual meeting failed to elect officers, then any householder was authorized to call a special meeting as in the case of the first organization of a district, and such called meetings could elect officers and exercise all the powers of annual meetings.

The act of 1838 devolved the duties of district treasurer upon the district clerk. The clerk was to be elected by the directors from their own number. This method of having the directors elect one of themselves district clerk, remains in force. The directors were elected for one year until 1842. Since that time they have been elected for terms of three years, one each year. The separate office of district treasurer was restored in 1851, but the law of 1853 made no separate sub-district fund, and the office was discontinued.

There was evidently an unwillingness on the part of competent men to accept these offices. In 1830, the law imposed the same penalties for refusal to serve as in the case of township trustees, but no one should be compelled to serve two years in succession. The township trustees were authorized, in 1833, to appoint district directors in case of vacancy. This power was given to the township clerk in 1838, and the law in that particular is so now. In 1830, the district officers were required to take an oath of office, and the next year it was made the duty of the district clerk to verify, by oath or affirmation, his enumeration of the youth of the district. Both of these requirements were repealed in 1833. The oath of office was restored in 1838; but it was not until 1873 that the law again required the officer making the enumeration to verify the same by his oath or affirmation.

The most important clause in any school law is that which declares who shall appoint the teacher. This power was given to the district committee by the act of 1821, and this feature of the school laws of Ohio has never been changed. In 1825, it was made the duty of the directors to employ teachers. This was repeated in 1853, when the former districts became sub-districts, and in the act of 1873 it was made the duty of the local directors, in every township district, to employ teachers.

The district committee, under the law of 1821, had power to build a school house, to employ a teacher, and to make assessments for expenses. It was the duty of the directors, under the law of 1825, to employ a teacher, to manage and superintend the concerns of the school, to call district meetings, to receive and expend all funds, and they, or any two of them, had power to make agreements for these purposes. In 1838, the powers of management and superintendence were expressed more in detail—to divide the district into sub-districts, to select and purchase sites for houses, to repair he houses and keep them in order, to provide fuel and to levy a small tax for repairs and fuel, to establish schools and to make regulations for their government, to classify the schools and assign children of different ages to attend at different seasons of the year. They must also perform all other lawful acts required by the district meeting or necessary to carry into effect the provisions of the law. Their annual written report to the district meeting must state the receipts and expenses, schools, teachers, salaries, number of pupils, branches taught, and other useful information. They were authorized to determine the branches taught in the schools, provided that instruction in reading, writing, and arithmetic should be given in the English language.

This rule as to the language was changed several times. In 1839, power was given the directors to determine the branches and languages taught, "provided the branches shall be such as are generally taught in common schools." This phrase has the air of a legislative compromise. The act also provided that children who desired to pursue their studies in German might go to another district for that purpose, and the same privilege was accorded to those who desired to pursue them in English, when there was no proper school in the district where they resided.

The law of 1825 did not stop with prescribing the duty of directors to employ a teacher, but also affixed a penalty for neglect of this duty. The same section which ordered the share of tax of undistricted townships to be distributed to the rest of the county, also ordered that when a district neglected for three years to employ a teacher, its share of the tax should be divided among the other districts of the township. Four years later, every district was required to keep a school in session at least three months every year, as a condition of receiving its share of money from the county treasury. The penalty for failure to have a school in session was omitted from the laws from 1838 to 1865.

The powers of taxation by local directors have been stated in previous pages. The disbursement of the funds of the district was given to the directors by the law of 1825, and when two years afterward it was made their duty to appoint a treasurer, he was under their control and removable at their pleasure. The principal duty of the district treasurer was the collection of district taxes. Detailed rules for performing this service, and as to his bond and his accounts, were given in the act of 1829, and repeated with little variation in subsequent laws. The funds distributed by the county were not paid into the hands of the district officers from 1825 to 1829, but were retained in the county treasury and paid directly to teachers on the certificate of the directors. After that, the moneys distributed by the county, or by the State from interest on the land funds, were paid directly to the district treasurers till 1838. The law of that year made the township treasurer the treasurer of all school funds of the township arising from lands, fines, interest, taxes, or state distributions, and he was to pay out the share of each district to the teachers, upon the order of the district clerk and one other director. This left all other school expenses to be provided for by district assessments or voluntary contributions. The district treasurer, who was clerk, could pay out the moneys in his hands only upon the written order of the clerk—to-wit, himself—and one other director. This was amended, in 1842, so that any two directors constituted a quorum for business and were authorized to draw all orders for money. In 1851, the signature of the clerk was again made requisite.

The law of 1838 constituted a separate school district of every incorporated city or town. Several cities and towns of the State already had in their charters special laws for the regulation of their public schools. Each city or town, except those governed by special laws, was to elect every year three school directors, who were to exercise the same powers and duties as other school directors, with especial authority to establish schools of different grades. The township trustees were authorized, with the consent of these directors, to attach adjacent parts of the township to the town school district. The clerk of the city or town was to be clerk of such town district, but not with the duties of treasurer. This was changed ten years afterwards, and the directors were authorized to elect one of their own number clerk, as in other districts. If the town were divided into sub-districts, then there might be one director elected from each sub-district.

In 1839, it was made the duty of the directors of town districts to provide evening schools for the instruction of young men and boys over twelve years of age who might be prevented by their occupations from attending the day schools.

From the earliest legislation about schools in Ohio, there has been a marked distinction between the laws for towns and those for rural districts. Beginning with 1808, the General Assembly every year granted charters of incorporation to several school companies; and in 1818 a general law was enacted whereby any six or more persons, associating themselves for the purpose of establishing a school, might become incorporated. Such schools were usually located in towns. Special acts of incorporation were afterwards enacted, and special and local laws were made every year, not only as to school lands, leases, and sales, but also as to local taxes for building houses, establishing libraries, or other purposes, and as to the powers and duties of officers, and even the boundaries of districts. One of the most important of these local laws was passed in 1847, "for the support and better regulation of common schools in the town of Akron." The next year, any town or city was authorized to adopt this act whenever two-thirds of the voters should petition the council to that effect. In 1849, a somewhat similar law was passed for the regulation of schools in cities and towns, which was to take effect in any city or town when a majority of the electors voted for it at an election held for that purpose. For a better account of these laws and of the more important laws relating to schools in particular towns and cities, the reader is referred to the chapters on Graded Schools and High Schools.

The general school law of 1853 begins with the declaration that every township in the State shall compose but one school district for all purposes connected with the general interests of education in the township. The districts of all previous laws were thenceforth sub-districts. All cities and villages of 300 inhabitants, with the territory annexed for school purposes, were excluded from the townships. If they were organized under the Akron law, or under the law of 1849, or under any special law, they remained unchanged by the law of 1853, except as to the duty to make annual reports of statistics. If they were not organized under either the Akron law, the law of 1849, or other special law, they were to be organized very much in the manner provided for such districts by the law of 1838. The board of education was to consist of three persons elected for terms of three years, one each year. The clerk or recorder of the city or village was to be clerk of the board. Here the previous history was repeated, for in 1862, the boards were authorized to appoint one of their own number clerk. They were to exercise the same powers and perform the same duties as other boards of education. The limit as to sex in the attendance at evening schools, for all youth whose avocations prevented them from attending day schools, was omitted in 1853, and the limit as to age was omitted in 1873.

The mode of organization of the sub-district of a township district, remained, under the law of 1853, the same as it had been for the district, as to number of directors, their term of office, the oath, the filling of vacancies by appointment by the township clerk, the calling of special meetings, and the election of clerk by the directors from their own number. With slight amendments, these provisions of the law remain in force.

The township board of education consisted, and still consists, of the township clerk and the clerks of the several subdistricts, the township clerk being clerk of the board but not entitled to vote.

The local directors retained the power to employ teachers, and to certify to the township clerk the amount due teachers for services, and it was the duty of the latter officer to draw an order on the treasurer of the township for the amount. To this was added the power to dismiss any teacher at any time, for such reasons as they might deem sufficient. The act of 1873 authorizes the local directors to employ teachers of the schools of the sub-districts, and to dismiss them for sufficient cause; and they "also have power to fix the salaries or pay of said teachers, which salaries or pay may be increased but not diminished in amount by the township board." The law of 1853 made it the duty of the local directors to make all necessary contracts for fuel, purchasing or leasing school house sites, renting school rooms, and making all other provisions necessary for the schools in their sub-districts. The only limit to this power was that the expense should not exceed the money distributable to the sub-district in proportion to its number of scholars, without first obtaining the consent of the township board of education. This was so amended in 1873 that all these duties of the local directors are performed "under such rules and regulations as the township board of education may prescribe."

The law of 1853 made every township board of education an incorporated body, as every board of directors had been since 1829; but the local directors, after 1853, were no longer incorporated. The title to all houses, sites, libraries, and all other school property of the township was vested in the board of education, with power to control the same to the best interests of the cause of education, and to sell unnecessary houses and sites. The regular meetings of the board are held in April and October, at or near the place of holding township elections. They may hold other meetings at their pleasure, and since 1873, special meetings may be called either by the clerk, by the president of the board, or by any two members, and may be held at any place in the township.

The board of education has control of any central or high school that may be established in the township, with power to employ, pay, or dismiss teachers, to build, repair, and furnish houses, to buy or lease building sites, or to rent rooms, or to do whatever else may be needed for such a school. High schools, before 1873, could only be established by a vote of the township; but now the board of education have power to establish schools of higher grade than the primary schools whenever they deem it proper.

The township board of education have power to change the sub-districts at any regular session, and it is now their duty to establish a primary school in each sub-district. Before 1873, it was their duty to establish in each sub-district a school of such grade as the public good might require; and they might regulate the grading of the scholars among the several schools. The act of 1853 provided for residents of one township attending school in another, when so situated as to be better accommodated in that way. Further, to meet such cases, in 1865, the formation of sub-districts composed of parts of several townships was authorized, and this was afterwards extended to allow sub-districts composed of parts of several counties. The act of 1859 provides for the united action of a village and township in establishing a central or high school, and the law of 1873 allows the transfer of a part or the whole of any school district to an adjoining school district, by consent of both boards.

The law of 1853 made it the duty of the local directors to visit the schools at least twice each term, with such persons competent to examine pupils in their studies as they may choose to invite; but the power to suspend a pupil for disorderly conduct was reserved to the board of education, unless the board authorized the directors also to exercise this power. The board had general powers to regulate the schools, and whenever the local directors neglected their prescribed duties, the board might exercise the special powers of directors in the sub-district. The board could also determine the studies to be pursued and the books to be used. The exercise of this power over text books was restricted in 1871, so as to prevent frequent changes. We shall speak hereafter of the power of the board to appoint a manager or superintendent. In all these details, it is seen how much power has been concentrated in the township board. The tendency of legislation continues in the same direction.

The present state constitution, adopted in 1851, has been understood to forbid local legislation as to schools, but to permit the local laws previously enacted to remain in force till repealed by the General Assembly. Laws previously enacted for the government of schools in several cities, towns, villages, and even country districts, remained in force till 1873. The Akron law also was in force in many places, and the law of 1849 in many others. The constitution also sanctioned school laws, to take effect upon the approval of local authorities, or upon adoption by vote of a district. An act was passed in 1867, providing for the formation of separate school districts, composed of one or more sub-districts, upon a vote of the majority of the voters. All of these acts were repealed by the act of 1873, and in their place a system was enacted which recognizes several distinct kinds of school districts; viz., city districts of the first class, being cities of over ten thousand inhabitants; city districts of the second class, being all other cities; village districts; township districts; and special districts, being those not included in the other classes, and which have been established by a vote of the people, or by some general or local law. Each district includes the territory attached to it according to law for school purposes.

The board of education of first class city districts consists of one or two members from each ward, elected for terms of two years, one-half each year. Such boards are required to hold meetings every two weeks, and they have power to fill vacancies that may occur in their number. The board of education of a second class city district, or of a village district, consists of three or six members, according as the district had a board of three or six members previous to the passage of the law, elected for terms of three years, one-third each year; but such board has power to make the number of its members the same as the number of wards in the city, and in that case, they are elected for terms of two years, one-half each year. Where the number is three, it may be ineased to six, by vote of the district.

The board in a special district consists of three members. Any special district is authorized, by vote of the people, to abandon its organization and become part of the township district in which it is located. The township board is organized as under the law of 1853, provided that when a township consists of one or two districts, all the directors are members of the board. Any township district may decide by vote to be governed in the same manner as a village school district—that is, it may abandon the plan of electing directors in sub-districts, with two sets of officers and jurisdictions more or less in conflict, and may place the control of all its school affairs in the hands of one single board elected by the whole township.

The powers and duties of all boards of education are not materially changed by the law of 1873, except as above stated in the case of township districts. Some strict rules are laid down as to the manner of conducting their business. Where money is to be paid or received, there must be entire publicity. Large sales must be by public auction duly advertised, and large contracts for labor or materials in building or repairs must be awarded to the best bidder after due publication. The records of the board must give the names of those members voting for or against every proposition to purchase or sell any property or to pay any money, and upon every appointment to office. No member of any board is permitted to have any pecuniary interest in any contract, nor can any member be employed for a compensation to discharge any duty except as clerk. The laws of Ohio never have provided any compensation to school directors or members of boards of education for their services as such directors or members, and since 1862 such compensation is expressly forbidden.

In 1846, local directors received authority to levy a small tax for the purchase of libraries and apparatus, and to make rules for their use. In 1853, the State levied a tax of one-tenth of a mill for the purchase of libraries and apparatus, to be purchased by the State Commissioner and distributed through the county auditors to the "clerks of the townships, boards of education, or other school local officers." It was made the duty of the several boards or local officers to preserve the books and provide for their use by the families of the district or sub-district. This tax was levied for seven years and was then repealed. The books were generally scattered and lost, except in some townships where the boards of education took pains for their preservation, and except in the towns and cities. As there was greatest loss and least use in the townships where the books were distributed in small lots among the sub-districts, the boards of education were authorized, in 1864, to collect all the books of one district in a central library. In 1867, the boards of education in cities were authorized to levy an annual tax of one-tenth of a mill on the dollar, the proceeds to be expended for books for a public school library. This act remains in force, and under its operation some very large public circulating libraries are growing up under the charge of officers appointed by the boards of education. In 1875, all boards of education were authorized to appropriate limited sums for the purchase of books and apparatus for the especial use of teachers and pupils.

The law of 1853 made it the duty of the township board of education to provide for continuing the schools in session six months every year. The act of 1873 limits the sessions of all common schools in the State to not less than twenty-four nor more than forty-four weeks in every year. A school month consists of four school weeks, and a school week consists of five school days. Under the amendatory act of 1864, if any board of education failed to estimate and certify to the county auditor the amount of tax needed to continue the schools of the district for six months, and to provide a suitable school-house in every sub-district, it was made the duty of the county commissioners to perform said office. The delinquent township, in 1865, also lost its right to a share of the state tax, and the members of the board who caused the failure became personally responsible for the loss. In 1873, the rule inflicting the loss on the school district was omitted, and the negligent officers were made liable to a fine of from twenty-five to fifty dollars, to be paid into the county school fund.

The law of 1853 exempted from sales on execution all school lots not over four acres in extent. Twenty years after, the exemption was extended to all common school property whatever, without limit. In 1860, boards of education were authorized, when they needed land for school house purposes and could not agree with the owner as to price, to institute judicial proceedings for fixing the price and appropriating the property.

The question of what language shall be taught, is disposed of in the law of 1873 by making it the duty of every board of education to cause German to be taught when demanded by seventy-five freeholders of the district representing not less than forty pupils who desire to study German and English together, but all branches taught in the common schools must be in the English language.

Every board of education is required to organize on the the third Monday of April in each year, by choosing a member for president, and all boards, except in township districts, also choose a clerk who may be a member of the board. In cities and townships, the city and township treasurer are respectively treasurer of the board of education. Other boards choose their own treasurer. The present number of school districts in the state is 1,942.

TEACHERS.

The legislation especially concerning the teacher relates either to employing, examining, educating, or paying him. The laws as to employing teachers have been detailed under the head of districts.

From the first schools, the existence of which was recognized in the act of 1806 relating to original townships, till 1825, there was no one to judge of a teacher's fitness except the parents, and for the last four years of that time, the district committee. The law of 1825 provided a way to assist the directors to judge of the competency of a teacher. The court of common pleas of each county was directed to appoint annually three suitable persons as examiners of common schools, whose duty it was to examine every person wishing to be employed as a teacher. The number of the examiners was rapidly increased. Two years afterwards, the court might appoint as many as it deemed expedient, not exceeding the number of organized townships in the county. After another two years, the number was not to be less than five nor more than the number of townships; and again, after two years, not more than double the number of townships. In 1834, the number of county examiners was fixed at five, and they were to appoint an examiner in each township with power to examine only female candidates. The law of 1836 provided for the election of three examiners of teachers in every township. In 1838, the original number of three county examiners was restored, appointed for terms of three years, and with power to appoint assistants in distant townships who should be governed by the rules prescribed by the county examiners. Since 1853 the probate court has appointed the three county examiners for terms of two years, which was restored to three years in 1873. The act of 1853 granted no power to the examiners to appoint assistants in remote townships. Since 1864, the probate court has had power to dismiss an examiner from office for immoral conduct or neglect of duty. By the law of 1873, no teacher of a normal school, or school for the education of persons as teachers, can be an examiner.

At first, the certificates issued to those candidates who were approved by the examiners were not limited by law. In 1829, they might be made valid for one year; after 1834, for two years or less. In 1836, the one year limit was restored, but in the law of 1838 it was fixed at not more than two years nor less than six months. This remains still in force, amended in 1873 so that certificates must be for either six, twelve, eighteen, or twenty-four months, thus ranking teachers in four grades. The Akron law, the law of 1849 for cities and towns, and various local acts provided for local boards of examiners to be appointed by the boards of education. The certificates issued by them were not required to be for any limited time until 1864, when the law required that such certificates must state the time during which they were to be valid. The act of 1873, superseding all these special acts, authorized boards of education of city and village districts having a population not less than twenty-five hundred to appoint a board of three examiners, which number might be increased to six or to nine in first class city districts. The term of office is three years. Certificates may be valid for one, two, or three years, and in first class city districts, for two, five, or ten years. These city boards of examiners are also authorized to secure the occasional aid of persons of knowledge in particular branches to assist them in conducting examinations.

At first, a certificate might be granted by a single examiner. Since 1829, two are required, or a majority of the board when there are more than three examiners; but under the law of 1838, one could examine and issue certificates, if, at the time and place appointed for a regular quarterly meeting of the examiners, one only was present. Before 1873, there might be special meetings; but since that year, all examinations must be at convenient places, of which public notice must be previously given, and two examiners constitute the necessary quorum.

No person, since 1825, without a certificate from the county examiners, could receive any money from the public treasury as wages for teaching; and since a few years after that date, a copy of the certificate must be given to the clerk or other officer who audits the teacher's claim for pay.

In 1825, no particular branches were named, a knowledge of which should be required by examiners. In 1831, the certificate must name the branches which the teacher was found qualified to teach, and no certificate should be given to any teacher unless he should be found qualified to teach "reading, writing, and arithmetic." Within the year this was amended to allow certificates to female teachers of their qualifications to teach spelling, reading, and writing only. This lower grade of certificate was omitted in the act of 1838, and the examiners were required to state what other branches the teacher was found qualified to teach, in addition to reading, writing, and arithmetic, and no teacher should be allowed to teach any branch not named in the certificate. In 1849, it was enacted that upon the written request of as many as three householders of a district that English grammar and geography be taught in the school, it became the duty of the directors to provide for such instruction. In the same act, the county examiners were forbidden to issue any certificate unless the candidate was found qualified to teach geography and English grammar in addition to the three branches previously requisite.

The act of 1853 required every teacher to be qualified to teach orthography, reading, writing, arithmetic, geography, and English grammar. The certificates of teachers of schools of higher grade must state the qualification to teach the additional branches. To these requirements, it was added, in 1864, that the teacher must possess an adequate knowledge of the theory and practice of teaching. In 1868, it was allowed to insert, in the certificates of teachers in German schools, German grammar in place of English grammar. The law of 1873 provides for special certificates to teachers of special arts or languages.

The law has always required every certificate to state that the examiners find the person to be of good moral character. In 1864, authority was given to the examiners to revoke a certificate held by an incompetent teacher or by one who neglected his duty.

In 1850, the General Assembly passed a law for the appointment of a state board of public instruction. So far as the statute book shows, this is one of the most important steps in all the history of Ohio school legislation. It provides for the election of five members of the board by joint ballot of the two houses of the General Assembly, to hold office for terms of five years, one to be elected every year. Each member, during the last year of his term, was to be styled State Superintendent of Common Schools, with the duties already assigned to that office as to statistics and reports. The board were to divide the State into four districts, in which the several members were to be district superintendents. Each one in his district was to aid the county examiners in the performance of their duties, and no certificate was to be valid without his signature. A list of questions to be used at the examinations was to be prepared every half year by the State Superintendent. Certificates were to be valid for one year; but upon the recommendation of a county board of examiners, countersigned by the district superintendent, the state board might issue a life certificate. Any certificate under this law should authorize the holder to teach a public school in any county of the State. This act never amounted to anything, because the General Assembly never appointed any members of the board. Each applicant for a certificate under this law was to pay one dollar, and each holder of a life certificate became subject to an annual professional tax of the same amount. These moneys were to defray the expenses of the system and of the publication of an educational paper to be called the "Ohio School Teacher," which was to be sent free to every one holding a certificate and to certain school officers.

This law remained a nullity, and certificates issued by county examiners in Ohio have never been valid outside of the county in which they were issued, nor have certificates issued by any local board of examiners ever been valid outside of the district.

In order to provide for a higher grade of certificate, the amendatory law of 1864 made it the duty of the State Commissioner to appoint a state board of examiners to consist of three competent persons who should hold their office for two years. This state board of examiners are authorized to issue "state certificates of high qualifications to such teachers as may be found upon examination to possess requisite scholarship, and who may also exhibit satisfactory evidence of good moral character and of eminent professional experience and ability." Such certificates are countersigned by the State Commissioner. They supersede the necessity of examination by any county or local board, being valid throughout the State during the life of the holder. This law remains in force.

Every applicant for a state certificate pays to the board a fee of three dollars. Since 1864, every applicant for a county certificate has been required to pay an examination fee. A part of the money is appropriated to the expenses of the examiners, but the greater part to the maintenance of county and city teachers' institutes. The legislation upon the subject of institutes for the instruction of teachers began in 1847, with an act to encourage teachers' institutes. An account of this law and of all subsequent laws on this subject is given so fully in a subsequent chapter as to preclude the necessity of any further mention in this place. This is all that has been done for the education of teachers in Ohio, except the power given to some boards of education to establish normal schools. This power has been exercised in some cities. For a full account of this, also, the reader is referred to a subsequent chapter.

In 1806, the law authorized the trustees of original townships to lay off the townships into districts for the purpose of establishing schools, and each division was to "receive a fair and equitable dividend of the profits arising from the reserved section, according to the number of inhabitants." This was repeated in 1810, but the division was to be according to the number of scholars and in proportion to the time they were taught. Four years later, the teachers were required to make certified lists of their scholars as the basis of the division, and the next year the clause was added, "whether the scholars had gone to school within or out of the township." This continued to be the duty of the teacher till 1831. There is no other legislation about paying the teacher previous to 1821. We may infer, from the frequent mention of voluntary contributions in the earlier laws, that much was done in that way until many years after the date last mentioned.

The committee, under the law of 1821, might cause the expenses of the school to be assessed on the parents or guardians in proportion to the number of scholars; but they might remit all or part to parents unable to pay, and the deficiency should be raised by tax. The law of 1825 devoted the revenue from land and the proceeds of the county tax exclusively to pay the wages of teachers, the township's share of the tax being divided among the districts in proportion to the number of families in each. The law of 1829 required the school to be kept open for three months and as much longer as the funds would pay the teacher, and if the funds did not suffice for three months, the residue, "if not raised by voluntary subscription," was to be paid by those sending in proportion to the number of scholars and time they attended. The act of 1831 repeats the above, and devotes to the payment of teachers and to no other purpose whatever, all money coming to the treasury of any school district for the use of schools. In 1833, the directors were authorized to apportion the money to divisions of the year so as to have a summer school and a winter school, and the act applied the previous rule to seasons instead of the year. This act allowed fuel to be bought with school money when the inhabitants neglected or refused to furnish it, thus infringing upon the rule which kept the fund sacred to the pay of teachers. In the same way, in 1836, the pay for taking the annual enumeration of youth was charged to this fund. The act of 1838 appears to restore it—the township treasurer being then made treasurer of all funds except district taxes, and it was his duty to pay out the money to teachers, no other purpose being named.

The law of 1838 omitted the subject of assessments; but it was enacted in 1839 that when the public funds were insufficient to support the school as long as the directors desired in any one year, the residue, if not raised by voluntary subscription, should be paid by those sending scholars in proportion to number and time. The teacher was to keep an account, and if the charges were not paid, the treasurer should collect the amount as other district taxes were collected; but it was expressly provided that no youth should on any pretence be refused admittance to school on account of inability to pay tuition. This section of the act was amended in 1848, making it the duty of the district clerk to ascertain the proportion to be paid by those sending to school, and to exclude from the calculation and apportionment the attendance of those whose admission was secured by the proviso of the amended section. There is no subsequent legislation about assessments on parents or guardians. The law of 1853 proceeds upon the principle that the schools of the State are to be supported entirely by the property of the State.

The devotion of certain funds to the pay of teachers is thus precisely stated in the act of 1853:

> "So much of the school moneys coming into the hands of the treasurer as may be derived from the state tax or from any township tax levied for the continuation of schools after the state fund has been exhausted, or from such school funds as arise from the sale or rents of section sixteen, or other school lands, shall be applicable only to the payment of teachers in the proper township, and shall be drawn for no other purpose whatever."

The act of 1873, superseding all the above, makes no distinction in school funds as to their purpose—apparently assuming that there no longer exists any necessity for such separation.

SUPERINTENDENCE.

The first clause in any law of Ohio that contemplated anything like supervision, was in the act of 1825. Any one or more of the county examiners of teachers might visit the schools in the county and examine the same, and give advice relative to discipline and mode of instruction. In the revision of the law in 1831, the clause as to advice was omitted. In 1838, their powers aside from examination of candidates were confined to determining what were good text-books and recommending the same.

The first formal effort to secure supervision was made in 1837, in the law to create the office of Superintendent of Common Schools of the State of Ohio. This officer was to be elected by a joint resolution of the General Assemby, for the term of one year, at a salary of five hundred dollars. He was required to take an oath of office to discharge the duties of the office with fidelity.

His duties were principally to collect statistics and report to the next General Assembly the following facts: the number of districts in each township of each county of the State; the number of white youth between the ages of four and twenty-one years, specifying the number of each sex; the number attending school within the year; the average time of their attendance; the time the schools were in session, distinguishing the time they were supported by the proceeds of the irreducible funds, the time supported by taxation, and the time supported by voluntary subscriptions; the amount paid to teachers in each district, township, and county, and from what sources derived; the amount paid for houses or repairs, distinguishing the amount from taxation and that from voluntary contribution. He was also to report upon the condition of the several school funds, and upon the operation and effects of the common school system, and to suggest plans for its better regulation and improvement. The law authorized circulars to county auditors and to local directors, and made it their duty to assist.

Next to the great influence upon public sentiment exerted by Mr. Lewis during the first year of his superintendency, the principal result of his labors appears in the school law of 1838. This act provided a more elaborate system of supervision and statistical reports. The township clerk of every township was made superintendent of the common schools in his township, and it became his duty to take, in every second year, the enumeration of all the white unmarried youth in each district of the township, male and female, between the ages of four and twenty years, and to deposit with the county auditor a copy of the list.

Upon the establishment of the various land funds in 1828, it had become necessary to make a rule for the distribution of the interest on these funds. The rents in the original surveyed townships had been distributed to the districts, at first, in proportion to the number of inhabitants; then in proportion to number of pupils attending school and time of attendance, and for several years in proportion to the number of families. In 1831, an enumeration was ordered to be taken annually, by every district clerk, of the unmarried white youth between the ages of four and twenty-one years. A report of this enumeration was to be made to the auditor of the county. The report was to state in what original surveyed township or in what school land district the school district was situated, as well as in what civil township. These numbers were the basis upon which the interest was distributed by the county auditors. In 1836, it was made the duty of all county auditors to report the number of school children to the Auditor of State.

The law of 1838 made the township clerk superintendent of the common schools of his township, and the county auditor superintendent of the common schools of the county. It was made the duty of the township superintendent to visit every common school in the township at least once a year, to examine the teacher's record, and all other matters he deemed important "touching the situation, discipline, mode of teaching, and improvement thereof." If the local directors whom he appointed in case of vacancy or failure to elect, refused or neglected to act, he was to exercise the duties of the board of directors, for which he became entitled to compensation out of the funds of the district.

The teacher's record referred to was a book to be provided by the district clerk, in which it was the duty of the teacher to enter the names of all the children, their ages, the date each one entered the school, length of time each one continued in school, and a table showing daily attendance. This book was to be open to the inspection of all persons interested. It was the duty of the teacher, as often as once in three months, to make an abstract of this record showing the whole number of boys and of girls enrolled and their average daily attendance, and to deposit the same with the clerk. It was unlawful to pay the teacher more than two-thirds the amount due for teaching, until this abstract was deposited.

It was the duty of the township superintendent to make the enumeration of all the unmarried white youth of the township between the ages of four and twenty years, and report it to the county auditor every second year. He was also to report to the county auditor, every year, an abstract of the district reports, showing the number of schools; the number of teachers, males and female; wages paid to each; length of school session in each district; number of pupils enrolled, male and female; average daily attendance; houses built and cost of each; value and quantity of school land in or belonging to the township and its annual rent; and such other information as might be thought important. His further duties in relation to taxes have been stated on a previous page.

It was made the duty of the county auditor, as county superintendent of common schools, to apportion the various funds according to law--the state fund and all fines and other moneys that were by law paid to the county treasurer for school purposes, among the townships and districts in proportion to the enumeration of youth ; the county tax, to each township the sum levied on the property of that township, among the districts thereof in proportion to number of youth ; the interest on school land funds to the school districts of the proper original surveyed township or other land district in proportion to the number of youth. These have always been the rules for distribution of these distributable funds. It was also the duty of the auditor to collect the fines and all other moneys payable for school purposes in his county, and to take all proper measures to secure to each township its full amount of school funds.

The auditor of the county was also required to make an annual report to the State Superintendent, giving an abstract of all the reports made to him from the several townships according to such form as the State Superintendent might prescribe. He was also to distribute to the townships and districts such circulars and blank forms as that officer might require. He was to be paid "from the county treasury," not from any school fund. This has been the rule generally in paying this officer, also in paying county and other treasurers for services connected with school funds.

The duties of the county auditor as superintendent of common schools have almost exclusive reference to finances and statistics, and not to any supervision of schools. Under all subsequent laws, these continue to be the duties of the county auditor.

The term of office of the State Superintendent was extended to five years by the act of 1838. Mr. Lewis resigned in 1840. The office was then abolished, and the duties devolved upon the Secretary of State. The salary of the office was increased to twelve hundred dollars. The duties as to collection of statistics and annual report were substantially the same as by the act of 1837.

It was also made the duty of the State Superintendent to ascertain and report the condition of all school lands in the the State, with the amount of funds due each township from lands and interest; to ascertain what lands were yet due to different townships, under the legislation of Congress, and to take measures to secure the location of such lands; and to furnish to the various school officers and to teachers forms for keeping their accounts and records and for making their reports. It was also his duty to investigate all trust funds and property for the support of education, except such as belong to chartered colleges, and he was authorized to examine books and papers of any trustee, and to institute legal proceedings in the name of the State of Ohio to enforce the faithful discharge of all trusts. One other duty was given to this officer in the following words:

"He shall cause to be printed for one year from and after the passage of this act, at the seat of government, a periodical to be called the 'Ohio Common School Director;' a sufficient of said paper shall be published at the expense of the state, at six different periods within the year, to furnish at least one to every district, which paper shall also be distributed by the township clerks; and the district clerk shall suffer all officers and residents of the district, and all the teachers of schools in his district, to have access to said paper, and to read the same to the schools, if they think proper; in said paper shall be printed all the forms to be observed in the different school departments, with such directions and explanations as may be deemed important; also statistical and other information, and such other articles, original or selected, as shall be thought most useful in promoting the cause of common school education."

The township trustees were authorized, by the amendatory act of 1839, to excuse the clerk from the duty of visiting the schools, or they might allow him a compensation for that duty not exceeding one dollar per district each year.

This was amended, in 1851, to make it his duty to visit the schools when directed by the township trustees. With this exception, the legal duties of superintendence remained nearly unchanged till the year 1853. An act of 1842 directed the State Superintendent to prepare and publish an edition of laws relating to common schools, with notes, directions, and forms for the guidance of county, township, and district officers. This act names the officer "Superintendent," though the office had been abolished two years. The act of 1848 speaks of this officer as "Secretary of State." These two acts contained many details intended to perfect the system of statistics and reports. The teacher was required to make his abstract and deliver it to the township treasurer on presenting his claim for wages, and he was to include a statement of the amount received for tuition from other than public funds. Until this report was made the treasurer was forbidden to pay the teacher. In 1851, it was made the duty of the district clerk to report to the annual district meeting a summary of the proceedings of the directors, number of schools, length of time in session, teachers, salaries, taxes, houses, and libraries. The officers of city schools and of all special districts were required to report the same as the officers of township districts.

In 1847, a law was passed allowing the appointment of a county superintendent of schools in certain counties. Very few counties ever acted under this law, and it has been repealed. No general law for county superintendence has ever been enacted by the General Assembly of Ohio.

The act of 1853, setting aside all previous laws on this subject, authorized every board of education to appoint one of their own number acting manager of the schools of the township, and to prescribe his duties as to management and supervision. Boards of education in city districts, under this law, had no authority to appoint any person superintendent who was not a member of the board, but it was customary to do so. The special laws for schools in various cities authorized such appointments. The act of 1873, codifying all these, authorizes any board of education to appoint a superintendent of schools. The act also authorizes the appointment of a superintendent of buildings, janitors, and other officers.

The report required of the teacher at the expiration of every term by the act of 1853, was to give the number of pupils admitted, male and female, average attendance, books used, branches taught, and number of pupils in each branch of study. Without such report no wages could be paid. The act of 1873 places the teachers and superintendents under the direction of the boards of education in the matter of reports. The board of every city district of the first class is required to publish an annual report on the condition of the schools, including their financial affairs.

The law of 1853 required the local directors to take or cause to be taken, every year, the enumeration of the unmarried youth of the sub-district between the ages of five and twenty-one years, noting white and colored, male and female, permanent and temporary residents, and to return a certified copy to the township clerk. The boards of education in all districts except township districts were charged with the same duty. The act of 1873 devolved this duty upon the clerk of the sub-district in township districts, and upon the clerk of the board of education in all other districts. The age was again changed to between six and twenty-one years, and those above sixteen years of age must be given separately. If the school district or sub-district is composed of parts of several original surveyed townships or land districts, the enumeration must be taken for each part separately. Abstracts of these enumerations are reported through the county auditor to the State Commissioner of Common Schools, and by him to the Auditor of State, who

6

is superintendent of the funds. He apportions the distributable funds according to the enumeration and the law, as stated in a previous page. Under the law of 1873, it is a misdemeanor punishable by fine or imprisonment for any officer through whose hands the enumeration passes to add to or take from the number actually enumerated. Every officer appointed to take an enumeration is required to be under oath that he will take the same truly, and when he reports the result he must verify it by affidavit.

According to the enumeration taken in 1875, the total number of school youth in the State of Ohio was 1,017,726.

The act of 1853 also required every board of education to report yearly to the county auditor such statistics as had been required by previous laws, and this duty is required, with increased detail, in the act of 1873. Treasurers are also required to report statistics of moneys received and disbursed. Abstracts of all these are sent by the county auditor to the State Commissioner.

The court appointing examiners must report their names directly to the Commissioner. Every board of examiners must report to him the number of examinations, applicants, certificates of each grade issued, fees received, and whatever else the Commissioner may require. For fear some useful item of information might be overlooked in the law, the act of 1873 makes it the duty of every school officer to report direct to the Commissioner any information he may require.

One of the great advance steps of the law of 1853 was to restore the superintendence of all the common schools of the State to the charge of a distinct officer elected for that express duty. The State Commissioner of Common Schools is elected by the qualified electors of the State every three years. In addition to his duties, just stated, in collecting statistics, he makes an annual report of the same, with plans for the management and improvement of common schools, and such other information as he may think important. It is also his duty to visit annually each of the nine judicial districts of the State, "superintending and encouraging teachers' institutes, conferring with boards of education or other school officers, counseling teachers, visiting schools, and delivering lectures on topics calculated to subserve the interests of popular education."

The State Commissioner is also required to exercise a supervision over the educational funds, and he has power, upon complaint in due form that school funds have been misapplied, to appoint a trustworthy and competent accountant to investigate the matter, in order that if there has been fraud, civil or criminal proceedings may be commenced against the delinquents.

PUPILS.

For whose benefit all these laws, all this care, and all this labor and expense? The preamble and first section of the law of 1825 are as follows:

"WHEREAS, It is provided by the constitution of this State, that schools and the means of instruction shall forever be encouraged by legislative provision, therefore,

SECTION 1. *Be it enacted by the General Assembly of the State of Ohio*, That a fund shall hereafter be annually raised among the several counties in this State, in the manner pointed out by this act, for the use of common schools, for the instruction of youth of every class and grade, without distinction, in reading, writing, arithmetic, and other necessary branches of a common education."

This was re-enacted in the year 1829, with the following words added:

"Provided, that nothing in this act shall be construed to permit black or mulatto persons to attend schools hereby established, or compel them to pay any tax for support of such schools; but all taxes assessed on their property for school purposes, in the several counties of this State, shall be appropriated as the trustees of said township may direct, for the education of said persons."

The same act, in another section, declares that the schools shall be open to all except blacks and mulattoes. The law of 1831 has the same preamble and section 1 as the act of 1825, but inserts the word "white" before "youth," and omits the proviso of 1829. The next section provides for a tax, omitting the property of blacks and mulattoes. The law of 1838 also directed no tax to be levied on the property of any black or mulatto person, and it declared that in all cases during the periods when the public money is applied to the support of schools, the schools shall be free for all the white children in the district. From 1831 to 1848, black and mulatto persons were simply let alone by the school laws, as if neither they nor their property had any existence.

In 1848, a law was passed to provide schools for colored children. It directed the property of black or colored persons to be taxed for school purposes the same as other property, a separate account to be kept by the county auditor, and the money to be paid for the support of separate schools for black or colored persons; but in districts where they were allowed to attend the common schools, the money was added to the common school fund of the district. Every city, town, or township containing twenty or more black or colored children of any age was constituted a school district for such children, with the same organization and officers as other school districts. If the number of children was over fifty, the district might be divided. If the number was less than twenty desirous of attending school, they should be admitted to the common school unless a written objection was presented to the directors signed by any person having a child in the school or by any legal voter. In that case, no school tax should be levied on the property of any black or colored person in such city, town, or township, and if any such tax had been already paid, it should be refunded.

The law of 1853 directs that when the number of colored school children in any school district exceeds thirty, there shall be established a separate school for them in such district, under the management of the board of education of the district; but if the average attendance is less than fifteen, the school shall be discontinued for any period not exceeding six months at one time, and if the number of children is less than fifteen, their share of school money shall be reserved and appropriated for their education under the direction of the township board. What should be done when the number of colored children in the district was between fifteen and thirty, does not appear. This was amended, in 1864, by substituting twenty for both thirty and fifteen, and providing for a joint district where the aggregate of colored children in two adjoining school districts is over twenty. The act of 1873 codified and superseded all other former laws, but this amended section of the previous law was left unrepealed.

The laws of Ohio have never expressly excluded from school either adults or children below the minimum age of enumeration. In 1834, it was enacted that adults might be admitted to the common schools upon payment of tuition. In 1839, the same privilege, upon the same terms, was extended to adults and to persons residing out of the district. This was repeated in 1853 and in 1873. The schools are free to all youth between six and twenty-one years of age, residents of the district. No pupil can be suspended except till the board of education or the local directors can be convened. No pupil can be expelled unless by a vote of two-thirds of the board of education or of the local directors, and after the parent or guardian of the accused has been notified of the proposed expulsion and been permitted to be heard against the same. The expulsion can only be for the current term.

CONCLUDING REMARKS.

In the foregoing sketch it has been necessary to omit any notice of projects of legislation. Only enacted laws have been examined. Any mention of the legislators who were most efficient in making these laws, has been omitted. Very few of the names are known to the writer, and it is presumed that they will be sufficiently noticed in the chapter on Biography. It has also been necessary to omit many details of secondary importance, and nearly all mention of local laws. It is proper to say, however, that the latter have constituted a very large and important part of the school legislation of the State from the time when the lands were leased to the present.

The statutes of 1821, 1825, 1838, and 1853 have been regarded, and with some reason, as new laws initiating new eras in school history. This is more apparent than real. Many of the most important laws were made as amendments to these four.

The law of 1821 provided a way in which people might unite in building school houses and employing teachers. It contemplated action of neighborhoods. The school lot in some corner of the forest would be of so little pecuniary value that a tax for its purchase was not provided for. The log house would cost more, and for that expense there would be needed some united action. This law was entirely permissive, and this has remained a characteristic feature of Ohio school laws. Township superintendence, county superintendence, teacher's institutes, tax for building houses, organization of high schools, the adoption of this or that law for a town, and various other matters have been left to the judgment or the caprice of the people most interested. The title of the act of 1821 was, "An act to provide for the regulation and support of common schools."

The law of 1825 was very different from the preceding. From beginning to end it had the tone of command—thus it shall be, and such shall be the penalty for neglect. This was the first law which levied a tax upon the principle that the property of all must help pay for popular education. The reader is impressed with the straightforward, earnest zeal which is evinced in all its sections. Its title was, "An act to provide for the support and better regulation of common schools."

Organization was the characteristic of the law of 1838. It provided system, with a head and various grades of supervision. It was entitled, "An act for the support and better regulation of common schools, and to create permanently the office of superintendent."

Between 1838 and 1853, many amendments to the general law were enacted and many special and local laws were passed. Some confusion existed. The law of 1853 restored the state supervision, initiated the township system, and established the rule that the property of the State must pay all the expense of public education. The features of that law are well expressed in its title, "An act to provide for the reorganization, supervision, and maintenance of common schools."

The school law of Ohio, as it exists to-day, is the result of more than half a century's slow growth. The progress has not always been forward. Many experiments—some unsuccessful—have been tried.

The law of 1873 is a codification. It is distinguished from all previous school laws in that it unifies to a large extent the various systems of local organization, and prepares the way for yet greater uniformity in the future.

CHAPTER II.

UNGRADED SCHOOLS.

The origin of the Common School System of Ohio may be traced to the ordinance for the government of the North-western Territory passed by Congress in 1787. The third article of that ordinance declared that, "Religion, morality, and knowledge being necessary to good government and the happiness of mankind, schools and the means of education shall be forever encouraged." Two years prior to the promulgation of this enlightened sentiment, Congress had provided for the division of the Western Territory into ranges and townships in order to facilitate the sale of public lands therein. Each township was sub-divided into thirty-six sections, and the sixteenth section in every township was set apart "for the maintenance of public schools within the township."

This grant of land for the support of schools was designed to encourage emigration to the unsettled regions of the then far west. The reservation of section sixteen for the maintenance of schools, and other provisions of a kindred character found in these early ordinances, indicate the sound judgment and far-sighted statesmanship of those who were instrumental in framing and passing them. It is difficult to determine to what extent the tide of emigration which soon rolled westward, was broadened and deepened by the inducements held out to pioneers by these grants, which by compact were made perpetual. History bears out the assertion that many of the early settlers were wholly indifferent to those educational privileges which a little zeal and energy on their part would have placed within their reach; and it is altogether unlikely that such were led to encounter the hardships and privations of pioneer life through the hope that their children's children would be the recipients of free instruction.

The *true* pioneers, those who formed, as it were, the vanguard of the army of emigrants, and who sought the western country for the purpose of finding permanent homes there, entertained far more liberal and advanced views on the subject of education than those who were quick to follow in their footsteps when the real advantages of the West as a place of abode became known. The early settlers of Ohio brought with them to their new homes the ideas and sentiments which prevailed in the older states from which they emigrated. If religion and education were regarded as of primary importance by the people of any state, their sons and daughters carried these ideas with them to their pioneer homes, and were swift to prove the force of their early teachings by their acts. The reverse was equally true. From states in which a low standard of moral and educational sentiment prevailed, came emigrants who remained as indifferent to the moral and intellectual welfare of their children as their fathers before them had been. Under such circumstances, the condition of education in the various settlements established before Ohio became a member of the Union, and in fact for many years after that event, was widely different. Intelligence became almost universal in the settlements established by the former class, while in settlements founded by the latter, the evil results of the settlers' apathy in educational matters were discernible for many years.

The settlement of Ohio began in 1788. In April of this year a little band of emigrants, under the auspices of the Ohio Company, landed at the mouth of the Muskingum river, and at once proceeded to lay out a town and erect rude dwelling-houses. These pioneers were the descendants of those sturdy Puritan Fathers who, in the winter of 1620, found a home in the dreary solitudes of New England. Possessed of many of the traits of character which so distinguished their forefathers, the settlers at Marietta were soon enjoying the advantages of a school ,and the regular ministrations of a preacher of the Gospel. The labors of the Rev. Daniel Story, as a teacher and a preacher, began as soon as the infant settlement was fairly under way. Before 1800 there were eight settlements established in the Ohio Company's purchase, in each of which, it is fair to presume from the known antecedents of the settlers, the subject of education received that consideration which the nature of the times would permit. A school of young boys and girls at Belpre, taught during the summer of 1790 by Bathsheba Rouse, is mentioned by some authorities as being the first school of white children opened in Ohio. It is a well authenticated fact that the Moravian missionaries had established Indian schools at different missions on the Tuscarawas, a tributary of the Muskingum, several years before the settlements at Marietta and Belpre were begun.

While these events were in progress within the purchase of the Ohio Company, a promising settlement was begun at a point on the Ohio river a short distance above Fort Washington, the present site of Cincinnati. This settlement was called Columbia. Near the close of the year 1792, Francis Dunlevy, who had achieved distinction in the Indian campaigns, opened a school in Columbia. This pioneer teacher afterward held important offices under the territorial and state government.

The first permanent settlement in that portion of Ohio known as the Western Reserve was not commenced before the year 1796, and two years later but few settlements were to be found in all that reservation. In 1802, a school was opened in Harpersfield which soon obtained a wide-spread reputation. This is supposed to be the first school established on the Reserve. The first teachers were Elizabeth Harper and Abraham Tappen. About the time the Harpersfield school was established, a school was taught by Anna Spafford in the cabin of one of the early settlers of Cleveland.

Thus we see that the pioneers who settled in south-eastern, south-western, and north-eastern Ohio, established and sustained schools in their settlements amid all the perils and misfortunes that environed them. Regarding the settlements in the interior of Ohio less definite information can be obtained. With few exceptions, schools were opened as soon as the settlements were established. As before remarked, the presence or absence of a school in any settlement was largely due to the previous condition and training of the settlers. There were no means of removing the lethargy of the indifferent and of stimulating the faint-hearted. Opportunities for learning the lessons of prudence and wisdom from the experiences of sister settlements were rarely afforded and less often improved in those early times. Each settlement solved the educational problem for itself. The wiser men of that period looked into the future and discerned the foreshadowings of something better than was likely to be enjoyed in their generation.

In the Territorial Legislature education was made the frequent topic of discussion, and although nothing was done for the support of schools, the utterances of that body were such as to leave no doubt of the high estimation in which educational advantages were held by the members. The convention which met in Chillicothe, in 1802, to frame a constitution for the State of Ohio, was composed of men who recognized the expediency and necessity of legislative action in regard to schools as a means of insuring the well-being of the new state. It was made the imperative duty of the legislature by the terms of the first state constitution, to encourage schools and the means of instruction by such legislative provision as would not be antagonistic to the rights of conscience. Another section of this instrument placed a prohibition on any legislative enactments that would tend to prevent the poor from participating equally in all the benefits arising from donations made by Congress for the support of schools and colleges. The ordinance of 1787 declared that "schools and the means of education shall forever be encouraged," but the first constitution of Ohio pointed out the manner in which this encouragement should be extended; namely, "by legislative provision."

From 1802 to 1821, legislative action regarding education, under the power conferred by the constitution, was confined to the passage of acts authorizing the incorporation of seminaries, religious and educational societies, and providing for the leasing of school lands. Nothing was done looking to the establishment of schools by means of general or local taxation. The tardiness of the legislature in carrying out the constitutional requirement by a system of state or local taxation, might have been owing to the confident expectation, which was general in the early days of the State's history, that the revenue arising from the lands donated by Congress would be adequate to sustain free schools throughout the State. How this hope was realized may be seen by study of our school legislation prior to 1828.

Yet it must not be understood that there were none to lift a voice in advocacy of an efficient system of common schools. The different men who held the gubernatorial office during the first twenty years of Ohio's existence as a state, were earnest in their endeavors to secure wise school legislation on the part of the General Assembly, and no inconsiderable portion of their messages was devoted to the consideration of educational interests. Private citizens were not lacking who endeavored to arouse the legislature to the importance of the trust confided to its keeping, and who were swift to denounce the abuse of that power over the school lands by which the children of a new generation were defrauded of their just inheritance.

While these agencies of a public character were at work for good or evil, private enterprise and private means were employed in giving to the pioneer youth of the State the simplest rudiments of a common school education. This was an undertaking of no small magnitude. The conditions of pioneer life are such as to render anything approximating to an adequate provision for schools and other means of instruction well-nigh impossible. The pioneer must provide for the physical wants of himself and his household before he is in a condition to give his attention to the demands of his higher nature. In a new settlement, a certain amount of material prosperity must be enjoyed by the people before they are prepared to introduce any of the more enlightened features of civilized life which are so beneficent in ministering to the mental and moral culture of the people of the older localities. The early settlers of Ohio, as a rule, were too busy in erecting rude habitations, felling trees, burning off the heavy timber, fencing the clearings, guiding the plow through rooty ground, and making passable highways to mill and market, to allow them to devote any attention to any other interest less pressing, and that could be deferred to a more convenient season. Hence it is not strange that school interests were often neglected. Muscular power could be used, and was indispensable, in improving a new country, in making money to pay for the homestead, and in meeting the demands of the tax-gatherer. So it happened that muscular power was respected and commanded a high premium, while mere intellectual force without bodily vigor was at a discount.

The pioneer schools of the northern and eastern sections of Ohio differed, in many respects, from those of the south-western portion of the State; the latter being settled by people from Virginia, Kentucky, and the Carolinas, who, probably, did not appreciate educational privileges so highly as did the settlers of the former, who were from the New England States where common schools, at that time, were far in advance of those in any other section of the Union.*

The teachers of the pioneer schools in south-western Ohio were selected more on account of their unfitness to perform manual labor than by reason of their intellectual worth. The few schools established in this section were taught by cripples, worn-out old men, and women physically unable or constitutionally too lazy to scotch hemp or spin flax. Educational sentiment was at a low ebb, and demanded from the instructors of children no higher qualifications than could be furnished by the merest tyro. Before school legislation and other instrumentalities effected salutary changes in the methods of school administration common to this locality, schools of worth were only to be found in the more populous centers. The estimation in which the teacher was held by the community at large was not such as to induce any young man or woman of spirit and worth to enter upon teaching as a vocation.

The teacher was regarded as a kind of pensioner on the bounty of the people, whose presence was tolerated only because county infirmaries were not then in existence. The capacity of teachers *to teach* was never a reason for employing him, but the fact that he could do nothing else was a satisfactory one. Under such circumstances, it would be vain to look for exalted qualifications on the part of the teachers. The people's demand for education was fully met when their children could write a tolerably legible hand, when they could read the Bible or an almanac, and when

*The writer of this chapter is indebted to Hon. D. P. Nelson, of Butler county, and Judge S. G. Barnard, of Medina county, for interesting facts relating to the pioneer schools of Ohio.

they were so far inducted into the mysterious computation of numbers as to be able to determine the value of a load of farm produce. This crude instruction was deemed amply sufficient; more than this was regarded as dangerous, since the idea had gained currency that education made boys lazy and tricky. It was also a popular belief that young ladies who were apt with pen or pencil, were in imminent danger of falling an easy prey to some designing knave who might entrap them by an epistolary correspondence which could never be detected by an illiterate mother. Girls seldom learned to write.

A brighter picture presents itself when we consider the state of educational sentiment in that section of Ohio peopled with settlers from New England. At an early day schools on the Western Reserve were in a thriving condition. Among the pioneers were found men who had received a liberal culture in schools and colleges second to none in the Union. Narrow and restricted views in regard to education found lodgment in the minds of comparatively few of the people. They were not oblivious to the value of education in a utilitarian sense, but their notions of utility were broader and more comprehensive than those entertained by their southern neighbors. They would not confine school instruction to those subjects, a knowledge of which would enable the child to provide for the wants of his physical nature alone, but would make it an important agency in arousing and strengthening the child's moral and mental attributes as well. The instruction which the child received at school bore early fruit, as seen in his improved conduct, manners, and morals.

The social status of the teacher was on an equal footing with that of the physician and the minister. Society welcomed him to its presence as an honored member. His periodic visits to the homes of his pupils were regarded as quite an event by each household, and great were the preparations that preceded his appearance to "board out" the share of any patron of his school.

The qualifications of the teachers were generally such as to command respect. Many of them magnified their office, and contributed not a little to the formation of that public sentiment which soon began to demand a practical recognition of school interests by the General Assembly. The teacher found board and lodging in the houses of his patrons. His evenings were spent with the family. If this plan did not give him the best opportunities for self-culture and preparation for the duties of the morrow, it was not without its advantages. Many an aspiring youth was led into new fields of thought by coming in personal contact with the master in the home circle; and the seeds of knowledge planted by the faithful teacher around the firesides of the pioneers, often sprung up into vigorous life, yielding a rich mental fruitage. The teacher became intimately acquainted with the habits and peculiarities of his pupils when they were acting independent of the authority exerted in the schoolroom, and was thus enabled to turn his knowledge of their traits of character to his own assistance and their profit. Parents were awakened to a new interest in their children's instruction, and were led to co-operate with the teacher in his efforts to promote that end by the quiet missionary work performed by the teacher when brought into such close personal relations with them.

In other respects than those instanced the pioneer schools of Ohio were not widely dissimilar. The schools were indeed independent. The teacher would draw up an article of agreement binding himself to teach a school in some specified house for a term of thirteen weeks, six days per week, and eight hours per day, for which the patrons agreed to pay him a stipulated sum, ranging from one to two dollars for each scholar subscribed, one-half payable perhaps in wheat at fifty cents per bushel, and the balance payable in money at the close of the term. As a rule, when twenty scholars were pledged the teacher's labors began.

The practice which prevails to a great extent at the present day, of employing a male teacher to teach a winter term and a female teacher to teach the summer term, was prevalent all over the State. The teacher was compelled to devote three-fourths of his time to labor of another kind, since the pittance saved from his school earnings was totally inadequate to supply him with physical comforts during the rest of the year.

The mode of government was simple. Moral suasion was not recognized by the pioneer school-master as an important element in school management. The neighboring forests were filled with fine sprouts, which were regarded as just the thing to sharpen the wits and brighten the moral perceptions of a pupil. Hickory oil was known to be a good lubricator for the mental friction of a school-boy, and its use in liberal quantities by the master or mistress was rarely the subject of complaint or criticism on the part of parents.

The text-books were such as had been brought from the old settlements—few of them designed or fitted for school use. Murray's English Reader with Introduction, Columbian Orator, American Preceptor, Testaments, and not infrequently old almanacs were in the hands of pupils as reading books. Dillworth's Speller and Webster's Easy Standard of Pronunciation were extensively used in pioneer schools. Pike's Arithmetic was the universal favorite, and the teacher who was unable to elucidate its mysteries as far as the "Rule of Three" soon lost the repsect of his pupils and patrons. Geographies and grammars were seldom seen in the hands of teachers and scholars. The instruction in most schools was very rudimentary, being confined to such subjects as reading, spelling, writing, and the simplest opertions in numbers. A pioneer reading-class was an important event in the programme of daily exercises. One pupil read from the family Bible, another from Poor Richard's Almanac, while still a third read thrilling passages from some highly-prized volume, such as Captain James Riley's Narrative of Shipwreck and Captivity among the Arabs. If the reader of the last chanced to possess some elocutionary power, the whole school, teacher included, suspended operations and with open mouths and eyes listened intently to the interesting narration. Spelling and reading were made specialties, and were regarded as the chief tests of soholarship. Spelling matches were second only in importance to the schools themselves. These were usually held at night, and were attended by old and young. A ride, or more frequently a walk, of six miles was an obstacle easily surmounted by persons wishing to enjoy the competition or witness the discomfiture of a rival school when its last champion was "spelled down."

The school-houses in which these busy scenes were enacted almost defy description. Were it not that after nearly three-quarters of a century of progress, many school-houses yet exist which have their prototypes in the pioneer school-houses, the attempt to describe the latter by any other than one who had a personal knowledge of them would be a difficult undertaking. The vacant cabin, which had been hastily constructed by some pioneer and vacated as soon as he had built a better or had left the settlement to seek a more favored locality, sometimes served as a school-house. Again, the settlers would exercise their ingenuity and architectural skill in building what they considered a suitable house for school purposes. As regards the material used in its erection, and the means of comfort provided for those who were to occupy it, the latter structure had few advantages over the former. It was formed of logs, sometimes roughly hewed, and was generally about eighteen feet wide by twenty-four feet long. The eaves were about ten feet from the ground, and the roof was covered with rows of clapboards held in place by long poles running lengthwise. The openings between the logs were chinked with pieces of wood, stone, or any other convenient material, and plastered with mortar made from the ground near by. This work was called "mudding" the house. The directors generally attended to this branch of repairs every fall, as the rains of spring and summer usually washed away the mortar, especially if straw or hay had not been used in mixing it.

The door was made of rough boards, hung with wooden hinges, and fastened by means of a wooden latch, to which a string was attached passing through a small hole above out into the open air. Access to the building was obtained by pulling the string, by which the latch was lifted, and exerting a little muscular force to overcome the friction of the rude hinges. The pioneers secured their houses from surreptitious entrance by pulling in the string. Thus it became proverbial that the "latch-string out" was a sign of hospitality. Tardy pupils who found no string outside, knew that the master was "at prayers" within, and waited silently and solemnly around the door until the latch-string appeared.

Some houses had rough puncheon floors, others only clay. These puncheons were thick slabs or plank split from large logs and hewed on one side, being from three to four inches thick and often lying upon the ground instead of upon "sleepers." Ventilation was perfect. In some cases, light was obtained by cutting out an entire log and pasting oiled paper over the opening—thus admitting some light and excluding some cold—again, window sash were fitted in openings made by cutting through three or four logs, and glazed in the usual manner. Sometimes the inside walls, instead of receiving the common coat of mortar, were covered with boards. These walls were bare of pictures and other ornaments, if we accept such rude efforts at portraiture as were made by the more ambitious and skillful pupils with no better material than chalk or a piece of coal taken from the wide-extended fire-place.

The school furniture was in keeping with the exterior and interior appearance of the building. By splitting a log six inches in diameter and fifteen feet in length, into halves, and mounting these upon four legs, flat side up, solid if not comfortable seats were made. The idea that a pupil's spinal column needed any support or that his feet should touch the floor, was utterly ignored by the mechanical geniuses who constructed the benches for the pioneer school-house. Next to the wall, on three sides of the room, the floor was often elevated for the benches of the larger scholars. The lower benches were in front. It was a well established rule of the school that pupils occupying the back seats should not put their feet on the persons or seats of the smaller pupils in front—a rule that had a wholesome effect in protecting those whose youth and size doomed them to occupy places on the front forms. The desks were only for the use of pupils on the back seats. These were formed by placing wide boards on long pins driven into the logs. The edges of these desks served as a sort of brace for the backs of those scholars whose size gave them a seat near the wall.

The scholars were required to face the teacher except on special permission or when writing. "Face to the wall" required a movement calling for much skill and judgment, on the part of the actors, to execute it surely and gracefully. A young lady, in complying with this order, was compelled to disturb the other occupants of the bench, perhaps by obliging them to rise, or to swing herself into her place in a very ungraceful manner. The boys swung themselves into the required position with wonderful alacrity. The movement was peculiar. A boy with arms akimbo and lower limbs extended would describe a half-circle, passing his feet between the seat and desk as he turned. An inexpert whose feet chanced to strike either seat or desk, was thrown to the floor as the result of misdirected motion.

In winter, immense logs blazed in the open fire-place which occupied a great part of one end of the building. A wall of rough stone against the side of the house formed a foundation upon which the chimney rested. The chimney itself was made of sticks placed upon each other like cobs in "cob-houses," chinked with mortar and thickly coated internally with the same material—the whole being kept in place by two naturally-crooked saplings, shaped like the runners of a sled, one end of each resting on a log in the building and the other on a joist.

The time and ingenuity of the builders of these primitive school-houses seemed to be exhausted when the main building was completed and furnished. Those adjuncts which are now regarded as indispensable features of every school-yard, were not always seen among the surroundings of the pioneer school-house. The sexes usually had their recesses at different times.

Such was the condition of education throughout the rural districts of Ohio prior to the passage of the first school law in 1821. Many schools of a higher character than those whose description has been attempted were to be found in the larger towns of the State. All schools were supported by the voluntary contributions of the people, as no tax had been authorized by the General Assembly, and as the lands donated for the support of schools had not yet produced any revenue of importance.

The influences which were effective in securing legislation in behalf of a common school system, emanated from a few wise, liberal-minded men in Cincinnati. Their efforts were ably seconded by the friends of education in Cleveland and other northern towns, between whom and the originators of the movement an extensive correspondence in reference to school interests was carried on. This concerted effort, together with the advanced views disseminated among the people through the agency of Solomon Thrifty's Almanac, published at Cincinnati under the proprietorship of Nathan Guilford, led to the passage by the legislature of the first general school law for Ohio. Although this law failed to effect any salutary reforms in the methods of school administration in vogue at that time, it paved the way for more efficient legislation in subsequent years. The school law of 1821 made provision for the division of townships into school districts in case a majority of the householders voted in favor of such organization; the selection of these householders as a school committee in each district so established, and the levying of taxes within a certain limit; the erection of schol-buildings in suitable and convenient localities, and the employment of teachers by such committee. In assessing taxes, the committee was authorized to remit the whole or any part of the taxes levied upon parents or guardians who were unable to pay their share of the assessment, the amount of which was determined by the number of scholars who had been in attendance at school. The effect of this *pro rata* assessment in those districts organized under the law, was to deprive the children of the poor of all school instruction. Pride acted as an effective bar to prevent the acceptance by the poor man of school privileges which were grudgingly paid for by his more prosperous neighbors.

The law of 1821 carried with it nothing more than a moral force. Under its authority, action on the part of the people was permissible, not obligatory. The law of February 5, 1825, was wider in its scope and more liberal in its provisions than its predecessor. For the first time in the history of the State, a county tax for the support of common schools was established by legislative authority. The people were slow to avail themselves of the opportunities for the establishment of a better school system afforded by the new law, and meager were the results secured for many years. It reached the country districts finally, and caused the organization of several districts and the erection of a better class of school-houses, but produced no material change in the management of the schools.

As late as 1825 there were no public schools, properly speaking, in Cincinnati, where, as we have seen, public sentiment was early manifested in favor of wise legislation in support of schools. The revenue derived from the county tax and the receipts from school lands were insufficient to maintain free schools for more than a few weeks in the year. In order to provide the necessary funds to keep the schools in session for a longer period, "rate bills" were assessed on all school patrons. In 1829, when the county tax was three-fourths of a mill, the whole amount of money apportioned to the directors of a rural district for the maintenance of a free school rarely exceeded $10. How could a free school be opened with only ten dollars of public money in the school treasury? This problem was solved by a public announcement, under authority of the directors, that upon a certain day a school would be opened for free instruction for a term of ten days. The appointed day came, and with it came scholars in search of free tuition. Many scholars, whom the teacher had never seen before and whom probably he never saw again, flocked to the school house and filled up every available seat. Ten days of anarchy ruled in the school-room. Those who were able to pay the assessment by which the school was sustained after the public fund was exhausted, did not, as a general rule, patronize the free school.

The law of 1825 provided for the appointment of examiners of schools by the court of common pleas. Teachers were required to obtain certificates of qualifications from these examiners before they could teach a district school. In this legislation is seen the first attempt to protect the children of the State from the results of incompetent teaching. The law secured the "instruction of youth in reading, writing, arithmetic, and other necessary branches of a common education." Applicants for certificates were examined in spelling, reading, writing, and in arithmetic as far as the "Single Rule of Three." Many teachers who had taught acceptably in the school-room, and whose fitness to discharge the duties of instructor had never been questioned by their employers, were unable to pass a satisfactory examination in these rudimentary branches. Among teachers and patrons the impression prevailed that the action of school examiners in fixing the standard of qualifications was needlessly severe.

Between the years 1825 and 1837, legislation accomplished little for the advancement of school interests. During this period the county tax was increased to one and one-half mills, with an additional half mill at the discretion of the county commissioners. In 1831, a new impulse was given to education by the organization of a College of Teachers at Cincinnati. The papers read before this body, which included among its members the most prominent educators of Ohio and neighboring states, were characterized by marked ability and profound wisdom. The influence of the College of Teachers was felt in securing a more general and a more efficient administration of the school law, in spreading abroad more enlightened views on the subject of a public school system, and in promoting the progress of higher education in the State. It was mainly through the discussions held at its sessions that the public mind was directed to the need of a Superintendent of Common Schools.

In 1837, a State School Department was established and Hon. Samuel Lewis became the first State Superintendent. The most authentic history of the common schools of Ohio from 1837 to 1840, is to be found in the three annual reports of Mr. Lewis published under legislative authority. For the first time, an attempt was made to obtain statistical information respecting the condition of the schools of the State as seen in the practical workings of the school law. Many county auditors, either through negligence or inability to obtain the required information, failed to make any returns whatever, while the reports of others were so inaccurate and incomplete as to convey no other information than that school affairs in many counties were badly administered.

Mr. Lewis became convinced that the common schools of cities and towns were poorer than those in country districts. The people of the rural districts took a deeper interest in the common school, because the means and opportunities for establishing and supporting private schools were not so abundant in the country as in the cities and towns. The patronage extended by the wealthy inhabitants of cities to private schools tended to bring the common schools into disrepute, and to fasten upon them the ruinous appellation of "poor schools." Those unable to provide for the instruction of their children, except through the agency of the common school, were not always willing to accept its privileges when such acceptance on their part was a sure means of exhibiting their poverty.

When the labors of Mr. Lewis began, Cincinnati was the only city in the State where free instruction was provided for all alike by local taxation. The chief difficulty experienced in cities where attempts were made to sustain free schools, resulted from the inadequacy of the school accommodations. The schools were kept in rented houses, often totally unfit for the purpose for which they were leased, and sometimes in the basement of churches. When the old order of things was superseded by the free school policy, new buildings became a necessity. The erection of suitable buildings for the accommodation of the large number of pupils that soon applied for admission to the free schools, greatly increased the burden of taxation and thus aroused the active opposition of many wealthy citizens. Nothing but the inherent strength of the free school policy and the courage and intelligence of its advocates secured its growth into popular favor under such circumstances.

Action under the school law was by no means uniform in towns, villages, and rural districts. The plainest provisions of the law regarding the use of the school fund derived from the county tax were frequently and shamefully violated. In certain districts the school fund would be allowed to accumulate until it was sufficient to sustain a school for a time of three months, and then a free school would be opened. Again, in other districts the public money would be used in part payment of school expenses, while the balance would be subscribed by parents at so much per scholar. Under the plan last mentioned schools were kept in session for longer time, but the poor were rarely allowed to participate in the greater amount of instruction thus secured. Sometimes the teacher was required to receive the children of those who were able to *prove* their inability to pay their proportional part of the cost of tuition; but if these so far overcame their feelings of pride as to seek school advantages under such conditions, the school-room was overcrowded and the teacher's efforts crippled thereby. The school-house of a district was rarely commodious enough to accommodate all the children living within the district, and not without reason did the wealthy class prefer the school supported by subscription to the free school with its crowded forms, impure air, and overworked teacher.

While pointing out the weak places in the school system as it then existed, and while exhibiting in the clearest light and the strongest language the abuses that had crept into its administration, Mr. Lewis did not hesitate to affirm that outside of New England no better schools could be found in the Union than those of Ohio. He found cause for congratulation and encouragement in the facts that the people were beginning to recognize the evils that had become associated with school management and seemed determined to remedy them; that public sentiment was demanding qualified teachers; that the instruction in the common schools was taking a freer range and a wider scope; and that substantial frame and brick school-houses were taking the place of the old pioneer relics and rented basements.

The school law of 1838 gave legislative sanction to many of the views advanced in Mr. Lewis's first annual report. Its main provisions remained essentially the same until 1853. A state school fund of $200,000 was established, a county tax of two mills was imposed, local taxes for building school-houses were authorized, and reports from teachers and school authorities were required. Under this liberal legislation the prosperity of free schools was assured, as more abundant means were provided for their support.

The three years' service of Mr. Lewis marks a bright era in the educational history of Ohio. His retirement from office in 1839 lost to the cause of free schools the active service of its ablest advocate.

From 1840 to 1853 the duties of State Superintendent of Schools devolved upon the Secretary of State. Between 1840 and 1845 there was an evident decline of school interest on the part of the people. The tables of school statistics in the appendix to this work will show, in part, manifestations of this decline.

In 1845, the first session of a teachers' institute in Ohio was held at Sandusky. It is no exaggeration to say that from that time until the present no instrumentality has been more effective in elevating the character of teaching in all schools, but more especially in ungraded schools of the State, than the teachers' institute. The College of Teachers, of which mention has been made, accomplished much for teachers engaged in the more advanced departments of education, and the State Teachers' Association, organized in

1847, has contributed largely to the same end; but the great mass of the common school teachers of the State have never been directly benefited by the able discussions and scholarly papers which have so distinguished these educational bodies.

The early schools of Ohio were from necessity ungraded schools. The graded system could not be established in pioneer settlements. The cities were the first to demand and secure such legislation as would enable them to provide for the instruction of a large number of pupils in one building. Classification, by which the work of instruction might be facilitated and rendered more effective, followed naturally. Before 1847, the cities of Cincinnati, Cleveland, Dayton, and Columbus had organized graded schools under special acts of the legislature. The value of the graded system of instruction, as evinced by the steady progress of the schools in these cities, received legislative recognition in the passage of the "Akron law," the law of 1849, and that of 1853, under which graded schools have since been established in all the cities and towns and in many of the villages of the State. Since the passage of these acts, the most energizing and vitalizing forces have been employed in placing the graded schools on a more elevated plane of progress than has been even approximately reached by the best and most favored ungraded or rural schools. During the last thirty years the most intelligent efforts of legislators and educators have been put forth in perfecting the graded systems of cities and towns, while the interests of the ungraded schools of the rural districts, if not forgotten, have been sadly neglected. In 1838, the schools in rural districts were more efficient than those of cities; but since that time the former have advanced by slow and almost imperceptible stages, while the latter have progressed with unparalleled rapidity. That there has been progress in country schools cannot be denied, but this progress has been due as much to the force of events as to any wisely-directed efforts put forth in their behalf. Educators and friends of education do not point to our ungraded schools when they wish to show the best fruitage of our common school system. The cities are altogether relied upon to sustain the credit of the State in all educational expositions.

The causes that have been instrumental in retarding the progress of ungraded schools are now generally known. They have not felt the effects of intelligent supervision; they have not been taught by professional teachers; and they have not been watched over by intelligent, capable boards of directors. It is frequently asserted, with some show of reason, that the ungraded sehools of to-day afford fewer facilities for the acquisition of a knowledge of the higher branches than they did a score of years ago. Before the schools of cities and towns afforded a more remunerative field of labor to the professional teacher, it was not uncommon to see a teacher of liberal culture in charge of a country school. The pioneer teacher was often the graduate of a good college. He was able to soar beyond the elementary fields of knowledge into regions comparatively unknown to the greater number of the common school teachers of a later day. His pupils caught something of the love for knowledge which actuated the master, and were thus led to aspire to a higher standard of scholarship than that limited by an acquaintance with the elementary branches.

The law by which the qualifications of teachers were measured by boards of county examiners, when faithfully enforced, secured the banishment from the school-room of many incompetent teachers; but it failed to recognize any distinction between the liberally-educated teacher and the one possessing no more book knowledge than was required to entitle him to a certificate of the lowest grade. The law widened the field of competition, and hastened the withdrawal from the ungraded schools of the State of the best educated and most capable teachers. Boards of directors were expected to supply teachers for their districts, and sometimes they set about the work in much the same way as they would conduct themselves in driving a sharp bargain with a cattle dealer for farm stock; only pausing long enough, before concluding the transaction, to satisfy themselves that the applicant was in possession of the certificate required by law. Of course such a state of affairs did not prevail all over the State. In many localities, any other than a thoroughly qualified teacher could not secure a school under any circumstances.

From 1825 to 1849, teachers were required to pass an examination in spelling, reading, writing, and arithmetic. To these branches were added, in 1849, geography and English grammar. During the last quarter of a century the law has demanded of the teachers of ungraded schools no higher scholarship than would enable them to show a moderate acquaintance with these rudimentary subjects. The people often manifest no disposition to find fault with a law which has the effect to supply abundant material from which to select cheap teachers. Under the present system of examination the supply of teachers greatly exceeds the demand, and as a consequence, the less qualified teachers establish the rate of compensation, while the more worthy are compelled to seek a livelihood in some more lucrative labor.

This excess of the supply of teachers above the demand is productive of another evil. The services of a good teacher are often dispensed with for no other reason than that the directors favor "rotation in office." Two young ladies are ambitious to become the teacher of the district school. The law kindly interposes no serious obstacle. Certificates are obtained by each, after many successive attempts, and the two aspirants for pedagogic honors present themselves before the local directors and ask employment at their hands. If the friends of these young ladies are equally influential and importunate, the directors are placed in no enviable position. A compromise is generally effected, by the terms of which both are assured of employment. The one selected is expected to vacate the teacher's chair at the end of the first term to make way for the installment of the other at the beginning of the second.

It is not difficult to form an idea of the nature of the instruction given in many schools when the meager qualifications of the teachers and the mode of their selection are known. The tendency of the instruction, in schools taught by such teachers, is to make pupils mere memorists of the language of the text books rather than to awaken and stimulate their mental faculties. Pupils are pushed rapidly forward in reading and spelling, and yet they rarely become either good readers or good spellers, because their teachers do not understand in what good reading and good spelling consist. The reading lesson accomplishes little for the pupils beyond an indifferent drill in vocal culture. It is not generally regarded as a means of cultivating expression and stimulating thought. The spelling-book is in the hands of every pupil. Whole columns of words are committed to memory and afterwards spelled in the spelling class, by pupils who have no idea whatever of their meaning or the use to which they might be applied. The idea that spelling could be taught in any other way or that it might prove a valuable auxiliary in furnishing new words for the pupil's vocabulary, has never dawned upon the mind of these exceptional teachers. Under their tuition, instruction in writing is confined to printing on slates until the pupil has attended school several terms. Grammatical instruction adapted to the wants and mental capacity of small pupils is rarely attempted. After several years of school life, during which he was permitted to set all grammatical principles at defiance both at the recitation seat and in his ordinary conversation, the pupil is required to supply himself with a text book, and at once enters upon the discouraging labor of committing its definitions and rules to memory.

Geography and arithmetic are taught in much the same way. The pupils are left in ignorance of the easiest combinations of numbers and the simplest notions of geography until they arrive at the age of ten or eleven years, when they obtain their first knowledge of these subjects through the medium of the text books. Language lessons, composition, object lessons, music, and drawing, now so generally taught in the primary classes of graded schools, do not receive that attention their importance merits in ungraded schools. Indeed, it sometimes happens that public sentiment does not uphold the teacher in giving any considerable portion of his time to instructing his pupils in these subjects. When such is the case, the branches enumerated in the school law fix the educational bounds beyond which the teacher is not at liberty to wander.

There are many teachers employed in ungraded schools who can not justly be charged with incompetency or lack of professional zeal. Such are struggling with commendable fidelity against the obstacles and discouragements which beset them. It is encouraging to know that their numbers are constantly increasing. Through their efforts the people of rural districts are becoming awakened to the real value of good school-houses, improved school furniture, and competent teachers, and to the justice of paying liberal salaries to professional teachers. Charts, maps, globes, and other means of explaining and illustrating the subjects studied by the pupils are to be found in schools taught by the better class of teachers. The skillful use of such material by the teacher rarely fails to convince school directors and school patrons of its value.

The school machinery in country districts is far too complicated to admit of effective action. To the multiplicity of sub-districts may be attributed many of the evils that have fastened themselves like an incubus upon the schools. Many school officers are engaged in performing various duties in reference to these sub-districts which could be more faithfully executed by a single board of education in each township. Local directors usually oppose such a consolidation of sub-districts as would place the schools of the townships on a more advantageous footing. Each sub-district must have its own school-house and its own teacher. Thus educational means and forces are dissipated without securing adequate returns.

The best interests of ungraded schools now demand the consolidation of the sub-districts, when it can be effected without the too great inconvenience of the people. Good school-houses are generally found in those districts which have forty or more pupils under instruction. A careful re-districting of a township by a township board of education would render it possible for each district to have a comfortable school-house, to keep the school in session for a longer period, and to secure the services of a competent teacher.

The worst features in the administration of ungraded schools have been pointed out. There are some brighter sides to the picture than those presented. Were it not that our graded schools are showing such excellent work, the results of the instruction in ungraded schools might not appear so meager and unsatisfactory. It is only when the two are brought into comparison that the defects of the latter are prominently seen. There is hope in the future in that the impression is becoming general that some wisely-directed efforts must be put forth, at an early day, in behalf of ungraded schools.

CHAPTER III.

GRADED SCHOOLS.

GENERAL HISTORY.

The greatest obstacle in the way of grading the schools, in the early history of popular education in Ohio, was the want of sufficient and suitable school buildings. The first schools opened in cities and towns were held in such rented rooms as could be obtained at the least possible expense. The furniture was made or furnished by common mechanics, who seldom considered whether or not it was adapted to the uses to which it was to be put. Single rooms were procured in different parts of the town, each room designed to accommodate all the children of school age within a specified territory. Under such circumstances, grading and classification were wholly impracticable. No decided progress was made in the general management of schools and the methods of instruction till suitable houses and convenient and comfortable furniture were provided. The cities and towns which were the first to erect good buildings with the necessary appliances, were also the first to enter upon plans which looked towards improvements in classification and instruction.

The school law passed by the General Assembly, February 5, 1825, contained the germ of the present school system, but it made no adequate provision for furnishing means for the erection of school houses. The organization of the public schools under the provisions of this act called out more or less opposition, especially in the larger cities and towns where private schools had been established and were in a prosperous condition. The friends of the public schools saw plainly that under an organization so feeble and inadequate, success in the establishment of an efficient system of free schools could not be attained. Cincinnati, the largest city in the State, felt most deeply the need of providing for the education of her youth. In the Senate of the General Assembly of 1828–9, Col. Andrew Mack introduced a bill for a special act to amend the city charter of Cincinnati, which bill authorized the city council to lay off the city into ten districts, and at the expense of the city to provide for the support of common schools; to purchase for the use of the city a suitable lot of land in each district, and to erect thereon a substantial school house; and in addition to the tax of one mill on the dollar for the purchase of sites and the erection of buildings, the city council was authorized to levy a tax of one mill on the dollar to defray the expenses for teachers and fuel. This bill became a law. It was at first received with decided opposition by men of property, and attempts were made to make the act exceedingly unpopular with the people. The influence of the wealthier classes caused the city council to delay in carrying out the provisions of the law, and it was not till the year 1836 that the buildings were completed and ready for occupancy. The houses were each forty by sixty feet, two stories high, with two apartments in each story. The upper stories were occupied by the girls, and the lower by the boys. The pupils of each department were divided into two grades.

This special act, which was the first passed in the State for the better support of public schools, gave Cincinnati an organization independent of the general school law. Improvements in management and instruction began with the occupancy of these buildings. The first attempts at systematic grading and classification in Ohio were made in these schools from 1836 to 1840. The size of the houses and the prevailing opinion that the boys and girls should be separated by brick walls, prevented the establishment of any more than two distinct grades. But this condition of affairs did not continue long. Albert Picket, Sen., and James H. Perkins, members of the school board, made a report in 1840, in which they presented a basis for defining the courses of study and the advancement of pupils in a graded system of instruction. The following is a synopsis of the course prepared by these gentlemen. As it is the first graded course of instruction in the Cincinnati schools, and the first in the public schools of Ohio, it is here presented.

SYNOPSIS OF COURSE OF STUDY.

GRADE I.

The alphabet, spelling words of one, two, three, and four letters; easy words of two syllables; spelling and reading easy sentences; oral instruction—teaching the pupils to use their eyes as well as their ears.

GRADE II.

Spelling; correct pronunciation; reading; modulation of the voice; accent, emphasis, stops and marks in reading; spelling sentences; simple tables in arithmetic; learning to count, etc.; writing after copies on slates and blackboards; oral instruction continued.

GRADE III.

Spelling; higher reading; analysis of words and learning their meaning; analysis of sentences; writing after copies on slates, blackboards, and books; copying words and sentences from books and manuscripts; oral, mental and written arithmetic; tables in arithmetic; oral instruction continued.

GRADE IV.

Spelling; reading and definitions; stops and marks; analysis of words and sentences; the nature and power of letters; modification and influence of words upon one another; writing after copies on slates, blackboards, and books; copying from books and manuscripts; higher arithmetic; geography and history of the United States, with maps; the definition of grammatical terms; simple parsing; classification of words and their constructive influence on one another; modern geography and history, with maps and globes; chronology; oral instruction continued.

GRADE V.

Analysis and definition of words; rhetorical reading; penmanship as applied to the forms of business, as copying from books or manuscripts, letter writing, bills, notes, receipts, etc.; higher arithmetic with all its kindred branches, as applied to business; English grammar, parsing, correction of false syntax, writing with grammatical accuracy; rhetoric and composition; modern and ancient geography and history, with maps and globes; algebra; geometry; trigonometry; mensuration; surveying; chemistry; botany; natural history; geology; natural philosophy, and rural economy. To these may be added, as circumstances may suggest, the study of the constitution of the United States, and all the higher branches of mathematics.

It was also recommended that the pupils in the last three grades should be required to read at certain intervals in the Bible, of which the authorized version without notes or comments should be used.

Such was the first graded course of instruction of which there is any record in the public schools of Ohio. Several years elapsed before the plan recommended was fully carried out; but the results obtained in the attempt to follow it, placed the Cincinnati public schools in the first rank among the common schools in the country, and made them the pride and glory of the city.

Another step in advance in grading the schools of Cincinnati was made in 1847, by the establishment and organization of the Central High School, and by the adoption of a course of study embracing the higher English branches, the ancient and some of the modern languages, besides drawing and vocal music. Classes were admitted to this school only once each year. The pupils at this time in the district schools were divided into three grades, and each of these grades into three sections. At stated times, upon passing a satisfactory examination, they were transferred from a lower to a higher grade.

The example of Cincinnati encouraged other cities and towns to efforts in a similar direction. The cause was also greatly aided by the indefatigable labors of Hon. Samuel Lewis, the Superintendent of the Common Schools of Ohio. In his second annual report he refers to the gradation of schools as follows:

"I am satisfied that, as the cause advances, experience will ultimately induce the union of several districts, so as to class all the scholars, leaving the small children to be taught in sub-districts by females, and having a central school of a higher order taught by a male teacher."

Before this time, 1840, a partial graded system had been established in New York, Boston, Providence, and Philadelphia. In these cities, provision was made for a class of primary schools for all under eight years of age. In Boston three distinct grades were recognized—primary schools for children from four to eight years, and grammar schools and writing schools for boys from eight to fourteen years, and for girls from eight to sixteen. Each grade had two departments, one for boys and one for girls, and each department had two divisions. The Latin Grammar Schools and the English High School constituted the third grade.

The progress made in grading in these older cities, and the good results which followed, had undoubtedly much influence in encouraging similar efforts in the schools of the growing cities of the West. Cleveland was the second city in the State which introduced a system of grading in the public schools. The first free school in this city was established in 1834. In 1837, the first board of managers was appointed by the city council and the free schools were organized. Under the provision of a special law two houses for public schools were built in 1840. Each building contained four rooms and accommodated two hundred pupils. The boys and girls, in accordance with the public opinion of the day, were separated. The schools were divided into two grades, distinguished by the names primary and senior. As the number of pupils increased, the lines of gradation were drawn more sharply and at shorter intervals. This was the condition of the schools until a high school was established in 1846. The grades were now distinguished by the names primary, secondary, intermediate, grammar, and high. The names for the different grades were afterwards very generally adopted in Northern Ohio, and have been retained in the Toledo schools up to the present time. Grading, in the Cleveland schools, was a growth and not a creation. The accommodations and the number of pupils which could be collected together, modified the plans adopted for the classification of the pupils. The growth of the schools into a systematic and efficient instrumentality for the education of the youth was rapid and substantial.

The third city, in the order of time, to take steps toward a system of grading, was Dayton. As the result of the labors of Hon. Samuel Lewis, State Superintendent of Common Schools, this city secured a special law similar to the law for Cincinnati. In 1839, two school-houses were built, one in the eastern and one in the western part of the city. In 1841, a city charter was granted to Dayton, and under its provisions a board of managers of public schools was appointed. The schools were divided into four grades, and designated as senior, junior, secondary and primary. This plan of grading was adopted in accordance with the number of rooms then at the disposal of the board of managers. In Dayton as in Cleveland, an outline of studies was marked out, and the pupils were transferred from a lower to a higher grade on examination; but no well defined course of study was prescribed for each separate grade, in Cleveland, till 1853, nor in Dayton, till 1858. The Dayton High School was established and organized in 1850. At this time the schools were well graded and in a prosperous condition.

Columbus was the fourth city to make an effort to better the condition of her public schools. Before 1847, for the want of suitable school accommodations, no system of grading could be adopted. In 1845, Columbus, by a special law, was made a separate school district. Three school houses, each containing six rooms, were erected during the year 1846, and were ready for occupancy in July, 1847. The board of education, deeming it of great importance that more attention should be given to the schools than they could devote to them, determined to create the office of superintendent of Public Schools. Thus Columbus was the first city in the State to create this office and to elect a Superintendent. Dr. Asa D. Lord, having been elected to that office, entered upon its arduous duties in May, 1847. He began at once to grade and classify the schools, which were at the time so unpopular and inefficient that the better and more influential portion of the citizens sent their children to private schools, which were in a flourishing condition. The grades were designated as primary, secondary, and grammar. Many pupils were found to be too far advanced for the grammar school grade. These were organized into a higher department, which at the close of the year became what has since been known as the high school. Soon after the grades were established and the pupils distributed to the respective grades for which they were found to be qualified, a systematic and consecutive course of study was prescribed by the board for each grade. Among the branches of study enumerated in the course, and not usually taught in the public schools at that early day, were music and drawing. Teachers' meetings were inaugurated for the first time, and other means adopted for the improvement of those employed as teachers by the board. So efficient did the schools become, under the judicious and able management of the superintendent, that at the beginning of the second year the prejudices of the people were removed, and many of the private schools were closed for want of pupils. The success of the schools was largely attributed to the wisdom of the board in providing for them efficient and able supervision. Before the lapse of five years, many other towns and cities followed the example of the board of education of Columbus, and placed competent superintendents at the head of their schools.

The public schools of Portsmouth were organized under a special law, and were graded and classified prior to 1844. The plan of grading was similar to that adopted in the cities already mentioned.

The first movement made in the northwestern part of the State towards the improvement of public schools, was at the village of Maumee, in 1842. A good building was erected and the schools opened, in 1844. The higher department was in grade a high school. Perrysburg is reported to have established under the Akron law, as extended in 1849, the first graded school in the Maumee valley.

By a special law passed in 1839, Zanesville was made one school district, by which the public schools were greatly improved; a thorough system of grading, however, was not adopted until 1849. The cities and towns whose schools were organized under special laws authorizing levies to be made for building school houses, were the first to make such improvements as rendered the public schools efficient. The results attained showed that such schools were actually cheaper and better than schools conducted as private enterprises.

The above are all of the cities and towns under special enactments for the regulation of schools prior to the act for the regulation of schools in the town of Akron, passed February 8, 1847. The progress which was made in grading, classification, courses of study, and in buildings, did much to commend the free school system to the good sense and intelligence of the citizens of the State. The success attained prepared the way for broader and more liberal legislation.

The impetus which the Akron law gave to the advancement of popular education in Ohio, as the first in which the principle of free graded schools was embodied, was so great that a brief statement of its principal provisions seems to be necessary. The author of the plan was Rev. J. Jennings, pastor of the Congregational Church of Akron. The law provided for the election of six directors whose term of service should be six years. It gave this board of education full control of all the schools of the town, which, by a union of the several school districts into which it was divided, became a single district, and authorized this board to establish in the district six or more primary schools and a central grammar school; to fix the terms of transfer from one grade to another; to make and enforce all necessary rules and regulations for the government of teachers and pupils; to employ and pay teachers; to purchase books and apparatus; to select sites and erect buildings; to certify to the town council the amount of money necessary for school purposes; to appoint three persons to act as examiners of teachers, and to appoint once each year public examinations at such time as the board might deem fit. The law was subsequently amended by limiting the tax for school purposes to four mills on the dollar each year.

The provisions of the law, at the time of its passage, were extended to the managers of the common schools of the city of Dayton. In 1848, the General Assembly of the State extended its provisions to every incorporated town or city in the State whenever two-thirds of the qualified voters petitioned the town or city council in favor of such extension. After the passage of this law the public schools of Akron were immediately organized. Two primary school houses were built, and M. D. Leggett, late Commissioner of Patents, was elected teacher of the higher department and superintendent of all the schools. This law and the operations of the first board met with strong opposition from many wealthy men, who, by their influence, succeeded in reducing the tax levy for school purposes from five to four mills on the dollar of the taxable property of the town.

In the winter of 1848–9, Hon. S. T. Worcester, Senator from Huron county, and one of the most earnest and able advocates of free schools in the State, introduced a bill entitled, "A general act for the schools in cities and towns." This law, which passed the General Assembly February 21, 1849, embodied the important features of the Akron law, and gave boards of education power to establish not only schools of primary and grammar grades, but a higher grade, and to decide what branches shall be taught in each and all grades. Boards of education were required, by a provision of this act, to keep the schools in operation not less than thirty-six nor more than forty weeks each year. In 1850, the provisions of this act were extended to incorporated townships, which should be recognized in law as single school districts with all the rights and powers conferred upon incorporated cities, towns, and villages. These two special laws, although bitterly opposed by property-holders in localities where they were enforced, gained over to the public school the influence of the majority of the intelligent and thoughtful portion of the people.

The decade between 1845 and 1855 was perhaps the most important and eventful one in the history of popular education in Ohio. It was a period of organization. The free public school was recognized as a political institution, necessary for the enlightenment of the people and the welfare and safety of the State. The time had come for putting into practical operation the carefully matured plans of a few earnest and scholarly men, expressing the convictions of many noble and intelligent citizens who had long believed that the highest good of the State required the education of the masses. During the ten years preceding 1845, the members of the "Western Literary Institution and College of Professional Teachers," had arrested the attention of the intelligent and thoughtful among the people of Ohio by their discussions of educational topics. The State Teachers' Association was organized December, 1847, and became a potent agency in harmonizing and uniting the efforts of the teaching talent of the State. About seventy cities and towns in different parts of the State established the free graded system within a year or two after the passage of the Akron law and the law of 1849. Among these were, Dayton, Toledo, Xenia, Chillicothe, Massillon, Marietta, Sandusky, Norwalk, Newark, Ironton, Salem, Circleville, Hamilton, Lancaster, Painesville, Elyria, Troy, Ashland, Plymouth, McConnelsville, Bucyrus, Tiffin, Akron, Warren, Eaton, and Athens. The schools in each city and town were generally divided into five grades, designated as primary, secondary, intermediate, grammar, and high. In the smaller towns, and also in the larger where the buildings were small and situated in the different parts of the town or city, two or more grades were placed under one teacher. Only in the cities which had erected houses capable of accommodating four or five hundred pupils was one grade placed under a single teacher. It was customary to connect with the high school the senior grammar school, and in villages, the whole grammar school department. The course of study required for its completion a period of eight or nine years before admission to the high school, and in the latter a period of three or four years. Following the example of the Columbus board, other boards of education employed a superintendent who was also teacher of the high school. The demand for text-books adapted to the different grades was soon supplied by authors and publishers, who appreciated the advantages which would result from a well graded series of text-books. The need of suitable school books was deeply felt, for the teachers, as a general rule, had received no professional training and possessed meager literary qualifications; consequently, they were poorly qualified to give oral instruction, which fact made good text-books a necessity.

Men were generally placed over the grammar school grades, and women over the intermediate, secondary, and primary. This seems to have been done, at first, for economic reasons; but experience proved that women were better fitted by natural disposition and temperament for teachers in all the grades below the high school than men. Comparatively few men are now engaged as teachers in grades below the high school.

In the year 1849 and 1850, a vigorous effort was made by the prominent educators of the State to extend to townships and small villages the system of graded schools. It was proposed to form a single district by the union of two or more districts, the inhabitants of which should unite in building one large school house for the accommodation of two or more departments. Hence the term "union school" as applied to the graded schools of the State. In accordance with a resolution of the State Teachers' Association, adopted at the meeting in December, 1848, a committee was appointed to prepare a report on the advantages to be derived from union schools, and on the best mode of organizing and conducting them. This committee consisted of Dr. A. D. Lord, Rev. S. S. Rickly, and Hon. H. H. Barney. The report was made and published, and had great influence in securing the amendment to the law of 1849 which extended the provisions of that act to townships and small villages. This class of schools has never met with the expectations of its friends.

Among the agencies used at this time for the better organization of schools, the elevation of the standard of the qualifications of teachers, and the introduction of better methods of instruction, none did more effectual work than the "Ohio School Journal," edited by Dr. Lord, and published at Columbus from 1846 to 1852. Lorin Andrews, Esq., chairman of the executive committee of the State Teachers' Association, in a report made December 30, 1851, and published in the Ohio School Journal, makes the following statements in regard to graded schools:

"The passage of the law of 1849, and the organization of so many union schools under it, constitute a higher era in the educational history of the State. These schools have greatly elevated the profession of teaching, by furnishing so many permanent and lucrative situations for teachers, and by requiring of them a much higher order of qualifications. They are largely supplying the place of normal schools, and are annually sending out well qualified, professional teachers into other schools of the State. They are the model schools of their various localities, and are rapidly introducing to the favorable notice of teachers and citizens, the best methods of teaching and classifying pupils. Finally, they are the forerunner, a kind of John the Baptist, crying in the wilderness and making the paths straight, for that more glorious and more comprehensive system of *universal free education*, which, before many moons shall wax and wane, like the impartial dews of heaven, will distil its blessings alike generously upon every son and daughter of this broad State."

The office of State Commissioner of Common Schools having been abolished by the General Assembly, the State Teachers' Association believed that the cause of education would be greatly advanced by putting in the field an active agent to aid in the organization of schools, to bring before the people of the State the advantages to be derived from a thorough system of public schools, to lecture before teachers' institutes, and to encourage educators who were struggling against the opposition of the enemies of popular education. In accordance with the convictions of the members of the State Association, Mr. Lorin Andrews was employed by the Association in the beginning of the year 1851, and he continued in its employ till the close of the year 1853, when he was succeeded by Dr. A. D. Lord who held the office till September, 1855. During the time these gentlemen acted as agents of the Association they conducted teachers' institutes in a majority of the counties in the State, and by public addresses aroused a deep interest in favor of a better organization and classification of schools. Many towns were persuaded to adopt the graded school system, new and better school-houses were built, and new life and energy were infused into those towns which had already adopted the system. The spirit of improvement aroused by the public lectures and individual labors of these bold, able, and noble men, the grand results achieved in the graded schools, and their unanswerable arguments in favor of free education prepared the way for the passage by the General Assembly of the general school law of 1853. The ungraded schools at this time made so bad a showing, as compared with the graded schools, that the feeling was unanimous that something ought to be done for their relief. It was claimed by the advocates of the graded system that it would educate more children, it would educate them better, and it would educate them cheaper.

The period between 1845 and 1855 will ever be a memorable one in the history of popular education in Ohio. The change which was brought about in public opinion and in the condition of the schools of the State, by the efforts of I. W. Andrews, Lorin Andrews, Lord, Cowdery, Harvey, Freese, Barney, and many others was without a parallel. Mr. M. F. Cowdery, in the annual address delivered before the State Teachers' Association, December, 1852, alludes as follows to the progress made in educational affairs:

"In three-fourths of the towns of Ohio, with a population of one thousand inhabitants and upwards, substantial school buildings have been erected by the free contributions of the people; the schools themselves have been more or less accurately classified, thus preparing the way in the best possible manner for all other practicable improvements; and, lastly, the confidence of the public in the capacity of the common school system to afford a suitable education to all, has been almost immeasurably increased."

At this period, or at the close of the year 1855, the free graded system was permanently established, met with the hearty approval, and received high commendation and support from an influential class of citizens who had been the enemies of any system of popular education supported at the expense of the State and by local taxation. The compensation of teachers was increased, and the lengthening of the school year to thirty-six weeks, and in many schools to forty-two, gave them permanent employment.

The accepted plan of grading was now the separation of the pupils, in accordance with their attainments, into five grades, designated as primary, secondary, intermediate, grammar, and high school. The pupils were transferred from a lower to a higher grade annually, on passing the required final examination in the prescribed studies of their grade. The examinations at this time used as tests for promotion and for transfer were largely oral. Outside of the larger cities little oral instruction was attempted, even in the primary grades; consequently, a greater number of different text-books was used in the lower grades than are now used in the primary schools. In many of the primary schools, the children were required to have text-books in spelling, reading, geography, and both mental and written arithmetic. In most of the graded schools, as then classified, no attention was given to penmanship in the first, second, third, and in some cases the fourth year of the school life of the child, nor was any provision made for drills in language as a preparation for technical grammar. Vocal music and drawing were not embraced in the courses of study, except in that of Cincinnati, Cleveland, and Columbus. The reading of the Bible was generally a part of the daily exercises.

The regular daily sessions of the graded schools were three hours in the morning and three in the afternoon, with a recess of fifteen minutes each session.

The buildings erected for school purposes, although substantial, were generally defective and inconvenient in their internal arrangements, poorly lighted, having no cloak-rooms, with narrow halls, and stairways, scarcely any means of ventilation, and inadequate heating apparatus. The furniture was severely plain, clumsy, and uncomfortable. The seats and desks were each made for the accommodation of two pupils. Each room was belted by an ungainly blackboard, so far above the floor in the rooms for the lower grades, that the children were compelled to stand on tiptoe to reach it. Seldom was any effort made to relieve the dingy walls with pictures or any kind of ornaments. What has been written gives a fair representation of the graded schools prior to the year 1855. There were, however, particular schools at the head of which were men strong in certain directions, and who were able to impress themselves upon the teachers, and to imbue them with their own notions of discipline, order, and methods of instruction, to such a degree, that their marked peculiarities distinguished their schools from other schools of the State. There were men of one idea who rode hobbies; men who tried to do so much that nothing was well done; and there were also men of broad scholarship, whose common sense and wisdom led them to do well what they did do, and never to go so far beyond the people as to defeat their own measures.

The succeeding twenty years may be characterized as the era of the growth and improvement in the graded schools as now permanently established. All opposition had disappeared. The free public graded school was a popular institution. A public exhibition or examination would call out an interested audience when nothing else would, and praises of the exercises would flow from every tongue. The improvement of the system was aimed at by educators in two ways: first, to raise the standard of the qualifications of teachers and to introduce better methods of instruction; second, to improve the grading and classification of the schools. What should be included in courses of study, the value of examinations and the methods of conducting them, how often examinations should be made, promotions, plans of school buildings, ventilation, heating, and discipline or school government formed fruitful themes for discussion and experiment. It is impossible to trace the progress of the improvement made during twenty years without extending this paper beyond the assigned limits. It will be sufficient to point out some of the great changes which have been made, or, rather, to show what the graded schools of Ohio now are, and leave the reader to compare them with the schools of 1855.

The need of normal schools was greatly felt by those who were placed at the head of schools and by those who aspired to become teachers. In the absence of them, other instrumentalities were devised. These consisted chiefly in giving incidental instruction in methods of teaching to those members of the public high schools who looked forward to the profession of teaching, through examinations in the branches required to be taught in the schools, teachers' institutes, and teachers' meetings, held at regular intervals for instruction in methods of teaching and discipline, and for conference in regard to all subjects pertaining to school work. By these agencies, the teachers of this State, many of whom are eminent in the profession, have received their training in professional work. At the meeting of the teachers, those who were not well informed in special studies, such as music and drawing, were able to obtain the needed instruction. Such meetings held weekly or even monthly, when well conducted, were the means of accomplishing much good in the way of exciting enthusiasm, inspiring confidence, and in creating harmony and unity of feeling and action. The teachers in a system of graded schools under an energetic and progressive superintendent, in a short time, by attending such meetings, became well qualified for their work, well informed in pedagogical science, and were soon able to work out for themselves the well-timed suggestions of their superior, and to put them in practice in their respective schools. Teachers of a certain grade were thus often led to investigate and experiment for themselves in particular lines of school management and instruction, and were put in a position to distinguish themselves in special work. Many superintendents endeavored to gather information wherever it could be obtained. As soon as any of these active and enterprising men heard a rumor that something new and good was being done in a neighboring city or town, where there were better opportunities for information and facilities for experiment, he made a visit to its schools, remained long enough to form an idea of what was being done, and then returned to present it to his teachers at the teachers' meeting. By this means, the graded schools in the smaller towns have kept abreast of the age in adopting the improvements made in the larger cities.

The grading of schools has depended largely upon the size of the town and its buildings. For a prescribed course of study covering a period of twelve years, it is necessary for purposes of close grading that the number of pupils be about six hundred. If these are gathered into a single building large enough to accommodate them, the problem of grading and classification is easily solved; or, if the high school and grammar school are placed in a central building, and the pupils of the primary grades in two different houses of four rooms, the grading will be easy. Eight primary schools of fifty pupils each are sufficient to form, from transfers and promotions in the primary grades, four grammar schools and one high school of sixty pupils. The above arrangement of buildings has been made in but few towns, and circumstances compel placing under one teacher two or more different grades. In the large towns and cities, difficulty in regard to buildings of sufficient capacity to accommodate at least the first six grades is seldom encountered. School men have generally found it a difficult matter to induce boards of education to consider the subject of grading and classification in their selection of sites and in the construction of school buildings.

No man in Ohio has studied more thoroughly the classification of schools, and done more during the last twenty years to bring about the degree of perfection which has been attained in the present system of grading, than Mr. A. J. Rickoff, now Superintendent of the Cleveland schools. Mr. Rickoff's attention was called to this important subject when, in 1854, he was the superintendent of the public schools of Cincinnati. When he entered upon the duties of his office he found two classes of schools in operation—the district schools and the high schools. He was requested by the board of education to make a report upon the expediency of organizing grammar schools as a part of the school system. To this end, he visited the prominent eastern cities and obtained from practical teachers their most advanced and approved plans of grading, with a view to economy and efficiency in instruction. In this able report he defines classification to be, "The arrangement of pupils according to proficiency and capacity for study, into grades, classes, or divisions. That system of schools is most nearly perfect which enables us to secure the nicest classification. It is at once the most economical and most efficient. The most economical, because it gives the greatest possible number of pupils to the teacher, and the most efficient, because it gives to each pupil the greatest possible share of the teacher's time and labor." In accordance with his plan, which differed in many points from any plan previously adopted, and on his recommendation, the grade known as the "intermediate" in the Cincinnati schools, was established. So perfect was the grading and classification of these schools at this time, that few essential changes have since been found necessary. The intermediate, as first established, consisted of two grades. By the recommendation of Mr. John Hancock, afterwards superintendent, another grade was transferred to the intermediate.

The district schools now comprise five grades, designated

by the letters D, E, F, G, and H; and the intermediate schools are divided into three grades, A, B, and C. The term intermediate, as applied in the Cincinnati schools, comprises the three grades next to the high school; in other parts of the State, it is applied to grades between the primary and grammar. The old nomenclature by which the grades were designated, has been abandoned, with a few exceptions, and instead of the names primary, secondary, intermediate, and grammar, the primary and grammar schools are designated by letters or the year, as D, C, B, and A primary, D, C, B, and A grammar, or as 1st, 2nd, 3rd, 4th, 5th, 6th, 7th, and 8th year. In Dayton, the 8th year is called the intermediate.

PROMOTIONS AND TRANSFERS.

The use of these terms in connection with schools is rather ambiguous. A pupil may be said to be promoted when he is advanced from one class to another in the same grade—for grades are sometimes divided into classes—or when he is transferred from one teacher to another in a higher grade. The word transfer is used in two different senses by school authorities; viz., when a pupil in a certain grade is sent to another teacher in the same grade, he is said to be transferred; also, when a pupil is promoted from a lower to a higher grade, by which he changes teachers, he is said to be transferred. In order to avoid confusion of terms, in this paper the word promotion has been used to designate the advancement of pupils from a lower to a higher class in the same grade and under the same teacher, and the term transfer to designate the promotion of pupils from a lower to a higher grade and at the same time to a different teacher—a change of teacher always being necessary to constitute a transfer. In most all of the graded schools of Ohio, the pupils are transferred annually. This usually occurs at the close of the school year. As a condition of transfer, the pupils are required to pass a satisfactory examination upon all the branches of study prescribed in the grade to which they belong. Transfers of individual pupils who show superior ability and attainments in the monthly examinations, are often made during the year. In some of the graded schools, each of the primary grades is divided into two or more classes. For example, a school of fifty pupils in the first year grade is divided into classes designated as A and B. The A class is a little in advance of the B. In this case, promotions are made from the B to the A class at any time, and transfers are made twice each year. Such a course becomes necessary in a system of schools where children who reach the legal school age are admitted twice in the year. The courses of study in the graded schools of Ohio are broad enough for the brightest and strongest pupils, and narrow enough for the dullest and feeblest. Seldom, if ever, with a competent teacher, is injustice done to any pupil for want of flexibility in the prevailing system of grading.

EXAMINATIONS.

In every well regulated graded school, the progress of the pupils in their studies is ascertained by examination tests, either oral or written, or both. From five to eight examinations are given the pupils each year besides the final examination for the annual transfer. The questions are prepared by the superintendant or by some one whom he designates. In many schools, ten years ago, the standing of each pupil, especially in the higher grades, was kept in a book which showed his record for each daily recitation. From this his preparation for promotion or transfer was ascertained. This plan has very generally been abandoned —periodical examinations being substituted for it. So various are the methods of conducting these examinations, and so different are the objects and aims of teachers in the uses which they make of them, it is not possible to give in approximation any general method which will represent even a small number of schools.

TEACHERS AND SALARIES.

About ninety per cent. of the teachers are women. Two-thirds of them have received their academic education in the high schools. As a reward for continuing long enough in school to complete the prescribed course of study in the high school, and for making a good record for scholarship and deportment, boards of education favor their appointment to positions as teachers in the schools. The adoption of this principle has done much towards securing a class of teachers of fair ability and tolerably broad culture. Still, the want of normal or professional training makes the first year's teaching an experiment at the expense of the children. The basis upon which the salaries of teachers are determined is by no means uniform. In some cities and towns, the salary is regulated by the grade of school taught, the minimum salary being paid to teachers in the lowest grade and the maximum to those in the highest; in others, the salary does not depend upon the grade taught, but is determined by the experience, tact, success, and ability of the teacher. The first principle is pernicious, because it holds out an inducement to seek positions in the higher grades at the expense of the lower in which the best teaching talent is most needed. Where this principle has been acted upon, the experienced and successful teachers have been gathered into the grammar schools, and the inexperienced and incompetent into the primary—this grade being regarded as a kind of purgatory to be passed in order to reach the paradise above. The compensation allowed women ranges from two hundred and fifty dollars to one thousand dollars per annum, that of men from six hundred to fifteen hundred dollars per annum. The high school is not included in this statement. Teachers in Ohio, as elsewhere, seek the market which pays the highest prices.

COURSE OF STUDY AND INSTRUCTION.

The instruction given in the primary grades is largely oral; in the grammar school grades, chiefly by text-books. The number of different studies is greater in the primary than in the grammar school—the principle governing the assignment of studies being that young pupils are capable of learning a little about many things and not much of any one thing, while those who are older and in grammar school grades, are able to think and to reason, and to learn a few things thoroughly. To illustrate, it has been demonstrated in some of the larger cities, that children in the first and second year who take the study of the German language in addition to the prescribed English branches, will accomplish as much as those who take English studies alone. Experience has also shown that children of the first year who are taught to read sentences both in script and print, will read more fluently at the close of the year than those who have been taught to read only from the printed page. Drawing, music, and lessons on objects aid rather than delay the pupils in learning to read, count, and write. Language culture is made prominent in all the graded schools of the State. From the lowest to the highest grade careful attention is given to the language of the pupils, to the correction of mispronunciation, incorrect use of words, or of faulty sentences. The truth is acknowledged and acted upon, that correct expression is valuable in itself and promotes correct thinking. Lessons in language, as now given, are systematic and rise gradually through the grades into the study of technical grammar, rhetoric, and a critical study of the best English classics.

In some of the graded schools, the first lessons in reading are given by or through the "word method," and subsequently by teaching the phonic elements of the language; in others, the phonic elements and the characters which represent them are first taught. Success has attended the use of both methods. In arithmetic, processes and operations are carefully taught before principles. In the first year, the pupils use counters and deal with concrete numbers. The subject is gradually developed, and the pupil seldom encounters difficulties which he cannot surmount.

Teachers have learned much, within the last ten years, in regard to oral teaching. It is now recognized that such teaching requires much preparation, patient effort, great resources, and quick perception on the part of the teacher. Fragmentary and unsystematic object teaching has disappeared. The elements of the natural sciences are now presented in a connected series of lessons which assist in laying a foundation for future scientific culture. While the pupils are trained to habits of observation and generalization, they are also given instruction which will be of permanent value should no opportunities be granted to pursue the study of these sciences beyond the mere rudiments.

The following synopsis of a course of study is given as a fair representation of that pursued in the graded schools of the State as they now exist. It embraces a greater number of branches or different subjects than is taught in some of the small towns, and perhaps a less number than is taught in some of the large cities.

SYNOPSIS OF A COURSE OF STUDY.

GRADE I.—FIRST YEAR.

Reading.—Words, elementary sounds, lessons read from charts, blackboard, book, in script, and from printed page. *Spelling.*—By sound and by letter all words in reading lessons and other exercises used in the grade; words spelled orally and by writing on slates and on the black-board. *Writing.*—On slates and with lead pencil on paper; copying from blackboard and from books. *Numbers.*—Counting to 100, treatment of numbers from one to ten. *Oral Lessons.*—Familiar objects, colors, verses, and maxims. *Drawing.*—Free-hand outline, from cards, blackboard, memory, dictation. *Vocal Music.*

GRADE II.—SECOND YEAR.

Reading.—From books, papers; definition, the use of words. *Spelling.*—By sound and letter, oral, and by writing. *Writing.*—On slates, blackboard, paper, in copy-book, small and capital letters. *Numbers.*—Addition, subtraction, multiplication, and division, tables, problems. *Language.*—Correction of faulty expressions, mispronunciation, uses of capital letters, punctuation marks, etc. *Oral Lessons.*—Animal, vegetable, and mineral kingdoms, verses, maxims, etc., etc. *Drawing. Vocal Music.*

GRADE III.—THIRD YEAR.

Reading.—Analysis of lessons, second or third reader used, definitions, expression, vocal drills, voice culture. *Spelling. Writing.*—Copy-book, pen and ink used. *Arithmetic.*—Notation, numeration, exercises in fundamental rules, problems mental and written, dry measure. *Language.*—Making sentences, compositions, describing objects, pictures, filling blanks, writing names. *Oral Lessons.*—The human body, characteristics of domestic animals, general structure, relative size, kinds of food, habits; buds, flowers, leaves, plants, trees; points of compass, school grounds, idea of distance, direction, etc., etc., *Drawing. Vocal Music.*

GRADE IV.—FOURTH YEAR.

Reading.—Enunciation, modulation, definitions, reading as an intellectual exercise. *Spelling.*—Oral and written exercises. *Writing.*—Copy-book of a graded series in penmanship. *Arithmetic.*—Text-book used, operations and processes in the fundamental rules, accuracy and rapidity in calculations, problems mental and written. *Language.*—The noun, adjective verb, pronoun developed, inflection of noun and pronoun, subject and predicate, abbreviations, quotation marks, picture lessons, letter writing, etc. *Oral Lessons.*—Swimming birds, scratchers, their characteristics; animals, ruminants, etc., etc. *Geography.*—The county, the State, journeys, making maps. *Drawing. Vocal Music.*

GRADE V.—FIFTH YEAR.

Reading.—Fourth or fifth reader, articulation, analyses of lessons, definitions. *Spelling.*—Oral and written. *Penmanship.*—copy-book. *Arithmetic.*—Properties of numbers, greatest common divisor, least common multiple, fractions, principles and rules. *Language.*—Subject and predicate, agreement of subject with predicate, participle, pronoun, preposition, conjunction, picture lessons, letter writing, punctuation, etc. *Oral Lessons.*—Leaves, parts, venation, roots, seeds, woody plants, trees, growth, etc., food plants, wheat, barley, rice, apples, peaches, etc., etc. *Geography.*—Text-book used. *Drawing. Vocal Music.*

GRADE VI.—SIXTH YEAR.

Reading.—Fifth or sixth reader. *Spelling.*—Use of dictionary taught. *Writing. Arithmetic.* — United States money, decimals, denominate numbers, tables, principles, compound numbers. *Language.*—Text-book used, exercises in composition. *Oral Lessons.*—Botany continued as in former grade. *Geography.*—Text-book used. *Drawing. Vocal Music.*

GRADE VII.—SEVENTH YEAR.

Reading.—Sixth reader and selections from the best authors. *Spelling.*—Oral and written, (text-books used in many schools), defining. *Writing.*—Copy-book, business forms, notes, receipts, etc. *Arithmetic.*—Text-book, principles, fractions, common and decimal, percentage, and applications. *Grammar.*—Etymology, parsing, syntax. *Physics.*—Of nature, gravity, states of matter, properties of solids, liquids, gases, forces, moving bodies, heat, expansion, thermometers, etc., radiant heat, light, electricity. *Drawing. Vocal Music.*

GRADE VIII.—EIGHTH YEAR.

Reading.—Selections from the works of the best English writers of prose and poetry—to be a thoroughly intellectual exercise. *Spelling. Penmanship. Arithmetic.*—Ratio, proportion, mensuration, rules, definitions, principles, etc. *Grammar.*—Technical parsing, analysis, syntax, practical exercises in composition and in forms of speech. *Physical Geography.* — Text-book followed. *United States History. Drawing. Vocal Music.* In some schools algebra is introduced in this grade.

HIGH SCHOOL.

First Year.—English grammar, algebra, chemistry, civil government, German, Latin, vocal music, and drawing.

Second Year.—General history, physiology, plain geometry, geology, natural history, physics, German, Latin, Greek, solid geometry, vocal music, and drawing.

Third Year.—Book-keeping and penmanship, trigonometry, arithmetic, astronomy, political economy, physical geography, rhetoric, English literature, botany, Constitution of the United States, German, Latin, Greek, vocal music, and drawing.

Fourth Year. — Psychology, astronomy, physics, Latin, German, Greek, reviews.

In most of the high schools of the State these subjects are distributed into four different courses, designated as English, German English, Latin English, and Classical. The pupils upon entering can elect any one of them.

In the above synopsis, the aim has been to give the subjects in the respective grades without any attempt at placing them in the order of their development. In the grades where text-books are used, the order of the text-book is generally followed, as for example, in a series of books on reading, geography, grammar, and arithmetic. The same may be said of the methods used.

There is no uniformity aimed at in the use of text-books in the graded schools of Ohio. The school authorities have been wisely left by the legislators to choose such text-books as in their judgment are considered the best.

Committees have again and again been appointed by the State Teachers' Association, to draw up a course of instruction adapted to the different grades of schools. Their reports have had much to do in bringing about numerous and important changes within the last twenty years. There are still men of influence and intelligence who oppose the introduction into courses of study of anything beyond what is known as the common branches, and who claim that botany, physics, vocal music, and drawing should not be taught at the public expense. The same persons oppose high schools on the same grounds. It is believed that the public sentiment of the people is, however, very largely in favor of the free public schools as they now exist, and that it will cheerfully support any measures calculated to enhance their efficiency and promote their progress.

CHAPTER IV.

HIGH SCHOOLS AND ACADEMIES.

EARLY HISTORY.

The early history of Ohio is very unlike that of Wisconsin, Illinois, and other recently settled states. The ox team and the flat-boat were the means of transportation and conveyance, not through prairies that welcomed their possessors with a crop of corn the first year, but through dense forests of giant trees which tenaciously claimed the soil as their own, and yielded it only to the most stubborn and prolonged warfare. Leagued with these was the red man, who had little conscience about destroying or appropriating the fruits of a soil he also claimed.

Many of the earlier inhabitants, also, had not enjoyed in the heart of an already advanced civilization the educational facilities possessed by the earlier immigrants to many states now settling. They were themselves, in part at least, from frontier portions of older states, with only a mixture of the refinement and culture then attainable in the eastern cities and villages. Books which can now be purchased in Kansas for a bushel of corn, would have cost these early settlers ten bushels at least.

We can not, therefore, as in the new states of to-day, expect to see the New England school, with its perfected system of support and instruction, springing up at once. Within the memory of men now living, however, has been developed by seemingly slow steps, and out of a public sentiment not a stranger to bitter prejudices regarding educational innovations, a system of instruction for the masses second to none on the globe, and superior to any known to the most privileged people of a half century ago.

Though one thirty-sixth part of the whole area of Ohio was, by the Congress of the Confederation in 1785, and by subsequent enactments by the Federal Congress in response to the territorial and state legislation, set apart for school purposes, little or no benefit accrued to the State from these lands until 1817 or 1818. Meantime the leaders of public sentiment, and without exception the men entrusted with the chief magistracy of the State, had been most active and large-hearted apostles of a popular system of education. Though many of their early public declarations on this subject seem only to point to a common school education for the masses, yet, as indicating the real sentiment of these leaders, it must be remembered that the Bill of Rights, in 1802, contains the provision that, "No law shall be passed to prevent the *poor* in the several counties and townships in this State from an equal participation in the schools, *academies*, colleges, and universities within the State, which are endowed in whole or in part from the revenues arising from donations made by the United States for the support of schools and colleges; and the doors of said schools, *academies*, and universities shall be open for the reception of scholars, students, and teachers of every grade without any distinction or preference whatever."

Thus in the very preface of our history as a State, is written the declaration, which, in the minds of thinking men, could have but one logical result. Whenever the State should be wise enough and rich enough to act upon the logic taught by republican institutions, not alone the mimimum skill to read and write, but the development of the power and habit of thought and consideration that come only with such exercise of the mental faculties as is incident to academical courses of instruction at least, was to be placed within the easy reach of all who would accept it. On this principle, the first General Assembly, in view of the appropriation of lands made by the General Government, not only established in 1802 the Ohio University "for the education of youth in all the *liberal arts and sciences*, for the promotion of education, virtue, religion, and morality," and declared that, "institutions for the *liberal* education of youth are essential to the progress of arts and sciences; important to morality, virtue, and religion; friendly to the peace, order, and prosperity of society; and honorable to the government that encourages and patronizes them;" but also connected with this institution a preparatory school. This school embraced studies similar in grade to those of our present *high schools*, and it is commonly understood that Hon. Thomas Ewing, leaving his salt kettles in the Kanawha Valley, here pursued his *high school* or *academic* course, with higher studies of the university, from which he was among the first graduates.

The history of the establishment of Miami University, in connection with the various discussions incident to the Symmes Purchase, and the provision therein made for the support of an educational institution, show conclusively that the early statesmen appreciated better than any other idea regarding education the relation which real culture—the strengthening of the mind for useful work, and the storing of it with available knowledge—sustains to the progress, peace, order, and prosperity of society.

The next legislative action making specific provision for educational work, was the incorporation of the "Erie Literary Society," in 1803, which resulted in the establishment of the Burton Academy.

In 1807, Dayton Academy was incorporated, and a building erected on lots donated for the purpose by the proprietor of the town. Up to the establishment of public schools in 1838, this academy seems to have furnished nearly the sole means of education to the children, and did much by its preparation of teachers to introduce improved methods of instruction into this part of the State. Its course of study embraced most of what is now included in the high school course and a preparation for college, and when in 1838 the question of the establishment of a public school was put to the people, much opposition was developed, owing to the doubt as to whether pure morals and thorough instruction could be secured in public free schools. Each governor in turn had urged the subject upon the attention of the legislature. In 1809, Governor Huntington used the following language :

"Suffer me, in this place, to call your attention to the state of our *seminaries* and schools of education, and to recommend them to the patronage and encouragement of the State; it is in a public as well as in a private point of view that the State is interested in the diffusion of learning and useful knowledge; where the means of education are extended, and the great body of the people are enlightened, the arts of designing and ambiiious characters can never succeed in undermining the liberties of the country."

Governor Meigs, in 1810, thus alludes to the subject in his inaugural:

"Correct education is the auxilliary of virtue; moral science will exalt the mind, while ignorance, the badge of mental slavery, debases it. Where the structure of government rests on public opinion, knowledge is of vital interest; public opinion, to be correct, must be enlightened, and *the culture of the understanding* is the preserver of republican principles. Man informed of his political rights becomes reluctant to renounce them. Tyrants govern the ignorant. Intelligence alone is capable of self-government."

Thus it is seen that the aim of these early statesmen was to afford the opportunity for something above the rudiments of knowledge. The necessity and practicability of a broad culture to such as should be ambitious to compass it, is indicated in all these early addresses. These appeals were certainly not unheeded by the people of the towns and villages of the State. Besides the seminaries above alluded to, an academy was established in Salem in 1809, one in Gallipolis in 1811, one also in Steubenville in 1814, one at Granville, one at Worthington, and one in New Lisbon about this time, and perhaps earlier.

No doubt many other seminaries were established, and did excellent work in the way of preparing young men for college and for active life, since Governor Meigs, in the same address from which the above extract is taken, proceeds as follows:

"Our schools and *academies* are advancing in improvement, and promise to sanction the hopes entertained of their utility."

From the earliest settlement of the city, Cincinnati afforded facilities for the education of such of her own children as possessed the money required for tuition, and was also prepared to invite such youth from neighboring states. Her seminaries of learning were in early days largely patronized by the people of the South. Cincinnati College, Kinmont's Academy, Dr. John Locke's Academy, Picket's Academy for young ladies, Mrs. Ryland's High School, Madison Institute, and the Academy of Fine Arts were among these private academies.

Thus, long before the subject of common schools had received efficient attention, arrangements were perfected for securing facilities for higher culture at the expense, in some way and to some degree, of the community. This state of sentiment is not surprising, since most of those engaged in the discussion of educational questions in these early days, were themselves men who enjoyed the benefits of intellectual discipline and knew its value. There is, accordingly, little in their addresses implying a belief that the mere ability to read a vote or to write one's name is of transcendent advantage to the individual or the commonwealth. They knew the value of quickening the intellect by study and mental conflict, and observed in the conduct of the men around them the results of bringing the lower nature into habitual subjection to the intellectual and moral. They therefore prized for themselves, their children, and the children of their neighbors the means of attaining these results. They declare that, "the wealth of a State is in her mind; and her true economy, not to say her duty, is to give full scope to native powers which lie within her sons."

Moreover, the early history of such as came from Eastern states would incline them to provide, in any system of education, for a course of study sufficiently extended to enlarge the faculties and secure correct and valuable mental habits. The public school system of New England was never a mere *common school* system. In 1647, Massachusetts provided by law that every township with forty families should provide a school where children might learn to read and write; that every township of one hundred families should provide a *grammar school* where youth could be fitted for the university, and that every township containing five hundred families should provide two grammar schools. These were called "grammar schools" until recently, and were the equivalent of our high schools in aim and purpose.

After the war of 1812 and the partial recovery of the State from its effects, the subject of general and of higher education became still more an object of interest in Ohio. In 1817, Governor Worthington recommended that a high school be at once established at the seat of government, at public expense, for the thorough education of poor boys for the work of teaching. He anticipated all the arguments that have been brought forward on this subject at a later day, by the broad declaration that if the State was to educate her youth, she would gain time and secure superior work if she took care that a sufficient number of persons were rendered competent, by proper moral and intellectual culture, to do the work well.

This suggestion not having been acted upon, in 1818-19 he presses the subject again in the following words:

"From a sense of duty to the State, I must again recommend the subject to your attention. Surely, nothing can be more important than information to the citizens of a free government like ours. Indeed, I feel convinced that a perpetuation of that freedom we now possess greatly depends on the means which may be used, under Providence, to produce that state of general information which will enable the people to appreciate the liberty they enjoy. * * The wealthy are deeply interested in such a state of things. Information and the practice of moral and religious principles never fail to produce order and secure rights of property in society. Information is common stock or national wealth; and in proportion as it is increased, are our means enlarged and national liberty secured."

The financial depression of the country immediately following Gov. Worthington's administration delayed action on these suggestions. Gov. Ethan A. Brown and Gov. Morrow repeated the recommendations made by former chief magistrates. During the administration of Gov. Morrow, in 1824-5, the first law making a tax for the support of schools obligatory was enacted. It imposed one-half of a mill on a dollar as a county tax, and did not, as is often asserted of the early laws of Ohio, restrict the teaching to the mere rudiments of knowledge. Among the most intelligent advocates of this measure was Mr. Nathan Guilford, of Cincinnati, who entertained the most enlarged views regarding the education of youth. His subsequent efforts in procuring high school facilities for the youth of his own city, render it improbable that such restriction could have been intended. He had a thorough acquaintance and sympathy with the New England system of primary and grammar schools in cities, villages, and townships, as is shown in the following citation:

"Nothing but free schools has ever succeeded in diffusing education among the mass of the people who cultivate the soil. The system scatters schools in every neighborhood, is within the reach of every farmer, and freely offers to the poor tenants of every cabin the means of instruction. The yeomanry of every country constitute its sinew and strength, and it is among them that those wholesome, honest, and home-bred principles are preserved, which constitute the safety and honor of a nation. A taste for reading and a desire for further information are thus created, and the result in New England, where free schools have long existed, is that in almost every town and village a respectable circulating library is to be found. Their common schools are the nurseries of the *academies and classical seminaries* which exist in almost every populous county, and which are the natural consequence of the common schools."

It is thus seen that in 1824, such men as Mr. Guilford regarded the elementary schools as the most enlightened educators of to-day regard them. While it seemed impracticable then to provide specifically for high school culture in the public schools, and while the effort for such provision seemed to take the direction of private or church schools, for the most part, there is in the early law no inhibition of such culture in the public schools. At all events, there seems to have been no hesitation, on the part of citizens imbued with the spirit to do so, to engage persons of liberal culture as instructors, and to introduce such subjects as natural philosophy, astronomy, algebra, geometry, engineering, the rudiments of Latin grammar, and other academic studies into the public schools. This law in its text is as general and liberal in this respect as that of 1838, and under the latter, instruction in the high school studies above ennumerated was not unfrequently provided for by boards of education.

But we are not left to these negative arguments to establish the fact of the existence at this period of most strong and intelligent sentiments in favor of fostering means for advanced education by the State. In December, 1826, Gov. Morrow thus urgently appeals to the legislature on the subject:

"With the tide of emigration which has so copiously flowed, were had a full supply of those qualified for the liberal professions. We have heretofore had the advantage of all the provisions made for education in the original states; but now, from the comparative density of population, and the wider range of settlement toward an extended frontier, that flow of emigration has ceased. The society is placed on its own ground, with its own means to cultivate native resources, physical, mental, and moral. The inquiry is interesting—are we prepared, from the present state of the public institutions of learning, to become independent in that respect of the older states in the Union? * * * It is true that much has been done for *general education* by the law for the regulation of common schools; that system, however, is defective, and the hope can scarcely be indulged that, with its present provisions, it can be brought into general use. It contains not sufficiently the principle of compulsion or *inducement* to insure its general operation; and experience has shown that without one or the other of these, the chance of its being carried into effect is in the inverse ratio to the necessity of its use. Should this system be improved by more perfect provision, and the fostering care of the legislature be extended to our *seminaries of learning*, giving them support as they shall have means, and the plans for internal commercial intercourse which are now in successful progress, be steadily persisted in, the flattering prospect is presented, that this State will rise to the exalted station, and continue to sustain that rank among the other states of the American Union, which by extent of territory, exuberance of soil, and salubrity of climate, she is entitled to hold."

Additional and most cogent arguments were presented on the same subject by Gov. Allen Trimble, who occupied the chair of state from 1826 to 1830. It is, indeed, remarkable that nearly every thought by which recent appeals on this subject have been strengthened, was most forcibly presented by the wise and patriotic men of fifty years ago. In one of his messages, he says:

"To afford to youth the means of instruction, and *to facilitate their march in the pursuit of useful knowledge*, has been the anxious care of the wise and good in every age and country; nor can the political condition of that country long continue prosperous and happy, where the *progress of intellectual and moral improvement is not commensurate with the development of its resources of wealth and power.* * * * No wise government should afford the means of instruction to a few in exclusion of the many, but should extend a *liberal* and equitable patronage. * * * It is a melancholy fact, that many of our young men have been and now are abroad, for want of the adequate means of instruction at home; the consequence of which is a constant drain upon the resources of the State of a large amount annually, which, if judiciously applied, would contribute salutary aid to some one of our home institions, *and enable the parent who sends one son abroad to educate two at home.*"

The only addition that has been made to this argument, so often presented more recently, is that the money spent at home would be doubly useful, even to the educated families, since by educating the neighbor's child as well, it creates an intelligent society without which even the most favored fall far short of full enjoyment. Even this will be found as a hint in a previous extract.

Subsequent statesmen, without regard to party, were equally zealous in their advocacy of similar views. We cannot refrain from adding one or two extracts among many that might be given, which bear directly on the subject of high schools. Governor Duncan McArthur, in 1831, thus speaks:

"A system of common schools that will impart to our whole population the benefit of a *competent business education*, would vastly promote the happiness of individuals and the prosperity of the State. The importance of perfecting such a system cannot be too firmly impressed upon your consideration."

Gov. Lucas, in 1836, is still more explicit:

"To perfect a system of public instruction, I am convinced that we must begin with common schools, and that the most effectual support that can be given to our academies, colleges, and universities, will be to raise the standard of common schools to that of preparatory schools."

Gov. Vance, in 1836 and 1838, and Gov. Corwin, in 1841, were both most earnest and able in their advocacy of every practicable improvement of our school system. Gov. Shannon, in 1843, remarked:

"The advantages and blessings of our common school system are beginning to be duly appreciated by all our citizens. It is not, however, all we should desire it to be. We should aim to improve our common schools, and give to them the capacity of imparting a *more enlarged and liberal education*; we should seek *to elevate the grade of public instruction*, so as to be in harmony with the progressive spirit which is now animating the civilized world."

Besides the information on the subject rendered available by the preservation of the executive messages, the logic of the events of the times and the testimony of many living witnesses clearly establish the fact that in large communities, and in many small ones, local talent was very active at this period in urging upon the people the necessity of higher culture than that embraced in a mere common school course. The organization of every college was the occasion of a thorough discussion of the subject of academic and preparatory education, not only at the seat of the college, but in whatever community the denomination or society seeking to support it was represented. As the various denominations by degrees succeeded in securing incipient endowments for collegiate or university instruction, they brought every community more or less thoroughly under the influence of the prevailing arguments on the subject. Thus the intelligent and impassioned appeals contained in the literature of Europe and America, as well as the thought of the best local talent, were made familiar to the understandings and effective on the hearts of every class of citizens in the State. Not only the agents of these institutions, who made the discussion of topics connected with higher education a specialty, but the local representatives of the churches and associations, vied with each other in their efforts to arouse their people to an appreciation of advanced culture.

We have thus endeavored to give an outline of the educational spirit which through years of hardship and toil animated the hearts of the earlier citizens of Ohio, and led by logical steps to the interesting era of which people now in active life know so much.

Effects follow causes. With a different early history, the present status of Ohio would have been widely different. It takes time and labor to enlighten and arouse masses of men, and the responsibility of those who assume to be leaders of public sentiment, might be clearly seen by a just comparison of the early history and present condition of other states with those of our own.

We have traced a constant and intelligent advocacy of enlarged provisions for popular education, based less on the plea of industrial and economical interests, powerful as these considerations might have been made, than on the broad principles of patriotism and humanity—the inalienable right of man to the means of mental and moral growth.

Up to this time, as has been implied, and for several years after, nearly all of what is now known as high school education was provided for in private schools and academies. These schools were often of a high character in their day, their instructors having the true spirit of patriotic educators, and many of them being thoroughly prepared for their work by graduation from the best colleges. Young men and women flocked to their rooms from a spirited desire to grow in wisdom rather than in accomplishments, and the brightest names of the State are of men who never enjoyed any other advantages than those afforded in these schools. Business men, lawyers, doctors, statesmen, clergymen, and teachers here received the inspiration of good and true sentiment, met with warm and manly encouragement, and often with little help from class-room drill, mastered most of the branches of study now taught in our best high schools. Such men as the late Governors Seabury Ford and David Tod, Rev. Dr. H. L. Hitchcock, the late learned and eloquent President of Western Reserve College, Judge Reuben Hitchcock, and many others, prepared for college, or for their professional studies in Burton Academy, in 1810–24. The seminary at Chillicothe was the great gathering point for the youth of the Scioto Valley, and many men of national reputation there formed their first habits of intellectual conflict. The same is true of the academies at Circleville, Dayton, and Springfield, and of many others, objects of reverence and grateful remembrance to many a once humble but ambitious and persistent youth, now strong in the possession of knowledge and of the discipline received in its acquisition.

An account of one or two of these early institutions may not be uninteresting to those who know some of the distinguished gentlemen who were students in them. We give, therefore, an extract from an address delivered at a picnic in Columbus, many years ago, by Hon. John R. Osborn, now of Toledo. After referring to the more primitive schools in Columbus—to the one taught by Joseph Olds, who, while teaching, prepared a manual on the principles of astronomy, and who afterwards became an influential lawyer; to another taught by Peleg Sisson, and containing several quite advanced students, thus justifying its enrollment in the list of early seminaries of the State, though the building afterward became the grocery of one Bezee, "who disgraced it by making it the arena of self-murder;" and to another opened in a frame building on Front street, not far in the rear of the present Neil House, and kept by Rudolphus Dickinson, who taught the languages to a class of boys—he says:

"Columbus as a town continued to grow, and the necessity for schools became more apparent, but as yet there was no school house proper. About the year 1821 or 1822, an organization was had for building an academy. The building was a single story frame house, consisting of two rooms; having in the then style of furniture, desks built around the sides of the room, where scholars could conveniently sit, with backs to their teacher, while their eyes unobserved might look out at the open windows, or else be employed with pocket knife upon the smooth surface of the desk. It was located on Third street, not far from the present Presbyterian Church. One of the earliest, if not the first teacher in this building, was A. G. Brown, a graduate of Ohio University, a gentle and kind man, a good scholar and a good teacher. I remember the Sullivants, McDowells, and Backuses from the western, and the Miners, McLeans, and Hoges from the southern districts."

Appropos to this is the statement among others made to the writer by Hon. E. D. Mansfield, LL. D., that the only seminary he ever attended was built of logs and over looked Mill Creek in Hamilton county. This was in 1811.

Another of the early educational institutions of the State, presumably an academy from the hint at philosophical apparatus, is thus described by Hon. Samuel Galloway:

"The roof on one side was trough-like, and down toward the eaves there was a large hole, so that the whole operated like a tunnel to catch all the rain and pour it into the school-room. At first I did not know but it might be some apparatus designed to explain the deluge. I called and inquired if the teacher and pupils were not sometimes drowned out. 'We should be,' was the answer, 'but the floor leaks just as badly as the roof, and drains off the water.'"

It is proper to remark that Mr. Galloway did not regard this as the best model of an educational edifice. The substantial, spacious, convenient, and comfortable school buildings, both public and private, that have come into existence within the last twenty years, are fitting evidences of the inspiring influence of his eloquence and that of his coadjutors, and of the spirit and enterprise of the citizens of Ohio.

As indicating the sentiment of the leaders of public opinion in the early settlements of Ohio, especially in such settlements as endeavored to establish and maintain this class of institutions, facts condensed from a well written history of the "Norwalk Academy" are given below. This history was written by a gentleman among the last to give up the plan of providing for higher education by academic institutions, and his account of the final abandonment of these schools for a graded system crowned by the inspiring influence of an efficient high school, may be taken as a true representation of the judgment and action of the enlightened citizens of every part of Ohio.

From the earliest settlement of Norwalk, Huron Co., in 1816, until 1826, small private schools, taught during the winter months, afforded the only educational facilities for the sparse population. In 1826, an association of gentlemen erected a three story brick building, the first and second stories for an academy, and the third for a masonic hall.

Rev. C. P. Bronson was the first principal, and an enrollment of ninety pupils was reported the first quarter. The tuition was as follows: reading, writing and spelling, per quarter, $1.75; arithmetic and English grammar, $2; higher English branches, $3; Greek and Latin, $4. Besides this, each pupil was to furnish "one-half a cord of wood or twenty-five cents in cash towards warming the building." After several principals had succeeded each other in the attempt to make the school pay, it united its fortunes to the common school, and thus made up a salary of $400 a year for the principal. In 1833, the Methodists bought the building and opened a school designed to fit young men for college or for active business, intending to make Norwalk an educational center for their denomination, the village then having a population of 899. They prosecuted the enterprise with vigor, and 189 pupils attended the second year, a large proportion of whom were of such age as "to possess unusual zeal in acquiring an education." In 1836, the seminary burned down, but the school found temporary retreat in church basements, and enrolled 137 males and 118 females.

In 1838, after much canvassing in the East and at home for funds, a building was erected, and Rev. Edward Thompson, afterwards Bishop Thompson, was principal, with Rev. Alexander Nelson as assistant. Luicus A. Hine, of Cincinnati, Judge L. B. Otis, of Chicago, W. H. Hopkins, Gov. Rutherford B. Hayes, and other distinguished men, were long students here, and doubtless look back with veneration on the old building and the dingy church basements where they pursued their studies, and will remember that good and thorough work was done there. Gen. Jas. B. McPherson was also a student in this school.

From the time of rebuilding in 1838, the institution had labored under a heavy debt, and as the Methodists had transferred their sympathies to the university at Delaware, it was sold to the Baptists, under execution, in 1846. Rev.

Jeremiah Hall as principal conducted the school, having 306 pupils in 1849, and was followed by A. S. Hutchins. The writer of the history referred to above says:

"It was a vigorous, popular, and thorough institution, aiming to qualify its pupils for the business of life, or fit them for entrance into the higher departments of collegiate study, and but for influences that had been agitating the public mind for several years, it might still have continued a valuable institution.

"The people of Ohio had become thoroughly awakened to a necessity of better and more efficient public schools. * * * In April, 1850, the question of adopting the union school system was submitted to a vote of our people, and by an almost unanimous vote it was adopted. A board of education was elected, and Mr. D. F. DeWolf appointed Superintendent.

"This system once fairly inaugurated, the private schools began to decline. The popular pride was concentrated in the support of the public schools. Our best citizens accepted positions in the board of education, and those who had been the most efficient in sustaining seminaries now became the champions of free schools, with the determination to make those of our village fully equal to any private school or seminary we ever had.

"The result of this state of feeling was, that in March, 1855, the Norwalk Institute was purchased by the union school district, together with library and apparatus, and Mr. Hutchins became the Superintendent of our public schools."

The names and statistics of thirty-one academies which are now found reporting more or less regularly to the State School Commissioner, and the names of 161 others known to have flourished in different parts of the State, are necessarily omitted for want of space.

RECENT HISTORY.

The law of 1838, making the school tax a state instead of a county tax, and creating the office of State Superintendent of Common Schools, was an event of great importance in the progress of the school work in Ohio. The world could hardly have presented a fitter man for the office than Hon. Samuel Lewis. So large-hearted that he could not refrain from laboring for the good of his kind, he turned, for the time being, all the resources of his nature into the interests entrusted to him.

Public spirit was everywhere aroused, and a general longing for a more thoroughly organized system and better individual schools characterized the period. Several of the colleges of the State were in a very active and flourishing condition. The disposition of the students to make their way by teaching a part of the time furnished excellent schools in many places for certain months of each year.

Educational journals were established, advocating improvements and imparting a large amount of knowledge and earnest persuasion on the subject from the pens of such men as Horace Mann, Henry Barnard, and others. Many of these articles abounded in telling facts regarding the advantages of education to the manufacturing and business interests of the country, gathered from the statements of leading manufacturers and men in active business. The Secretaries of State who succeeded Mr. Lewis as *ex officio* superintendents of common schools, were also efficient, and each in turn, by his carefully collected statistics accompanied by eloquent reports and appeals, co-operated with every effort of the people, the teachers, and the legislature to promote improvements in the system of education. Teachers' associations in various parts of the State were active, individual benevolence was ready with its contributions, and the tide of popular feeling set strongly in the direction of abandoning the system of select schools and private academies for a more generous, more practicable, and more efficient system of higher instruction. This was especially true of the decade from 1845 to 1855. Of course, the actual progress in a state so large and variously peopled as Ohio, seemed slow to those who constantly directed their most earnest thoughts to the subject; but when considered from the point of view now reached, embracing the wonderful change in public school edifices and other physical appliances, together with the advantages that have accrued to systems of instruction in consequence of the retention in the profession, by better salaries, of the skill and wisdom secured by years of apprenticeship and experience, the revolution has really been most rapid and complete. The awakening during this decade is, in this view, remarkable and well worthy to be remembered. It has been pronounced by men of other professions as superior to any results effected in any country, even in this age of rapid changes.

The Hon. Samuel Galloway, in his report of 1847, uses the following language:

"It is manifest from an extensive correspondence with influential and intelligent gentlemen in different parts of the State, that there exists an abiding determination to invigorate and perfect our common school system. It is equally apparent, that any legislative action to advance this object will be hailed with enthusiasm, and aided by a zealous co-operation.

"There are some practical evidences of improvement, which indicate the coming of a brighter day. Within the past year, several teachers' associations, or institutes, have been formed under encouraging auspices. In one or two of our cities and in several towns, large and commodious houses have been erected, and other extensive preparations made for a more perfect organization."

The interest taken in educational progress by prominent citizens of Ohio was probably never so marked as during this decade. The influence of Mr. Lewis and his successors in office, led strongly to this result. The personal influence of several leading educators of that day was also remarkably efficient in the same direction. Among these will be remembered the names of Dr. Asa D. Lord, of Lake Co., Lorin Andrews, of Ashland, M. D. Leggett, of Akron, M. F. Cowdery, of Sandusky, Andrew Freeze, of Cleveland, T. W. Harvey, of Lake Co., Milo G. Williams, of Springfield, J. C. Zachus, of Dayton, Reuben McMillan, of Columbiana Co., W. N. Edwards, of Troy, M. F. Hollenbeck, of Maumee, Dr. Joseph Ray, I. J. Allen, H. H. Barney, and others, of Cincinnati, and in the latter part of the decade,

Rev. Anson Smyth, of Toledo, A. J. Rickoff and Cyrus Knowlton, of Cincinnati, Hon. J. D. Cox, of Warren, and President I. W. Andrews, of Marietta College.

Intelligent teachers and school authorities in the larger cities opened correspondence with the boards of education and other friends of the cause in eastern cities. The answers to these letters were published in the newspapers and educational journals. Much light concerning the organization of schools was thus disseminated, and much interest awakened on the subject.

Among these instances, H. H. Barney and Dr. Lord, at the time of the establishment of the high schools of Cincinnati and Columbus, in 1845–6–7, opened an extensive correspondence with those who had witnessed the elevating and energizing effect of high schools upon all the departments of the common school system. We have recorded our belief that reforms are never the result of a spontaneous uprising of the people, but that effects everywhere follow causes. As illustrative of the *means* of carrying on the work of improvement, and in accordance with the wish of the writer to support his assertions by documentary evidence, several extracts from the letters as first published in the "Public School Advocate, and High School Magazine," are inserted. These extracts will further indicate that the high schools of Ohio are the result of a well matured conviction in the minds of the early friends of education as to their essential importance in a system of public school instruction. They show that the schools are in no sense an after-thought engrafted on the common school system of Ohio, but *a recognized necessity to the existence of such a system.*

The formers of public sentiment knew then, as well as we know now, that those states or communlties which had attempted to sustain a system of common schools without free high schools, had signally failed, and that in the nature of things they must fail, since they could not secure the co-operation of the better classes of society. They understood, and often declared, that if the "better classes" should ever become interested in public schools, it would be because they saw in them the means of educating their children up to the point generally required by them, more cheaply and better under their own eyes than abroad. The high school was with them, therefore, the very point in issue. Failing in this point, the whole question of the existence of an efficient common school system would have been lost.

The following accounts of the influence and important advantages of high schools to a system of common schools as such, are therefore as useful to-day as they were when the sentiments were penned. The experience of all Ohio cities has confirmed their truth. They form an important part of the history of the high schools of the State, though written in other states, since they form an important part of the arguments by which these high schools were finally established.

Hon. Charles McClure, then Superintendent of Public Instruction in Pennsylvania, in speaking of the High School of Philadelphia, said:

> "The influence exerted by the High School of Philadelphia upon other schools, is very apparent and highly beneficial. The pupils of the lower schools look forward to admission into it as a most desirable promotion, which operates as a stimulus to excite them to an earnest application to the acquisition of learning. This influence pervades all the other schools, and without it I cannot believe the school system could be so eminently successful as it now is in Philadelphia. A strong argument in support of this opinion is found in the fact, that in the first nineteen years after the introduction of the public schools in this city, there were but *seven thousand pupils;* whereas, in six years from that time, the number of pupils was increased to nearly *thirty-five thousand.*"

The following is from the report of the Controllers of the Public Schools of Philadelphia:

"The influence of the high school upon the other schools *is believed to be worth more than all it costs, independent of the advantages received by its actual pupils.* * * * * The privileges of the high school are held forth to the pupil as the reward of successful exertion in the lower schools. They are kept constantly and distinctly in view, and operate as a powerful and abiding stimulus to exertion through all the successive stages of promotion. * * * * The influence is felt by those who do not reach the high school quite as much as by those who do."

The following is from a gentleman of Providence, R. I.:

"The high school was the only feature of our system which encountered much opposition. When first proposed, its bearings on the schools below, and in various ways on the cause of education in the city, was not clearly seen. But now it would be as easy to strike out the whole, or any other feature in the system, as this. Its influence is seen in giving stimulus and steadiness to the workings of the lower grade of schools; in giving thoroughness and expansion to the whole course of instruction; in assisting to train teachers for our city and country schools, and in bringing together more advanced pupils of either sex, many of whom, but for the opportunities of this school, would enter on the duties and business of life with an imperfect education."

A gentlemen from Brattleboro, Vermont, writes:

"The high school has now taken deep root in the affections of the community, and is sustained and cherished by the most ardent exertions and wishes of all. In the same school-room, seated side by side, according to attainments, are children representing all classes and conditions of society. * * * * Envy and jealousy have given place to kindness and respect. Such was *not* the case when we had four select schools in this town, not one of which now remains."

Robert Kelly, President of the Board of Education of New York city, said:

"The reciprocal action of the 'Free Academy' (the Free High School) and the common schools, is highly advantageous to both. It benefits them by the introduction of uniformity, by exhibiting in immediate comparison the skill of teachers, as evidenced in the preparation of the candidates they furnish for the Free Academy; by raising up among the people a body of well prepared teachers, * * * * and by the incitements it constantly presents to the industry of all the scholars in the common schools."

Mr. Havemeyer, Mayor of the city, said:

"To hold out the strongest of honorable incentives to diligence in improving the opportunities afforded by the common schools; to generate a salutary emulation among the vast numbers whose education is to be received, and whose characters are to be formed in them, is an object of the greatest importance. And how can this be so fitly and so wisely done as by the establishment of high schools, by holding out the assurance that those who avail themselves most faithfully and effctually of the advantages offered in the common schools, shall have the opportunity of gratuitous instruction in the higher departments of learning? It acts most beneficially upon the whole mass of those who are embraced in the inferior departments. For my own part, I cannot regard with indifference anything which is calculated to improve our system of public instruction. It is our chief security for good government, and the protection of the rights of persons and property."

The following extracts are from equally high authorities:

"The influence of the high school has been to produce a greater degree of thoroughness, and a better attendance in the common schools. It opens to the poorest child an avenue by which he can be admitted to the realm of knowledge, not as a charity, but as a right, and without humiliating conditions."

"The influence of the high school is decidedly manifest in elevating public sentiment in reference to the advantages of common schools, and the value of general education. It presents also a powerful and abiding stimulus to the scholars in the lower schools, to greater diligence and effort, to qualify themselves to gain admission, so that even our grammar schools are far better than our best schools, public or private, before this system was introduced. Nor can the benevolent mind contemplate, without high satisfaction, its results in imparting a gratuitous education of an elevated character to hundreds of children, whose means are totally inadequate to secure it in private schools."

Extracts of a similar nature might be greatly multiplied from these letters.

It cannot be too strongly impressed upon the minds of the present generation, not only that our school system has been most considerately shaped, but that our State itself differs from other states in the Union in consequence of the powerful and persistent efforts of those who assisted to form public opinion in the crisis of her history. It is difficult to realize that in many parts of our State there existed as much indifference as then characterized those states which are now far behind Ohio in evidences of intelligence and thrift. It is equally difficult to accept the truth that but for such effort Ohio would have continued in this condition, as other states failing or refusing to make equal efforts have done. Until we do realize this, we cannot estimate our debt of gratitude to the noble men of the past, nor can we be sufficiently awake to the necessity of like action to preserve and enlarge for others the blessings we enjoy.

Appeals to pride, to interest, to patriotism, to humanity, and to the religious sentiment, were multiplied as the field of labor enlarged and the people manifested a disposition to act. Mr. Galloway's report for 1846, contains the following:

"No one possessing the pride proper for a citizen can abase himself by entertaining the idea that other states whose resources render them less capable of high achievement, shall tower above Ohio in all those enduring elements which indicate advanced civilization, and invest human nature with imperishable renown.

"There are considerations which show that popular education, a distinguishing privilege of our institutions, is also our highest policy. Intelligence is the life of successful enterprise."

Vigorous correspondence on the subject was also established, by the state superintendents, with all parts of the state. County auditors and others were called on for their views, and their letters during those years, constitute a large body of well expressed popular sentiment in favor of the improved system of public schools. These sentiments, by the distribution of the Superintendents' Reports, reached large numbers of citizens in every county of the State. Coming as the expression of popular sentiment in their own state, these views awakened an interest in all portions of Ohio, and its different regions vied with each other in securing good leading teachers and good school buildings.

According to the measure of previous intelligence in each community, and sometimes without reference to this intelligence, but under the influence of a few leading minds, the whole state moved forward many degrees in their interest, as manifested by liberal appropriations for high school houses, on well considered plans, and in commanding and convenient localities.

Some of the individual members of other professions, and of the higher ranks of teachers, who during this period were especially active in their efforts to promote public high school education, deserve at least a passing notice. Among those who contributed by their pens in the journals, or by addresses at important local associations of teachers, should be named Hon. George Willey and Hon. Harvey Rice, of Cleveland, Rev. Asa Mahan, D. D., Rev. Chas. G. Finney, D. D., Rev. Edward Thompson, D. D., Rev. W. C. Anderson, D. D., President of Miami University, I. W. Andrews, L. L. D. President of Marietta College, Rev. E. N. Gerhart, D. D., of Heidelburg College, Rev. James Fairchild, D. D., of Oberlin, Hon. James Monroe and Dr. N. S. Townsend, of Lorain Co., Hon. Samuel T. Worcester, of Norwalk, Prof. Harris and Prof. F. Merrick, of Delaware.

The eloquence and personal efforts of such men all over the state, did much to render the subject of advanced education in the public schools popular, and thus to strengthen them where they had been organized, and to facilitate their general introduction.

We cannot forget, nor fail highly to appreciate the generous public spirit of railroad officials in their patriotic disposition to advance the cause of public education, by a free use at this time, of their power to reduce fare for delegates to and from teachers' institutes and associations. They thus contributed greatly to assist in arousing public sentiment, informing the people, and facilitating an intercourse among teachers, which has proved to them the very soul of improvement.

Besides all this, inducements were offered in different places for the sessions of these associations, the enterprising citizens feeling richly repaid for the gratuitous entertainment of the members, by the lectures and other means made use of in these meetings to stimulate an interest in the subject of popular education in their communities. Not only were teachers entertained at their annual gatherings, but feted by boat rides and social levees, so kindly did the hearts of the people incline to invite this progress. This greatly encouraged the teachers and stimulated them in their work. In other cases, leading citizens devoted their time and talent to the work of improving their schools, in many cases not waiting for special legislation or for any change of general laws, but proceeding at once, under the law of 1838, to establish high school departments in connection with the common schools.

EARLY HIGH SCHOOLS IN SMALLER PLACES.

In the winter of 1842–3, the people of Maumee, then a flourishing village, held a meeting at which Gen. John E. Hunt presided, and the present Chief Justice Morrison R. Waite, Dr. Horatio Conant, Oscar White, and others were present, and voted a tax to build a suitable house for schools, including a high school. In the winter of 1843–4, a good public high school was established in this house, by Thomas Lane, A. M., a superior teacher from Canandaigua, N. Y. This school has been kept up till this day. A new school house, a brick structure, erected in 1869 at a cost of $30,-000, is "a model school building with model heating arrangements."

Among the high schools organized under the general law of the State, there was one in the village of Fitchville, Huron Co., which may, perhaps, be taken as the representative of popular sentiment in many other places then containing enterprising eastern families, some of whom, in the decay of these smaller places, have found their way to railway centers, and have lent their aid to larger and more permanent enterprises. In September, 1846, the writer of these pages found completed in this then enterprising village, a beautiful two story school building, supplied with the most approved furniture and with a room for apparatus. In the upper room of this house there was opened a high school, in which were taught all the branches then commonly taught in preparatory schools. Public exhibitions of the school soon supplied many pieces of apparatus, and for several years the school turned out a goodly number of young men and women with a high school education.

Time and space would fail to mention other schools of this character which within the knowledge of the writer came into existence about this time in different villages in the northern part of the State. No doubt many were established in other parts of the State also. Thus, while the larger towns were still practically oblivious to the advanced education of all children except those of parents rich enough to patronize the academies, these smaller towns were already awake. The existence of similar enterprise in other small towns, is indicated in reports of Hon. Samuel Galloway. In 1847, he said:

> "Frequent representations are made to this department, of the oppressiveness of many directors in prohibiting any branches being taught in the schools over which they have jurisdiction, except reading, writing, and arithmetic. This they have the power to do, by a strict construction of the present law. It is strange that men should so stultify themselves by an irrational exercise of power, and virtually limit the advancement of pupils. It may be suggested as a sufficient corrective of this grievance, that more enlightened men may be chosen by the people, if those in power act unworthily."

SANDUSKY HIGH SCHOOL.*

Hon. Eleutheros Cooke, Henry F. Merry, and Hon. Foster M. Follet of Sandusky, besides taking an interest in the subject of education throughout the State, were active, with others, regarding the schools of their own city. In 1844, they found the public schools worthless, and reorganized them. The building intended for the high school was first occupied for the purpose in 1845. The branches then taught in it were reading, spelling, writing, arithmetic, grammar, geography, Latin, French, philosophy, chemistry, and physiology—algebra and astronomy being added the next year. Tuition expenses for the school year were $808.61. In 1847 and 1848, principals were paid $35 per month. In November, 1848, M. F. Cowdery, already a teacher of large experience and excellent reputation in Lake county, was employed to take supervision of all the schools of the city, which still worked under the general law of the State. He acted in this capacity till July, 1871, with the exception of a few months. Mr. Cowdery was also principal of the high school till 1852, his wife, a lady of ripe scholarship, experience, and judgment, being his first assistant. Under this management, the high school soon became noted throughout the State. Many teachers of that day made pilgrimages to it, and received their first definite ideas of a well managed and well taught school. It did much to aid in the development of public sentiment in favor of public high schools.

The citizens for many years entertained peculiar views regarding the study of languages in the public schools, and excluded them, but the progress of events restored them in due time. This high school has generally maintained a good reputation, and for twenty years and upwards has been

*In the preparation of the following summaries of particular high schools the writer is in great part indebted to the local "Histories of Educational Work."

regarded by the intelligent citizens of Sandusky as an essential part of the public school system of the city. The strongest testimonial of the value at which it was estimated, was given in the erection, in 1866–9, of a building for the high school, at a cost of $85,500. Between 1855 and 1873 the high school graduated 176 pupils, of whom 48 were young men. The graduates are occupying prominent posiions in business, and in professional and social circles. A large number of them have engaged in teaching in the city schools and elsewhere.

The following are the names of the Principals of the High School: M. F. Cowdery, 1848–52; S. S. Colton, 1852–67; A. Phinney, 1867–9; N. S. Wright, 1869–71; E. S. Wellington, 1871–3; Miss E. Patterson, from 1873 to the present time.

CLEVELAND HIGH SCHOOLS.

In the spring of 1846, the Mayor of the city, George Hoadley, Esq., in his inaugural address to the council, made the following recommendation:

> "I earnestly recommend to your favorable consideration the propriety of establishing a school of a higher grade—an academic department—the pupils to be taken from our common schools according to merit. This would present a powerful stimulus to study and good conduct. The poorest child, if possessed of talents and application, might aspire to the highest stations in the Republic. From such schools we might hope to issue the future Franklins of our land."

Accordingly, on the 22nd of April, on motion of J. A. Harris, it was voted that a high school for boys be established, and that suitable rooms be rented and fitted up for its accommodation. Basement rooms in a church on Prospect Street were rented. Andrew Freese, of the Prospect Street Grammar School, was appointed Principal, and the school went into operation July 13, 1846, with 34 pupils. The number of pupils for the year was 83.

The school register contains the following observation by the principal, under "General Remarks;"

"April 19, 1847.—*Fourteen* girls were admitted this term. They do not come up the standard, and I doubt the policy of admitting girls at all into this department."

The rules of the board took it for granted that girls were not capable of mastering the higher mathematics, and hence they were permitted to advance only to "quadratic equations" in algebra. This was the limit for girls until 1854, when Mr. E. E. White took charge of the school. The first class of girls permitted to take the full course in mathematics stood *considerably higher*, on the average, than the boys!

It was thought by some that the high school had been illegally established, and the expediency of opening such a department was doubted. Accordingly the "high school question" became one of lively debate among the people. Those who opposed the school—chiefly the heavy taxpayers—said that no other city or town in the West maintained a school of this character, and while they were willing to be taxed to maintain common schools, they did not desire to support public high schools and colleges.

The city council appointed a special committee to examine the subject. A majority of this committee reported that in their opinion the school was established in violation of law, and that "it is inexpedient to support a high school at the charge of the common school fund." A dissenting minority report was also submitted.

The friends of the school now appealed to the people through the newspapers. A mass meeting was called, and Dr. Fry, of the St. Clair Street Grammar School, J. A. Briggs, Esq., and Bushnell White, Esq., ably advocated the measure. The legality of this measure was ably sustained by an appeal to the law of 1838, which provided that directors of schools in any incorporated town, city, or borough might establish schools of different grades, and ordain such rules for the duties and discipline of such schools as they might think conducive to the public good. The board of school managers, consisting of Messrs. Charles Bradburn, T. P. Handy, Samuel Starkweather, and William Day, in their report for that year to the city council, argued the expediency of this enlargement of the common school system, saying in conclusion:

> "It is our firm conviction, that the system is essential to the success of our public schools, and that it is the only way in which they can be made in truth what they are in name, *common schools*—common to all; good enough for the rich, and cheap enough for the poor—such schools as will meet the wants of all classes in the community."

No action of the council was taken on the committee's report; but in the following winter, 1847-8, the friends of the school secured a law by which the city council was "authorized and required" to establish and maintain a high school department. The battle was over, but partly by reason of unfriendly feelings toward the school, and partly, perhaps, from ignorance of its needs, appropriations by the council were inadequate for its support, being barely sufficient to keep it in existence. For two or three years the outlay of money per annum was about as follows: rent of basement, $100; fuel, $25; incidentals, $25; salary of principal, $500; salary of one assistant, $250. Total expenses $900. The average number of pupils for three years was 80; so that the cost per scholar was low enough, one would suppose, to satisfy the most scrupulous in matters of expenditures. It did not do so, however. Fault was found, and the school was pointed to as an unnecessary extravagance. The work of the school was done by two teachers up to the fall of 1852, when an additional assistant was employed. The course of study embraced the branches usually taught in high schools, excepting the languages, which were not added until 1856. The teaching force was small, and classes had often to be heard out of school hours.

The necessities of the school were pressing, and the efforts put forth by teachers and pupils to supply them were courageous. The boys of the school from time to time purchased a few pieces of apparatus to illustrate natural science, until the collection was worth upwards of $500. They earned this money by giving lectures, chiefly upon chemistry, and by doing small jobs in surveying. Occasionally they received donations of money from their friends. They purchased material and laid up with their own hands a brick laboratory. "There is scarcely a principle in mechanical philosophy, or other physical sciences, that they did not illustrate by machinery of their own construction." They published a small monthly paper. This yielded much fun and some money, and was useful in other ways. A gentleman of Cleveland to whom the writer is indebted for most of the facts in this sketch, remarks:

"These matters seem trifling, and are so, in themselves, but they belong to the history of the Central High School, as showing how that department was *developed* out of the growth below, was a *necessity* of that growth, and therefore normal. The enterprise and pluck of the boys of that day, mostly poor, is something phenomenal; and the unflagging exhibition of spirit, in their pursuit of knowledge under difficulties, had more to do with satisfying all classes of people that such an institution ought to exist and be maintained by the city, than all the arguments that had been made in its behalf. Opposition gradually died out. Leonard Case, the wealthiest man in the city, held a warm interest in this school, and on one occasion made the "boys in the basement" a handsome donation by way of encouragement.

"Subsequent classes have pursued a greater number of studies, and in some instances advanced further in the branches taken than did those embraced in the first catalogue. But in history, general reading, English literature, ready and correct writing of the language, inextemporaneous speaking or lecturing, and especially in debate, no class is recollected to have equaled it. In the class were many who are now eminent in the city as professional or business men; others, in new homes, have achieved distinction; and others still have occupied high official positions, and done the State and the nation distinguished service. They made the school a miniature world of work and conflict, and they grew by every struggle. It scarcely admits of question that the earnest, practical spirit of teacher and pupils, more than compensated for the increased facilities of the present day."

The lot on which the present high school building stands was purchased in 1850, and in the following year a cheap wooden structure was put up on it for the temporary accommodation of the school. The Central High School building was erected in the spring of 1856.

Cleveland has now a high school in the central, one in the western, and one in the eastern part of the city. No other city in the Union seems to manifest more pride in its public schools. Though she has had difficulties to contend with, her public schools from the first have been blessed with active, enthusiastic, persistent, and intelligent friends. They are now provided in all the departments with excellent buildings and apparatus, with well qualified teachers and a liberal supply of vigilant supervision. As in other cities, the lower grades owe their superiority to the successful establishment of the high school, and the consequent final enlistment of intelligent classes of society in the public school system.

Andrew Freese, Dr. Theo. Sterling, W. A. C. Converse, and S. G. Williams, Ph. D., have been Principals of the Central High School. Dr. Williams is now Principal of this school, and Superintendent of the three high schools.

CINCINNATI HIGH SCHOOLS.

Cincinnati had among its first settlers a number of enterprising, intelligent men, who would be likely to see to it that facilities for the education of their own families were not wanting. Yet, up to a late period, comparatively little really effective work was done for the promotion of common schools in the city. What schools of this name existed were maintained in inferior out-of-the-way houses, and not until annual processions of the children of these schools developed the fact to the astonished citizens that they were really human, and capable of being washed clean, dressed neatly, and kept so for at least a gala day, was any attention bestowed on them. Through these and similar means the schools gradually came into notice, and they rose in importance, until in February, 1845, a special law was secured for the thorough reorganization of the schools throughout the city. Up to this time, excellent seminaries, which have been heretofore noticed, had existed for those who could afford to pay tuition in them. But no public high school was opened in which the children of rich and poor alike could enjoy superior advantages, until 1847.

The first high school established in Cincinnati as an adjunct of the common school, was the "Central High School." It commenced operations July 27, 1847, in the basement of the German Lutheran Church, on Walnut Street. Those early and staunch friends of education, Chas. S. Bryant, Bellamy Storer, William Goodwin, Dr. John A. Warder, and D. R. Cady, constituted the committee on whose report the school was established.

Its first principal was Hon. H. H. Barney. It commenced with an attendance of 39 boys and 58 girls, but shortly grew to large proportions. Its curriculum of study consisted of moral and political science, belles-lettres, and composition, ancient and modern languages, ancient and modern history, natural philosophy, penmanship, chemistry, botany, anatomy and physiology, vocal music, book-keeping, etymology, reading, and declamation. This high school was discontinued in 1851, when the Woodward High School, and the Hughes High School were established.

ORIGIN OF THE WOODWARD AND HUGHES HIGH SCHOOLS.

William Woodward was an upright farmer, of frugal habits and simple tastes, a good, true, and humane Christian man. Long before his death, he found himself possessed of wealth by the approach of the corporate limits of Cincinnati to a farm which he owned, and to which he had moved from Connecticut when Cincinnati was a hamlet. He and his friend Samuel Lewis had consulted together regarding the education of youth and its relation to human happiness, and especially to the welfare of his country. He had no hesitation in determining that it was his duty to render actual assistance, then much needed, in furnishing educacational facilities for youth who could not procure them for themselves. He transferred to trustees that part of his farm lying nearest to the city as an endowment for the establishment and maintenance of schools—providing in his deed of trust, that orphans and the children of widows should have the preference of admission to the school. Mr. Lewis being the chief manager of the trust, the revenues were well husbanded, and a successful school was kept up for some time. The State common school system was afterwards inaugurated, and rendered this, as a lower grade school, superfluous. On the advice of Mr. Lewis, the conditions of the trust were so modified by Mr. Woodward as to allow of the establishment of the "Woodward College or High School." On the union of the high schools and the common schools, the original Woodward High School building was taken down, and the present beautiful building erected, which is a monument to his memory and creditable to the taste and judgment of the board of education.

Mr. Woodward lived to witness the full success of his scheme, and to enjoy the heart-felt gratitude and ever-increasing esteem of his fellow-citizens and countrymen.

The farm of Thomas Hughes, an Englishman by birth, and a practical shoemaker until his death, joined that of Mr. Woodward. The latter had little difficulty in directing the mind of Mr. Hughes into his own channel of thought. As a result, he bequeathed his land to William Woodward, William Greene, Nathan Guilford, Elisha Hotchkiss, and Jacob Williams, in trust. The land was leased on a perpetual ground rent, and the accumulation of a fund awaited, sufficient to erect a building for a school to be supported by the future revenues. Losses and delays were occasioned by failures and consequent lawsuits on the part of parties to to whom the interest in these leases had been sold. Matters were finally adjusted, and the city was put in possession of the annual revenues.

In 1852, these two funds were united and merged in the city school fund—the Hughes fund amounting to $12,000 or $13,000. The Hughes High School building was erected at a cost of $23,000. The reports now show the annual receipts from the two funds to be from $11,000 to $12,000.

These funds greatly facilitated the supply of early educational advantages to the youth of Cincinnati, and now afford the means for securing special conveniences or special instruction without burdening the tax-payers. Hon. H. H. Barney became Principal of the Hughes High School, and Dr. Joseph Ray Principal of the Woodward High School, in 1852. Under these eminent teachers the schools at once assumed a position of great dignity among the educational institutions of the country. They did much to attract the attention of educated and influential citizens of the State to the subject of public high school education. It was now no longer doubtful that the public high schools, supported by appropriations of the public funds sufficient to secure the services of the most accomplished educators of the land, must possess facilities for imparting thorough culture unknown to any other schools, and under such relations to the family and other social privileges as are congenial to every intelligent parent. The warm and hearty support of these schools, with the active co-operation of such men of culture as Wm. Goodman, Dr. James La Roy, Rev. Jas. H. Perkins, Hon. Samuel Lewis, Nathan Guilford, Wm. Greene, the Hon. Bellamy Storer, E. D. Mansfield, E. S. Brooks, and others of the highest social position, did much to overcome the prejudices of more common minds, and to place the public schools of the State on the highest plane of respectability. The best families patronized the schools. They were visited from all parts of the State. The cities that had not secured public high schools felt an additional impulse to act in this direction, and "the people's schools" were regarded as in all repects the most desirable institutions to foster. All that had been claimed for them in the earlier discussions of their merits was realized.

The Principals of the Hughes High School have been H. H. Barney, Cyrus Knowlton, J. L. Thornton and E. W. Coy. The Principals of the Woodward High School have been Dr. Joseph Ray, D. Shepardson, M. Woolson and Geo. W. Harper.

AKRON HIGH SCHOOL.

As marking still further the growing sentiment of the times, and as largely contributing to this growth and to the facilities for meeting its demands, the action of the people of Akron is highly interesting. The following account of the condition of the schools of that village up to 1846, needs only a change of names to be applicable to a large number of cities and villages of that era:

> "There were, in 1846, 690 children between the ages of four and sixteen, of whom there was an average attendance in public and other schools of 375. During the summer of 1846, one of the district schools was taught in the back room of a dwelling-house, another in an uncouth, inconvenient, uncomfortable building, gratuitously furnished. Private schools were taught in rooms temporarily hired and unsuited to the purpose. Reading, writing, spelling, arithmetic, and grammar were more or less attended to in these schools."

Rev. J. Jennings, then a young man, and pastor of the Congregational Church of Akron, is credited with giving definite direction to the new influences. Meetings of the citizens were held, Mr. Jennings actively collected information, and a definite plan of procedure was agreed upon. Hon. L. V. Bierce and H. B. Spelman were especially prominent in securing the required legislation. The result was the "Akron School Law," afterwards so largely adopted by the other cities of the State. True to the dictates of enlightened reason, the first thought was the establishment of a high school as a point of attraction and permanent interest. A pleasant lot of two and a half acres was purchased, and a house fitted up for a grammar school, or incipient high school, in the summer of 1847. M. D. Leggett, late Commissioner of Patents, was employed as a teacher of this high school and superintendent of all the schools, at a salary of $500 a year. In 1849, many tax payers opposed the provisions of the first law, as conferring too much power with respect to taxation. This power was then restricted to four mills on the dollar. Houses had to be built and lots paid for, and the consequent forced parsimony of the board of education lost to them the services of Mr. Leggett. The branches taught in the high school were the higher common English branches, history, algebra, geometry, trigonometry, physiology, natural philosophy, mental philosophy, chemistry, book-keeping, and phonography. Botany and English literature came in at a later day. Compositions and declamations were required once in four weeks. Latin and Greek were taught during the first two years, and were then dropped, in opposition to the sentiment of the citizens, but in accordance with the prevailing sentiment of the board, "that a good practical English education is all that any one has a right to expect or exact at the hands of a generous public." As if the "generous public" would be giving this instruction asked for to any others except to this same generous public itself. Accordingly, in August, 1865, Latin and Greek were again admitted by resolution of the board.

The superintendents were for some years also principals

and teachers of the high school. Their work was, indeed, mainly that of instruction in this department. Several "new periods" marked the development of these schools, however. In the eleventh annual report, the board declared their conviction that "the low wages principle was not the best economy." They also expressed a grave doubt whether their schools have maintained their relative rank in the State. Acting on this view, in 1857 a principal was engaged at $1,000 a year.

Another "new period" was reached in 1868. With new men and new business success and prosperity, larger and more liberal views had come to prevail. Akron had no institution or interest it cherished as it did its schools. "The board cast about for teachers who had obtained a really high rank in the profession. There were not many such, and the demand was large."

Finally, together with a general superintendent at a salary of $2,500 a year, Mrs. N. A. Stone, of state wide reputation as a teacher and discipinarian, was employed and put in charge of the high school, at a salary of $1,500. The leading features of an improved management of the high school under Mrs. Stone, were thoroughness in preparing lessons, an animated, accurate, and full recitation of them, and more polite deportment.

The high school graduated its first pupils in 1864, and has graduated 86 in all. The average attendance in the high school, in 1875, was 112. Musical instruction runs through this and the other grades.

Miss Maria Parsons is now Principal of the High School.

COLUMBUS HIGH SCHOOL.

In 1847, through the intelligent advice of Dr. A. D. Lord, Superintendent, the board of education of Columbus opened a school for the accommodation of the most advanced pupils, under the immediate direction of the superintendent, who devoted half of each day to teaching. Before the close of the year, this school became so large that the academy building on Town Street was rented for it, and another teacher was employed. This was the origin of the Columbus High School, and the board, at the close of 1848, made gratifying mention of the change in public sentiment within two years.

Better families now eagerly patronized the high school and soon afterward the lower grades. With teachers meetings, improved methods of instruction and discipline were instituted. In 1848, a course of study was adopted for the high school, and under the efficient management of Dr. Lord this school offered to the poor and rich alike far better facilities at a less cost than those which had hitherto been enjoyed by the rich alone.

This high school has not only gradually advanced with the general progress of methods of instruction, but has contributed to that progress, especially in later years, and in the particular department of physics, more perhaps than any other high school in the State. In this respect, it can probably divide the honors with the earlier achievements of the Cleveland high schools already recited. It has numbered among its principals and teachers some of the most active and efficient educators of the West, who have maintained, and some of them in an eminent degree, the reputation of the school. The most satisfactory results have followed a liberal provision for skilful special teachers in this school. With several able assistants, among those most prominent, T. C. Mendenhall, now Professor of Physics in the Agricultural and Mechanical College of the State, the Columbus High School has done much to add to the reputation of the public high schools of Ohio. It has not only effected this directly through the scholarship of its own classes, but by inspiring and directing to better efforts many a novitiate or long-time groveler in the profession. Its four years' course of study embraces the ordinary academic course, including zoology and botany, and thorough instruction in music and drawing, the latter a recent addition to the course. It offers a diploma for any one of four courses: English, German, Latin, and Classical.

The following are the names of the Principals of this school: Dr. A. D. Lord, 1847–53; A. Samson, 1853–55; J. F. Follett, 1857; Horace Norton, 1857–61; Geo. H. Twiss, 1862–4; Jonas Hutchinson, 1864–6; H. S. Westgate, 1866–8; Chas. R. Payne, 1868–70; A. Brown, 1870–2; E. H. Cook, from 1870 to the present time.

DAYTON HIGH SCHOOL.

In 1847, the board of education procured the extension to Dayton of the provision of the Akron school law. In 1848, the principals of the school petitioned the board for the privilege of teaching some of the higher branches, to meet a want expressed by many of their more advanced pupils. They stated that many of their best scholars were drawn from the public to private schools from the lack of this instruction. They therefore desired to introduce the elements of algebra and geometry, and perhaps physiology and natural philosophy." A committee of the board reported that it would not be wise to introduce such instruction in the district schools, but recommended the establishment of a high school. It was not, however, until 1850 that decisive action was taken. On April 15, 1850, the school was opened, James Campbell being Principal. In the fall of 1850 it was removed to the "academy building," the free use of which was granted by the trustees to the board of education. In June, 1857, this property was donated to the board of education, and during the same year the old building was removed and the present high school building erected.

The course of study, now occupying four years, has been enlarged from time to time, until it embraces all the branches usually pursued in the best city high schools. Latin, or its eqivalent—German or French—is *required* to be studied by all the pupils. Greek is taught, but comparatively few desire to study it. A large number of pupils has been prepared for college in the high school, and many of them have taken high rank in their classes. In 1857, the salary of the principal was $1,200; in 1867, $1,500; in 1875, $2,000.

In 1857, the total enrollment of pupils in the high school was 101; in 1867, 154; in 1875, 238. The first class was graduated in 1854, and consisted of two members; the class of 1864 consisted of 32 members. The total number of graduates is 122 males and 238 females.

A citizen of Dayton refers to the graduates of the school in the following manner:

"The graduates of the first class are now teachers in our public schools and have always ranked among the best. No one familiar with our city, can glance over the list of graduates, and trace their history as teachers in our schools, or as filling prominent positious in business circles and society, without being impressed with the noble work accomplished by this school."

The following gentlemen have been Principals of this High School: James Campbell, 1850–8; John W. Hall, 1858–66; William Smith, 1866–72; Charles B. Stivers, from 1872 to the present time.

THE TOLEDO HIGH SCHOOL.

The first school-house was erected in Toledo in 1834, and up to 1849 the entire public school system of the town was comprised in three district schools, having, in the year 1849, an enrollment of 389 different pupils, the enumeration of youths from 5 to 21 being 1010. In the spring of 1849, the citizens, after some discussion of the subject in the papers, adopted the main features of the Akron law. They at once established a graded system of schools. In the spring of 1852 the report shows 38 pupils in a high school taught in a temporary building provided for it.

In the meantime a lot, 480 by 200 feet, then worth $8,000, and now $80,000, was purchased. In 1854, the main part of a well-proportioned and really beautiful, though plain, high school building, in the Italian style of architecture, was completed. It was 56 by 112 feet in size, and three stories high. A wing was added in 1859, making the whole building, with lot and furniture, worth $175,000. It contained six large study rooms, an assembly room 56 by 88 feet, and twenty-two smaller rooms for recitations, laboratory, and offices. It seated 712 pupils. A part of the rooms have been devoted to the grammar schools from the first.

The course below the high school embraced a period of eight years. The classification and course of study in the high school in 1866, were as follows:

Fourth class.—Arithmetic, grammar, elements of algebra, and botany; or for a Latin-English course, instead of English grammar, two terms of Latin lessons.

Third class.—Natural philosophy, universal history, botany, algebra, physical geography; or in place of algebra, Latin grammar and translations into Latin.

Second class.—Geometry, rhetoric, astronomy, chemistry, English history, political economy, zoology; or Latin grammar, translations into Latin, Sallust, or Virgil, in place of geometry, astronomy, and chemistry.

First class.—Geology, Paley, trigonometry, surveying, mental philosophy, moral science, logic; or Latin composition and Cicero's orations in place of trigonometry and surveying.

A classical course also prescribed for second class, Latin as above, and Crosby's Greek grammar and lessons; and for first class, Latin as above, and Anabasis, Homer, and Greek composition. In all the classes, penmanship and vocal music under special teachers; reading, spelling, composition and declamation, weekly; tri-weekly debates and lectures; daily physical exercises and moral instruction; drawing, painting, and German, optional.

This course has been somewhat modified since, by adding French as optional, and putting physical geography a year earlier, also United States history. It dropped Paley, logic, and surveying; added a through course in physiology; substituted a complete course of English literature for moral science, and introduced a full course of historical reading running through the whole high school.

As representative of the growth of the public school system in the State for the last twenty-five years, and the present ratio of attendance, the following table is inserted. It shows the population of Toledo, and the actual enrollment and average attendance in the high school of that city, for each period of five years since 1850, with an accompanying year to show the rate of increase more clearly:

Year ending Aug. 31.	Population.	Enumeration.	No. Pupils Enrolled.	Average Attendance.
1850............	3,829	1,010	......	......
1854............	....	2,122	72	......
1855............	....	2,979	93	......
1859............	....	3,044	108	94
1860............	13,768	3,388	123	102
1864............	....	4,147	86	61
1865............	....	5,392	70	43
1869............	....	8,875	147	117
1870............	31,584	9,248	167	133
1874............	....	10,611	293	234
1875............	....	11,468	306	245
1876............	54,000	14,541	......	344

The following table exhibiting the number of pupils in each study in the high school, during 1874–5, is inserted as an average exhibit of the work being done in the high schools of Ohio:

Reading	306	Chemistry	57
Spelling	306	Natural Philosophy	57
Writing	306	Mental Philosophy	38
Arithmetic	306	Astronomy	38
English Grammar	306	Geology	57
Composition	306	Rhetoric	38
Vocal Music	306	English Literature	38
Physiology	328	German	89
Physical Geography	128	Latin	42
General History	306	French	63
Botany	85	Drawing	146
Natural History	85		

The two sexes are seated in the same room. The halls, or passage ways, however, are at different sides of the room, so that the sexes are entirely separate except in the study and recitation rooms. This is believed to be the rule in all the high schools of Ohio, although there are known to be some in which the sexes are seated in different rooms for study, but reciting together.

The high school graduated its first class of three pupils in 1857. Its whole list of graduates comprises 86 gentlemen and 196 ladies. Of these, 79 have been or are now teachers in the public schools of the city. Large numbers are occupying leading positions in the manufacturing, commercial, and professional interests of Toledo. Very few of these have failed to reflect credit on the school, and many of them have honored it in an eminent degree.

Ever since its thorough establishment, persons of superior scholarship and experience and good moral culture have stood at the head of this high school system—in all cases graduates of our first-class colleges. They have at all times been assisted by ladies of superior endowments and social and moral excellence, at salaries varying from $600 to $1200 a year. The breadth and thoroughness of scholarship, and of accomplishments even, attainable in the school, have left no inducement to the citizens to seek aid from private schools. The methods of instruction have advanced with the general improvement in the art of teaching, and with the advancement of science, as both are indicated by the text-books and in treatises on teaching.

Besides this, it is thought that some special points of progress have been made in the practice of illustrating by drawings the various lessons in the physical and natural sciences. This practice is carried through all the grades, from the crude drawing of the first shell or leaf in the oral lessons of the lower grades to the really perfect drawings of animals, and of plants and their parts, in the high school. The practice not only incites to practical efforts in the drawing classes, but greatly facilitates the acquisition of a definite knowledge of the sciences themselves. Since 1856, speciar instruction has been given in drawing.

Another peculiar characteristic of this school consists in the fact that from 1859 to 1869 an ample room was fitted up with a complete set of aparatus and used as a fixed gymnasium. It received classes of each sex separately from the upper departments of the school, which classes were conducted by a competent master. The citizens, during this time, took great interest in these exercises. Since the room was forced from this use to the purpose of a study room, free gymnastics have been required in all the schools, and most of the people seem satisfied with them. The young men of the city have not abandoned the gymnasium, however, but have secured other quarters for it.

Still another characteristic of the school, worth mentioning, perhaps, is the voluntary military organization connected with it—the Myers Cadets, consisting of a full company of 83 pupils of the public high school, thoroughly drilled, armed, and uniformed. A band of 16 pieces and a drum corps of 20 members, are also uniformed and furnished. The whole expense of this equipment was the donation of J. W. Myers, Esq., a former member of this high school. Admission into and retention in this company are conditional on regular attendance and orderly deportment in the school, and on abstinence from tobacco, intoxicating liquors, profanity, and ungentlemanly conduct.

Great credit is due to the board of education and to several individual members in particular, for the interest they have manifested in whatever pertained to the advancement of this school. Gen. C. W. Hill has for twenty-six years devoted a larger proportion of time to the buildings and schools than, perhaps, any other official in the State has done. Dr. Bliss, Dennison Steele, Lucius Wadsworth, Alonzo Rogers, and J. W. Myers, all now dead, were exceedingly attentive to the wants of the teachers and schools. John R. Osborn, Matthew Shoemaker, Calvin Cone, J. M. Gloyd, and others, have given the schools strong support on important questions of law, or in financial straits.

With scarcely an exception, after the graded system was inaugurated, the intelligent citizens of Toledo united to establish and support the high school. The wealthiest families took great pains to conform to the most exacting requirements as to the attendance of their children, and thoroughly supported the authority of the teachers. They cheered the instructors and pupils by their frequent presence in the school. They contributed addresses on public occasions, and in every way evinced their interest and pride in the school. Dangerous opposition has sometimes developed, but up to the present time the greater the dangers of this kind, the more hearty has been the support of the intelligent citizens.

R. M. Streeter, A. M., Mary E. Dennison, a graduate from Antioch College, and A. A. McDonald, are at present Principals of the High Schools of Toledo—each having separate and exclusive charge of distinct grades.

GENERAL SUMMARY.

In the above sketches of particular public high schools, the attempt has been made to exhibit the gradual development of such schools in the State, first giving the previous condition of schools in the larger communities, and in such smaller ones as have become historic by their early special efforts in the work of progress. In doing this, the opportunity has been improved to present what is known of any special characteristics of the schools referred to. Indeed, the general progress of the system of teaching in the State has resulted from the interchange of special experiences and views among educators, through institutes, associations, and the "Ohio Educational Monthly," or from visits to different schools. Hence, many items which were specialties in particular schools for a time, have so long since become general in the State that their origin has been forgotten. Happily very little jeasousy exists among teachers in this regard. All are glad to be able to contribute to the general improvement of the schools of the State.

The greater part of the account of the high schools of Cleveland and Cincinnati has been condensed from manuscripts kindly furnished from these cities. The accounts of the Dayton, Columbus, and Sandusky High Schools, are the result of personal knowledge and a perusal of early reports and recent "Local Histories." A large number of interesting facts might be added to the above regarding many other schools of the State, whose early friends are entitled to equal credit.

Massillon was among the earliest to move in the improvement, Mr. Arvine Wales and Dr. Bowen being among the most active promoters of the interest, and Lorin Andrews and T. W. Harvey being the first principals. Urbana turned its flourishing seminary into a public high school on the adoption of the Akron law, in 1849, with W. D. Henkle as principal. The Troy High School, under Mr. W. N. Edwards; the Perrysburg High School, under A. D. Wright and Edward Olney; the school at Xenia, for many years under Mr. Geo. S. Ormsby; that for twenty years under Mr. Joseph Welty, at New Philadelphia; those at Youngstown, Zanesville, Warren, Hamilton, Salem, Circleville; these, and many others, have histories of great interest, and have done their full share in perfecting the system of instruction, and rendering the high school system of Ohio a success.

The whole number of high schools in the State is not less than two hundred. This is indicated, at least, by the large number of additions that have by correspondence been made to the list contained in the State Commissioner's report.

Well built and commodious high school edifices are not confined to the few largest cities of the State. Sandusky has a high school building costing over $80,000. Bucyrus, with some 5,000 inhabitants, has a house costing over $60,000. Wauseon, Napoleon, Maumee, Perrysburg, Tiffin, Findley, Kenton, Lima, Fremont, Wooster, Galion, Mansfield, Lancaster, Portsmouth, Chillicothe, Gallipolis, Newark, Steubenville, Salem, Akron, Painesville, Elyria, Oberlin—indeed most of the leading towns of the State—have houses well adapted to the size of the respective towns, and costing from $10,000 to $40,000 each. Many of these houses, if not all, are, however, built to accommodate not only the high schools, but other grades also. It has been found impossible to give statistics as to high school buildings alone. The following shows the progress in expenditures for public school buildings since the establishment of high schools was begun.

The cost of lots and of school houses built was—

In 1851	$109,303
In 1860	341,273
In 1871	703,084
The total value of school houses in the State was, in 1874	18,829,586
In cities and villages	11,214,369
Increase in the former from 1873 to 1874	1,170,310

PRESENT SENTIMENT IN OHIO REGARDING HIGH SCHOOLS.

Extensive observation and correspondence, together with current printed testimony, authorize, it is believed, the following statements

1. The great mass of such citizens of the leading towns of Ohio as give any attention to educational interests, have had but one sentiment, for many years, regarding the necessity of a good high school to the success of a system of public schools. They have not doubted the superior advantages attainable with the same teachers in a school for which most of the members are regularly and carefully prepared in such lower grades as have a logical relation to this school, and under a management responsible for the work of each department in its relation to other departments.

2. The average age at which classes now reach the higher departments indicates the saving of time effected by a system of instruction related in all of its parts.

3. The age at which pupils enter the high school from the lower grades is also generally taken as an indication of the increased number of youth who are likely to pursue the elements of the higher branches of study, and the statistics showing the attendance upon the high schools bear out this suggestion.

4. The influence of the high school on the attendance and enthusiasm of the pupils in the lower grades, as attested in eastern cities, is fully appreciated and affirmed by friends of general culture in Ohio.

5. Recognizing the fact that for the large mass of even enterprizing citizens, the limits of school life for their children are from six to sixteen or eighteen years of age, they also see that any attempt to provide a system of education for these classes, must be much more efficient, complete, and economical of time and money, if the whole period of school life is embraced under one system.

6. The sentiment is believed to be gaining ground through the influence of these schools, that it is poor economy to withdraw pupils from school before the powers of the mind have been sufficiently developed to be put to substantial work. The relative growth of faculty and

power, under the more enlarged influence of high school studies, is beginning to be better understood. As the desire to secure these results, both in sons and daughters, is becoming more general, the necessity for the high school in close connection with the lower grades of schools becomes more and more generally apparent. Youth are frequently exhorted by citizens to continue a course of study for which the lower grades have so well prepared them to pursue with advantage. The falling off in numbers between the grammar and high school is accordingly diminishing.

7. The proverbial uncertainly concerning the continued existence of private high schools and academies, owing to failure of funds or change in the circumstances of the proprietors, and their frequent want of ability to meet the increasing necessities of the community, have also shown the public high school to be desirable.

8. The individual or associative management of private academies, which may render them the most desirable to the few immediately connected with their management, so often renders them undesirable to the public at large that they have ceased to be generally regarded as the best means of supplying the educational wants of the community.

9. Those who have given the subject liberal and serious consideration, observe that it is of the utmost importance that people should be so related to each other that they may know each other well, and that the different classes may have an opportunity to assimilate. This is especially desirable when contact can be secured under such circumstances as to give the better classes of sentiments the controlling influence. In a high school, to which pupils go directly from their homes for a few hours each day, the best culture of the community is brought, for the time being, to bear on that which may possibly not be so good. Yet this is done without rendering direct association of the refined

with the uncultivated a thing of necessity. Whatever untoward influences may reach these schools in the form of individual coarseness is under the restraint, not only of the teachers, but also of the better class of pupils, who have their individual and family character and their position in society to sustain, and who are seldom less refined at school than in their homes. Hence the history of high schools has never exhibited a tendency to demoralize the well bred, but their influence in improving the uncouth is well established and understood. This state of things, exhibiting an important gain without corresponding loss, every sentiment of patriotism leads our citizens to cherish.

10. While single private academies may be highly successful, it has hitherto been impossible, and in the nature of the case it must continue to be so, to bring them into such relations to each other as to secure concert of action and that harmony and progress in methods of instruction so desirable in a progressive age and among a people constantly changing their residences and even their occupations. No one can conceive that education could, under this system, become economical, thorough, and universal. These last two considerations show that public high schools are alone adopted to the genius of our republican institutions.

11. The argument regarding the education of their children under their own eyes, and under such circumstances as to secure to them the society of their children, has, to well constituted parents, practically but one side. Those who have sent to these schools have ceased to manifest nervous anxiety regarding the question of caste and social rank in them, or regarding the influence of such associations as their children are likely to meet in the public high school. They observe that their home culture, if such culture is imparted, is of avail to maintain excellence under any test ever applied in these schools. The pupils, living at home and passing immediately from their association with the teacher in the

study or class rooms to the society of their parents, are considered far more safe than in boarding schools, where the hours not employed in study are spent among people who have little personal interest in them, and among pupils who, though of wealthy parentage, perhaps, are as likely to be vicious as any who reach the high school, if not more so.

12. The subject of moral culture is strongly insisted on by the rules of all the boards of education, and is considered to be quite as attainable in these as in any other form of high school. In most places in the State no rule exists regarding the reading of the Bible at the opening exercises of the school; nor is any such rule considered necessary, long established precedent permitting teachers to do as they please in this particular, though no comment regarding the Scripture lessons would be tolerated, especially if of a sectarian character. Of moral culture, its importance and practicability, Mr. John Eaton, in a report printed by the Toledo board of education, and expressing, it is believed, the sentiment of that board, and substantially that of all Ohio boards of education, fitly remarks:

"That teachers should neither indulge, nor the people acquiesce, in neglecting this department of education, is painfully manifest. There is hardly an issue of the daily news that does not contain some record of the corruption of public or private virtue. We cannot expect honesty or uprightness in the State if they are not inculcated in the schools. The fallacy that makes all moral instruction sectarian, has too long held sway; the friends of man and of truth should free themselves from its power.

"The culture of the moral nature is not more sectarian than the culture of the intellect; the activity of conscience, than the activity of memory; nor is the law of love to God and man more sectarian than the law of gravity—to teach the law of right, than to teach that two and two make four."

13. It is believed that the settled existence of these schools practically carries with it the settlement of the important question regarding their relation to higher institutions of learning. In the same communities with these schools can

not, except in larger cities, exist other schools seeking to prepare pupils for the higher institutions. The practice of continuing pupils in these schools until their courses of study are finished, and then sending them to academies to complete a preparation for college, can not become general. The question of their leaving before the course is completed, involves the whole matter in issue. It remains for the colleges of necessity to provide the means of supplementing any demand they may make on pupils as requisites for admission. The interest of the colleges and of the communities alike require that this question shall be so treated by the colleges as to secure as large an attendance of our youth as possible in these higher institutions. The special knowledge and high culture of the professors in our first-class institutions of learning, should be made much more largely available in the cultivation of our youth. Every motive of patriotism and interest appeals to the true friends of higher education to cultivate the most affectionate relations to these schools, and to tax their wisdom to adapt all parts of our existing system of instruction to each other. The same generous enthusiasm which has secured the improvements already made, can realize all that remains to be done. Nothing is so much to be feared as the notion that the work of importance has all been accomplished.

Indeed, in proportion as the present public high schools usurp the place of the earlier academies, they will feel the need of that intelligent direction and warm-hearted advocacy for whose influence, in the days of less enlightenment and more popular prejudice the true friends of education can never be too grateful. No doubt can exist as to the superiority of a public graded school system, out of which shall naturally grow the high school, all under such management and systematic organization as will secure a logical order of sequence in classes and studies from the lowest to the highest grades, and that, indeed, all the intrinsic elements of a good school can be made to subsist under these conditions much more certainly than in connection with the old plan. But it is a matter of great concern whether the State will ever be able to draw around its institutions that warm and enthusiastic individual support which nourished into life, against so many opposing circumstances, the higher schools of the earlier days. There is, just now, great danger that the popular ardor which originated under the glowing eloquence heretofore referred to in these pages, and which carried the community forward to the adoption of the system which promised so much, and is capable of so much, may die out under the mistaken confidence that the system is good enough to run itself. Whenever it is forgotten that a correct and vigorous public sentiment is indispensable to success under any system of education, then laws and legislation will be powerless to secure an efficient system of schools. There is no strong hand in this country to enforce the best of systems. An earnest people alone can secure it; an apathetic people, never. It is of the nature of education itself to create this interest and to teach its importance. It would be a source of great mortification and real embarrassment, if, for the want of this vitalizing influence, our schools should lose their freshness and vigor of spirit.

CHAPTER V.

HIGHER EDUCATION.

The first organized white settlement within the present limits of Ohio, was made in the year 1788. Two years before this, March 1, 1786, in response to a call in the public prints signed by Generals Putnam and Tupper, several citizens of Massachusetts gathered at the "Bunch of Grapes Tavern" in Boston and after consultation organized the Ohio Company of Associates.* The men connected with this movement were, for the most part, soldiers of the Revolution who had given long and weary years to the service of their country, and had found when victory and peace had come, the new nation bankrupt and themselves greatly impoverished.

These men had government certificates of indebtedness, or army warrants—but there was no money in the treasury with which to pay them. They were strong men, full of energy and hope, and they determined to invade the great wilderness northwest of the Ohio river, and build them new homes and plant a new State if the government would sell them land and take army warrants as payment in whole or in part.

Gen. Rufus Putnam, a man of great strength and worth of character, who had won and retained the esteem and confidence of Gen. Washington during the war, was the acknowledged leader of the movement. Rev. Manasseh Cutler, LL. D., aided by the Hon. Winthrop Sargent, was the

*The Bunch of Grapes Tavern stood on a site now occupied by the New England Bank, on the south side of State street and the upper or western corner of Kilby street.

chief agent of the company in negotiating with Congress for the purchase of land. Hon. Nathan Dane, a personal friend of Mr. Cutler, and the representative in Congress of most of the members of the Company, took a deep interest in the matter of providing a territorial government for the contemplated settlement in the West. Thus originated the peerless Ordinance of July 13, 1787.

The two most notable features of this ordinance were Article VI excluding "Slavery and involuntary servitude" from the western territory, and Article III asserting that, "Religion, morality, and knowledge being necessary to good government and the happiness of mankind, schools and the means of education shall be forever encouraged." Thus liberty and learning were to enter the territory hand in hand. The clause relating to education was not accidental, it was inserted by those who were wise enough to comprehend the work they were doing for the great future. Dr. Cutler visited Congress and took an active interest in the subject of the ordinance, and at the request of the committee having it in charge, suggested such modifications and changes as seemed to him suitable to fit the instrument to be the charter under which the proposed colony could best plant itself in the West. A man of liberal culture and of comprehensive views, he combined the wisdom of the statesman with the sagacity of the diplomatist and so impressed himself upon the members of Congress that he secured a prompt passage of the ordinance in such shape as he wished. It is said that within three days after Dr. Cutler's appearance before Congress the ordinance was prepared and passed.* By this ordinance, the Northwest was placed at the first, upon a vantage ground of freedom, and the States formed from this territory have become among the most influential of the nation.

*For a history of this ordinance and of the part taken by Manasseh Cutler in its formation and passage, see an article in the North American Review, April, 1876, written by Frederick Poole, Esq.

In the contract made by Messrs. Cutler and Sargent with the Board of the Treasury in October, 1787, for the purchase of the land for the Ohio Company, it was stipulated that lot number sixteen of each township within the bounds of the purchased tract, should be set apart for the maintenance of public schools, and that two complete townships should be given perpetually for the purposes of a university. The devotion of section sixteen in each township of the public domain to school purposes had been previously made a part of the Government plan of disposing of its western territory, as appears in an act passed by Congress May 20, 1785, for the survey of lands north of the Ohio river.

The setting apart of a section in each township for schools, contemplated in 1785 and realized in 1787, became the rule of the government in the disposition of all territory subse quently surveyed and given to settlement.

The suggestion of the division of lands into townships of six miles square and of devoting a part to schools, is found in a letter of Gen. Rufus Putnam to Gen. Washington, dated June 16, 1783. At that early day soldiers of the Revolution contemplated removing to the West, and two hundred and fifty officers petitioned Congress for a grant of land.

The aggregate pecuniary value of one thirty-sixth part of the public lands is enormous, and the proceeds of the sales of these school sections have been of great help to the cause of education, but it is believed that the fact that the education of the people was thus honored by the nation and made a matter of especial care, has been of even more value. Thus popular education was in the earliest days of the Republic placed before the people as something of great worth. The States of the West have followed the example of the general government and by taxation contributed most generously to the same cause.

To Dr. Manasseh Cutler and his associates of the Ohio Company belongs the credit of securing two townships of land for the purpose of higher education and the endowment of a university. This was accomplished in the contract for land signed October 27, 1787. These townships became the endowment of the Ohio University located at Athens, Athens County, the history of which will be given hereafter.

Later in the same year, 1787, Hon. John Cleves Symmes, a citizen of New Jersey, doubtless stimulated by the example of the Ohio Company, entered into negotiations with Congress for a tract of land lying between the two Miami rivers, and secured a contract which provided for the setting apart of one township of land for a literary institution. This contract was modified by an act of Congress in 1792, and by it 1,000,000 acres were to be sold. The patent for these lands was executed by President Washington, September 30, 1794. The college township did not after all come from this purchase, but was subsequently given by Congress to the State of Ohio, in March, 1803, to be selected and located west of the Great Miami river. The State at once appointed commissioners to locate the township. They selected the township which is now Oxford, in Butler county. This was a direct grant of land by the general government for a university. In the case of the two townships set apart for a similar purpose within the limits of the Ohio Company's purchase, it has ever been claimed that in effect the donation came from the Company and not from the United States. This is shown in the following extract from Harris's Tour published in 1803:

> "Congress, in 1787, covenanted with the Ohio Company to give these lands perpetually for the purpose of a university; therefore, that Company consider themselves the virtual donors, and with the utmost propriety, for this stipulation made a part of the consideration for which they contributed to pay a certain price for the other lands."

From the foregoing statement it seems that universities were deemed important to the well being of the future State of Ohio by those who first planted the State.

The two institutions of learning thus early provided for did not go into actual operation for several years.

OHIO UNIVERSITY.

At this institution, the first instruction was given in June, 1809. It continued as an academy for several years under the care of Principal Lindley, but grew more like a college until 1822, when a full faculty was organized. The degree of Bachelor of Arts was in some cases afterwards conferred upon those who had been students during this transition state of the institution. By the triennial catalogue, Thomas Ewing and John Hunter were the first graduates, having completed their course in 1815. Mr. Ewing afterwards greatly distinguished himself as jurist and statesman.*

The first President was Rev. James Irvine, A. M. His successors, all able men, have been Rev. Robert G. Wilson, D. D., 1824-39; Rev. Wm. H. McGuffey, LL. D., 1839-43; Rev. Alfred Ryors, D. D., 1848-52; Rev. Salmon Howard, LL. D., 1852-72; Rev. Wm. H. Scott, A. M., 1873, to the present time. Classes have been graduated every year since 1815, excepting the years 1817, 1818, 1821, 1835, 1846, 1847, 1848, and 1849.

The whole number of graduates has been—Bachelors of Arts, 255; Bachelors of Science, that is, those who have completed a partial or scientific course, 43. So far as the records show, the ratio of graduates to freshmen is 25 per cent. Among the graduates there have been many who have won for themselves honorable positions in the learned professions and in public life. Although it was in the hearts of Dr. Cutler, Gen. Putnam, and their associates to unite religion with learning in the university, yet there has always been the broadest freedom and toleration. In the earlier days

*G. S. B. Hempstead, M. D., an eminent physician of Portsmouth, who also received the degree of A. B., claims to have completed his course of study before Mr. Ewing. Dr. Hempstead is still living

the presidents were Presyterians, but of late they have belonged to the Methodist church. President Scott in his Historical Sketch of the institution says, "The university is not sectarian and no effort is made to inculcate the doctrine of any particular creed or denomination; but care is taken to promote sound and healthy religious sentiments. Students are required to be present at prayers in the chapel every morning, and a lecture is delivered every Sabbath afternoon at which attendance is required."

The two townships of land set apart for the endowment of the university, are Athens and Alexander, Athens county. They contain something over 46,000 acres. If these townships had remained in the original forest, without a cabin in them or a road through them, the value of the lands today would be a munificient endowment of the university. It was the original purpose to secure to the institution the benefit of the natural and necessary rise of the lands from the general development and growth of the State and country, without regard to the special improvements made on them by the lessees. To secure this benefit provision was made for occasional re-appraisements of the lands.

The first act of legislation establishing the university was passed by the Territorial legislature in January, 1802. Section 11 of this act vests in the board of trustees townships eight and nine in the fourteenth range for the "sole use, benefit and support of the university, with full powers to divide, sub-divide, settle and manage the same by leasing, * * * providing that no lease shall be made for a longer term than twenty-one years." Section 14 exempts the college lands and the buildings from territorial and state taxation.

In 1804, the State legislature passed a new act modifying in several respects the territorial act of January, 1802. This act provides for the sub-division of the lands of the two townships, those included in the town of Athens excepted, by three disinterested and judicious free-holders under oath, appointed by the trustees. It provides that these free-holders "shall estimate and value the same as in their original unimproved state, after which the trustees shall proceed to make out leases of the lands * * * for the term of ninety years, renewable forever, on a yearly rent of six per centum on the amount of the valuation so made by the said freeholders, and the land so leased shall be subject to a revaluation at the expiration of thirty-five years, and to another revaluation at the end of sixty years from the commencement of the term of each lease, which revaluation shall be conducted and made on the principles of the first, and the lessee shall pay a yearly rent of six per centum on the amount of the revaluation to be made, and forever thereafter on a yearly rent equal to and not exceeding six per centum of the amount of a revaluation to be made as aforesaid at the expiration of the term of ninety years aforesaid, which valuation the trustees and their successors are hereby authorized and directed to make." It also provides that "the said corporation shall have power to demand a further yearly rent on the said lands and tenements not exceeding the amount of tax imposed on property of the like discription by the State, which rents shall be paid at such time and place, to such person and collected in such manner as the corporation shall direct." It was further provided that "the lands in the two townships, appraised as aforesaid, and the buildings which are or may be erected thereon shall forever be exempted from all State taxes." Very few if any leases were taken under the provisions of this law.

On the 21st of February, 1805, the legislature passed an act to amend the act of 1804. Five persons were appointed appraisers of the college lands, and it was enacted that "the said trustees shall lease the same to persons who have or may apply agreeably to law, for a term of ninety-nine years, renewable forever, with a fixed annual rent of six per centum on the appraised valuation; provided, that no lands shall be leased at a less valuation than at the rate of one dollar and seventy-five cents per acre, * * * and that so much of the aforesaid act, passed the 18th day of February, 1804, as is contrary to this act, be and hereby is repealed."

In 1807, the clause limiting the minimum valuation to one dollar and seventy-five cents per acre, was also repealed. Under the acts of 1804 and 1805 the lands were leased. Some degree of uneasiness was felt by some of the lessees with their leases, as shown by a petition signed by Robert McKinstry and thirty others, addressed to the board of trustees of the university April, 1810. The petitioners prayed for a modification of the form of their leases, and stated that, at "any rate, they would pray that the following clause in the latter part of said leases in their printed form might be totally expunged; viz, 'Together with such other sums as may from time to time be legally assessed on said lands,' and that all who now hold leases with the said clause therein may have liberty to surrender the same and take out new leases with that alteration."

A committee of the trustees consisting of Samuel Huntington, Jessup N. Couch, and Leonard Jewett, to whom the petition was referred, recommended that its prayer be granted. In a memorial of the lessees presented to the legislature in 1842, it is stated that this report of Judge Huntington and others was accepted and adopted by the board of trustees.

In 1826, the legislature passed an act authorizing the trustees to sell any lands not encumbered with leases, and also "to convey to any lessee of lands in said college townships the fee simple of such leasehold lands, on such lessee paying to the treasurer of said board such sum of money as will yield at an interest of six per cent. per annum, the sum which is yearly reserved in said lease." Under this act about 2,000 acres have been sold, or changed from leasehold to fee simple.

At the expiration of thirty-five years from the taking of the leases (the earlier ones), the board of trustees took measures, as contemplated by the law of 1804, for a revaluation of the leased lands. At the April meeting of the board in 1841, Col. William Medill introduced resolutions for this purpose, and five members were appointed to consider the subject and report at the next meeting in August. The report was in favor of a revaluation, and a subsequent committee was appointed with authority "to enter into an arrangement with the lessees, or any of them by which the question of the powers of the board may be submitted in an agreed case to the proper tribunals."

Such a case was agreed upon, that of *Festus McVey and others* vs. *the Ohio University*, which was taken to the Supreme Court of Ohio in bank upon demurrer, in December, 1841. It was argued by Hon. John Welch for the complainants, and Messrs. Ewing, Stansberry, and Hunter for the defendants. Judge Hitchcock, in giving the decision, held:

"The question which is presented to the court for consideration in this case is within a very narrow compass. It depends entirely upon the construction of the act of February, 1804, "Establishing a university in the town of Athens," and the act amendatory thereto, passed February 21, 1805. Other questions are argued by the complainants' counsel, but they do not properly arise in the case. Whether any provision was made in the lease for revaluation is a matter of no consequence. The lessors refer in the lease to the law under which they act, as the authority conferring upon them the power to make the lease, and it was incumbent upon the lessee to know the extent of this authority. Unless the lease was in conformity with the law, it was one which the trustees had not power to make, and the complainants' title would fail. The complainants cannot avail themselves of the allegation of having purchased without notice, for they are bound to be acquainted with the title under which they claim."

Then follows a statement of the provisions of the act of 1804 and of the amendatory act of 1805.

"If then we can ascertain wherein the two acts differ, or wherein the latter is contrary to the former, we ascertain to what extent the former is repealed.

By the act of 1804, the lands were to be appraised by three freeholders; by that of 1805, by five individuals named in the law. In this particular there is a difference. By the former law the land was to be leased for ninety years renewable forever; by the latter for ninety-nine years, renewable forever. Here is another difference.

By the former law, the trustees were authorized to lease all the lands; by the latter only such as could be appraised as high as one dollar and seventy-five cents per acre; and here is another difference.

The two laws are contrary, the one to the other, in the mode of appraisal, in the duration of the lease, and in the quantity of land to be leased. To this extent the former was repealed. We have sought in vain for any other matter in which they conflict.

It may have been the intention to have repealed all that part of the former law which related to the valuation and leasing of the land. But such intention cannot be gathered by any known rule of construction, and, of course, we are not authorized to declare that such effect is produced."

The case was therefore decided in favor of the trustees of the University.

On the 17th of December, 1842, the lessees of the college lands presented a memorial to the legislature, praying for relief, to which a reply of the board of trustees was presented on the 30th of the same month. These papers were submitted to the standing committee on the judiciary in the Senate. A majority of this committee reported adversely to the memorial of the lessees, and a minority report in their favor was presented by Eben Newton. The legislature passed the following act, entitled,

"An act to declare the true intent and meaning of the first section of the act entitled an act to amend an act to establish an university in the town of Athens, passed February 21, A. D., 1805."

"SEC. 1. *Be it enacted by the General Assembly of the State of Ohio*, That it is the true intent and meaning of the first section of the act entitled 'An act to amend an act entitled an act establishing an university in the town of Athens passed February the twenty first, eighteen hundred and five,' that the leases granted under and by virtue of said act and the one to which that was an amendment, should not be subject to a revaluation at any time thereafter as was provided for in the act to which that was an amendment."

Since the passage of this act in 1843, there has been no

other legislation on the subject of the revaluation of the lands, and the trustees have made no further efforts in this direction.

The history of the management of these college lands by the State as trustee for the university is an unfortunate one. When it was found that it was impossible to lease wild lands at a price equal to or greater than that of surrounding lands, *if subject to future revaluations,* it would have been the part of wisdom to hold the lands until they had risen in value. But they were already largely occupied by settlers without title, or "squatters," who were anxious to obtain legal rights to them. This produced no little pressure both upon the trustees of the university, and upon the State, the higher trustee. The trustees, furthermore, were anxious to realize funds in order to put the university into operation, and perhaps they were as unwilling to wait as were the people who desired the lands. In those days of small salaries and cheap living, the $4,000 to $5,000 to be obtained from the leases appeared to be a large sum. The action of the State was premature, and there should have been in the legislature enough men of wisdom and foresight to prevent the haste and consequent waste in the disposal of the lands.

In the act of 1804, there was added to the article authorizing the leasing of the college lands the following clause:

> "Provided always, that the corporation shall have power to demand a further yearly rent on the said land and tenements not exceeding the amount of the tax imposed on property of like description by the State."

The corporation has never availed itself of this proviso and collected such rent from the lessees, although asserting the right to do so at different times. In 1844, it asked legislative aid to enforce the collection. On March 30, 1875, the legislature passed a mandatory act in general form, requiring the trustees "to demand and collect said rents for the support of said institution." The act took effect July 1, 1875. This year (1876) the trustees will doubtless "demand and collect" such rents, or attempt to do so. The lessees of the university lands petitioned the Legislature of 1875–6 to relieve them from this payment. No such relief was granted.

The aggregate valuation of the university lands for taxation is $1,060,000, while the valuation for rental is "scarcely $70,000." Should the university succeed in obtaining the amount of the state tax on the one million dollars of valuation, now paid neither to the State nor to the institution, it will nearly double the present college revenue from the lands.

MIAMI UNIVERSITY.

The second institution of higher learning established in the State was the Miami University, at Oxford, Butler county, the origin of which has already been referred to The township of land granted to the university by the United States was located and registered in 1803. The legislature passed an act to establish the university February 17, 1809, and the first meeting of the board of trustees was held on the 7th of June, in the same year. The university, however, was not opened until November, 1824. There are eighteen trustees chosen by the legislature to serve for nine years. The first president was Rev. R. H. Bishop, D. D., who held the office from 1824 to 1841. His successors were Rev. George Junkin, D. D. (1841–4), Rev. E. D. McMaster (1845–9), Rev. W. C. Anderson, D. D. (1849–54), Rev. J. W. Hall, D. D. (1854–66), Rev. Robert L. Stanton, D. D. (1866–71). He was succeeded by President Hepburn, who remained only a short time. These were all learned and able men. Since 1872 the institution has been closed, but it will be reopened whenever its financial condition will warrant it.

The history of this university is one of much interest. Few institutions have done better work or sent forth so large a proportion of graduates who have become eminent in the various walks of life, but there has been a long struggle with financial embarrassment.

The legislation of the State deprived it of the revenues it ought to reap from its endowment, as will be seen hereafter when the history of the State control of the university is presented. So important were the tuition fees, to make up for want of larger endowment, that in many of the catalogues we find the following notification: "Tuition and room rent must invariably be paid in advance, and no deduction or drawback is allowed, and if not paid by the student it is charged to the faculty, who are made responsible to the board for it"—the latter clause sometimes printed in italics and sometimes in capitals. It is to be hoped that few colleges have ever been compelled to make a similar demand upon a poorly paid faculty.

The whole number of graduates from 1824 to 1872 inclusive, is 966. Of the 699 graduates from the beginning to the year 1860 inclusive, 198 became clergymen and 187 lawyers, being in each case nearly 27 per cent. The graduates, in unusually large numbers, have reached positions of distinction as governors, senators, congressmen, cabinet officers, foreign ministers, professors in theological, literary, and medical institutions, editors, teachers, business men, etc. It is doubtful whether any college in the land can show a relatively greater proportion of distinguished graduates. In the triennial catalogue of 1867, there is a roll of honor giving the names of 233 students who were connected with the army or navy in the service of the United States during the late civil war. These were not all graduates, but all had been students. On this roll are three distinguished "war Governors"—Richard Yates, Governor of Illinois, who was connected with the institution, but afterwards graduated at Jacksonville College, Illinois; William Dennison, a graduate of the class of 1835, Governor of Ohio in the first year of the war, and Oliver P. Morton, Governor of Indiana, who was a student in 1843. Hon. Chas. Anderson, a graduate of 1833, Colonel of the 93d Ohio Regiment, was elected Lieutenant Governor and became Governor after the death of Governor John Brough, in 1865. There were thirty-five field officers from the grade of major to major general, nineteen surgeons and assistant surgeons, and seven chaplains. Professor R. W. McFarland left his chair of mathematics and served during the war as Lieutenant Colonel of the 86th Ohio Regiment, and afterwards returned to his professorial duties. Among the captains, we find the name of Whitelaw Reid, the successor of Horace Greeley as editor of the "New York Tribune." Probably more than twenty graduates have become presidents or professors of colleges.

The catalogue contains the following information relative to religious instruction and worship:

> "Instruction in religion and morality, is, according to the charter, among the objects for which the university was established. For this provision is made. Bible classes are instructed by the Faculty every Sabbath morning. * * * The students are required to attend daily worship in the chapel and also on the Sabbath a public religious service in some one of the churches of the town."

The endowment of the university was a township of land. On the 17th of February, 1809, an act was passed authorizing the trustees to "divide, sub-divide and expose the same to sale in tracts of not less than 80 nor more than 160 acres and for the terms of 99 years and renewable forever, subject to a revaluation every 15 years, always considering the land in an unimproved state for the purpose of valuation, and provided that the land shall be offered at auction at not less than $2 per acre, and the tenants or lessees shall pay 6 per cent. per annum on the amount of their purchase."

On the 6th of January, 1810, or less than one year after, the next legislature passed an act to amend the foregoing act declaring "That so much of the 10th section of said act as requires a revaluation of said lands every fifteen years, is hereby repealed, together with so much of said act as comes within the purview of this act."

By an examination of the records it appears that a large number of the members of the legislature which passed the first act, belonged to the succeeding one which repealed it. The Senate was composed of the same persons in both years, with only a change of two members, and in the House twenty members out of forty-nine were the same men. The Senator and the three members of the House from Butler county in which Oxford is located, were the same individuals in both legislatures. The only explanation, attainable, of this legislation so self-contradictory and in the end so disastrous to the university, lies in the fact that during the year 1809 very few if any leases were taken, on account of the revaluation clause. But there was no pressing need to dispose at once of the lands. The university did not need the money, for it did not go into operation until November, 1824, or fourteen years after the passage of the law of 1810.

The university now receives from its lands—farming lands and village lots, $5,600 per annum.

It is not to be wondered at that the alumni and friends of the university, however rich as individuals they may be, should be unwilling to add to the endowment of an institution under the control of a State which has shown so little wisdom in the management of its great trust. It should be stated however, that in 1867 nearly $30,000 were contributed chiefly by the trustees, for a new college building and for general improvements. The buildings are now in good order. They are finely situated in a beautiful and well kept campus of one hundred acres.

OHIO AGRICULTURAL AND MECHANICAL COLLEGE.

On the 2nd of July, 1862, the Congress of the United States passed "an act donating lands to the several States and Territories, which may provide colleges for the benefit of Agriculture and the Mechanic Arts." By this act, the quantity of land to be given to each State was proportioned to the number of its congressional members, 30,000 acres to each member. The proportion offered to Ohio was 630,000 acres. There being only eighty acres of public land in Ohio "subject to sale at private entry at one dollar and twenty-five cents per acre," land scrip for 629,920 acres was to be issued by the Secretary of the Interior and placed in the treasury of the State. The assignees of this scrip might locate the same "upon any of the unappropriated lands of the United States subject to sale at private entry at one dollar and twenty-five cents per acre." The act providing that the proceeds of the sale of these lands shall be safely invested, and the interest "shall be inviolably appropriated by each state which may take and claim the benefit of this act, to the endowment, support and maintenance of at least one college, where the leading object shall be, without excluding other scientific and classical studies, and including military tactics, to teach such branches of learning as are related to Agriculture and the Mechanic Arts, in such a manner as the legislatures of the States may respectively prescribe in order to promote the liberal and practical education of the industrial classes in the several pursuits and professions of life."

At a special meeting of the State Board of Agriculture called by Gov. Tod in December, 1862, that board recommended the "acceptance of the grant, under the provisions of said act, by the legislature of the State and the early establishment of the college contemplated." In January, 1864, the same board presented to the General Assembly a memorial, entitled a "Memorial of the Ohio State Board of

Agriculture in favor of accepting the lands granted by Congress in aid of instruction in Agriculture and the Mechanic Arts, and in favor of the speedy establishment of an agricultural college."

On the 9th of February, 1864, the legislature accepted the congressional grant in the following formal enactment:

> "*Be it enacted by the General Assembly of the State of Ohio,* That the assent of the said state is hereby signified to the aforesaid act of Congress and to all the conditions and provisions therein contained, and the faith of the State of Ohio is hereby pledged to the performance of all such conditions and provisions."

On the 15th of March, 1865, the State Board of Agriculture passed a resolution recommending to the legislature to provide for the sale of the land scrip, "at a price not less than eighty cents per acre," and to appoint "a commission to receive propositions for acquiring an experimental farm." It was also resolved "that we, as the representatives of the agricultural and mechanical interests of the State, do earnestly protest against any division of the fund arising from said grant."

On the 13th of April, 1865, the General Assembly passed an act for the sale of the land scrip "at a rate of not less than eighty cents per acre," and for the appointment by the Governor of five commissioners who shall report a suitable location for the college or colleges, and such propositions and inducements as may be offered for the establishment of more than one such college. The commission was also to present a detailed plan for the organization of said college or colleges. This commission reported in favor of dividing the proceeds of the lands, giving one half to Miami University reorganized, and the other half for the endowment of a college to be located in the northern part of the State. A minority report designated College Hill, near Cincinnati, as a desirable location.

In March, 1868, a joint committee, composed of four members of the Senate and eight from the House, was appointed to make investigation, receive propositions, designate a location of the college, and report to the legislature. In 1869, this committee reported in favor of Urbana, Champaign county, as the most desirable location. A minority report recommended Wooster, Wayne county.

On the 22d of March, 1870, the General Assembly passed "An act to establish and maintain an Agricultural and Mechanical College in Ohio." This act provided for the appointment of a board of trustees—one from each congressional district—the appointment to be made by the Governor. The president of the State Board of Agriculture was to be a member *ex-officio*. This board was authorized to locate the college upon lands—not less than one hundred acres—the same to be reasonably central. They were to judge of the relative merits of the various propositions and inducements presented by counties, towns, or individuals for such location, and to organize the college and elect its president and professors.

In order to secure full competition and generous offers for the location of the college, the General Assembly on the 18th of April, 1870, passed an act authorizing the several counties of the State to raise money to secure such location. On the 11th of May, 1870, the board of trustees met for the first time, and was organized by the election of Hon. V. B. Horton, President, R. C. Anderson, Secretary, and Joseph Sullivant, Treasurer. On the 13th of October the board made a final location of the college on the Neil farm in the suburbs of Columbus, three hundred thousand dollars having been voted by the county of Franklin as an inducement.

The location, in the fertility and beauty of the lands, is an admirable one. The farm of 320 acres was bought, a large and handsome college building and two dormitories were built, and the laboratories equipped with apparatus, all from the Franklin county donation. The land, now within the corporate limits of Columbus, is rising rapidly in value.

Under the act of April 13, 1865, to "provide for the sale of the land scrip," which fixed the price of the lands at 80 cents per acre, comparatively little land was sold. Other States offered for sale similar lands, and the market was overstocked. It was the strong desire of many who had watched carefully the progress of the West, and marked the inevitable rise of lands in value, that the lands should be carefully and promptly located. Parties were willing to take all the land scrip at eighty cents per acre, if a comparatively short time could be given on payments, no title to pass until full payment was made. They wished to locate the lands *at once*, and had already investigated the more desirable districts for such location—districts in which lands have since risen very greatly in value. If such purchasers had failed in their payments, the lands would have remained for future sale by the State—a fortunate thing, since every year of delay in the sale of well located lands added many thousands of dollars to their value. But the land-scrip commissioners, consisting of the Auditor, Treasurer, and Secretary of State, felt constrained to reject such offers, the law, in their opinion, not making provision for other than sales for cash. This was in the latter part of 1865. Few sales were made. On the 5th of April, 1866, the General Assembly passed an act to amend the act of April 13, 1865, by which the whole matter of sale was left to the discretion of the commissioners, only they were to make prompt and vigorous efforts to effect sales. They were "authorized to sell or cause to be sold said land scrip at the best price they can obtain for the same, and to employ a suitable person or persons to aid them in making such sales, and to pay such persons such commissions on sales made by them as they may deem adequate to secure prompt and vigorous efforts to effect sales." They were authorized to sell scrip of not less amount than for 50,000 acres on four equal payments, the fourth to be due at the end of six years, and scrip for not less than 10,000 acres, with three years time on the last payment.

In obedience to the letter and spirit of this law, the lands were promptly sold during the year. Five hundred and seventy-five thousand five hundred and sixty acres were sold for fifty-three cents an acre, of which 400,000 were sold to one man, and 125,760 to another. The total proceeds of sales, independent of interest, was $340,906.80. The House of Representatives, in January or February, 1868, passed the following resolution of inquiry: "*Resolved*, That the land-scrip commissioners of this State be and they are hereby requested to inform this house at as early day as practicable, why the land scrip belonging to this State was sold, part of it on time, for less than fifty-three cents an acre, while the government of the United States was selling lands at one dollar and twenty-five cents an acre; also, to report the date of each sale, the name of each purchaser, the terms of each sale," etc. The commissioners responded to this resolution of inquiry, denying that any scrip had been sold for *less* than fifty-three cents, and defending themselves from reproach for selling the scrip at the low prices obtained, by quoting the law requiring "prompt and vigorous efforts" to make sales, etc.

We have in this unfortunate history the third case of the disposition by the State, of lands granted to it by the general government for the support of colleges. For the Ohio University at Athens there was a grant of two townships, for Miami University one township, and for the Agricultural and Mechanical College 630,000 acres. To the latter have since been added the unsold lands in the Virginia Military District. These college lands are more in the aggregate than all the lands given to the State for common schools. How wisely or unwisely the school lands have been managed by the State we may learn from the chapter in this volume devoted to School Legislation. Fortunately, many of the school lands remained in the possession of the State until they had risen somewhat in value before they were sold.

Some indeed, are yet unsold and pay a rental to the State. The annual income from these lands from interest and rents is from $230,000 to $240,000, while that from a larger quantity of land given for colleges is only about $40,000. The larger part of these lands—the 630,000 acres, were pressed to sale upon a market temporarily overstocked.

There was doubtless much pressure brought upon the legislature to sell the lands. So far as the records show, it was of an open and honorable character. Many of the leading agriculturists of the State expressing themselves through the State Board of Agriculture, and in other ways, urged from the first a "speedy sale" of the lands. As we have seen, this board first recommended to the legislature to fix the minimum price at 80 cents an acre, which recommendation was acted upon. This price not being readily obtained, the General Assembly ordered the sale of the scrip at the best price to be obtained. This secured the desired sale and brought to the treasury for the Agricultural and Mechanical College a little over $340,000 for 630,000 acres. A state lives on through centuries, and so does a university. Each could afford to wait a few years to realize the millions which were sure to come from the munificent grant of the national government. Nor was the land perishable property needing to be sold at once.

The proceeds of the sale of the scrip were placed in the treasury of the State, the interest being compounded semi-annually. Dr. Henry S. Babbitt, treasurer of the college, reported the "principal derived from the proceeds of the sales of the land scrip and the accumulations thereto up to January 1, 1874, $470,307.28." To this are added other funds derived from other sources, making the whole available fund "something over $500,000, the annual income from which slightly exceeds $30,000." The total value of the endowment and property of the college exceeds $1,000,000.

Congress having given to the State of Ohio all unsold land

in the Virginia Military District between the Scioto and Little Miami rivers, the proceeds of the sales of these lands were given to the college by an act of the General Assembly passed March 26, 1872. Something has already been realized from this source.

The college was opened for instruction in September, 1873. Edward Orton, A. M., was chosen President, and there are now seven professors, two assistant professors, and one instructor. President Orton at the time of his appointment was President of Antioch College and also one of the assistants on the geological survey of the State. He has had much experience as an instructor.

The following departments of instruction are enumerated in the Catalogue for 1874–5:

> "Physics; Chemistry; Zoology; Botany; Geology; Agriculture; Mathematics; English, French and German Languages; Latin and Greek Languages; Political Economy and Civil Polity; Mechanical and Free-hand Drawing."

The objects of the college, briefly stated, are,

> "1st. To furnish a general education by which the youth of Ohio shall be fitted for the several pursuits and professions in life. The sciences that bear on practical life are to be made especially prominent in this education, and for such branches the college is bound to make ample provision, but no departments of study that enter into a well balanced scheme of general training, are to be purposely excluded from it.
>
> 2d. To provide opportunity for those who wish to pursue special studies."

Tuition is free but charges are made for room rent and incidental expenses. Young ladies are admitted on equal terms with young men.

The college is too young to have graduates in any of its courses. It is in its various laboratories, chemical, physical, and zoological, well equipped. The geological cabinet contains the collections made in connection with the recent geological survey of Ohio.

By an act of the General Assembly passed April 16, 1874, the number of trustees was reduced to five, and new appointments were made by the Governor and confirmed by the Senate. The term of office is five years, one member retiring each year. The following persons were appointed; Alexander Waddle, Warren P. Noble, William Larwill, Ralph Leete, and Joseph Sullivant. Mr. Leete is the president of the board, and Joseph Sullivant, secretary. Mr. Sullivant, in addition to the usual duties of secretary, has charge of the buildings and grounds, audits and allows all necessary accounts, etc., for which he receives an annual salary of $2,000. Dr. Henry S. Babbitt has been the treasurer of the college from the first.

The whole number of students on the Catalogue of 1874–5 is 66. They are not grouped into classes. Of the 66, a little more than one-half (36) are from Columbus. In the "*Fifth Annual Report of the Board of Trustees to the Governor*," President Orton in a report to the trustees dated November 15, 1875, states that the whole number in attendance is 99 and of this number 58 are from Franklin county, chiefly from the city of Columbus. The President states that, "the conditions of admission to the college remain unchanged. Entrance examinations are made in arithmetic, geography, English grammar, and elementary algebra." Prof. Mendenhall in the Department of Physics and Mechanics reports 38 students, the great majority of whom are in the elementary course. Eight are working in the Physical Laboratory. Prof. Norton, in the Chemical Department, reports six students in analytical chemistry. In the Department of Latin and Greek, Prof. Wright reports:

Students in Latin of the first year class	8	
Students in Latin of the second year class	3	
		—11
Students in Greek of the first year class	4	
Students in Greek of the second year class	2	
		— 6

Prof. Tuttle, in the department of Zoology, reports 30 registered in the class of elementary physiology and 6 in the advanced course of zoology. Prof. Colvin, in the department of Political Economy, Civil Polity, and Accounts, reports 15 students in political economy and civil polity, and 35 in the study of accounts. No detailed reports of the number of students in the other departments is given. There are no public religious exercises of any kind in the institution.

KENYON COLLEGE.

On January 24, 1826, the General Assembly of Ohio authorized the faculty of the Theological Seminary of the Protestant Episcopal Church in the Diocese of Ohio, which had been chartered December 29, 1824, to add a college department and confer degrees in arts and sciences, under the name and style of the President and Professors of Kenyon College in the State of Ohio. In 1839, the General Assembly authorized a separate faculty for the college, and from that time the two faculties have been distinct.

The first President was the Right Rev. Philander Chase, Bishop of Ohio. This gentleman resigned the presidency and episcopate in 1831, and was succeeded by the Right Rev. Charles P. McIlvaine. Bishop Chase afterwards removed to Illinois, where he was chosen Bishop in 1835. Bishop McIlvaine was president of the college from 1831 to 1840. His successors have been Maj. D. B. Douglass, LL. D. (1840–44), Rev. S. A. Bronson, D. D. (1845–50), Rev. Thomas M. Smith, D. D. (1850–53), Lorin Andrews, LL. D. (1854–61), Charles Short, LL. D. (1863–67), Rev. James Kent Stone, A. M. (1867–68), and Eli T. Tappan, LL. D. (1868–75).

The history of the college presents many features of much interest. Bishop Chase first sought to establish a theological seminary. In 1817, he left his parish in Hartford, Conn., and came to Ohio, where the next year he was elected Bishop and was consecrated as such in Philadelphia February 11, 1819. His diocese included the whole State of Ohio, but he had only two or three clergymen as co-laborers in the vast field. To secure an educated ministry for the West he determined to establish a theological seminary, and to obtain funds he visited England in 1823. He was well received and found friends and contributors in Lords Gambier, Kenyon, and Bexley, Sir Thomas Ackland, the Right Hon. Dowager Countess of Rosse, Mrs. Hannah Moore, and others. He returned with gifts amounting to $30,000, and the General Assembly of Ohio granted a charter to him and his associates for a seminary December 29, 1824. The seminary was first located on the Bishop's farm in Worthington, Franklin county, but subsequently 8,000 acres of wild land were purchased in Knox county, for $18,000, to be the permanent site of seminary and college.

The town where the institutions were located was called Gambier after Lord Gambier, and the college was named Kenyon after Lord Kenyon. The building afterwards erected for the use of the theological seminary was called Bexley Hall after Lord Bexley. Rosse Hall is named after the Countess of Rosse. In1827 Bishop Chase obtained $25,000 in the eastern States. In the meantime the college had opened well, students were present in considerable numbers and were well instructed by an able faculty. But there were financial troubles. Eight thousand acres of wild land brought little or no income. Expensive buildings were to be erected and a faculty supported. In 1831, Bishop Chase brought the difficulties before the diocesan convention of the State, but the action of the convention was not satisfactory to him and he "peremptorily resigned both the presidency of the seminary and college and the episcopate of the diocese, and forever severed his connection with the institutions which he had so ardently and faithfully labored to establish."

The Bishop was a man of great executive energy and of undaunted will. His plans were noble and comprehensive, but the difficulties in his pathway were very great. Bishop McIlvaine succeeded Bishop Chase to the presidency of the college. Bishop McIlvaine was a remarkable man, full of gifts and graces. If less intense and imperative than Bishop Chase, he had more tact and discernment of men. His first work for the college, after thoroughly surveying the ground, was to go to his eastern friends and obtain funds. In 1833, he brought to the rescue of the college $30,000. This saved the institution. In 1835, he visited England chiefly, for rest and health, and brought back $12,600 for the erection of a building for the theological department. He also received valuable gifts of books for the library.

In 1841, he resigned his position as president of the college, and thenceforward the faculty of the college became distinct from that of the seminary, although both were under the control of the same board of trustees. In 1842, Bishop McIlvaine visited the Eastern States and obtained $29,517, which, with $6,000 raised in Ohio, brought temporary relief. In 1850, a portion of the lands which had hitherto been a great burden and expense to the trustees, was sold. All the debts were paid and a "bright day dawned on Kenyon." Not long after this, (in 1854) Lorin Andrews, LL. D., who for many years had been favorably known in Ohio in connection with popular education, was elected to the presidency of the college. He was an excellent president. His personal magnetism drew and retained students, and his fine executive capacity caused the affairs of the college to move on regularly and smoothly. President Andrews on hearing of the fall of Fort Sumter almost instantly offered his services for the suppression of the Rebellion. He was made the Colonel of the 4th Regiment, Ohio Infantry, and at once entered upon active military service among the mountains of West Virginia. In the early autumn of September, 1861, he died of fever contracted in the camp. He was a rare man, full of all noble impulses and deeds.

Bishop G. T. Bedell, the associate and successor of Bishop McIlvaine, although never president of Kenyon, has proved to be one of its foremost friends and benefactors. By his efforts he has very largely increased the endowment. In 1866 he recounts "the recent subscriptions to the college as amounting to $140,000, of which over $100,000 have been paid."

The present estimated value of the lands, buildings, libraries, apparatus, and endowments at Gambier, including seminary and college, is about half a million of dollars. The financial history of Kenyon is essentially like that of many other western institutions. Few have any distinct conception of the wearying labors and of the many discouragements which are the portion of those who would found a college. We are reminded of the familiar words of Virgil: "*Tantæ molis erat Romanam condere gentem.*"

The presidents since President Andrews have already been named. President Tappan, the last incumbent, a successful professor of mathematics in the Ohio University for several years before his appointment to the presidency of Kenyon, has recently resigned the president's chair and taken charge of the mathematical department to which he is drawn by his tastes and for which he has peculiar fitness.

Kenyon College has always done good literary work, and has sent forth many graduates who have given an excellent account of themselves in professional and public life. Hon. Edwin M. Stanton who has had few peers in history as a war minister, received his education at Kenyon. Hon. R. B. Hayes, the thrice chosen governor of Ohio, was a graduate of the class of 1842. Hon. David Davis, of the Supreme Court of the United States, and Hon. Henry Winter Davis were also graduates.

There is at Kenyon as at nearly every other college in Ohio, a preparatory department. Attendance in the college chapel at daily prayer is obligatory on all the students.

Since 1873 the board of trustees has been constituted as follows: The Bishops of the two dioceses of Ohio and the assistant Bishop, if there be one of the diocese which includes Gambier; the President of Kenyon college; four clergical and four lay trustees whose successors shall be chosen by the board of trustees for terms of ten years; three clerical and three lay trustees whose successors shall be elected by the diocesan convention for terms of three years; and two clerical and two lay trustees to be chosen by the alumni, who shall hold office for four years.

The aggregate number of volumes in all the libraries of the seminary and college is about 19,000. The whole number of graduates up to 1872, is 452.

WESTERN RESERVE COLLEGE.

By its original colonial charter, Connecticut had a claim to lands lying west of Pennsylvania. These lands were ceded to the United States, except a strip lying contiguous to the Pennsylvania line, 40 leagues in length. This tract became known as the Connecticut Western Reserve and was often popularly termed New Connecticut. Connecticut afterwards sold this land for $1,200,000, and the proceeds of the sale were set apart as a school fund. Naturally, Connecticut people settled in New Connecticut. They brought with them notions, material and immaterial, and among the latter were two, faith in God and faith in themselves. "*Qui transtulit sustinet,*" the motto of the Connecticut coat of arms, represented their religious faith. They brought with them educated ministers and teachers, and with stout hearts entered upon the work of subduing the forest and creating themselves homes.

As early as 1801, an unsuccessful attempt was made to obtain a charter for a college from the Territorial Legislature. In 1803, a renewed attempt succeeded. The Territory had meanwhile become a State, and its legislature granted to the "Erie Literary Society" college powers. An academy was opened at Burton, designed to be the germ of a college. Afterwards the presbyteries of Grand River, Portage, and Huron, which included the congregational element under the "Plan of Union," appointed commissioners to select another location and Hudson was chosen and a new charter obtained, February 7, 1826. It was to be an independent college free from ecclesiastical control, the charter making the board of trustees a close corporation with power to fill vacancies.

The design of this college is thus well stated by the author of the Historical Sketch furnished the Centennial Educational Committee: "The objects proposed by the founders were to educate pious young men as pastors for our destitute churches, to preserve the present literary and religious character of the State and redeem it from future decline, and to prepare competent men to fill the cabinet, the bench, the bar and the pulpit. The clerical portion of the founders were most of them graduates of Yale College, and the others of Williams and Dartmouth. The lay portion were from Connecticut, having been reared under the shadow of the influence of Yale College. Those famous colleges of New England were therefore their models, the objects they achieved were the ends sought for here by the same means." The college was opened in 1826, and a freshman class formed. The institution was to be in character and methods a copy of Yale, and so thorough and genuine has been the instruction afforded that no one can say that there has been any blur in the copying.

The first president was the Rev. Charles Backus Storrs, of a Massachusetts family that has won for two generations ministerial honors. He had for several years been pastor of the church at Ravenna, and was a man of marked ability as a preacher. He became persident in 1830. He had lived and preached in the South and, perhaps as a result of personal observations there, became a strong foe of slavery and his speeches against it were characterized by great boldness and vigor. He died in 1833 at the age of 39 years having occupied the chair of president only three years.

He was succeeded by Rev. Geo. E. Pierce, D. D., a native of Connecticut and a graduate of Yale, who was president of the college from 1834 to 1855. He devoted himself to the work of building up the college, and was untiring in his labors. His selections of a faculty were the wisest and no college, east or west, could boast of professors of finer culture and ability. It was the trying problem assigned to President Pierce, one which needed to be solved anew every year, how to support this large number of able men. It is to be feared that the meager support they received would lead to the belief that the problem was never more than half solved. It was the old struggle through which Harvard, Yale and Amherst and all our best American colleges have in their time passed.

Rev. Henry L. Hitchcock, D. D. succeeded to the presidency in 1855. A native of the Reserve, a son of one of the most eminent judges of the State, a graduate of Yale, for many years an honored pastor of a leading church in the capitol of the State, for many years a trustee of Marietta College—a profitable experience to him—a wise and good man, he brought to the presidential chair unusual adaptations to the place and the hour. In a few years he removed all financial embarrassments and added one hundred and seventy-five thousand dollars to the permanent funds of the college. In 1871, he resigned his office, but served the college as professor until his death in 1873. A true college is a tree of centuries. It is believed that Western Reserve, thanks to the labors and gifts of its many devoted friends, is now rooted for the ages. President Hitchcock has been worthily succeeded by Rev. Carrol Cutler, D. D.

The founders of the college had in view a theological department and a professor of theology was appointed as early as 1828, and other professors soon after. This department was continued until 1852, when it was given up. The professors were unusually able men and afterwards filled high positions in eastern theological seminaries and colleges. In 1844, a medical department was established, located at Cleveland. It is well equipped with buildings, library, museums, etc., and has a faculty of eminent physicians and scientific men. It has granted the degree of Doctor of Medicine to 1,250 young men.

There is attached to the college at Hudson a preparatory department in which young men are thoroughly fitted to enter the college classes.

The college has libraries containing an aggregate of 12,200 volumes, a good working laboratory and a good cabinet of minerals, and fossils.

The number of graduates is 404. From an examination of the table of statistics it appears that of all who have entered the freshmen class 50 per cent. have graduated. This is a large proportion.

DENISON UNIVERSITY.

This university is located at Granville, a pleasant village in Licking county. It was first incorporated by a charter granted by the General Assembly, December 13, 1832, as the Granville Literary and Theological Institution. In 1845, the name was changed to Granville College, which in June 25, 1856, was again changed to Denison University, to commemorate a donation from Wm. Denison, of Adamsville, Ohio. At a meeting of the Ohio Baptist Education

Society, at Lebanon, May 1830, it was resolved to undertake the establishment of a college, and the institution resulted from the action of this society. For several years there was a theological department in the interest of the Baptist denomination, but it was given up, and of late years the only departments have been the collegiate and the preparatory. There have been several modifications of the board of trustees. In 1873, the board was reorganized under a general law of the State affecting the incorporation of colleges, from which time the university was "to be managed and controlled by thirty-six trustees, to be chosen exclusively from members in good standing and full membership in regular Baptist churches in the State of Ohio, who shall hold their office only so long as they retain such membership; five at least to be resident freeholders of Licking county." The board is a close corporation, with power to fill vacancies.

The university, though under the control of the Baptist denomination, claims to be unsectarian and to teach no denominational dogmas.

The first president of the university was Rev. John Pratt, a graduate of Brown University in 1827. For six years from 1831, he occupied the post of president, and afterwards, for twenty-two years, held the chair of Ancient Languages. A man of careful and exact scholarship, he gave to the college a character for thoroughness which it yet retains. He is still (1876) living. The name of Prof. Pascal Carter, long associated with Prof. Pratt, deserves honorable mention for thorough scholarship. Pres. Pratt was succeeded by Rev. Jonathan Going, D. D., a graduate of Brown University in 1809, who held the office from 1837 to 1844. These were the years of the greatest prosperity of the theological department, and to this department Dr. Going devoted his time and energies, while the college proper was under the supervision of Prof. John Stevens, D. D. Prof. Stevens, a graduate of Middlebury College in 1821, has been a pillar of strength to the university as well as to the denomination in the State. His professorial life is almost co-extensive with that of the institution. He is now professor emeritus and resides at the university.

Rev. Silas Bailey, D. D., LL. D., a graduate of Brown University in 1834, held the office of president from 1846 to 1852. He was succeeded by Rev. Jeremiah Hall, D. D., who was president from 1853 to 1863. Dr. Hall came to the college at a critical time, when funds were low and friends were divided in counsel. He secured harmony and greatly contributed to the welfare of the college.

His successor was Rev. Sampson Talbot, D. D., a graduate of the university in 1851, who held the office from 1863 to his death in 1873. He was loved and honored, and the value of his labors for the college in advancing its financial and literary interests can hardly be over-estimated. His successor, Rev. E. Benjamin Andrews, entered upon the duties of his office the present year (1876).

The whole number of volumes in the college and society libraries is a little over 11,000. The cabinet contains collections illustrating mineralogy, geology, conchology, zoology, and archæology.

The whole number of graduates in the classical course is 176. Besides these, twenty have taken what is called the scientific course, which includes a year and a half of Latin, one year of French, and eighteen weeks of German. It retains the mathematics and the scientific instruction of the college course with some modifications. It requires three years for its completion.

The table of statistics shows that the ratio of graduates to the number of freshmen is something like 25 per cent.

OBERLIN COLLEGE.

This college was located at Oberlin, Lorain county, in 1833, and received its charter under the name of the Oberlin Collegiate Institute, February 28th, 1834. The name was changed to Oberlin College in 1850. It was in its inception to be an institution of distinct type. Moral and religious elements, combined with a zealous spirit of reform, were to be united with intellectual training. The plan was first suggested by Rev. John Shipherd, one of the first trustees. That the institution might be exempt from any external contamination and be free to work out its methods, it was planted by itself "in a dense and unbroken forest eight miles from Elyria and thirty-three from Cleveland." The college and the village to grow up around it, were to be of the same name, and both were to exemplify the spirit and life of the famed Swiss pastor whose name was adopted. The founders and the first colonists were of Puritan New England stock. The board of trustees is a close corporation, and fills without any external interference, all vacancies which may occur in its membership. The members were at first brought together by common sympathies and similar judgments, but the charter does not require them to hold any designated creed.

The plan of the institution contemplates a Theological Seminary, and this is Congregational, and indeed, the members of the faculty have probably always been of that denomination. But there is no ecclesiastical supervision.

In the spring of 1835, President Asa Mahan and Professors C. G. Finney, John Morgan, and Henry Cowles entered upon their duties in the institution. President Mahan remained in office until 1850, when he was succeeded by Professor Finney, to be succeeded in turn in 1866, by Professor J. H. Fairchild, the present incumbent. All the gentlemen above named have proved themselves to be very able men.

From the first, students of both sexes were admitted, and in the winter of 1834–5, the doors were opened to all without distinction of color. These were peculiar features and attracted no little attention. With the admission of colored students was combined a decided and an aggressive anti-slavery spirit. The students were armed for the great moral conflict which was beginning to agitate the nation. The very name of Oberlin became a power in the land. There went forth from the little village planted in the forest a voice which reached distant and unwilling ears and compelled attention. The voice came not from the college as a merely literary institution, but rather from the all-pervading spirit of the place—from teachers, pupils and patrons whose religion was largely philanthrophy, and whose philanthrophy was intensely religious. In a word, Oberlin was a noble and potent ism with a college attached. Thus it continued for nearly thirty years, until the war put an end to slavery in the land and the amendments of the Constitution gave equal civil rights to all. Since the war the college has made decided progress as a literary institution, and is doing a good work, one of constantly increasing magnitude, in the cause of higher learning.

The admission of young ladies to the college course of study has, in the opinion of the faculty, been attended by no injurious results, and the plan of co-education is pronounced an unquestionable success. Such ladies are under the special supervision of a lady principal and a ladies' board. While young ladies have constituted more than one-third of the whole number in attendance upon the schools, not a very large number has attended the regular college course, or graduated from it. Of the regular graduates ladies have constituted thirteen per cent. The number of colored students has always been small, and few have graduated. Wilberforce University under the care of the African Methodist Episcopal Church, now draws this class largely to itself. Other colleges in the State also receive colored students. But to Oberlin must be accorded the credit of fighting the first battle for the right of the colored race to college education in Ohio.

There are two courses of study; the Classical and Scientific, or "College" course; and the Literary. "The former embraces the studies usually pursued in American colleges, so arranged that after the freshman year the student can give a classical or scientific character to his course by a system of elections."

The literary course omits all the Greek of the classical course, and part of the Latin and mathematics. This course is the one generally pursued by young ladies. Below these courses above named are the classical preparatory school and an English school.

The aggregate attendance in the various courses and schools has always been large. The average number of students of all grades from 1834 to 1852 was 462, and from 1853 to 1876, 1,150. Of the latter number 32 per cent. were "in departments above the preparatory." The whole number of graduates, exclusive of theological students, is 757, of whom 100 were ladies, or an average of 18 each year since 1834.

The college has done good literary work, and its course of study corresponds with that of similar institutions. It has sent forth many graduates who have won honorable distinction in public life. Hon. J. D. Cox, Major General during the war, and afterward Governor of Ohio, was a graduate of Oberlin. A large number have entered the ministry. Many have became presidents and professors in colleges, and a large number teachers.

Connected with the college is a Conservatory of Music, organized in 1865, which is largely attended. The course requires for its completion from two to four years. The average attendance during the last seven years has been 266. The thorough training here given makes this department one of great usefulness and value.

There are five literary societies, three in the Classical, and two in the Literary, departments. No secret societies are permitted by the college laws and none are supposed to have ever existed.

There is an Alumni Association, organized in 1839. This association appoints three corresponding members of the board of trustees, who have all the privileges of regular members of that body except that of voting. A Gymnasium Association affords to its members every needed facility for physical training under competent instructors.

The institution is well furnished with buildings. Of these, the most imposing and beautiful is the Council Hall. The aggregate number of volumes in the college and society libraries is 14,600.

A cabinet affords ample means for illustration in the departments of geology, mineralogy and natural history. There is also a good supply of apparatus for class illustration in the departments of physics and chemistry.

Oberlin like the other colleges of the State has been compelled to struggle with poverty. The founders of the college early indulged in a mild form of speculation, in buying nearly 6,000 acres of land near the site of the institution, for one dollar and a half an acre and selling them for two dollars and a half. Arthur Tappan, well known for his philanthropy, gave $10,000 for the erection of Tappan Hall. Charles French of Cleveland, gave by bequest $5,000. The benefactions to the college have never been in very large sums.

Thirty thousand dollars were raised in England about the year 1840. From the Historical Sketch we learn that, " In 1850 a movement was made to secure an endowment of $100,000 by the sale of scholarships guaranteeing free tuition to the holders. The work of securing pledges was accomplished in a little more than a year. These scholarships were of three classes, one entitling the holder to tuition for six years, another for eighteen and the other perpetually. The prices of these scholarships were $25, $50, and $100. This measure which has been unprofitable to some colleges, was eminently wise and successful here. The money thus secured has been safely and profitably invested and the income from it is much more than the college ever received from tuition."

The estimated aggregate value of the property of the college in lands, buildings, money, etc., is $500,000. Of this only $145,000 produce revenue—$115,000 for the college and $30,000 for the theological department.

The manual labor system was tried, but the hopes of its friends were not realized, and compulsory labor is now one of the traditions of the early years of the college. This tradition is probably no where so well preserved as on the college seal, the motto of which is "Learning and Labor."

MARIETTA COLLEGE.

The charter of this college bears date February 14, 1835. As with many other colleges, it grew out a successful chartered academy. The town of Marietta being the Plymouth of Ohio we should expect to find among the trustees of the college persons bearing historic names. There have been eight trustees from the direct descendents of Gen. Israel Putnam, Gen. Rufus Putnam, Rev. Dr. Manasseh Cutler, and Gen. Benjamin Tupper. The three last mentioned acted an important part in the affairs of the Ohio Company which made the settlement at Marietta in 1788. Among the present trustees we find the names of Douglas Putnam, Esq., and Douglas Putnam, Jun., direct descendents of Gen. Israel Putnam; Hon. Wm. R. Putnam, a grandson of Gen. Rufus Putnam; Hon. Wm. P. Cutler and Gen. Rufus R. Dawes, the first a grandson, and the second a great grandson of Dr. Manasseh Cutler; and A. T. Nye, Esq., a grandson of Gen. Tupper. The first president of the board was Hon. John Cotton, M. D., a graduate of Harvard, and a descendent of Rev. John Cotton, a famous clergyman of Boston, in the Colonial days.

The board is a close corporation. No religious qualification is required for membership and no denominational control of any kind is possible. Various religious denominations have been represented in the faculty, the Congregational and Presbyterian more largely than any other. The college has always been under decided moral and religious influence. The first President of the college was Rev. Joel H. Linsley, D. D., a graduate of Middlebury College, Vermont, and at the time of his appointment, the pastor of Park Street Congregational Church, Boston. He resigned a successful presidency in 1846. Henry Smith, D. D., a graduate of Middlebury College, who had been Professor of Languages from the very beginning of the institution, was chosen his successor. His administration was marked by great ability. He remained until the winter of 1854–5, when he resigned to accept a professorship in Lane Theological Seminary. He was succeeded by I. W. Andrews, D. D., the present incumbent, who had been the professor of mathematics since 1839. President Andrews graduated at Williams College, Massachusetts, in 1837. Thus it appears that all of the presidents, except the first, were chosen from the professors of the college.

The institution has been a college and nothing else. Its aim has been to have a full and thorough four years' course of hard study and to get as many young men through it as possible. The Historical Sketch states that "Marietta has no hesitation in declaring a decided preference for the methods adopted at Yale and Williams over those of Charlotteville and Ithaca." There is connected with it the usual preparatory school, called the academy, but this is all. For a few years there was a partial course called, but not aptly, scientific, in which Greek and perhaps Latin were omitted. This has been discontinued for many years.

The first class graduated in 1838. The whole number who have completed the course and received the degree of Bachelor of Arts is 404. Many of these have filled positions of usefulness and honor. The Historical Sketch, which is very full, states that, "the number of graduates is to the number of freshmen as 66 to 100. Of the graduates, 37 per cent. have been clergymen; 25 per cent. business men; 17 per cent. lawyers; 8 per cent. physicians; and 8 per cent. professional teachers."

The college has never sold scholarships below the regular tuition rates. There are thirty endowed scholarships of $1,000 each. The grounds are beautiful and shaded, and the buildings are well adapted to meet the needs of the institution.

The aggregate number of volumes in the several libraries is 27,000. For this large and excellent library there is a large and handsome library building, erected by the Alumni.

The value of the property of the college may be estimated at a little less than $300,000.

The people of Marietta and of its immediate vicinity have given to the college $163,000. The trustees have given $135,000. One of them, Douglas Putnam, Esq., who has already given more than any other individual, offers an additional $50,000 when the same amount is raised from others. Col. John Mills has given between $20,000 and $30,000. Few colleges have had a more devoted and generous board of trustees. The home friends of the institution have ever been very warm friends.

The cabinets — mineralogical, geological, conchological, etc. — contain over 30,000 specimens, and the department of physics is well supplied with apparatus. There is also a well furnished laboratory.

The institution was never more prosperous than at the present time, but it needs additional endowment.

OHIO WESLEYAN UNIVERSITY.

This institution is located near the center of the State, at Delaware, Delaware county. It was incorporated March 7, 1842. It is controlled by twenty-five trustees, divided into five groups of five each. The Alumni choose the members of one group, and the four Methodist Episcopal Conferences—the Ohio, the North Ohio, the Cincinnati, and the Central Ohio—choose the members of the other four groups. The period of office is five years, and in each group one member retires and a new one is elected annually.

The college buildings occupy a campus of thirty acres, which is being planted by Rev. J. H. Creighton with all the species of trees and shrubs adapted to the climate. The estimated value of the property of the university is $381,888.

The endowment has been contributed by the Methodist denomination, and mostly in small sums. An effort is now on foot to raise $100,000 as an additional endowment, of which about one-half has been secured. The nominal tuition fee is $30 a year, but such tuition is never received, as appears from the following statement: "Scholarships can be purchased at the university at prices as follows: Perpetual, $500; twenty years, $100; ten years, $50; six years, $30; four years, $20; and two years, $15." Probably all the students attend on scholarships.

The aggregate number of volumes in the libraries of the college is 12,920. These volumes are preserved in a suitable library building. The museum contains large and valuable collections in botany, zoology, mineralogy, geology, etc. A laboratory affords facilities for chemical manipulation under the supervision of the professor of chemistry.

The whole number of graduates is 625, of whom 170 have become clergymen, 142 lawyers, and 60 physicians. Over 50 have held positions as presidents or professors in colleges.

The university has been fortunate in its presidents. The first was Rev. E. Thomson, D. D., L.L. D. He was a native of England, but educated in this country, partly at Canonsburgh, Pa., and partly at Philadelphia, where he took the degree of M. D. He was a man of ability and of popular address. He was elected president in 1846, and remained at the head of the institution for fourteen years. He resigned in 1860, and was elected one of the bishops of the M. E. Church in 1864. He was succeeded by Rev. F. Merrick, A. M., who had been a professor in the institution during the previous fifteen years, occupying successively the chairs of Natural Science and of Moral Science. He had had even earlier experience in teaching as Principal of the Amenia Seminary, N. Y., and as professor of Natural Sciences in the Ohio University. He was for a time an assistant on the geological survey of New York, and geological sections prepared by him appear in the published report of the First District. He held the position of president from 1860 until 1873, when he resigned. He has not left the institution, however, but remains as lecturer on natural and revealed religion. The university is greatly indebted to him for its prosperity. The present President is Rev. C. H. Payne, D. D., elected in the summer of 1875. He is a graduate of the Wesleyan University, Connecticut, and has been a successful pastor in the Methodist Church. He came to Delaware from the pastorate of St. Paul's M. E. Church, Cincinnati.

The Ohio Wesleyan University has ever had a strong hold upon the affections of the people of the M. E. Church in Ohio. It has educated a large number of preachers for its pulpits, many of whom, combining the spontaneity and freedom of the olden time with the liberal culture and mental discipline of the university, have become preachers of a high order.

The university disavows all sectarianism. The Historical Sketch states this point strongly, as follows:

"The objects of the institution are not in the least sectarian. It aims, however, to give a full, healthy, moral and Christian education. It has had members of all denominations among its students; it has graduated Roman Catholics. It has not a single Methodist book in its course as a text-book. * * * Chapel worship is held every morning—consisting of Scripture-reading, singing and prayer. The professors usually officiate in turn. The teachers are generally Methodists, though there have been among them Presbyterians and Quakers."

ST. XAVIER COLLEGE.

This institution grew up from a parish school connected with the first Catholic church established in Cincinnati. The school commencing about the year 1821, was changed October 17, 1831, by Rt. Rev. E. D. Fenwick, D. D., the first Bishop of Cincinnati, into a literary institution called the Athenæum. For this institution a building of brick was erected with tower and spire, which in those early days attracted attention by its imposing character, and, perhaps, not less by the strange inscription carved upon its front—"*Athenæum Religioni et Artibus Sacrum.*" The institution did not altogether flourish, and in 1840 Most Rev. Archbishop J. B. Purcell, D. D., gave it to the Fathers of the Society of Jesus. It then became St. Xavier College, and in 1842 was chartered by the General Assembly and received the usual university privileges.

Students from abroad generally boarded in the college, and day scholars were received from the city. The boarding department was discontinued in 1854. In the pleasantly written Historical Sketch of the institution, it is claimed that in addition to the high character of its teaching, the retention of "corporal chastisement," too much neglected elsewhere, "induced many Protestants to prefer it to many of their own seminaries for the education of their sons."

The classical may be regarded as the central department

of the college, and the degree of Bachelor of Arts is given, followed after two years spent by the graduate in literary pursuits, or one year devoted to philosophy, by that of Master of Arts. "The classes," says the Historical Sketch, "though differently named, agree substantially with those of non-Catholic colleges: philosophy, rhetoric, poetry and humanities corresponding respectively with the senior, junior, sophomore, and freshman classes of other institutions." French and German are obligatory in the academic course. In 1867, a part of a new college building was erected on the corner of Seventh and Sycamore streets. This part is in dimensions 120 feet by 66, and the entire building, completed according to the design, will be a structure of architectural beauty and of great size, quiet eclipsing the glory of the former Athenæum so honored in its day. The motto over its door, *Ad Majorem Dei gloriam*," grandly dedicates the whole.

It may be interesting to know how funds are obtained for such a structure. The Historical Sketch says:

> "Toward this undertaking one zealous clergyman subscribed $10,000, another $1,000, and a Catholic layman of the city, who is always foremost in works of charity, donated $1,000. These sums, with a few smaller amounts, were all the aid received from without; the remaining funds, amounting to about $130,000, were the result of years of saving and economy in the management of the college finances."

The chief source of income is the tuition fee, $60 a year for each student. If the above statement is calculated to arrest the attention of college trustees and college treasurers, what will our college professors say to the following:

> "The professors receive no salary whatever, and dovote their talents and life to the cause of education. They live at the college, are unmarried, lead a common life, indulge in no superfluities, and sometimes even stint themselves in what they might legitimately claim, when the circumstances of the college demand such sacrifice. Had St. Xavier College to pay the professors salaries such as their abilities warrant and other institutions pay, it could not live a day."

The Sketch gives an account of the preparatory training of these professors, which we condense. After completing a collegiate course, they are "tried two years in a novitiate to see whether they will suit the Society and the Society will suit them, and if the satisfaction is mutual, they are permitted to take vows by which they bind themselves to the Society, and agree to accept any of its usual ministrations for which they shall be found fit. * * * During two more years they repeat their rhetoric and poetry, studying the classics both ancient and modern very minutely, with a view of preparing themselves afterward to *teach* these branches or any others." They then make a thorough study of Christian philosophy for three years, not neglecting literature, and pay special attention to the physical sciences and mathematics. It rarely happens that any one is applied to teaching till he has finished this preparatory training; and then he usually begins with a lower class, and advances upward year by year. After a period varying from four to five years, they are ordained clergymen, having previously applied themselves exclusively to theology during a space of three or four years, and then usually resume the labor of teaching."

There is at St. Xavier a corps of eighteen professors, with Rev. E. A. Higgins the efficient president, at its head.

The whole number of graduates is 230, and the number of students in attendance last year (1875) was 274.

The library of the college numbers 14,000 volumes, and contains many rare and valuable works.

The museum contains collections of conchological, geological and mineralogical specimens, sufficiently large for the purpose of class illustration. A suitable provision of philosophical and chemical apparatus has been made. Music and drawing are taught by professors of these branches living in the city of Cincinnati.

The Historical Sketch declares that the faculty "never

tamper with the religious belief of any student, and studiously avoid influencing him in any way except by the example of a good life."

WITTENBERG COLLEGE.

This institution is located at Springfield, Clarke county. It received its charter from the General Assembly, March 11, 1845.

Its ecclesiastical connection is with that branch of the Evangelical Lutheran Church represented in the religious body known as the "General Synod of the United States." The board of directors is appointed by the following Synods: the Synod of East Ohio, the Synod of Miami, the Wittenberg Synod, all in Ohio, and the Synod of Northern Indiana, and the Olive Branch Synod, in Indiana. The synods by which directors are chosen fix their time of service and are the only tribunal to which they are responsible. There are now thirty-six members of the board, thirty-four representing synods and two from Clarke county, as provided for in the constitution.

There is a theological department which has held a prominent place in the institution. The institution had its origin, as so many others in the West have had theirs, in the religious and educational wants of the denomination it represents. Its establishment, according to the Historical Sketch, "was demanded for the education of a ministry sufficient in number and with an evangelical spirit who would stem the tide of formalism" at that time invading the Lutheran Church.

Wittenberg College possesses a beautiful campus of forty acres in the suburbs of Springfield, and has a productive endowment fund of one hundred and twenty-five thousand dollars. The total value of its property, exclusive of library, cabinet, apparatus, etc., is estimated at $175,000.

The libraries in connection with the college contain 8,000 volumes. The philosophical and chemical apparatus is said to be sufficient for class illustration, and the cabinet contains many valuable specimens.

Aside from the theological, there are no other departments than the collegiate with the necessary preparatory course attached. Preparations are made to open a department of Civil Engineering at the beginning of the winter session of this year. Wittenberg College is strictly a *college* and has ever done good work in a thorough and unpretentious way.

Rev. Ezra Keller, D. D., a graduate of Gettysburg College, Pennsylvania, in 1835, a man of strong intellect and of rare moral worth, was the first President. He died in 1848. He was succeeded by Samuel Sprecher, D. D., LL. D., a gentleman of profound learning and high Christian character. The simple genuineness of his scholarship has left its mark upon the institution. He still retains the professorship of Mental Philosophy. The college has worthily honored its own work in appointing in 1874 as the successor of Dr. Sprecher, Rev. J. B. Helwig, D. D., a graduate of the class of 1861.

There have been 261 graduates of the college, an average of 10.44 each year, and 145 from the theological department. The whole number of students in the four college classes, as given in the catalogue of 1874–5, is 65, that in the preparatory 66. There is a select course in which there are 22 pupils, chiefly from Springfield. The names of young ladies are found in the catalogue in connection with the preparatory and select courses, but none appear in the college classes nor among the alumni.

From the triennial catalogue of 1874–5, it appears that ninety-six of the graduates have entered the ministry. Eleven have become college professors.

President Helwig, in his Historical Sketch of the college, has with filial affection delineated the character and labors of his predecessors, Doctors Keller and Sprecher. In his tribute to the latter we find the following significant statement:

> "The light which shone from that banner of truth lifted up by Luther in the Wittenberg of Europe, has had its lustre brightened by Dr. Sprecher, the teacher of the Wittenberg of America, and without fear of successful contradiction, we hesitate not to declare that the 'General Synod of Lutheranism' of the 19th century is moré fully in accord with the teaching of the sacred scriptures than was the Lutheranism of the 16th century."

BALDWIN UNIVERSITY.

This institution is located at Berea, Cuyahoga county. Its existence is due to the generosity of John Baldwin, Esq., a citizen of Berea, who gave to the North Ohio Annual Conference of the Methodist Episcopal church lands, buildings, etc., for its endowment. In September, 1844, Mr. Baldwin offered fifty acres of ground, including grind-stone quarries and water privileges, on which he engaged to erect a brick building 72 feet by 36, to be finished in the fall of 1845. In the June following, he offered fifty village lots to be sold at a fair valuation and the proceeds funded for the use of the institution. These offers were accepted by the Conference, and a charter for the Baldwin Institute obtained in December, 1845. The board of trustees was organized January 21, 1846, and the institute was opened with male and female departments, on the 9th of April following, with Rev. H. Dwight as Principal. In 1855, the trustees acting under the direction of the Conference, secured a change in the charter and the name was changed to Baldwin University, by which it is now known. The first President was Rev. John Wheeler, D. D. His successors have been W. D. Godman, D. D., and A. Schuyler, LL. D., the present incumbent. In 1858, a German Department was organized under the care of O. Henning, Ph. D. In 1863, this department became a separate institution under the name of the "German Wallace College" in honor of Hon. James Wallace who gave the building it occupies. The two institutions still continue practically united, the same instructors teaching in both. Students in one are entitled to free tuition in the other. The German Wallace College is patronized largely by the German Methodists of the State.

In 1865, a College of Pharmacy was organized as a part of Baldwin University, with a professor of Pharmacy and Practical Chemistry, and another of Toxicology and Materia Medica. Mr. Baldwin appears to abound in noble deeds in behalf of the institution. The Historical Sketch states that "in addition to his original grant, he paid for many years the interest on ten thousand dollars which had been appropriated to the support of a professorship. In the winter of 1867, he donated forty acres of stone quarry, worth at least three thousand dollars per acre, or in the aggregate, one hundred and twenty thousand dollars. This princely gift has placed the institution on a solid foundation—literally has founded it upon a rock." The university has three buildings, two of brick and one of stone, the latter being used for a chapel and recitation rooms. Twenty thousand dollars are subscribed for the erection of a ladies' hall, which is now in progress.

The institution is entirely out of debt and possesses assets to the amount of $190,000. It has a good working apparatus worth fifteen hundred dollars and a library of two thousand volumes.

There are fifteen trustees chosen by the Conference. They are divided into three classes of five each, one of which retires every year.

The whole number of alumni is 189, and the present senior class numbers 15. The institution appears to be in a healthy and prosperous condition. Two of its professors are ladies, one occupying the chair of Mathematics and the other that of Rhetoric and English Literature. The President, well known as a mathematician and an author, is professor of Philosophy and Applied Mathematics.

The department of mathematics is evidently a strong one in this institution, while the whole course of study appears to be excellent and thorough.

There is also a scientific course of five years, embracing the same sciences and mathematics as the classical course, but with less Latin, and with French instead of Greek.

OTTERBEIN UNIVERSITY.

This institution is located at Westerville, Franklin county. It originated with the desire to secure to the church of the United Brethren, a ministry of higher culture and to advance the cause of learning among the people of the denomination. Some of the people looked with a measure of suspicion upon higher learning as having an infidel tendency, and putting the matter before their minds in an antithetical way, preferred religion without learning, to learning without religion. Fortunately there were good men in the church who wanted both. These men had learned what some other denominations had previously learned, that the day had passed when ignorance, however pious and zealous, could be an acceptable teacher of the profound doctrines of the christian religion. The founders of Otterbein university disregarded the old prejudices and resolutely set to work to educate the sons as the most ready way to enlighten the fathers.

The university was chartered in 1849, although a board of trustees had been previously appointed which held its first meeting April 26, 1847. Two conferences, Sandusky and Scioto, were represented in the board, three members from each. In 1847 the academy called the Blendon Young Mens Seminary, located at Westerville, was bought, and academical instruction given, Wm. R. Griffeth being the Principal.

The history of the institution in its financial aspects is not unlike that of most of the other colleges. There has been the usual struggle with poverty. The denomination in Ohio is not a rich one, and has never been trained to look upon the endowment of colleges as either a privilege or a duty, and the work of building up the institution progressed slowly. In 1870 a disastrous fire swept away a large edifice which contained the chapel, libraries, recitation rooms, society halls, etc. The loss was estimated at $50,000, relieved by an insurance of $20,000. In the college library were over 3000 volumes, and all were burned. A degree of distinction had been given the library by a copy of the *Sinaitic Manuscript* presented by the Emperor of Russia. This was burned. The trustees and friends of the university met the calamity bravely and raised funds for a new building, which is much larger and finer than the one lost, it being in extreme length 170 feet, and in depth 109 feet. The presidents of the university have been as follows:

Rev. Wm. Davis, 1849 to 1850.
" Lewis Davis, D. D., 1850 to 1857.
" Alexander Owen, 1858 to 1860.
" Lewis Davis, D. D., 1860 to 1871.
" Daniel Eberly, A. M., 1871 to 1872.
" H. A. Thompson, D. D., 1872 to the present time.

President Lewis Davis who was president for eighteen years, stands out with great prominence among the founders and guides of the institution. He had faith in God and faith in final success, and with this wealth of faith an indomitable will and an indestructible hopefulness. He was one of the first trustees and was thoroughly devoted to the great work of laying the foundation of an institution designed to be a blessing to his church and to mankind.

There are four courses of study, the Classical, Scientific, Ladies and English. The ladies course is quite similar to the scientific. Preparatory instruction is given but there is not for it a separately organized department with special teachers.

No discrimination has ever been made against colored students. Such discrimination could not well be made by an institution representing the church of the United Brethren which has always been hostile to slavery and forbidden slave-holders the rite of communion. In 1859 there was an effort to exclude such students and two of the six members of the executive committee voted in favor of such exclusion, at least until the board of trustees should pass upon the question. They were never excluded.

The manual labor system was at first adopted, requiring all the students to perform a certain amount of daily labor, but it failed as signally at Otterbein as at the many other colleges in the West, where it was tried.

All the students are required to attend chapel exercises once a day, and religious services on Sabbath morning, unless excused to attend some other church in the village. There has always prevailed a strong religious influence in the institution. The whole number of graduates reported is 150, of whom 50 are young women. This number represents only a small part of the whole number who have studied for a longer or shorter time at Otterbein.

President Thompson makes the following gratifying statement: "Throughout the length and breadth of the church, our influence has been felt for good. We have helped to furnish teachers for nearly all its other schools and colleges. Our sons have entered its ministry and have put into it a new life and power. We have furnished editors for its journals, and teachers for its first theological school. We have just reason to thank God and take courage."

HIRAM COLLEGE.

This institution is located at Hiram, in Portage county. It is under the auspices of the religious denomination called the Disciples, or sometimes Christians. There being many of this faith on the Western Reserve, and there being no literary institution of their kind nearer than the one at Bethany, W. Va., founded by the late Alexander Campbell, the desire for one became general and grew into a confessed want. They set about the matter in earnest in 1849, and March 1, 1850, secured a special charter from the General Assembly for the Western Reserve Eclectic Institute.

President Hinsdale has given so distinctly the peculiar aims of the founders in his Historical Sketch, that we quote his words:

"(1.) To provide a sound scientific and literary education.

"(2.) To temper and sweeten such education with moral and Scriptural knowledge.

"(3.) To educate young men for the ministry.

'One peculiar tenet of the religious movement in which it originated was impressed upon the Eclectic Institute at its organization. The Disciples thought that the Bible had in a degree been obscured by theological speculations and ecclesiastical systems. Hence, their religious movement was a revolt from the theology of the schools, and an overture to men to come face to face with the Scriptures. They believed also that to the holy writings belonged a larger place in general culture than had yet been accorded to them. Accordingly, in all their educational institutions, they have emphasized the Bible and its related branches of knowledge. This may be called the distinctive feature of their schools. The charter of the Eclectic Institute, therefore, declared the purpose of the institution to be, 'The instruction of youth of both sexes in the various branches of literature and science, especially of moral science as based upon the facts and precepts of the Holy Scriptures.'"

The institute was incorporated as a stock company, the amount of capital stock being limited to $50,000 divided into shares of $25 each, to be used exclusively for the purposes of education. The stockholders elect the board of trustees, limited by the following provision: "No stockholder shall have more than four votes for $100, six votes for $200, seven for $300, and eight for $400 or more." President Hinsdale thus writes: "As it is an open question how college boards of trustees should be elected, it is proper to add that in Hiram the stockholders' plan has always worked well."

The institute always prospered as to members, but the elective plan being in operation, and students generally chosing their studies, little attempt was made to enforce a regular curriculum. The institute conferred no degrees.

The first principal was Rev. A. S. Hayden, 1850–57. He was succeeded by Hon. James A. Garfield, a graduate of Williams College (1856) who held the office greatly to the advantage of the institution from 1857 to 1861. The subsequent principals were H. W. Everest, C. W. Heywood, A. J. Thompson, and J. M. Atwater.

In February, 1867, the board of trustees changed the name to Hiram College, and the college as such began its life and work the following August.

The first president was Rev. Silas E. Shepherd, A. M., who retained the office only one year and was succeeded by Prof. J. M. Atwater, A. M., who had previously held the chair of Ancient Languages. He was followed in 1870 by B. A. Hinsdale, A. M., the present incumbent. President Hinsdale had been professor in the institution for several years previously. Under his supervision the college has been more prosperous than ever before.

There are, besides the regular classical course, several other courses, viz.: the Latin and scientific, requiring five years for its completion, including the preparatory studies; the scientific course which omits both Latin and Greek; the ladies' course of four years; a teacher's course of two years; and a commercial course of one year. There is also a Biblical or partial theological course.

There have been forty-two graduates, as shown by the published table of statistics. The degree of Bachelor of Arts is given to those who graduate from the classical course, that of Bachelor of Philosophy to those who graduate from the Latin and scientific course, and Bachelor of Science to those who graduate from the scientific course. Diplomas are bestowed upon those who finish the other courses.

The ratio of graduates to the freshmen is 43.75 per cent.

The financial condition of the institution is given as follows:

The buildings, grounds, apparatus, etc	$25,000
The endowments	65,000
Total	$90,000

The various libraries contain in the aggregate 2,528 volumes. There is a "small but well selected museum."

To those who desire special Biblical instruction, "the leading tenets of the Disciples have been taught, but all attempts to exercise over the body of the students a peculiar denominational influence have been carefully avoided."

HEIDELBERG COLLEGE.

This college is located in the city of Tiffin, Seneca county. It was founded in 1850 by direction of the Synod of Ohio of the German Reformed Church, now known as the Reformed Church in the United States. Its charter was granted by the General Assembly of Ohio, February 13, 1851.

The board of trustees is elected by the Synod of Ohio, and is composed of twenty-four members, six of whom are chosen each year.

The college buildings, consisting of the main college edifice, the ladies' hall and a president's house, are situated in a beautiful campus of nine acres within the corporate limits of the city. The endowment, derived chiefly from individuals in sympathy with the Reformed Church, amounts to about $100,000, one half of which has been paid for scholarships. About $60,000 of the whole yields revenue. The remainder is in notes payable at the death of the donors, without interest. In 1872, R. W. Shawhan of Tiffin, gave the college 6,000 acres of land in Missouri, from which no income is derived as yet.

There are two courses of study, the regular Classical or College course, and a Scientific course. The latter embraces a period of three years. There is, besides, a preparatory department. Young ladies are admitted to all the courses on equal terms with young men. The results of such admission are regarded as entirely satisfactory. Few young ladies, however, have taken the Classical course, preferring the shorter Scientific or English course.

The libraries of the institution contain about 5,000 volumes. The cabinet contains many specimens of fossils, minerals, etc. Among the other apparatus is a telescope of five inch aperture, made by Alvan Clark and Sons. There are three literary societies, the Excelsior, the Heidelberg, and the Delphian, which have libraries and hold meetings for debates, compositions, orations, etc. The whole number of graduates since 1854 is 138. In the same time there have been 772 freshmen, making the ratio of graduates to freshmen a little over 20 per cent. The last graduating class of eighteen members gained one over its freshman number.

The college is under religious, but not sectarian influences. "No sectarian instruction is required or given by the college." There is a religious exercise each morning in the chapel and public worship is conducted on the Sabbath.

The faculty consists of a president and five professors and an instructor in vocal music. The President is Rev. G. W. Williard, D. D., who is also professor of Intellectual and Moral Philosophy, Logic and Evidences of Christianity.

WILBERFORCE UNIVERSITY.

This institution is located near Xenia, Green county, and was established for the education of the colored youth of the State and of the country.

It was organized under the general law of Ohio, April 9, 1852, and a board of trustees appointed, of which the Rev. John F. Wright was the president. At this time it was under the auspices of the Cincinnati Conference of the Methodist Episcopal Church. Rev. Richard D. Rust, A. M., was the President and Professor of Theology and of Natural Sciences. The institution had many evils to contend with. The colored race in the North rested under a heavy burden of prejudice, the result of the long years of vassalage to which their brethren in the South had been subjected. Self assertion and the thrift growing out of it were well nigh impossible, and hence the colored people of the State were poor and almost friendless. To be their special friend and helper required an unusual degree of philanthrophy and moral firmness. The Methodist Episcopal Church deserves great credit for undertaking to do what they did. Very considerable numbers of students of both sexes received more or less training and mental discipline, and were fitted to go out as teachers or preachers among their own people. The catalogue of 1859–60 give the names of 207 students. It continued under the supervision of the Methodist Episcopal Church until 1863, when the property was sold to the African Methodist Episcopal Church. This property consisted of fifty-two acres of land in the vicinity of Xenia, with several buildings which had been originally erected for the accommodation of visitors to the medicinal springs which are found on the premises. A new charter was obtained, and Bishop D. A. Payne, D. D., Rev. James A. Shorter, and John G. Mitchell constituted the legal corporation. The board was afterwards enlarged by the additions of persons designated by the conferences of the A. M. E. church. Several men of great distinction have been honorary members of the board. Among these we find in the catalogues the names of Chief Justice Chase, Major Generals O. O. Howard, Saxton, and Butler, Frederick Douglass, Prof. J. M. Langston, Hon. Charles Sumner, Rev. George B. Cheever, D. D., and Hon. Gerrit Smith. Many of these gentlemen have taken a deep interest in the welfare of the institution. Bishop Payne still remains its honored head. He was educated at Gettysburg, Pennsylvania. He possesses peculiar fitness for the position, and has made many friends for himself and for his philanthropic enterprise. His success in securing pecuniary aid has been considerable, although more endowment is greatly needed. Among other gifts we find recorded $1,800 from the Society for the Promotion of Collegiate and Theological Education in the West, $4,000 from the American Unitarian Association—a peculiarly noble gift when we remember the strongly "evangelical" character of the institution; $500 from Hon. Gerrit Smith; from Chief Justice Chase during his life time, $250 and a legacy of $10,000; from the Freedman's Bureau $3,000, and from the same by special act of Congress $25,000. In the evening of April 14, 1865, the main college edifice was burned. This was the evening when throughout the North there were rejoicings and illuminations over the final overthrow of the great rebellion, and nearly all the colored people of the college and vicinity had gone to Xenia to participate in the rejoicings. It was an incendiary fire, but its origin was not attributed to prejudice against the colored race, which does not prevail in the region of Xenia, but to revenge, on the part of a student who had been subjected to discipline. There was an insurance of $8,000 on the building. A new edifice of fine appearance and well adapted to its uses has been built.

There are several departments of instruction. The great

and original purpose of the institution was to give young men literary and theological preparation for the ministry. Hence the theological department is the prominent one. There is a classical department in which Latin and Greek are taught, and the usual studies of a college course.

A scientific department gives the studies of the college course with the omission of Latin and Greek, but with the addition of French and German.

For the training of teachers there is a normal department.

A law department has been planned, and will probably be established soon.

The library contains 3,000 volumes.

MOUNT UNION COLLEGE.

This institution is located at Mount Union, Stark county. It grew out of a seminary established in this place by Rev. O. N. Hartshorn in 1846. It was chartered as a college, March 11, 1853. Among the "leading provisions," as given in the Historical Sketch, it is stated that, "the college shall not be a close corporation; that the trustees hold their office during three years, one-third of the number, determined upon being elected each year; that in electing trustees, any candid person, religious denomination, or philanthropic organization donating to the college money or property shall be respectively entitled to one voice or vote for a trustee for every twenty-five dollars actually donated to the college by said persons, denomination, or organization."

There is a large central building for instruction connected with which is an observatory, and it is in contemplation to erect a new and capacious museum building. There are, belonging to the college, two large buildings devoted to boarding purposes.

It is impossible to obtain from the Historical Sketch the aggregate value of the college property. The college has been fortunate in having in its board of trustees three gentlemen, each of whom has endowed a professorship by the generous donation of $25,000. These gentlemen are C. Aultman and Jacob Miller of Canton, and Lewis Miller of Akron. Many donations of smaller sums have been received, and also deeds of lands. The museum is estimated by President Hartshorn to be worth $251,000. Two grants of silver mines, one in Arizona and the other in Montana, are mentioned among the assets.

The chemical and philosophical apparatus is adequate to the wants of the professors and students. There are also appliances for instruction in astronomy and geography. The observatory contains a telescope imported from Europe.

There are four leading courses of study, Classical; Liberal Literature and Arts; Philosophical, and Scientific. Besides these, are the Normal, Music, Fine Arts, and Business departments. The studies preparatory to admission in the classical course are chiefly English studies including algebra (Ray's II part completed) and geometry, with the addition of Harkness' Latin Grammar and Boise's Reader. The Latin and Greek are optional in college, the alternative studies being German and French.

Students may enter at any time and pursue any studies for which they are qualified. Such as have not studied Latin or Greek are admitted to regular and proper standing in the college classes, when equivalent acquirements in mathematics, literature, and natural sciences can be shown.

The Historical Sketch says: "If a student need be absent during the summer season, the fall, winter and spring terms will still give him opportunity to do a college year's work; or, if he attend all four terms, he can complete a four years' course in three calender years."

Young ladies are admitted to all the courses of study.

The institution has been commended to patronage by the Pittsburgh and West Virginia Annual Conferences but it disavows all sectarian character.

The aggregate number of the graduates of the college is not given in the Sketch. There is, however, an enumeration with a classification of the students from 1858 to 1875 inclusive.

Under the head of "Science, Literature and the Arts," which we suppose includes the "Classical" and "Philosophical" in the courses already mentioned, we find a total of 2,107 freshmen, 842 sophomores, 361 juniors, and 454 Seniors. This gives a ratio of seniors to freshmen of 21 per cent. The loss in passing from the freshman to the sophomore class is 60 per cent. For the last seven years there has been a gain in the aggregate number of seniors over that of juniors of 31 per cent. Such a gain is unusual in colleges where a rigid system of classification is followed. It may here be explained by supposing that those who make the four years' course in three years are not classified as juniors.

The President of the college is Rev. O. N. Hartshorn, LL. D. He has been with the institution from the first as its head, and has ever inspired its growth. He deserves great credit for his indomitable energy in the prosecution of an enterprise to which he has devoted his life.

ANTIOCH COLLEGE OF YELLOW SPRINGS, GREENE COUNTY, OHIO.

This institution, as its name imports, is located at Yellow Springs, Greene County. It originated with a religious denomination called "Christians," which is to be distinguished from the Disciples or Christians who established Hiram College. The name Antioch was chosen, because, in the ancient city of that name the disciples were first called christians. It was incorporated under the general law of Ohio, May 14th, 1859, under the simple name of "Antioch College," but April 19th, 1859, was reorganized as "Antioch College of Yellow Springs, Greene County, Ohio." It was the original plan to raise an endowment fund by the sale of perpetual scholarships, at the price of $100 each, and to establish an institution in the state of New York, but the success in selling scholarships in Ohio having been far greater than in New York it was decided to locate the college in the former State. To secure the location at Yellow Springs, the citizens of the place pledged a pleasant site of twenty acres of ground and $30,000 in money. This offer secured the location, and four buildings were subsequently erected, a large and handsome central hall, called Antioch Hall, two dormitories and a president's house.

It was a singular provision in the articles of incorporation that the trustees were to be elected by the holders of scholarships, each scholarship being entitled to one vote, but no one holder could cast more than ten votes. The first meeting of the holders of scholarship for the election of trustees was held in the college chapel Sept. 4th, 1854, when thirty-three trustees were chosen. Among these were many eminent men of the East, such as Horace Mann, Moses H. Grinnell, and Peter Cooper, who, although not "christians," sympathized in the new enterprise. The officers of this board of trustees were: Hon. Aaron Harlan, President; Elias Smith, Vice President; Wm. R. King, Secretary; and Hon. Wm. Mills, Treasurer.

Two years before this, Horace Mann having consented to become the president of the college, was elected to that office Sept. 15, 1852. At the same time five professors were elected, one of whom was a lady, Miss R. M. Pennell.

The college did not go into operation until Oct. 5th, 1853. Young ladies were admitted on equal terms with gentlemen to all the privileges of the institution.

At an early date colored students were received by President Mann, although forbidden to receive them by the president of the board of trustees. In this Mr. Mann was sustained by the faculty and the doors have never been closed to such students. The college started upon its career prosperously, and the first graduating class (1857) numbered fifteen—twelve gentlemen and three ladies. The fame of Horace Mann as the distinguished Secretary of the Massachusetts Board of Education, as a member of Congress, and as a man of progressive and liberal views, had preceeded him to the West and the college at once became popular.

But difficulties awaited the young institution. By the charter "two-thirds of the board of trustees and a majority of the board of instruction must be members of the Christian denomination." The endowment fund was to be raised by the sale of scholarships, and the building fund by special contributions. The former fund proved to be inadequate to the support of the faculty by an annual deficit of nearly $10,000, and the latter fund was soon exhausted, and the buildings were mortgaged to secure a large additional debt. In 1857, nearly $40,000 of the fund derived from scholarships had been "borrowed" to pay various expenses. This condition of affairs necessitated an assignment of the property. In 1859, the property was sold at two-thirds of an appraisment of $65,000, to T. H. Palmer, Esq., of New York. He assigned it to provisional trustees and by them it was assigned, April 22, to the trustees of a new corporation known as "Antioch College of Yellow Springs, Greene County, Ohio." Money was raised by subscription from "Christians" and Unitarians to pay the debts. In the new charter twelve of the twenty-four trustees were to be from the denomination of "Christians." The board was to be a close corporation. The college was now free from debt and it resolved to keep free. There was, however, no endowment and the faculty were supported chiefly by subscriptions. On the 5th of Aug. 1859, President Mann died. He was succeeded by Rev. Thomas Hill, D. D., who entered upon his duties in January, 1860. He was a man of wide learning and an eminent mathematican, and afterwards became the President of Harvard University. In 1860, a class of 28 was graduated. In 1861, the great civil war began and nothing could be done in providing funds for the wants of the institution. President Hill resigned in June, 1862, and at the same time or soon after, the faculty resigned. At the request of the trustees, Prof. J. B. Weston did not leave, and instruction was given to such students as remained. During this interim there was one graduate each year. By this time the harmony between the two donominations had become disturbed, and it was deemed best that one or the other should control the institution. The Unitarians agreed to surrender everything to the "Christians," if they would raise $50,000 for the aid of the college within a year, which time was extended to two years. This was on condition that afterwards, the Unitarians should have a similar privilege of trial. The money was not raised by the "Christians." Then the latter denomination made the attempt and succeeded, having raised $100,000 by June 21, 1865. Thus the college passed into the hands of the Unitarians. The charter was revised and all sectarian tests eliminated. At the same time a faculty was appointed. Prof. Austin Craig, D. D. was acting president for a year, when Rev. G. W. Hosmer, D. D., an eminent pastor of a Unitarian church of Buffalo, N. Y., was elected president. He proved to be a wise and able officer. He resigned Jan. 1, 1873, and was succeeded by Prof. Edward Orton. The latter resigned at the end of the college year, to take the presidency of the Ohio Agricultural and Mechanical College, at Columbus. Since that time Prof. S. C. Derby has been the acting or temporary president.

Since its last reorganization the college claims to be entirely unsectarian in character, and at this time, among its faculty and teachers are members of five different religious denominations.

The whole number of graduates is 133, of whom 87 are

gentlemen and 46 ladies. They have furnished from this number 12 ministers, 22 lawyers, 5 physicians, 4 editors, some presidents and professors in colleges, and a large number of teachers. Of the ladies three are connected with college instruction, two are physicians, and one is a preacher.

The total productive endowment is $123,000, so invested as to yield an annual income of between $11,000 and $12,000. Twenty thousand dollars of this fund were a bequest of Mrs. Sarah King, of Taunton, Mass. A prospective fund from a noble bequest by Hon. David Joy, of $40,000, to be devoted chiefly to women needing aid and to students of color, is reported.

The library contains about 5,000 volumes. The department of physics is well supplied with the most approved apparatus, and the chemical laboratory is also pretty well equipped. There is a telescope of 5 inch apperture, a prismatic reflecting circle, chronometer, etc., for instruction in astronomy.

The mineralogical and geological cabinets are sufficient for class illustration.

The number of students given in the Report of the Commissioner of Schools for 1875 is 70. Of these 34 are gentlemen and 36 ladies. The number of graduates in the same year was 4, two of each sex.

The course of study is full and excellent. Thorough preparation for admission to the freshman class is required. This may be obtained in the preparatory department, which is needed here as at the other colleges of the State.

Greek, both in the preparatory school and in college, is optional, but an equivalent is required. The study of Latin and Greek is not prescribed after the end of the sophomore year.

UNIVERSITY OF CINCINNATI.

Mr. Charles McMicken, who died in 1857, gave by his will to the city of Cincinnati, property, then valued at $500,000, for the purpose of founding two colleges in Cincinnati, one for the education of young men and the other for women.

After four years of litigation the property came into possession of the city in trust. In order to make the property productive it was necessary to make improvements upon it, which with annuities to be paid consumed the revenue. In 1870, the legislature passed an act, in general form, by which Cincinnati could establish a university and receive funds, etc., in trust for such a purpose, and in 1871 a board of trustees was selected, of which Hon. Rufus King was the President. This board consists of 19 persons appointed by the common council, six of whom shall be nominated by the board of education of the city. The term of office is six years. The care of the McMicken estate was transferred to this new university board.

There has been established by the aid of the McMicken fund a School of Design and an Academic Department. To these have been added the Cincinnati Observatory. There are some special endowments of the School of Design and of the Observatory, but these are under the care of the trustees of the university.

The Academic Department has already professorships of Mathematics, Astronomy and Civil Engineering ; of Physics and Chemistry ; of Ancient Languages and Comparative Philology, with instructors in the German and French languages. Appointments have quite recently been made to fill two additional professorships—of Philosophy and History, and of Modern Languages and Belles-lettres, and two others are in the process of formation. Instruction in this department is free to youth of either sex who are *bona fide* residents of Cincinnati. To other students the tuition is

$60 per annum for the full course or $30 for a single study. As yet the studies are largely elective as shown by the following list of the numbers pursuing the several studies:

Latin	8	Trigonometry	13
Greek	11	Calculus	9
German	22	Descriptive Geometry	8
French	19	Engineering	8
Physics	16	Chemistry	22

The whole number of students represented in the above list is 51, which were all in attendance at the close of December, 1875.

The courses in Civil Engineering, Physics and Chemistry are full, and all needed apparatus, instruments and laboratories have been provided. If to these could be added other thorough courses in science and technology, the university would meet a want long felt in the West.

In the Fifth Annual Report of the Trustees, three distinct courses are mentioned; the Classical with the degree of Bachelor of Arts; the Scientific with the degree of Bachelor of Science, and the course in Civil Engineering with the degree of Civil Engineer.

The School of Design has already reached a position of great usefulness and of no little popularity. The whole number of pupils enrolled in the year 1875 was 402, of whom 242 were in classes in drawing and design, 133 in wood-carving and 27 in modeling. There is a teacher of drawing with three assistants, a teacher of wood-carving and another of modeling. It is the hope to add instruction in special studies both in the fine and useful arts, and thus to make the school one of the highest value.

The Cincinnati Observatory with which the honored name of Prof. O. M. Mitchel will ever be associated, is also under the care of the trustees of the university. The present Director is Ormond Stone, A. M. The instruments are of the first class and additional ones will be provided when needed. Instruction in astronomical work will be given to such as are fitted to receive it.

The report of the Commissioner of Schools for 1875, gives in its list of Ohio Colleges several from which the Centennial Committee has received no historical sketches. These are Capital University, located at Columbus; Urbana University, Urbana; One Study University, New Market Station, Harrison county; University of Wooster, Wooster; Buchtel College, Akron; German Wallace College, Berea; McCorkle College, Bloomfield, Muskingum county; Muskingum College, New Concord, Muskingum county; Ohio Central College, Iberia, Morrow county; Richmond College, Richmond, Jefferson county; Wilmington College, Wilmington, and Xenia College, Xenia.

Some reference is made to the German Wallace College in the account of Baldwin University.

A catalogue of Wooster University has been received, from which it appears that in addition to the preparatory department, there are three college courses, viz: the Classical, Philosophical, and Scientific. In these are enrolled, respectively, 106, 15 and 22 students. To these are added 23 in partial courses. The Philosophical is the regular classical course with the omission of Greek and with the addition of German; the Scientific course adds German but omits both Latin and Greek. Attached to the university is a Medical Department located at Cleveland.

The President of the university is Rev. A. A. E. Taylor, D. D. There are twenty-four trustees appointed by the four Ohio Synods of the Presbyterian Church. Four professorships have been endowed by the generous donations of $25,000 each, from the following persons: B. J. Mercer, Esq., Mansfield; E. Quinby, Jun., Wooster; J. H. Kauke, Esq., Wooster, and W. D. Johnson, Esq., of Clifton.

The library contains 3,000 volumes. The cabinets, apparatus, etc., are said to be ample for purposes of illustration.

CONCLUSIONS.

It is evident that Ohio has not only enough colleges and universities but more than enough. The whole number, as given by the U. S. Census Report for 1870, is thirty-three. The Ohio School Commissioner's Report for 1873 gives thirty-six. The reports for 1874 and 1875 give twenty-nine. There are doubtless some from which no returns have been received by the Commissioner. From 1803 to 1860, fourteen universities and forty-two colleges were chartered. Quite a number have been chartered since. Possibly the whole number of births might be ascertained, but unfortunately for the statistician, the deaths are not reported. The mortality rate is large. Some die at a very young and tender age, others linger for years, so long indeed, that no interest is felt in their demise.

In Ohio there is great looseness in the use of the term university, and the proper distinction between the university and the college is seldom made. This distinction is thus given by President Mark Hopkins:

"Of a university, the conception is not uniform either in this country or abroad. In England, the university is a collection of colleges with endowments, partly for instruction and partly for investigation and the origination of knowledge; and it is this last that is thought by some to be the special function of the university. Of this we have little or nothing in this country. In Germany, the university is a collection of learned men and of books for the instruction of *men*. It comprises professional schools, and also offers lectures and facilities of instruction in every branch of related knowledge, and of this last again we have nothing. In this country, a university is sometimes simply a college; sometimes a college with one, or two, or perhaps three professional schools attached, and sometimes it is a mere huddle of studies, from the primary department up, perhaps to the college, perhaps to the professional schools. The underlying idea seems to be that of a great intellectual variety shop, where all may go, and stay as long as they please, and buy what they want.

"From all these the college differs radically, and the American Christian college from all others. It is not a German gymnasium. It is broader. It is not an English college. It is more varied in its studies, and is open to all. Like our form of govornment it has shaped and is shaping itself to our wants. Its object is not to fit men for business. In that it differs from institutions below it, and from professional schools. It has a prescribed course of study, regulates hours, enforces attendance, and proposes not merely intellectual culture, but also some care of morals, and of the formation of character. Its object is not simply knowledge, but wisdom. In all this it differs from the university. Its students are young men in the last stage of their progress towards free manhood, and it proposes to give them a *liberal education*. It is the only institution we have that represents that idea. Its object is the improvement of man as man. It is to discipline the mind symmetrically and furnish it richly. * * * * It would devise such a course of study and provide such teachers as would prevent the prevalent narrowness and one-sidedness, and the clashing that comes from sects and hobbies, and as would do the most that can be done in four years in forming young men at that stage to a complete symmetrical manhood. This is the problem of the college."

In Ohio we have colleges and nothing more. Some of these have a medical department attached, as Western Reserve and Wooster. Several institutions have theological departments. Ohio and Miami Universities have never been anything than colleges. There are now besides these, eight other institutions named universities, mentioned in the Commissioner's Report, not including the University of Cincinnati, now beginning to organize its special departments. To these, the Report adds the names of nineteen colleges. This is by no means the whole number. Naturalists tell us, that in descending from man, the head of the animal kingdom, through the gradations of animal forms, it is impossible to determine where animal life ends and vegetable life begins. So with Ohio institutions of learning. No one doubts the true character and value of the highest and best, for they are recognized and honored by learned people everywhere, but when we reach the border land, the "no mans land," between the college and the school, the power to distinguish appears to be lost and the puzzle becomes a difficult one. The difficulty is all the greater because the problem is not to discern between a low type of a college and a high type of a school, but rather between very low types of each. Our best high schools know their limitations, and are too genuine and honest to assume to be what they are not. In the educational growth and progress of the State the institutions of doubtful classification must pass away.

The State of Ohio, unlike some of the older States, exercises no supervision over higher educational interests, and does nothing to prevent the multiplication of colleges. The whole matter is as free as banking or the establishment of manufactories.

The motives for the establishment of colleges are various. Many have originated in a simple desire to secure for the State higher learning and culture and make it possible for the sons of Ohio to obtain an education of the best kind at home. In institutions thus formed, moral and religious influences have always entered as an element deemed essential in the formation of character. Denominationalism and sectarianism have had no place in them.

Some colleges have originated in a desire to advance the interests of a denomination. This is a powerful motive. While there are comparatively few who see the importance of higher learning for its own sake, the various churches are full of those who can readily see the importance of building up their denominations. This is in itself laudable, and often leads to noble sacrifices and large benefactions. But there should be some limitation to this method of promoting education. True learning can not always be made to flow in narrow race-ways leading to denominational wheels. It is something broad and universal in character. There is nothing in the mathematics, nothing in the classics, nor in natural and physical sciences, nor in mental or moral philosophy, bearing upon questions of church order or of doctrine. "The undevout astronomer is mad," but not more mad than the devout one who should attempt to make the stars teach Presbyterianism or Episcopacy, or baptismal regeneration. The usual college text-books contain no denominational tenets. Such text-books could not well be written, for there is an imperative sense of the fitness of things to restrain authors from introducing sectarian notions, and it would be just as impossible for such authors, as college teachers, to urge in the class-room what they would not publish in text-books. So incongruous is denominational instruction in a college, that most colleges, even those under ecclesiastical control, disavow every trace of sectarianism.

St. Xavier College, under the auspices of the Society of Jesus, says in its Historical Sketch, "They never tamper with the religious belief of any student, and studiously avoid influencing him in any way, except by the example of a good life." Heidelberg College, whose trustees are elected by the Synod of Ohio of the Reformed Church of the United Sates, declares that "no sectarian instruction is required or given." Denison University "managed and controlled by 36 trustees to be chosen exclusively from members in good standing and full membership in regular Baptist churches in the State of Ohio, who shall hold their offices only so long they retain such membership," says in its Historical Sketch that the "university is not sectarian and does not teach denominational dogmas." The University of Wooster, one of the youngest of the institutions of the State, devotes the whole of the second page of its catalogue of 1874 to the following announcement: "The University of Wooster, founded, owned, and controlled by the Ohio Synods of the Presbyterian Church of the United States of America, its aim to secure the highest form and grade of literary, scientific, and Christian education, through trained, experienced, and thorough teachers under constant and positive religious principles and influences, without sectarianism or restriction of freedom of opinion."

The Ohio Wesleyan University, controlled by four Ohio conferences of the Methodist Episcopal Church, by which four-fifths of the trustees are elected—the Alumni electing the other one-fifth—declares in its Historical Sketch that "the objects of the institution are not in the least sectarian. It aims, however, to give a full, healthy, moral and Christian education. It has had members of all denominations among its students; it has graduated Roman Catholics. It has not a single Methodist book in its course as a text-book. Chapel worship is held every morning, consisting of Scripture reading, singing and prayer. The teachers are generally Methodists, though there have been among them Presbyterians and Quakers."

As a rule, all the colleges of the State disavow sectarianism, and make such disavowal the basis of an invitation to students of all religious faiths to come to them. Such an invitation, given in all honor and good faith as we must believe, utterly precludes the possibility of manipulating the legitimate college influences for the special advantage of a sect. All, or nearly all the colleges of the State claim to exert a healthful religious influence, an influence all the purer and better from being unmixed with sectarianism.

With these facts admitted, it is unfortunate that there are in Ohio so many colleges of denominational origin, when with a broader view of the subject of higher learning, combinations could have been effected, which without any sacrifice of religious influence, would have given us institutions of greater strength and dignity and of ampler facilities for affording a broad and generous culture. The denominational name, which, as the colleges themselves acknowledge, can never be legitimately stamped upon a student as such, and is not to be found in text-book nor upon the walls of lecture-room or chapel, appears to be retained by some at least, only as a name to conjure with among the churches for the purpose of securing money and students. This entire misconception of the true function of the college has led to such a multiplication of colleges in Ohio that all are hindered and many are dwarfed. There are not men enough of eminent and finished scholarship to fill all the 245 professorships.* These men are generally poorly paid and are overworked. The circumstances surrounding them are depressing, and those who may have an ambition for high achievement, generally find themselves so straitened for the want of large libraries or scientific equipment that they become despondent. There are of course many exceptions to this in men who keep themselves fully up to the progress of the age in literature and science.

Another effect of multiplying colleges has been a competition productive of friction and irritation, and sometimes leading to a resort to methods incompatible with the wisdom and dignity which should characterise institutions devoted to high learning. Scholarships at absurdly low rates have been sold whenever persons could be found willing to buy. This has diminished the regular and legitimate revenue from tuition, and professors have been insufficiently paid. Of course the intelligent people of the State will place little value upon that which the colleges themselves hold so cheaply. This competition has sometimes led to the lowering of literary standards, and students are admitted to some colleges with very slight preparation. The distinction between the college and the grammar school is often not a little blurred. Rigid classification is not always observed, and students are admitted into some colleges as into a great pasture, to graze where they please and, perhaps, as much or as little as they please. Few, comparatively, complete the

*Statistical Report of the Secretary of State, 1873, gives 30 colleges and universities and 245 members of Faculties and 110 Instructors.

full course of study. By the report of the Commissioner of Schools for 1875, it appears that the whole number of regular college students reported is 3063 and the whole number of reported graduates is 357, or 11 per cent.

It is true that some of the best colleges of the State have been small and have graduated small classes. They have been contented to be small and genuine, preferring this to volume where volume might show inflation or adulteration. Such colleges should be made larger, they deserve to be. Having been faithful in a few things, they should be given rule over many things.

There is no good reason why the young men of Ohio should leave the State to secure a thorough liberal education. Such an education can be obtained at home at less expense and with less danger to morals. Cases are not wanting where our young men, who have been sent to some of the older colleges of the East, have returned with deeply rooted prejudices against all Western institutions without discrimination, and by their influence have done much to prevent our educational progress; in this, presenting a marked contrast with many natives of the East, graduates of eastern colleges, who, on making new homes for themselves in Ohio, desire to make the State of their adoption as great in its educational, as it is in material development. If colleges in Ohio need endowment or equipment of any kind, it is the duty of the citizens of the State to supply it. The public free schools of Ohio are among the best of the land, made so at an annual cost to the people of over eight millions of dollars. There is no reason why our people should not make its colleges strong and great. They need more generous endowment and the means of employing professors of the highest culture and attainments, and of furnishing them with every facility for study and instruction. Such endowments will come. They are already beginning to come, and many of the colleges can now gratefully point to names of noble benefactors. Some of these colleges were wisely planted and under careful nurture have already become firmly rooted. We may confidently believe that in the second Centennial year of the Republic it will be found that these institutions have been generously cared for and have become centers of wide influence for the advancement and elevation of the Nation.

CHAPTER IV.

NORMAL SCHOOLS.

The State of Ohio has, from its earliest history, been second to none in advanced ideas upon education, and in the zeal and well-directed activity of its large body of leading teachers and school officers.

As early as the year 1817, before Connecticut or Massachusetts began to agitate the question of State Normal Schools, Gov. Worthington, of Ohio, opened his message to the General Assembly by the recommendation to establish a thorough system of elementary education. In order to render such a system efficient, he argues that teachers must be employed "whose moral character and other qualifications fit them to enlighten the minds and to shape the morals of the rising generation. If we expect in our youth 'religion, morality, and knowledge,' suitable teachers must be employed to produce this effect." He then makes the following recommendation for the establishment of a State Normal School, which was probably the *first official recommendation of the kind made in the country:*

"With a view to effecting this desirable object, I recommend to the consideration of the General Assembly the propriety of establishing, at the seat of government, a free school, at which shall be taught the different branches of an English education, at the expense of the State, to such number of boys, the children of parents unable to educate them, and no others, as the Legislature may deem proper; that whenever young men thus educated shall become qualified for that purpose, they shall, when proper salarfes are furnished them, have the preference of employment in the public schools of the State, and shall be obliged to serve as teachers of schools until they are twenty-one years of age; and afterward, so long as they conduct themselves well, shall have the preference of employment."

Although these recommendations of the Governor were not carried into effect by the General Assembly, they quickened thought and provoked discussion. During the succeeding twenty years the interests of the common school system were the special care of the State. Early in the year 1836, the General Assembly of Ohio passed a resolution to the effect that Calvin E. Stowe, then professor in Lane Seminary, Cincinnati, "be requested to collect, during his tour in Europe, such facts and information as he may deem useful to the State, in relation to the various systems of public instruction and education which have been adopted in the various countries through which he may pass, and make report thereof, with such practical observations as he may think proper, to the next General Assembly."

A very elaborate report was made by Prof. Stowe, under date of December 18, 1837. Under the head of Normal Schools, he recommends:

"First: The science and art of teaching should be made a regular branch of study in some of the academies and high schools.

"Second: In populous towns there should be large model schools, under the care of the most able and experienced teachers that can be obtained; and the candidates for the profession, who have already completed the theoretic course at the academies, should be employed in this school as monitors or assistants, thus testing all their theories by practice, and acquiring skill and dexterity under the guidance of their head masters. While learning they would be teaching, and no time or effort would be lost.

"Third: To give efficiency to the whole system, to present a general standard, and a prominent point of union, there should be at least *one* model teachers' seminary at some central point—as at Columbus—which should be amply provided with all the means of study and instruction, and have connected with it schools of every grade, for the practice of the students under the immediate superintendence of their teachers."

The recommendation of Prof. Stowe suggested the plan of

opening the Western Reserve Teachers' Seminary at Kirtland, Lake county, in 1838. This excellent normal school was under the management of Dr. Asa D. Lord for eight years from the spring of 1839, and sent out a large number of teachers into the better class of schools in Ohio and elsewhere. Its influence remains to this day in the professional career of some of the prominent educators of the State.

In the year 1837, the office of State Superintendent of Common Schools was created, and Samuel Lewis was elected to its duties, which he discharged for the following three years. No educator, not even Horace Mann himself, to whom Massachusetts is indebted for her normal schools, ever felt more deeply the necessity for a body of trained teachers for the schools than did Samuel Lewis. He believed it to be the duty of the State to provide suitable instruction for those who were to have the care of its youth. His superior devotion to the educational interests of the State, and his acknowledged wisdom, procured for him the distinction of being the subject of the following resolution, passed by the General Assembly of Ohio, March 19, 1838.

"*Resolved by the General Assembly of the State of Ohio*, That the Superintendent of Common Schools be, and he hereby is requested to report to the next General Assembly:

"I. Upon the expediency of establishing a State university or universities, for the education of teachers and other students.

"II. If he shall deem it expedient to establish such university or universities, then upon the subjects of the proper system therefor, and the proper location thereof.

"III. Also, upon the proper mode of supporting the same, the probable expense thereof to the State, and such other views and information in relation to the subject generally, as he may deem it proper to communicate."

In compliance with this resolution, Mr. Lewis made a most valuable report, February, 1839, in which he considers the resolution as embracing two distinct propositions, viz.; the establishment of a university for "teachers," and a university for "other students." Under the former of these propositions, he considers the following questions :

"1. Is there a deficiency in the number of teachers in our State?

"2. Are there any defects in the qualifications of those now filling the place of teachers?

"3. What are these defects?

"4. What measures are now adopted to supply a proper number of teachers of sufficient qualifications, and how far will such means supply the demand?

"5. What additional measures are required and will a state institution be the best means to effect the object?"

The following extracts are made from the discussion of the last question:

"It may now be considered a settled question that there is something peculiar in the art of governing and teaching a school, which may be taught or learned as any other art or profession. There are, to be sure, many excellent self-made teachers, who have become so by long experience and labor, as there are many self-made men who are eminent in all the professions, and in neither case can it be pretended that the success of one man, without superior advantages, would justify us in abolishing those institutions which are intended to aid students in such professions, or that because a few succeed in spite of their disadvantages, therefore all men can do so. If one man has learned to govern a large school with very little corporal punishment, he can teach another with ordinary capacity the same art. If one man has learned how to adapt his instructions to the great variety of minds presented in the school-room, he can teach others to do so. If he has learned a mode of approaching each mind, in such a manner as to wake it up and secure at once a love of himself and the study; if he has found the art of making children reason at an early age; these, as well as all other important acquisitions in the business of teaching, can be imparted to others of ordinary capacity. Heretofore teachers have all acted without associated effort, each sought his own and no other interest, his experience died with him, and no record was preserved of improvements, as in other professions. To this cause may be attributed the lack of improvement in a profession so important to all our interests, individually and collectively.

"With the experience of other nations and other states, as well as the success which has attended individual experiments in our own State before me, I have made up my mind, that with teachers educated for the business, sufficient to supply all the districts in our State, we should, with the same money that is now expended, secure to our children an education far exceeding in amount, and far superior in quality to what is generally furnished. The advantages of associated power are felt in every other department, and may also be felt in this. That the interest of the people demands some provision for the preparation of teachers, I have no doubt; but what shall be the specific plan ultimately to be adopted by the Legislature, is a matter much more difficult to decide.

"One plan is, to have county seminaries, by appropriating to each county a certain amount of money, on condition that the counties would severally add an equal sum or any other proportion, and thus furnish a central high school for this purpose in each county under such regulations as may be prescribed.

"Another plan is, to divide the State into some eighteen or twenty educational districts, and establish a normal school at some central point in each district.

"Another plan proposes to appropriate certain sums of money to each of the different colleges that will undertake to organize in their institutions a teachers' department, and instruct a certain number of persons as teachers of common schools.

"A fourth plan is, to make a commencement by establishing at Columbus one normal or model school for the preparation of teachers.

"An experiment may be made here with very little expense, and until the experiment is made, it may not be prudent to expend a large sum for buildings or otherwise. Buildings for the present could be rented, or what would be better, as the city of Columbus is about to erect large school-houses, it would, no doubt, willingly allow the State to use three or four rooms for the teachers' school. As the students would all be teachers, they could, without additional expense, instruct all the youth in the city according to the most approved system. Indeed, a normal school can not successfully be established, unless it be in connection with schools of the different grades from primary schools up to those esteemed the highest. If some plan like this should be adopted, it would require not more than three professors, until the success attending the enterprise should induce an extension of the work. The students attending should all be admitted free of tuition charge, and the benefits made equal. Each county should be entitled to send one at least. A difficulty is presented in providing boarding and other expenses. But few of those who are to become school teachers have the means of paying heavy charges, even if the tuition is gratuitous, nor is the inducement to become a teacher at present so great as to justify very heavy expenses for this purpose. Females would probably form a large number of the students for teachers, if they had the means for support while attending. Under these circumstances it would certainly be well to make provision for boarding, say one student from each county, whenever the Legislature should feel authorized to appropriate as much money as should effect such a purpose; but this could not probably be done until one or two years experience convinced the people generally of the great advantage resulting to them from such a course. In the mean time, an appropriation of five thousand dollars per year would purchase the apparatus and employ three professors. This would be sufficient to secure instruction to at least one hundred students.

"The only real objection that can be anticipated is in the expense, and possibly the apprehension that the people would not sanction such an outlay; but whatever doubt may exist as to the university, it is scarcely possible that there should be any here. The cry of poor teachers is universal, and in some places teachers can not be had of any qualification. This want is sensibly felt by the people, and if there is any reasonable assurance that the proposed measure would supply the deficiency, or contribute to such a result, surely it would be approved of. However much the citizens of the State may complain of expenses incurred for purposes not general in their benefits, they have never complained of such expenditures as evidently carry with them corresponding advantages to the whole people; and if the advantages of an institution for the improvement of common school teachers can be made to appear beneficial to the cause of general education, it would be an unjust reflection upon the intelligence and public spirit of the people, to anticipate their objections to it. * * * *

"It is proper that one objection should be anticipated and answered. It may be said that if there are a thousand teachers required, and the want still increasing, the establishment of normal schools will fall too far short of supplying the demand to justify the expense. We answer that the benefit of these schools will not be limited to the number directly taught in them. The instruction of some eighty or one hundred teachers, if confined in fact to the furnishing of that number, would render the expediency of the measure doubtful; but it should be recollected that every one who shall go out from this institution, will go prepared to teach on the same plan, and his or her pupils will, to a greater or less extent, acquire the same knowledge. Each teacher thus instructed will be competent to take charge of a similar institution whether of a private or public character. But all this will not be the great advantage; the moral influence of such a model school will be felt by thousands who will never enter the walls. When a standard of this kind is erected and sustained, it will be looked to from every board of township and county examiners in the State; enterprising young teachers will aspire to reach, if not to excel, the perfection of the model, and thus, in a short time, very great improvement will be seen everywhere. * * * *

"The decision of the people of this State through the Legislature, on the best mode of supplying good teachers of common schools, is looked to with the utmost anxiety by the friends of popular education in other states, as well as our own. Education, after having been confined to a comparatively small number for many hundred years, has been gradually spreading its influence and increasing its votaries for some years past. until it has in our State visited every dwelling, from the most splendid building to the humblest cottage; and just in proportion as civil liberty extends an influence, has the love of learning manifested itself. Liberty and general intelligence are 'twins tied by nature; if they part, they die.' As a people, we all know this, and it is thought that all are anxious to have such measures adopted as will secure the best teachers for our children. We are no longer willing to employ a teacher who does not know much, merely because our children do not know much. * * * *

"The decision of this subject has to do with the best interests of that great body of people who can not hope by wealth to exert much influence in society,—whose only hope is in their mental and moral influence. Eight hundred thousand children call on the fathers of the present day to place in their hands the power that well-directed learning gives. Their fathers and mothers are ready to be their surety, that if they can be furnished with this intellectual and moral armor, they will, while we live, and following our example when we die, aid in carrying forward the great works connected alike with the happiness and glory of our country."

In 1840, after three years of service, Mr. Lewis resigned; the office of Superintendent of Schools was abolished, and its duties transferred to the Secretary of State. William Trevitt, the Secretary of State upon whom these duties first devolved, in his report made January, 1841, takes up the recommendation of Mr. Lewis, and urges upon the attention of the General Assembly the necessity for some immediate legislation providing for the special education of teachers. The following is an abstract of this valuable report upon this subject:

"Many of the older and more wealthy states,* have established sev-

*It is not certain to what Mr. Trevitt referred in this passage. Massachusetts was the only state which had a State Normal School at this date. She, through the almost superhuman efforts of Horace Mann, had had one in operation at Lexington—now the Framingham school—for eighteen months; one at Barre—now the Westfield school—for sixteen months, and one at Bridgewater for four months. New York was the next to open a State Normal School, which she did not do till 1844.

eral teachers' seminaries, usually called normal schools, which are said to have produced the most beneficial results. The establishment of these seminaries is the only effectual means for extending the knowledge of the art of teaching, and placing this department of public instruction on that elevated ground that its vast importance demands.

"The delicate and responsible task of cultivating the human intellect is of the deepest importance to the State, therefore our teachers should have at least as good qualifications as those of any other profession; for, 'whatever may be the inherent vigor of the plant, it can never become flourishing and fruitful till it meets with a suitable soil and culture.' The establishment of these institutions is a subject, in my humble opinion, entitled to the serious consideration of the Legislature, as well as of the friends of education throughout the State. Without competent teachers, good schools cannot be expected, and without adequate provision, we can never expect a sufficient number of well qualified teachers for the wants of this great and growing State.

"This subject is, by no means, new; the late indefatigable Superintendent of Common Schools, Samuel Lewis, Esq., two years ago, urged upon the Legislature the propriety of establishing 'model schools.' Another distinguished gentleman (Prof. Stowe) called the attention of the Legislature to the importance of the subject in 1837; but as no action was had upon it from their recommendation, it is fair to presume that the Legislature felt averse to the project, at least at that time.

"All will agree that it is impolitic to increase the number of our institutions of learning beyond our means of support, and that we already have a number commensurate with our wants can not for a moment be doubted. This being the case, might not some of those now in existence have a teachers' department connected with them, as one branch of instruction, without detriment to the institution? It strikes me, that the above or some other plan for accomplishing this desirable object is worthy of attention."

Here follows a quotation from the report of the Board of Commissioners of Common Schools for the State of Connecticut, for the year 1840, in which it is declared impossible to make "an adequate provision for the supply of the requisite number of teachers, who shall be at once capable of teaching in the best manner all that the pupils of our common schools are capable of learning, and of conducting the order and government of their institutions according to the most approved methods, without the establishment of *normal* schools devoted exclusively to the education of teachers in the principles and practice of their profession, and guided by men eminent for their talents and practical wisdom."

This is followed by the suggestion that if the State is not now prepared to erect and sustain seminaries of this elevated character, the work might be introduced by opening teachers' departments in the various seminaries of the State.

Reference is made to the success of the State Normal Schools recently opened in the State of Massachusetts, and further quotations are made from the Secretary of the Board of Commissioners of Common Schools of Connecticut, commending the use of the academies of the State for teachers' classes as a temporary expedient for the education of teachers.

The policy of the State of New York is also referred to. "In sixteen of these academies, departments for the education of teachers were organized, to which 490 students resorted for special instruction in the science and art of teaching, in 1839."

Mr. Trevitt was succeeded by Mr. Sloane, during whose administration of three years whatever of practical conviction or enthusiasm for normal schools had been developed by the earnest labors of his predecessors, was dissipated. He opens his school report for the year 1841, with the flattering statement that, "We have now at our command everything necessary to the entire success of the system, and if it fails, it must be for the lack of wisdom and courage." In his meager reports for the following years, 1842–3, he asks for nothing for teachers, but tells us that, "Much less inconvenience will result from a few years submission to even an imperfect system, than from too frequent changes adopted without the sanction of experience."

The successor of Mr. Sloane, Samuel Galloway, in his school reports for the years 1844–5–6, while he deplores the lack of preparation on the part of teachers, both as to literary and professional acquirements, gives the preference, as a remedy for the evil, to "more rigid examinations for teachers' certificates, teachers' institutes and associations, and a teachers' journal." He also recommends the opening of special departments in the colleges and universities of the State for the education of teachers. In the report of 1846, he says:

"The most approved and efficient plan for elevating the profession of teachers is the establishment of normal schools. This is an institution which characterizes advanced educational effort and improvement, and can only vigorously thrive in popular governments, where abundant means and a high degree of general intelligence prevail. When subordinate and more necessary agencies have succeeded in inculcating upon the public mind enlarged and correct views of the nature and benefits of full intellectual and moral cultivation, then this higher instrumentality may be added, and it will become a similarly appropriate relation to a highly improved system of education that the locomotive and steamship do to the extended business, enterprise, and resources of a high state of civilization. It is unnecessary to discuss the utility of seminaries for teachers, or to indulge enthusiasm by a description of the advantages bestowed upon public schools in Prussia, Holland, Switzerland, or other lands where the experiment has been fully tested. We are not ready, pecuniarily or intellectually, for their adoption. The most practicable and economical mode of securing these benefits, in a limited degree, would be to provide a special department in our colleges and higher institutions of learning for the education of teachers. It would certainly be a commendable measure if those who preside over our State universities would organize such departments, and present inducements to indigent but worthy men to qualify themselves as teachers. A measure of this kind, vigorously and liberally prosecuted, would return, in a few years, a manifold remuneration for the patronage bestowed."

The following year he is emphatic in his recommendation of teachers' institutes, but makes no reference to a normal school. In his report for the year 1848, however, he puts himself unmistakably upon the side of normal schools. Under this head he writes:

"This is a topic connected with common school education which merits attention and consideration. Those institutions exist wherever popular education has attained an elevated position, and to their influence may its progress to a great degree be attributed. Their necessity and utility are alike shown by the judgment and observation of the wise, by the experience of practical educators, and by argument based upon the character and effect of such institutions. Cousin, in his report upon the state of education in Holland, says: 'I attach the greatest importance to normal primary schools, and consider that all future success in the education of the people depends upon them.' Prof. Bache, a gentleman distinguished for his attainments and experience in the subject of education, in his report on education in Europe, remarks: 'When education is to be rapidly advanced, seminaries for teachers afford the means for securing this result.' The plan has been adopted and is yielding its appropriate fruits in Holland, Switzerland, France, and Saxony, while in Austria, where the methods of preparing teachers by their attendance on the primary schools is still adhered to, the schools are stationary. Similar testimony afforded by Hon. Horace Mann, Prof. Stowe, and the superintendents of schools in many of the States, might be adduced.

"All who have tested these schools by an active participation in their management, and by a full experience of their influence and results, earnestly recommend their adoption. They assert that an adequate supply of competent teachers could not be obtained until this mode of preparing them for the office had been secured. This experience is what might have been anticipated. Individuals do not successfully and reputably pursue other vocations without previous study, discipline, and careful preparation, and why should the business of teaching be an exception to the general rule which obtains in other employments. * * * *

"It is also obvious that a generously patronized and energetically conducted normal school, located at the seat of government, would become a standard and model of education throughout the State, and give dignity and influence to the profession of teaching. A few well qualified graduates of such an institution, alive with the spirit and adorned with the full attainments of their vocation, as 'leaven leavens the whole lump,' would soon impart their energy to multitudes of the same calling. A few men in any profession may happily determine its character for centuries. * * *

"It is manifest that the requisite capability to teach successfully can not be fully attained unless the candidate can secure the lessons and example of men of wisdom and experience in matters of education.

"This important aid may be partially obtained in teachers' institutes and other associations of a similar kind, but it cannot be fully realized except in permanent institutions, liberally endowed, and controlled by men possessing the highest attainments in the theory and practice of teaching. In view of the utility of normal schools, as evidenced by the unanimous recommendation of all who have witnessed their operations and results—in view of their intimate and indispensable connection with the consummation of the highest designs of popular education, and especially in view of present necessities, which demand an immediate supply of competent teachers, the establishment of a central normal school by legislative appropriation is urgently recommended for your attentive consideration."

Mr. Galloway was succeeded as Secretary of State by Henry W. King. Nine years had elapsed since the report of Mr. Trevitt, and still there was no State Normal School, and really less prospect of one than ten years before. Mr. King in his report for 1851, after acknowledging the value of the labors of the State Teachers' Association, through the Chairman of their Executive Committee, Lorin Andrews, who had been acting the greater part of the year as their State agent, and through their normal classes, and the service to education rendered by the teachers' institutes, adds:

"Should this [the teachers' institute] prove insufficient, as it probably will, to furnish a better class of teachers as rapidly as the increasing demands of the State require, it may be necessary, eventually, to resort to the aid of normal schools, such as have been established in some of the other states, for the express purpose of providing for this want which has been felt elsewhere as well as here. * * * * Certainly no good reasons can be given why schools should not be established for the professional education of teachers. * * * * It is respectfully suggested that ample provision should be made for the eventual establishment of such a number of normal schools as time and the further progress of our school system shall seem to demand."

At a meeting of the State Teachers' Association held in Springfield in the summer of 1850, this body passed a resolution to the effect that the State should provide for a normal school and a State Superintendent of Common Schools. An act was passed by the General Assembly March 14, 1853, organizing a separate school department, and creating the office of State Commissioner of Common Schools. Hon. H. H. Barney was the first incumbent of this office, entering upon his duties in 1854. But no official action gave any promise of legislation for a normal school.

The leading teachers of the State felt that some steps must be taken towards the establishment of such a school, and at a meeting of the Ohio Teachers' Association, held July, 1854, Dr. A. D. Lord, Chairman of the Executive Committee, presented a report in which he advised the establishment of a normal school under the auspices of the Association. Much discussion was provoked, the members disagreeing as to whether the duty of the education of teachers belonged to the State or to the Teachers' Association, or whether it should not be left entirely to private enterprise.

As the result of this discussion the following resolutions were adopted:

Resolved, That the Executive Committee be instructed to report at our next annual meeting, a definite plan for a normal school under the auspices of this Association.

Resolved. That said committee be authorized to take such action as it may deem proper for the purpose of determining the practicability of raising funds for the establishment of such normal school.

The first resolution was presented by Lorin Andrews; the second, by Rev. J. M. Trimble.

At the following meeting of the Association, held in Cincinnati, December, 1854, Lorin Andrews submitted a report strongly urging action, but suggesting no plan. He stated to the Association that Cyrus McNeely of Hopedale, Harrison county, would give grounds and buildings to the value of $10,000 for normal school purposes if the Association would accept them and sustain a school there. A discussion followed which resulted in a reference of the proposition to the Finance Committee with instructions to entertain any other propositions that might be made, and to report at the next meeting.

At the next meeting, held in Cleveland, August, 1855, upon motion of W. G. Williams, of Delaware, a committee of eleven was appointed to take possession of the McNeely property on behalf of the Association. This committee consisted of Dr. A. D. Lord, Lorin Andrews, M. D. Leggett, M.

F. Cowdery, Geo. K. Jenkins, John Hancock, Cyrus McNeely, James Taggart, Samuel Paul, John M. Black, and Edwin Regal.

The property was accordingly transferred to the Association at a valuation of $11,600, on condition that the Association pledge itself to raise $10,000 for the support of the school. The school was opened in the autumn of 1855, with John Ogden, of Delaware, as Principal. The Teachers' Association made praiseworthy efforts to raise the sum it was pledged to furnish, but failed to do so, and Mr. McNeely generously withdrew the condition, and gave a title free of all conditions save that the property should be devoted to no other than school purposes.

The Association soon found itself unable to meet the running expenses of the school, and December 30, 1857, at an annual meeting held in Columbus, Eli T. Tappan introduced a resolution, "That the General Assembly be memoralized upon the need and propriety of making the McNeely Normal School a state institution." The resolution was adopted, and in response to this memorial, Mr. Canfield, Senator from Medina county, presented a bill, February 15, 1858, requiring:

"1. That there be established and organized, as soon as practicable, an institution for the training and education of common school teachers, to be denominated 'The Ohio Normal School.' 2. That the Governor, by and with the consent of the Senate, appoint immediately after the passage of this act, five trustees to whom shall be intrusted the management and control of said institution. 3. That said trustees take possession of the McNeely Normal School property at Hopedale, and locate the said institution thereon, and cause such accommodations to be made and such buildings to be erected as shall be necessary; and to defray the expenses incurred the sum of ten thousand dollars be appropriated."

The bill, after having been read a second time, was considered in committee of the whole. On February 23, on motion of Mr. Canfield, the bill was referred to the Committee on Schools and School Lands, with instructions to report, after a personal examination, the value of the property, its adaptation to the purposes of a normal school, the character of the location, and all other matters the committee should deem important. On March 31, Mr. Canfield made his report, signed by all the members of the committee. After a description of the property he says:

"Whatever may be the final action of the Legislature upon this subject, the liberality of Mr. McNeely in so worthy a cause can not be too highly commended. Whether the donation so generously proffered shall be received, and the expenses of the school be incurred by the State, is a question which the committee prefer to refer to the consideration of the Senate, rather than to express any recommendation of its own.

"Upon the subject of normal schools generally your committee has but one opinion. The efficiency of our common schools is dependent upon the character and qualifications of the teachers. The importance of accomplished teachers is so great that we believe it to the interest of the State, as well as its duty, to provide all reasonable facilities for accomplishing that object as rapidly as is consistent with true economy."

The bill was reported back to the Senate, and on motion, postponed till the first Monday in January, 1859. It was never called up, but on January 4, 1859, Mr. Dawes, of Morgan county, introduced into the House a bill to provide for the establishment of normal schools in each of the several congressional districts of the State, whenever a majority of the electors of any such district should vote for such a school. This bill having passed a second reading was referred to the Committee on Common Schools, which never reported upon it.

The Teachers' Association, finding it could hope for no immediate aid from the State, and being unable to carry the financial burden of their school, employed a principal upon condition that he should have the entire management of the school, which render it self-supporting. This was the relation which the McNeely Normal School essentially held to the Teachers' Association until July, 1875, when the board of trustees agreed to transfer their claim to the property to any responsible party that would take possession of it for school purposes and relieve the Association from all legal claims for indebtedness thereon.

At a meeting of the Ohio Teachers' Association, held December, 1855, a resolution was passed calling for the appointment of a committee of five to draft a petition to the Legislature in behalf of normal schools. The following day, Alfred Holbrook, Principal of the South-western Ohio State Normal School, reported a petition soliciting the General Assembly to divide the State into four normal school districts, and to enact that a normal school having been established in any one of these districts by an incorporated body of teachers, with property suitable for school purposes, as determined by the State Commissioner of Common Schools, the Legislature should appropriate to each such school the annual sum of $5,000, to be applied in payment of teachers' salaries, on condition that two pupils from each county in the district be entitled to free tuition. Mr. Holbrook was authorized to present this petition to the General Assembly; but this effort to secure state aid also failed, and the South-western State Normal Association finding it impossible to meet the financial demands of their school at Lebanon, allowed it to pass into private hands.

In the report of Commissioner Barney for the year 1854 he states that, "School legislation seems to award them [teachers' institutes] a preference over normal schools as the best and most available agency for the preparation of teachers." In his report for the succeeding year, after refering to the success of the Swiss schools, and stating that this success is due to the professional education of their teachers, he pertinently asks, "How long will it be before each of the nine judicial districts of Ohio will sustain its normal school?" He then recommends that the General Assembly of Ohio take into consideration the establishment of a suitable number of normal institutions. He proceeds:

"In a State like Ohio, requiring annually over 20,000 teachers, it must be apparent to all that it woufd require a score of normal schools to *educate* as well as to *instruct in the theory and art of teaching* that number of teachers. But four such schools, properly located, endowed, and organized, and undertaking to do no work that does not properly belong to them, would furnish all the facilities which are now demanded for the special training of teachers.

"The experience and observation of the last fifteen years may be regarded as having settled one principle, at least, in respect to normal schools, and that is the work which they should undertake to perform. The normal school is not a substitute for the common school, high school, academy or college, though many pupils, and, in some degree the public, have been inclined thus to treat it. There should be no instruction in the departments of learning, high or low, except what is incidental to the main business of the institution, yet some have gone so far in the wrong course as to suggest, that not only the common branches should be studied, but that tuition should be given in the languages and the higher mathematics. A little reflection will satisfy us how great a departure this would be from the just idea of a normal school. * * * * *

"When, therefore, the time shall arrive for establishing in this State similar schools under the patronage of the government, great caution should be observed lest they depart from their proper sphere and become mere academies or high schools, with a sort of normal class appended to them; for such a departure would cause a misapplication of the public funds, by educating a few individuals in particular localities instead of imparting the theory and art of teaching to large numbers who would go forth to instruct and enlighten the thousands of youth in the common schools of the State!"

Mr. Barney congratulates the State upon the gift of Mr. McNeely to the State Teachers' Association of "buildings admirably adapted to school purposes, and spacious and beautiful grounds," and warmly recommends that state aid be granted the institution. He also mentions the Southwestern Normal School enterprise at Lebanon, in terms of the warmest commendation.

In the report for the following year, Hon. Anson Smyth, Mr. Barney's successor, emphasized all that had been said upon the subject of normal schools, and sketched the work which should be done in them. He closes his discussion by recommending that "a committee be appointed to inquire into the practicability of establishing normal schools, to make a report in due time."

In the report of 1860, Mr. Smyth says:

"Ohio stands almost alone among our Northern States in doing nothing for the special training of the teachers. The State has done well in enacting a general school system which is by many considered superior to any other in the country. For the erection of school-buildings and the payment of teachers it has made most liberal provision. Nothing further in these particulars could be asked or desired. But for the education of teachers for our schools, the State has never yet, so far as I know, appropriated a dollar. There is a difference of opinion among the most successful educators of the State in regard to the policy of state normal schools, and for the last four years there have been no petitions for their establishment in our State. The normal schools already mentioned are private enterprises and are self-supporting. But with their limited means they can accomplish but little towards supplying 20,000 teachers."

Hon. E. E. White, in his report for the year ending August 1, 1864, presents an argument in favor of making a school for the special training of teachers a department of the Industrial College. This is based upon an official interpretation of the act of Congress donating lands for the establishment of such colleges in the several states. His report upon this subject concludes as follows:

"A favorable opportunity for establishing in this State, one or more normal schools or departments, of a high order, now presents itself. The incorporation of such a feature in the proposed Industrial College, has not only official sanction, but weighty reasons in its favor. The teaching of the primary facts of agriculture in our common schools may thus be secured, and the practical education of the industrial classes otherwise promoted. The measure is confidently commended to the favorable consideration of the General Assembly."

As the result of these efforts on the part of the School Commissioners and other promoters of education, the following joint resolution was passed by the General Assembly March 13, 1865:

"*Resolved by the General Assembly of the State of Ohio*, That the Commissioner of Common Schools. be, and he hereby is authorized and requested to report to the Governor, to be by him laid before the next General Assembly, the organization and the results of the best normal schools in this country, and so far as may be practicable in other countries; and also the best plan of organizing one or more efficient normal schools in this State."

In compliance with this request of the General Assembly, Mr. White prepared and submitted in January, 1866, a full and able report upon Normal Schools, their organization in this country and abroad, their results, and their necessity; and presented "A plan for providing Normal Instruction in Ohio."

He starts with the proposition that, "A system of professional training for the teachers of the State to be in the highest degree efficient, must place such training within reach of every teacher. It must also provide facilities of a high character for the training of a superior class of teachers whose example and influence shall vitalize the profession and lift it up to a higher standard."

The three agencies which he recommends for the accomplishment of this work are, County Teachers' Institutes, District (Judicial) Normal Institutes, and a State Normal School. The latter he discusses as follows:

"To complete the system of professional training recommended, there should be established at least one State Normal School of a high character. No system of institutes, however complete and thorough, can alone accomplish what is needed. The length of their sessions is, at best, too limited, and the course of training too partial to raise up such a class of model teachers as are needed to lift common school instruction out of the deep ruts of routine, and to impart to it vitality and power. We need teachers trained by superior methods, that they, in turn, may become the teachers of teachers, and both by example and precept lift up the profession to a higher and truer standard. In short, we need a normal school that shall be able to go beyond mere scholastic training and model examples of skillful teaching; that shall unfold thoroughly and systematically the *why* as well as the *how* of education—that shall teach its history, its philosophy, its methods.

"It is true that one normal school, however complete and thorough, will not be adequate for the accomplishment of a tithe of what is needed. But we must make a beginning, and, as all experience teaches, one thoroughly equipped normal school will prove more efficient and valuable, even for the State at large, than two inadequately furnished for their mission, and consequently feeble and superficial in their influence and training. Besides the complete success of one normal school will soon prepare the way for the organization of another.

"The cost of establishing a first-class normal school in this State will depend, of course, upon the cost of the grounds and buildings. The experience of several other states leads me to hope that these will be given by some community as a *bonus* to secure the location of the institution. The citizens of McLean county, Illinois, subscribed one hundred and forty-three thousand dollars for the sake of getting the Normal University of that State located in the county. Hon. Josiah Quincy, of Boston, purchased a building and presented it to the Normal School at West Newton, Mass., now removed to Framingham. The city of Oswego has purchased and fitted up a fine building for the State Training School of New York. Other similar instances might be named,

"The annual expense of maintaining a normal school of a high character, when once established, will be about $12,000. The current expenses of the Illinois Normal University, Michigan State Normal School, New Jersey State Normal School, and the New York State Normal School at Albany, are respectively about $12,000 a year. This sum will be needed in this State.

It will thus be seen that the actual cost of maintaining the entire system of normal and institute instruction which I have recommended, is only about $20,000, ($8,000 for institutes), a sum altogether insignificant when compared with the grand object it is to promote. The law making the appropriation may, with propriety, be entitled, 'An act appropriating $20,000 to keep the half of $3,000,000 from being squandered on incompetent teachers!'"

"It is now nearly thirty years since Hon. Samuel Lewis, then State Superintendent of Common Schools, submitted to the General Assembly of Ohio, in answer to a resolution, a "Report on State Institutions for the Training of Teachers and others," in which he recommended the establishment of a State institution for the professional training of teachers, sustaining his recommendation by a cogency of argument worthy of the great cause he sought to promote.

"Since the date of Mr. Lewis' report, which presented to Ohio the enviable opportunity of becoming the American pioneer in the professional training of teachers, normal schools have been established by *sixteen* states—Ohio being outstripped by states that have not a tithe of her wealth or population. Even new-born Maryland has made the normal school an essential element of her new free school system. Indeed, states that have been peopled since the General Assembly of Ohio passed the resolution referred to, have now their normal schools. Massachusetts is paying more than $22,000 annually for the support of her normal schools and institutes. New York pays annually from $20,000 to $25,000 for her normal schools, about $17,000 for teachers' classes in academies, and from $10,000 to $15,000 for institutes. Illinois, even while the late civil war was raging, appropriated, in two installments, $97,000 to pay, in part, for the magnificent building now occupied by her Normal University.

"Why, in a matter so fundamental and vital as the supplying of her schools with qualified teachers, should Ohio longer fail to be the peer of her sister states? An efficient system of professional training for the teachers of the State is imperatively needed to infuse new life and vigor into the schools and elevate the standard of public instruction. I would most earnestly commend this subject to the favorable consideration of the General Assembly."

Soon after the presentation of this report, and before any action was taken upon it by the General Assembly, Mr. White was succeeded in office by Hon. John A. Norris. Mr. Norris, in his report for the year ending August 1, 1868, presents again the necessity for the establishment of some systematic means for the instruction of teachers in the theory and practice of teaching. He recommends the plan of Mr. White as both feasible and economical, and as having received the sanction of the great body of the leading friends of education in Ohio. After quoting the report quite fully, he adds: "The foregoing plan for the instruction of teachers is admirably adapted to meet the wants for which it was proposed. It is designed to reach every teacher in the State, and should it be adopted the advantages that would follow are incalculable."

In the report for the following year, Mr. Norris commends to the favorable consideration of the legislative authorities of the State, among other important measures, a provision for "a broad and comprehensive system of professional instruction and training for teachers."

Hon. W. D. Henkle, the successor of Mr. Norris. in his annual report for the year 1869, says:

"It is evident that a school system is incomplete in which no adequate means are provided for the education of teachers. Teachers' schools are just as necessary as law schools, medical schools, and theological schools. The need of such schools should not be lost sight of in our efforts to give theoretical perfection to our school system."

In his report for 1871, Hon. Thomas W. Harvey, the successor of Mr. Henkle, also advocates the establishment of normal schools. He says:

"Every facility for acquiring the desired training should be ungrudgingly afforded all teachers who desire to fit themselves thoroughly for usefulness in their profession. The normal school will enable the ambitious and persevering to secure thorough and systematic training. It should be a purely professional school. Academic instruction, except such as may be incidentally given in the illustration of methods, should be dispensed with, that the science of education and the art of teaching may receive exclusive attention.

"There should be two courses of study in this institution—an elementary and an advanced course. The elementary course should provide for instruction in the best methods of teaching the common branches of an English education, and the philosophy upon which such methods are founded; for practice in the use of methods; for instruction in the details of school classification and management, in educational history and legislation, and in the duties and responsibilities of teachers, patrons, and school officers. The advanced course should be thorough and complete, providing for instruction in all matters relating to pedagogics. Those who finish it should be familiar with the development and practical working of educational systems wherever established; should be able to criticize text-books intelligently, and to teach others how to supplement them, or supply their deficiencies with oral instruction; should be acquainted with school architecture, that under their direction school-houses may be hereafter erected, convenient in arrangement and economical in construction; in brief, should be thoroughly prepared to perform all the duties of a first-class teacher or superintendent. The labors of such as these will soon lift our teachers out of the ruts of routine, and their advice give tone and direction to educational effort throughout the State."

In the following year, Mr. Harvey again recommends the establishment of a State Normal School, with two courses of instruction—an elementary and an advanced course. He maintains that such a school would send out a body of trained teachers into cities, villages, and country schools, who would organize and teach normal classes, and conduct institutes, and so carry the influence of the school to the remotest portions of the State In due time it would become the acknowledged head of our school system, controlling, stimulating, and directing all educational effort—an educational Mecca to which earnest, enthusiastic teachers would make frequent pilgrimages.

In his annual messages for the years 1872 and 1873, Gov. Noyes refers to the Ohio and Miami Universities, located at Athens and Oxford, as being embarrassed financially, and recommends that one or both of these institutions be made available for normal instruction. He suggests that the funds of both might be united so as to afford support for one as a university, while the other could be made a normal school, supported entirely by the State, or normal schools could be substituted for both. He believes the common schools want, most of all, carefully instructed teachers, and if the Ohio and Miami Universities were devoted to this purpose, with very little state aid both would be abundantly supported.

The foregoing body of official recognition of the necessity for state provision for normal school instruction and urgent pressure of its claims, certainly has not its counterpart in the record of any sister state. Extending over a period of sixty years, the claims of normal schools were never more forcibly or intelligently presented than in Ohio by Gov. Worthington, Calvin E. Stowe, Samuel Lewis, E. E. White, and others. The question can not fail to occur, Why, then, has Ohio no State Normal School in this year of grace 1876?

Ohio from its earliest history had a strong body of educators; men of practical insight, breadth of comprehension, and positive opinions. These men saw work to be done in every direction, and burned with intense zeal, each man to do his part. They gave freely of their time and money to advance the cause of education. Men of this character do brave work, but do not co-operate as readily as those who are narrower and less ardent. There have been from the beginning, differences of opinion as to the ends most important to be first secured, and the best plans for promoting every interest pertaining to the schools. Each measure—State superintendency, county supervision, teachers' institutes, school libraries, and normal schools—has been in its turn the object of extreme solicitude; and frequently one of them has for the time come into an unforeseen but unfortunate competion with another.

Mr. Stowe's report was, without doubt, too early for legislation, and that of Mr. Lewis for the year 1838 was followed by a year of intense anxiety to save the advanced legislation which had been already secured. At its expiration, he was obliged to resign his office on account of impaired health. The office of State Superintendent of Schools was thereupon abolished, and attention was diverted to other school interests which were jeopardized, and at the time seemed to demand precedence in thought and action.

The efforts of the teachers of the State to establish and conduct normal schools in their associate capacity, had quite contrary to their expectations, a tendency to discourage legislation. While their efforts towards self-help were, in themselves, commendable, they developed and tended to establish the opinion which largely prevails in the State at the present, and to-day is a formidable obstacle in the way of any legislation for normal schools, that teachers, like other professional men, should provide their own professional education. The failure of the State Association to carry forward its enterprise in the McNeely school, and of the South-western Association at Lebanon, while it taught its friends the lesson that no such enterprise can succeed without assured funds to support it, did not inspire them unitedly and persistently to push their claim for professional education by the State, but resulted, to a great extent, in an abandonment of the whole project and a general feeling of discouragement in regard to normal school interests.

At the same time, these normal schools passed into the hands of private parties and became the progenitors of and models for a score of private normal schools which have sprung up all over the State. While no educator questions the impossibility of such schools, however excellent in themselves, accomplishing the work which a State Normal School of a high character could and should accomplish, in giving tone and impulse to all the educational interests of the State, the idea is quite prevalent among legislators that the professional work demanded is being satisfactorily carried on by private enterprise, and if the State does not intermeddle, the supply and demand will in time, somehow, regulate themselves.

The war delayed any agitation of this interest during its continuance, and when, after many years, public attention was again concentrated upon the necessity for a State Normal School, and the General Assembly had requested Commissioner White to prepare a plan for the professional education of teachers, it unfortunately occurred that very soon after he presented his report his term of office expired. His successor could not immediately take up the work where he had left it; the auspicious moment passed, and no bill calling for action upon the subject was introduced into the General Assembly.

Other pressing school interests, as the immediate availability of the teachers' institutes, the urgent necessity for efficient county supervision, etc., have from time to time diverted the attention of the men most earnest to promote the educational affairs of the State, just as the movement for normal schools seemed about to culminate in legislation.

As soon as the educators of Ohio shall unite in the demand for the establishment of a State Normal School, and press their claim to State recognition and legislation with an unyielding tenacity—which they have never yet done—the State of Ohio will have such a school.

While the centennial year of our nation finds Ohio without a State Normal School, it does not find her destitute of the means of professional education for teachers. Besides the professional work done in the teachers' institutes, there are a large number of private normal schools, and several city normal and training schools, which are doing more or less strictly professional work, and normal classes are instructed in several of the colleges. The following sketches of some of these schools represent the general character of all.

PRIVATE NORMAL SCHOOLS.

These schools vary as to their degree of efficiency and in the amount of professional work done. The oldest school of this kind in the State is the

MCNEELY NORMAL SCHOOL.*

The McNeely Normal School is located in Green township, Harrison county, Ohio. It originated in a visionary scheme of the proprietors, growing out of a theory that boarding-schools are pernicious in their influence, and that children, before they reach their majority, should not be removed from parental authority and family influences. They believed that the practice of parents in transferring such fearful responsibilities to school teachers and boarding-house keepers, is contrary to nature and dangerous in the extreme.

*The writer is indebted to Cyrus McNeely, Esq., for this sketch of the history of this school.

They fully believed too, that all of this danger might be avoided; that proper co-operation on the part of the citizens, even in the most rural districts, could secure all the facilities necessary to meet the wants of children, until they reach that period of life when nature makes them responsible for their own success or failure.

In making the experiment, a farm of about two hundred acres, remote from town and village influences, was selected and devoted to the work.

This farm was divided into large lots and sold out for improvements. A ten acre lot in the centre was reserved, and made the site of the "model country district school." A convenient, beautiful, and substantial building was erected, sufficient for the accommondation of two hundred children, and the grounds were tastefully and beautifully ornamented. These improvements were made in the year 1850–51. The school was inaugurated in 1852, under the charge of Edwin Regal, assisted by Dr. G. L. Work and Miss Rebecca McGrew.

The struggles with boards of education, which had no conception of what a school ought to be, the prejudice of the community against all innovations upon the old routine of a country school, soon convinced all concerned that there was a mistake in depending upon the co-operation of the citizens of Green township to carry forward such a work to success.

The Principal of the school, Mr. Regal, during this struggle with the neighborhood, made a trip to New England for the purchase of a library, apparatus, etc., and after spending a few months in one of the Massachusetts normal schools, conceived the idea of carrying forward the enterprise as a normal school. The proprietors cheerfully seconded this purpose, and every effort was put forth to make the new departure a success. They entered upon this new scheme, humiliated by the so sudden bursting of the anti-boarding-school bubble, but not knowing how to go forward without boarding facilities. A benevolent lady of the town of Cadiz, Mrs. Eliza Hogg, came forward unsolicited to the aid of the work, and volunteered to create boarding accommodations for the young ladies. In the spring of 1855, she erected on a plat of six acres of ground, which she bought for the purpose, the boarding-house known as Pumphrey Hall—a very substantial and comfortable building, sufficient for the accommodation of forty young ladies.

While these and other improvements were in progress, the "Ohio State Teachers' Association" embraced the theory that it could, as an association, establish and carry on a normal school. It was decided to tender to the Association the school property at Hopedale—for that, almost by intuition, became the name of the locality—on such conditions as should put the school entirely within the control of the Teachers' Association and enable it to test the wisdom of such an undertaking.

The Association accepted the property, and organized their school in the fall of 1855. They elected a board of trustees, and incorporated the institution under the general laws of Ohio. Its corporate name is the "McNeely Normal School of Ohio."

Mr. John Ogden, of Delaware, was made Principal, and Mr. Edwin Regal was retained in the academic department. Miss Betsey M. Cowles was put in charge of the model school. In less than two years the Association found itself hopelessly in debt, and with no power to curtail the expenses. Fruitless appeals were made to the Legislature for aid to carry forward the work. Politicians seemed utterly blind to the absurdity of paying out millions of money every year to teachers whom every body knew to be incompetent, and yet making no provision to remove the incompetency. The Association finally lost its interest in the enterprise and the school tacitly reverted to the management of Mr. Regal, who had been in charge for three years before the Association undertook the work. At the time Mr. Regal resumed the management, which was in the year 1859, he was assisted by Prof. Brinkerhoff, of Franklin College. Under the charge of these two men—who have alternately acted in the capacity of Principal for seventeen years—the "McNeely Normal School," has reached a degree of excellence and power second to no school in eastern Ohio.

The records of the school show an aggregate attendance of nearly five thousand pupils. A large proportion of them are practical teachers. But notwithstanding all the school has done and is doing for the general cause of education in the State, it is not, and cannot be, in the highest sense a "normal school." If the Legislature had given to it, even one thousand dollars a year, or if it had given to it the control of the public school which grew up about the movement, it could have had a "model practice school." But it did neither. So the lessons still given upon the "theory and practice of teaching," for lack of practical application to teaching as a business, are largely lost.

More than twenty-five years of labor and over forty thousand dollars of the capital of the proprietors have been given to these educational experiments. Had either scheme succeeded, their ambition would have been satisfied; as it is, they have an excellent academic institution which in beauty of location, in school appointments, in curriculum and faculty compares favorably with any other in the State. That it is not an ideal normal school is the fault of neither the proprietors nor the teachers. They are pained that the field they have striven so diligently to cultivate, is still a desert, and that such a multitude of young and inexperienced teachers must still blunder on under the weight of their tremendous responsibilities without the assistance of even a model to look at.

The school has a four years' Academical Course, comprising

all the higher English branches, and a four years' College Course corresponding in its curriculum with the older colleges in Greek and Latin, to which Hebrew is added in the senior year. The registration for the year ending June, 1875, was 178.

FACULTY.—W. Brinkerhoff, A, M., Principal, Mathematics and Natural Sciences; Rev. J. M. Jamieson, A. M., Latin and Greek Languages; N. Battelle Collins, A. B., English Grammar, English Literature, Rhetoric, and Ancient History; W. S. Poulson, English Department, Penmanship, Book-keeping; Mrs. Anna E. F. Collins, Assistant Teacher in Latin and Modern History; Charles H. Laizure, German Language; Mary E. Parry, Assistant Teacher in Arithmetic and Algebra; Mrs. Julia M. Lobdell, Instrumental Music—Piano, Organ, and Melodeon; John W. Fogle, Sen., Vocal Music; Mrs. Mary A. Brinkerhoff, Principal of Ladies' Department.

NATIONAL NORMAL SCHOOL.

The second Normal School of Ohio was located at Lebanon, Warren county. In the summer of 1855, a three weeks' institute was called by John Hancock and A. J. Rickoff, of Hamilton county, J. P. Ellinwood, of Butler county, Chas. Rogers, of Montgomery county, E. C. Ellis, of Brown county, and others. The institute was held in the buildings of the Miami University at Oxford, Butler county. During its progress an organization was effected called the "South-western State Normal School Association." Its object was to establish and sustain a State Normal School in south-western Ohio until aid could be obtained from the State. The first trustees of the Association were A. J. Rickoff, of Cincinnati, Charles Rogers, of Dayton, and E. C. Ellis, of Georgetown.

These trustees selected Lebanon as the place best adapted to the location of the school. The trustees of the Lebanon

Academy transferred their building and lot to the Normal School trustees with an agreement to furnish eighty pupils for five years to aid in sustaining the school.

Alfred Holbrook was elected Principal. The South-western State Normal School opened Nov. 24, 1855, with about ninety pupils from Lebanon and vicinity, and some four or five from other localities. There were three teachers employed besides the Principal. For the first year the finances were managed by an agent appointed by the trustees.

Hon. H. H. Barney, in his report for the year 1855, thus refers to this school:

> "The organization resulted from a general concert of action among those engaged in the instruction of youth, and is auxiliary to the Ohio State Teachers' Association. It has a favorable location, and commodious buildings have been already secured. The first session has elapsed with seventy pupils in attendance, and all the indications of future usefulness are very satisfactory. The terms are so arranged that while some young persons can pursue a regular course in training—study and practice in the experimental school—others already engaged as teachers can, during the interims of their own schools, attend a session of eleven weeks, more or less, without interfering with those pursuing a regular course of study, the latter being not unlike the plan of the McNeely institution. This temporary arrangement gives opportunity for teachers permanently engaged, to adjust the terms of their own schools, so as to attend a part or the whole of a session of eleven weeks at the Normal School, while others not permanently engaged can enter the Normal School at any time that may suit their convenience, and after devoting a reasonable time to preparation, will doubtless find full compensation for the expense in a more ready demand for their services. Tne organization of the South-western Normal School seems to be well considered."

It proved however to be unmanageable by the Association, and at the end of the first year was given over into the hands of the Principal, Mr. Holbrook. Several additional teachers were employed and two definite courses of study—a common and a high school course—were adopted. The enrollment for the year was 257.

In 1864, several collegiate studies were added and a Business Department opened. In 1870, the name of the school was changed from the South-western Normal School to the National Normal School. This school under the management of Mr. Holbrook has attained unexampled prosperity, the enrollment for the year 1875 having been more than 1,600 pupils. The courses of study are:

Teachers' Course.—This ordinarily requires two terms of eleven weeks each, in order to obtain a teachers' certificate, and three terms for a diploma. This shorter course prepares teachers to manage a grammar school, as well as any of the lower grades, with success. The branches pursued are English grammar, arithmetic, geography, map drawing, physiology, United States history, penmanship, objective drawing, elocution, and the art of school teaching and school management.

Business Course.—The Business Course requires two or three sessions. Many combine the Teachers' and Business courses, which can be done by giving an additional term. Three terms are generally sufficient for the completion of both courses.

Engineers' Course.—The Engineers' Course requires three or four terms. This fits young men for any possible form of county surveying, also for managing a squad of men in railroad engineering. Many combine the Business Course and the Engineers' Course. This can generally be done in three or four terms.

Collegiate Course.—The Scientific Course requires one year of fifty weeks, besides two or three terms in the Preparatory Department.

The Classic Course requires an additional year of fifty weeks.

There is also a Preparatory Department in which the common English branches are tanght.

BOARD OF INSTRUCTORS.—Alfred Holbrook, President; R. H. Holbrook, W. J. Stevens, G. W. Worthen, Warren Darst, W. F. Harper, L. T. Loer, L. R. Marshall, John Neuhardt, L. C. Crippen, J. B. Graham, Miss Irene Holbrook, Miss Anna Holbrook, Miss Ida Hardy, Miss Mary Owens, Miss Allie Johnson, Miss Ida Neff.

THE WESTERN RESERVE NORMAL SCHOOL.

The Western Reserve Normal School is located at Milan, Erie county, Ohio. It originated as follows: In the winter of 1830–31 there was an extensive revival of religion throughout the churches of the Huron Presbytery. Among the converts were several young men who desired to study for the ministry; but as there was at that time no school on the Reserve, west of Hudson, in which young men could prepare for college, Mr. Judson, the Presbyterian minister at Milan, set about trying to establish a school in which both sexes could be educated, but especially for the preparation of young men for college. The subject was discussed in the Presbytery, and a board of trustees appointed.

At the next session of the Legislature, an act of incorporation was obtained for this board. The school was called the "Huron Institute." It was proposed to raise four thousand dollars, and locate the school in Milan, provided the inhabitants would raise one-half of this amount, the churches of Huron Presbytery being responsible for the remainder. The people of Milan more than redeemed their pledge.

The Rev. E. Barber was employed as the first teacher, and the Huron Institute opened its first session, April 20, 1832. The school soon became very popular, and for many years held its place in the front rank as a preparatory school. In the meantime the country became more thickly settled, and other schools divided the patronage.

In 1858, the trustees leased the Institute building to Rev. A. Brainard and S. F. Newman. The character of the school was now changed from a preparatory school to a school for the training of teachers, and the name from the "Huron Institute" to the "Western Reserve Normal School.". Mr. Brainard resigned after one year, leaving the school in the care of Mr. Newman. From the years 1864 to 1867, Miss Delia Palmer taught with Mr. Newman, as assistant. In

1870, Mr. Newman resigned, and the board leased the build- to Miss Palmer, and she has occupied it till the present time, with an unexpired lease of three years yet to come.

The great aim of the school has been the training of teachers, especially "district school" teachers. During all this time, the school has had no financial support either from the State or from individuals, but has been supported by the tuition fees of pupils alone.

There is no model school attached to it, but the young teachers usually remain till they are able to pass a county examination, when they commence to teach, alternating teaching and attending school till they finish the course. In this way many of them are able to obtain and hold some of the best situations in the high schools of the surrounding country. Others who have stopped short of the full course of the high school, are now occupying the no less important positions of common school teachers.

The present centennial year of the nation, and almost the semi-centennial of the school, finds it in a more prosperous condition than ever before.

Teachers' reviews are an important feature of this school. They are held in November and March, each session being two weeks in length. These reviews are conducted largely in writing, and are confined to the branches usually taught in the district schools. Forty ladies and twelve gentlemen availed themselves of this department of the school last year. The enrollment upon the ordinary course was 126.

COURSE OF STUDY.

First Year.—Mental arithmetic, written arithmetic, geography and map drawing, English grammar and analysis, penmanship, United States history, vocal music, teachers' class.

Second Year.—Algebra, physiology, botany, penmanship, Latin grammar and reader, natural philosophy, vocal music, teachers' class.

Third Year.—Algebra, astronomy, vocal music, Cæsar, part of Virgil, general history and penmanship.

Fourth Year.—Geometry, trigonometry, chemistry, Virgil finished, geology, general review of common English branches.

TEACHERS.—Miss D. Palmer, Principal, Mr. E. N. Hawley, Assistant, Miss A. L. Simpson, Mrs. J. Bliss Palmer.

ORWELL NORMAL INSTITUTE.

This school is situated in the village of Orwell, Ashtabula county, Ohio. For twelve years previous to 1865, the school had been an academy, but having become weak and comparatively unsuccessful, the citizens of Orwell pledged themselves to give $400 annually for its support, if H. U. Johnson, Esq., the present principal, would take hold of the enterprise and make the school a success. This he was induced to do, and the school was opened under its present name, September, 1865.

The work is necessarily largely academic. The courses of instruction are a Preparatory, consisting of elementary studies; an Elementary Course of two years, consisting of the common English branches; an Academic Course of three years, including the higher mathematics, Latin, French, German, and vocal and instrumental music; and a Business Course, consisting of arithmetic, grammar, penmanship, and book-keeping.

The prospectus of the school thus sets forth its work:

"The design of this institution is to furnish a thorough course of disciplinary study, both theoretical and practical, to those who propose assuming the responsible duties of the school-room. With this view the courses of instruction have been arranged, and classes are organized in theory and practice of teaching. The members of these classes are alternately required to give instruction, subject to the criticisms of their fellows and the principal. In this way most of the advantages of a model school are secured.

Persons desiring to teach, having thoroughly completed the preparatory studies, will receive a certificate signed by the board of teachers. Those completing any one of the courses, or its equivalent, will be graduated with appropriate diplomas.

"The Business Course is calculated to furnish young persons who have not two or three hundred dollars to spend at a commercial college, with such training, as, when once engaged in business, speedily to comprehend its details."

Many young persons, fitting themselves for teachers' positions, avail themselves of the facilities afforded by this school. The summary of attendance for the year ending June, 1875, is: gentlemen, 106; ladies, 76—total, 182.

Board of Teachers.—H. U. Johnson, Principal, Miss Mary Crowell, Miss M. Alferdine Bedell, Miss Vesta M. Johnson, C. C. Case, W. A. Johnson.

NORTH-WESTERN NORMAL SCHOOL.

This school is located in the village of Ada, Hardin county. It originated as follows: In the spring of 1866, Mr. H. S. Lehr came to this village and proposed to the school board to teach for sixty dollars per month the first year, provided that he should be allowed to use the school building for a select school when the public schools were not in session, and that, should he prove successful in procuring foreign scholars, the citizens of the town and vicinity should assist him in erecting buildings suitable for normal school purposes. His proposition was accepted.

In a short time, the limits of the old frame school-house were outgrown, a commodious brick building was erected, and wages were made commensurate with the prosperity of the school.

In the fall of 1870, after Mr. Lehr had taught four years, the foreign students amounted to 120, and the school-house was again found to be too small. The propitious time for asking the citizens for the promised help seemed to have arrived. A meeting of the citizens of Ada was therefore called, at which Mr. Lehr proposed that he would furnish $3,500 toward the erection of a building for a normal school, if the citizens would furnish $4,000 and donate three acres of ground suitable for the location of the building. The citizens accepted the proposition, but instead of $4,000 they raised about $6,000, and wished him to increase his part of the funds in proportion. Not being able to comply unassisted, he associated with himself two partners, J. G. Park and B. F. Neisz.

The building was at once commenced, and in the fall of 1871 was sufficiently advanced in construction to admit of dedication, and was formally opened August 11, 1871, with an enrollment of 147 pupils.

H. S. Lehr, A. M., B. F. Neisz, B. S., J. G. Park, and Theodore Presser were the first faculty.

The first year the school was very successful. The union school of the village was consolidated with the Normal School, which was a financial advantage to the latter. The next year, a serious financial difficulty seemed inevitable, growing out of the failure of the citizens to redeem their pledges. Mr. Neisz left the school. Before the close of the year an amicable adjustment was concluded, the entire indebtedness was paid off by the citizens, and the buildings, grounds, etc., were placed in the hands of the faculty free of encumbrance. Mr. Rutledge was soon after added to the faculty. The school has been steadily increasing in prosperity since that time.

In the autumn of 1875, arrangements were made with Prof. J. Fraize Richard to consolidate the North-western Normal School, located at Fostoria, Ohio, with the North-western Ohio Normal School at Ada, both to be continued under the corporate name of the latter, and to be superintended by H. S. Lehr as principal.

Arrangements were made in the month of January, 1876, to commence the erection of a building for a musical conservatory to be conducted in connection with the Normal School. The citizens contributed about $7,000 to this enterprise.

The building is to be 45 by 90 feet, three stories above the basement. There will also be built, during the summer, a large boarding hall containing 100 rooms.

The institution is owned by the faculty, and is under the immediate control of the same, both as regards its finances and its management.

There are three courses of study: the Normal or Teacher's Course, the Scientific, and the Classical. Besides these, there are special courses for music and commercial science.

The school is well supplied with maps, charts, cabinets, philosophical and chemical apparatus, libraries, and instruments for leveling and surveying. There are two literary societies in connection with the school, each of which has a large collection of well selected books, supplying the students with all the miscellaneous reading necessary.

There is also a library in connection with the institution, consisting of text-books, works on theory and practice of teaching, statistics, etc. The text-books are rented to students, while all other books are free to any wishing to use them.

The enrollment for the last school year was 359—201 gentlemen and 158 ladies. The enrollment for the year 1876 will be at least 500 different students.

The whole number of graduates since the foundation of the institution is 23—14 gentlemen and 9 ladies. Of these, all but two are engaged in teaching.

Corps of Teachers.—H. S. Lehr, Principal, J. F. Richard, J. G. Park, G. W. Rutledge, Mollie Schoonover, Mrs. E. D. Richard, W. D. Woodard, Mrs. Hattie Rawley, W. H. Pontius.

OHIO CENTRAL NORMAL SCHOOL.

In the summer of 1871, the property known as the "Worthington Female Seminary," situated in the town of Worthington, Franklin county, Ohio, including three acres of ground, buildings, etc., valued at about $12,000, was purchased, and a school opened the following September under the joint principalship of Messrs. William Mitchell and John Ogden, with the title of "Ohio Central Normal School."

A course of study was adopted, embracing careful reviews of the common branches and the study of such other branches as are usually taught in the higher grades of schools.

This course was made supplementary to the Professional Course, which included the study of the best authors on education and teaching, the school laws of the State, and a careful comparison of principles and methods of teaching, in a course of lectures extending through each term, two each day, of which a careful abstract was made by the pupil-teacher. This, together with teaching exercises, discussions, and the writing of theses on the various topics relating to teaching, constituted the leading idea of the school, and the study of branches was made illustrative of principles and methods.

The attendance the first year, in the Normal School proper, was 111—52 gentlemen and 59 ladies; the second year, 178—94 gentlemen and 84 ladies.

The number graduated the second year, was 8—4 gentlemen and 4 ladies, all of whom, with one exception, entered soon upon the duties of teaching, some of them in the best schools in the State.

The following year the school was under the joint principalship of Messrs. John Ogden and M. H. Lewis, Mr. Mitchell having entered upon another profession. The attendance this year was 215—105 gentlemen and 110 ladies, with a graduating class of 8 gentlemen and 9 ladies, 16 of whom entered upon their duties as teachers. The course of study remained substantially the same.

In January, 1875, Mr. Lewis withdrew, leaving the entire management of the school to the present principal, assisted by Rev. Charles H. Young, A. M., Miss Clara M. Semple and six tutors of the senior class. The attendance this year was 214—111 gentlemen and 103 ladies, with a graduating class of 10 gentlemen and 10 ladies. A large majority of these have already found positions in schools in various parts of the State.

The school is now under the same principalship, with about the usual number in attendance, and with a marked and steady progress to a higher standard of excellence.

The Normal Institute, or summer session of five weeks, constitutes a prominent feature in the operations of this school. This is held during the months of July and August of each year, thus accommodating a large number of teachers from graded schools, whose terms of employment will not permit their attendance at any other time.

The course of study and lectures for this annual normal institute embraces the following: 1. A review of the common branches. 2. The higher mathematics. 3. Physiology and mental science. 4. Experimental physics. 5. Primary instruction and drawing. 6. Language lessons and composition. 7. Principles and methods of instruction.

CITY NORMAL AND TRAINING SCHOOLS.

The City Normal and Training Schools of Ohio are devoted exclusively, or nearly so, to professional instruction in the theory and practice of teaching. There are four of these schools in the State—in the cities of Cincinnati, Cleveland, Dayton, and Sandusky, respectively. They contemplate a post high-school graduate course in preparation for the schools of the city in which each is located. The following sketches of these schools will indicate their origin, character, scope, and intention.

THE CINCINNATI NORMAL SCHOOL.

The City Normal School of Cincinnati was organized September, 1868. It originated in a felt need of better teachers in the lower grades of the city schools. As vacancies in teachers' positions occurred in the higher grades, promotions were made from the lower, the time of the children being considered more valuable with advancing years. The vacancies constantly made in the lower grades by these promotions, were filled with inexperienced girls, and so these grades came to serve the purpose of training schools for teachers for the upper grades.

For several years, the Superintendent of Schools and some of the most progressive members of the Board of Education had felt that some measures must be adopted to prevent the great waste of time and labor in the primary schools through inexperience and lack of professional knowledge. Accordingly, in the summer of 1868 the board voted to open a school for the training of candidates for teachers' positions in the primary grades of the Cincinnati schools.

Notable among the men whose influence gave impulse and character to the movement were John Hancock, Superintendent of Schools, H. L. Wehmer, and J. B. Powell, Esq., members of the Board of Education. The action of the board was unanimous in favor of its establishment.

The school was located in the Eighth District schoolhouse, where it is still in operation. At its opening, two ordinary school-rooms were set apart for its use—one for normal school instruction, and one for practice with children. The second year three rooms were occupied, and now seven school-rooms are devoted to the normal school work—two for normal instruction and five for practice in teaching.

The expenses of the school are paid from the common

schoool fund of the city. Tuition is free to all candidates who state it as their intention to enter the Cincinnati public schools as teachers ; to others, it is $60 per annum.

Pupils, to be admitted to the school, must be graduates of the Cincinnati High Schools, or of some school of similar standing, or hold a teacher's certificate from the Cincinnati board of examiners of teachers, or have passed an equivalent examination before the Normal School committee. The subjects upon which an examination is instituted for a teacher's certificate, are mental and practical arithmetic, English grammar, geography, United States history and general history, reading, spelling, natural philosophy, anatomy and physiology, music, drawing, and penmanship. No certificate is issued to an applicant whose average of correct answers in grammar, geography, or written arithmetic, is less than 70 per cent., or whose average on the whole number of marks is less than 70 per cent. This is the lowest standard of admission to the Normal School.

There is but one course of study, pursued at option in German or English, for German or English positions respectively. The peculiarities of this course are: first, it is planned with reference to a definite purpose—the management and instruction of the lower grades of the Cincinnati public schools; second, it is broad in that it aims to discuss principles of education and deduce *methods* from them, instead of teaching them empirically; third, it is entirely professional. It consists of methods of teaching all the subjects pursued in the lower grades of the Cincinnati schools, together with the history of education, school-management, mental philosophy, and the philosophy of education. Special attention is given to penmanship, music, and drawing.

This study is supplemented by practice, each pupil spending about ten weeks—the time varying somewhat with the size of the classes—in the management and instruction of one of the ordinary lower grade city schools. This time is spent *consecutively*, and is designed to familiarize the pupil-teacher with the every-day routine of school work in all its phases, as far as this can be done in the time allowed. Critic-teachers have constant oversight of the work of the pupil-teachers, and make daily criticisms and corrections. The pupil-teachers are marked weekly in a register, open to all, upon the following items: punctuality, promptness, personal bearing, neatness (in person and work), correct use of language, improvement of time, ability to control, ability to instruct, ability to criticise, and ability to profit by criticism.

A diploma from the school secures to its holder the preference over an inexperienced teacher in appointment to a position, there being a rule of the Board of Education that no such person shall be employed while a graduate of the Normal School awaits appointment. It also secures $100 per annum additional salary until the maximum salary is reached. If the graduate teach seven years—the time required to arrive at the maximum salary—she will have received $550 more for services than if she had secured a position without a Normal School diploma.

The first principal of the school was Miss Sara Dugane, called to this position from the City Training School of Boston. She resigned at the expiration of the first year, and was succeeded by the present incumbent, Miss Delia A. Lathrop, then principal of the City Normal School of Worcester, Mass.

The number of pupils in the school for the year 1874–5 was 78—60 English and 18 German. The number enrolled in the practice school was 355. There were 41 graduates of the Normal School—35 English and 6 German. Since the organization of the school there have been 240 graduates.

INSTRUCTORS.—Delia A. Lathrop, Principal; George H. Borger, German Instructor; Helen E. Thorndick, English

Instructor; Clara A. Burr and Pauline Rulison, English Critics; Josephine Knaff, German Critic.

DAYTON NORMAL SCHOOL.

The Dayton Normal School was organized in 1869 to supply the want of better trained and more skillful teachers for the schools of the city. The majority of those seeking positions as teachers came directly from the schools, and being, in many cases, not even graduates of the High School, were found to need further training for the special work of the teacher than was afforded by the ordinary academic course.

It was also found that a system of graded schools adapted to the wants of a growing city, must make provision for a class of pupils having peculiar requirements. A large number of children enter school at the earliest possible age, and leave it as soon as they are large enough to earn their living. It was apparent that mere text-book instruction did but a small part of what was possible in the education of these pupils, and that there was need of methods of instruction which could not be employed with any degree of success by teachers who had not previously studied the principles upon which such methods are based, and acquired some degree of skill in their use.

The organization of a new school district, with a new building and a corps of picked teachers, presented a favorable opportunity for the establishment of a normal or teachers' training school which would meet this necessity.

The school began in September, 1869, with a class of 28 pupils, and was placed under the charge of Col. F. W. Parker, the principal of the district, with Miss Emma A. H. Brown, as assistant, who gave her entire time to the instruction of the pupils in the theory and practice of teaching.

The pupils were to be not less than sixteen years old. They were to pledge themselves to teach in the schools of Dayton not less than two years, and their salary for the first year after their graduation was fixed at $450, the third grade. Graduates of the High School were admitted with out examination, all others being required to pass a satisfactory examination in the common English branches.

The course of instruction lasted one year, and included a department of theory and one of observation and practice. The work of the theory department consisted of a general review of the academic branches and the study of methods of teaching, school economy, and criticism lessons. In the department of observation and practice, the pupils having by observation become familiar with the methods of the teacher under whose direction they were placed, were put in charge of classes, at first under the direction of the regular teacher; afterwards, as they developed confidence and ability, they were put in entire charge of the room.

The pupils were divided into two classes, devoting four weeks each to theory and practice alternately—one class being engaged in theory work while the other was in practice. Four rooms of the primary grade were specially set apart as practice rooms, and placed in charge of Miss M. J. Brown, a teacher of long experience in teaching these grades, under whose oversight the work of the rooms was carried on by the normal pupils. When any of these showed special fitness for teaching advanced grades, they were given opportunity for observation and practice in other rooms of the building, under the direction of the regular teacher in charge of the room.

In September, 1871, Colonel F. W. Parker having been appointed assistant superintendent of instruction, Miss Emma A. H. Brown was made principal of the Normal School, being also principal of the district, and Miss M. J. Brown continued as critic-teacher in charge of the first, second, and third year rooms, the plan of the school in other respects continuing as before. At the close of the school year 1872–3, Miss Emma A. H. Brown resigned her position, and Mr. Wm. Watkins was appointed principal of the district and also placed in charge of the Normal School.

This year some radical changes were made in the organization of the school. The principal taught the senior class of the grammar school, and gave instruction in theory to the normal pupils, attention being chiefly given to the review of the academic branches, the eighth year class of the grammar school and the class of normal pupils reciting together for this purpose. The practice department was largely reconstructed and confined mainly to observation. The critic-teacher was placed in charge of a single room of the primary grade, and, as occasion called, the normal pupils were distributed through the various grammar schools of the city for observation and as much practice as there was opportunity to obtain.

One of the reasons for this change in the practice department was the objection made by patrons of the grammar school to its continuance, the opinion having gained some prevalence that the children were retarded in their studies by being placed under the instruction of the normal pupils. While the truth of this was not admitted by the friends of the school, nor was there any evidence of it in the examinations, yet the Board of Education saw fit to defer to what it considered an expression of popular opinion from those directly interested, and made the change described as an experiment.

The results of the year's work were not such, in the opinion of the board, as to justify a repetition of the experiment. It was found, that to give proper attention to the work of the theory department required the entire time of the principal of the Normal School, and that the entire work of supervising and instructing the normal pupils in the department of observation and practice should be placed in the hands of a single person specially designated and qualified for that purpose. Accordingly, at the commencement of the following school year (1874–5), the school was reconstructed by appointing Miss Jane W. Blackwood, for some time an assistant in the Cincinnati Normal School, as principal, and Miss Lucy K. Rice, a graduate of the Oswego Normal School, as critic-teacher. The principal was placed in entire charge of the school, and gave the needed instruction in the theory department, and the critic-teacher was placed in charge of two rooms of the grammar school of the first year grade, being responsible for the proper advancement of the children in their studies and the supervision and guidance of the normal pupils in the work of observation and practice. The school still continues under the charge of these two ladies, whose work is eminently satisfactory.

The plan of the school as at present conducted, in addition to a general review of the academic branches, aims at giving such a degree of mental discipline and familiarity with professional work as will fit the pupils to assume successfully the responsible duties of the teacher. They are made acquainted with principles of education and methods of instruction, are confirmed in habits of accurate study, thought, and expression, are taught to be prompt and self-reliant in the use of their faculties, and are made acquainted with the practical duties of the school room. The entire class spend the first half of the year in the work of the theory department, in which the pupils are required to be proficient before they go into observation and practice. The standard fixed for the admission of pupils insures such proficiency in the academic branches as enables the greater part of the time to be spent upon professional work. The final examination of the pupils for graduation is conducted by the city board of examiners, in conjunction with the superintendent of instruction, the president of the Board of

Education, and the committee on teachers and examinations. Diplomas are given to those who have given evidence of teaching ability, and have passed a successful examination.

The number of graduates since the organization of the school is as follows:

1869-70	9
1870-71	13
1871-72	19
1872-73	11
1873-74	11
1874-75	8
Total	71

Of these, forty-four, or about one-half of all the teachers employed, were teaching in the Dayton schools at the close of the last school year.

The results of the establishment of the Normal School may be stated briefly as follows: first, the furnishing of a much better class of material from which to select teachers; second, a general raising of the standard of attainment and efficiency among the teachers; third, the increase of a spirit of professional pride and enthusiasm; and fourth, the maintenance of a thorough and efficient system of primary instruction, impossible without such an auxiliary.

CLEVELAND CITY NORMAL SCHOOL.

This school is located in the central part of the city of Cleveland, on Eagle street. It was established in August, 1872, and Alex. Forbes elected principal. The inability of Mr. Forbes to accept the position at the time it was tendered, caused a delay of two years in the opening of the school, which did not take place until Sepember, 1874.

The school is free to all residents of the city between the

ages of sixteen and twenty-one. For non-residents and those over school age, an annual tuition of $20 is charged. It is supported from the public school fund, and is under the control of the Board of Education. The pupils are mostly graduates from the Cleveland High Schools.

Only one class has been graduated. This class numbered twenty-six members. Twenty-five of them are now engaged in the schools of the city of Cleveland, and one in the Colored High School, Washington, D. C. The average attendance is about forty.

The course of study embraces a review of all the branches of study in the common schools, and a discussion of methods as based on mental philosophy. The pupils also practice in actual teaching in the schools. The practice department includes the three lowest grades of the primary schools. The purpose of the course is to prepare pupils for *teaching*, not for any particular grade of school work. All vacancies occurring in the schools of the city are temporarily supplied by pupils from the Normal School.

INSTRUCTORS. — Alex. Forbes, Principal, Miss Julia E. Berger and Miss Kate E. Stephan, Critic Teachers.

THE SANDUSKY TRAINING SCHOOL.

The Sandusky Training School went into operation in September, 1873. It had its origin in the need of professional training for teachers. The means at the disposal of the Board of Education did not justify the expense incident to the establishment of a normal school. The city of Sandusky requires about seven new teachers per year, eighteen per cent. of the whole number employed. It was believed that by grouping these persons in one school, and placing them for a time under the direction of a skillful teacher, thoroughly competent to instruct in normal principles and methods, much of the evil of this change of teachers would be overcome.

Persons who are candidates for positions as teachers receive instruction for one year; they are then given positions as pupil-teachers at the nominal salary of fifteen dollars per month. At the end of one year's service as pupil-teachers, they receive a certificate stating the fact of their instruction in normal methods, etc. The salary of the normal teacher is paid with the difference between the salaries of the pupil-teachers and the average salary of the regular teachers.

After a trial of one year, the board employed an additional normal teacher, who has assisted in normal instruction and has had charge of the experimental department.

Graduates of the High School are preferred as candidates for the Training School, but others of good qualifications are accepted. The year of training is devoted to the study of methods and school management. The experimental school consists of the four lower grades of the public schools, located in a building apart from the other schools. Each pupil-teacher keeps her grade an entire year under the supervision of a general critic-teacher.

Persons who have finished the normal course of study are preferred in the appointment of teachers.

The names of the present teachers are Miss Alice Chenoweth, and Miss Hulda M. Gazlay.

CHAPTER VII.

TEACHERS' INSTITUTES.

Generous provision for the maintenance of a system of common schools has been made, at different times, by the General Assembly of Ohio, but legislative foresight has not provided adequate means and agencies for the professional training of teachers. Normal schools, fostered and sustained by state patronage, have never formed a part of the educational system of the State. Attempts have been made to remedy this radical defect. The history of their failure can be found in the chapter on Normal Schools. The imperative needs of some agencies by which all teachers, especially those who labor in the rural districts, could be made the recipients of instruction and training in matters pertaining to the responsible duties of their calling, led to the formation of teachers' associations, and finally to the employment of the Teachers' Institute as the best available aid in this kind of educational effort.

The first association of teachers for mutual improvement in the State was organized in Cincinnati in 1822. It was probably the second of the kind in the United States. It had but a brief existence, more than one-half of its fourteen members engaging in other pursuits or removing from the city within the year. In 1829, about twenty teachers organized "The Western Literary Institute and Board of Education" in that city. The first annual meeting was held in 1830. In 1831, this association assumed the title of "The Western Literary Institute and College of Professional

Teachers." The objects of the College, as stated in its published proceedings, were, "to promote the cause of education, to foster a spirit of intellectual culture and professional skill among its members, which will fit them for enlarged usefulness to themselves and their fellow-men, and to establish the name and character of a liberal profession." The plan proposed by which these objects were to be accomplished, was thus stated:

"It is contemplated by the College to form district associations, or school institutes, throughout the country, and to have delivered in them courses of lectures by persons appointed for the purpose, embracing subjects of a literary and practical nature, with appropriate illustrations of the most successful modes of teaching, and to lay before school committees, parents, and teachers, all the important information that can be collected from any source."

This association held annual meetings until 1845. It did not succeed in establishing a "school institute" in any county except Hamilton, in which an association was formed that met quarterly or oftener for many years; but, by its discussions and the publication of the addresses delivered at its annual meetings, it created a wide-spread sentiment in favor of liberal culture, and aroused public attention to the necessity of universal education in a republic. It was not a teachers' institute, as that term is now applied; but, as it showed the benefits and advantages that might be derived from combined action, and awakened an interest in professional education among teachers in various sections of the State, a history of teachers' institutes would be incomplete without a statement of the character and aim of the organization, and an allusion to the earnest efforts of those belonging to it to create and maintain an *esprit de corps* among the members of the profession in the West.

In the fall of 1853, a course of lectures and exercises, very similar in plan and method to that given for several succeeding years in county teachers' institutes, was given to the students of the Western Reserve Teachers' Seminary, at

Kirtland, Lake county, and to such teachers in the vicinity as chose to attend. The course was continued two weeks. The exercises were conducted by Dr. A. D. Lord, principal of the Seminary, assisted by the teachers associated with him in the management of that institution. A similar course was given at the close of the fall term in 1844—the time occupied being one week.

It is believed that these were all the efforts made previous to 1845, aside from the formation of teachers' classes in a few of the higher institutions of learning and the organization of a few local associations of teachers, to provide, in a practical way, for normal instruction. However inadequate these efforts may have been, and however far they may have fallen short of accomplishing the object intended, they had the effect, in many localities, to create a sentiment in favor of the improvement of the schools both in town and country, and to convince the more thoughtful that such improvement depended largely upon the employment of teachers trained in some manner to do their work intelligently. They thus prepared the way for the general adoption of the agency to which attention is called in this chapter.

COUNTY TEACHERS' INSTITUTES.

A County Teachers' Institute is an association composed principally of teachers resident in the same county, or it is a meeting held by such an association. The term is most frequently used in the latter sense. The organization of an institute is perfected by the adoption and signing of a constitution and the election of certain officers. The institute generally determines, in committee of the whole, the character and amount of the work to be undertaken, and quite frequently designates the course to be pursued in attempting to secure its accomplishment; but it is the usual practice to entrust the arrangement of details and the general management of business affairs to an executive committee. Annual sessions are now held in most counties, varying in length from four days to six weeks—four days being the legal minimum. Experienced educators are generally employed to conduct the exercises. They are assisted, in most instances, by teachers belonging to the association. During these sessions, the branches of studies pursued in the schools receive a partial review, methods of school management and discipline are discussed, and methods of instruction presented and elucidated. In the evening sessions, if any are held, popular scientific lectures are delivered, the relations, duties, and responsibilities of teachers, pupils, and patrons discussed, and the value and importance of education pressed upon public attention.

The first meeting of an association of this kind in Ohio, and perhaps in the West, was held in Sandusky, Erie county, in September, 1845. The exercises were conducted by Hon. Salem Town, of Ithaca, N. Y., assisted by Dr. A. D. Lord, principal of the Western Reserve Teachers' Seminary, and M. F. Cowdery, then an assistant teacher in the same institution. Hon. Ebenezer Lane, Rev. L. Howe, and other men of influence in Sandusky took an active part in the exercises. A marked interest was manifested in the proceedings, both by the teachers present and the citizens of Sandusky and vicinity. About one hundred teachers were in attendance. The second session was held in Chardon, Geauga county, in October, 1845. It was conducted by Dr. Lord, M. F. Cowdery, and M. D. Leggett. The number in attendance was one hundred and fifty. The leading citizens of the county regarded the institute with great favor, and expressed a desire that a similar session should be held the following spring. These two sessions are worthy of special notice, as they were the first successful attempts made in the State to awaken a permanent interest in normal instruction among the teachers of the common schools. They were experiments, and, doubtless, there were serious defects in their management; but their exercises were, in the main, exceedingly interesting and profitable. Those who conducted them were zealous and energetic, and their names soon became familiar to every well-informed teacher in the State.

In 1846, teachers' institutes were organized and sessions held in the counties of Ashtabula, Geauga, Lake, Lorain, Richland, Trumbull, and Warren. Two sessions were held in Geauga county, and two in Lake—one, in the latter county, under the auspices of the Western Reserve Teachers' Seminary. The number in attendance was, in the aggregate, about one thousand. In his report for the year 1846, Hon. Samuel Galloway, Secretary of State, and *ex-officio* Superintendent of Common Schools, in referring to these institutes, uses the following language:

> "Were this same instrumentality extensively adopted in Ohio, it would breathe the spirit of a new creation upon our common school system. These associations must tend to promote a professional spirit and independence—an enlarged view of the dignity and responsibility of the teacher's vocation—ambition to attain the highest standard of attainment which may be exhibited by any teacher—imitation of the best modes of instruction and discipline, and active co-operation in all that is calculated to promote general intelligence."

In 1847, institutes were held in the following counties: Ashland, Ashtabula, Delaware, Geauga, Hamilton, Lake, Medina, Summit, Stark, Trumbull, and Warren. Two institutes were held in Summit county, and the counties of Stark and Wayne held two joint institutes.

The State Teachers' Association was organized at Akron, Summit county, in December, 1847. The executive committee of this Association, in January, 1848, made conditional arrangements for holding institutes in one-half of the counties in the State the following spring. The propositions of the committee were accepted by the following counties: Ashland, Columbiana, Huron, Licking, Richland, Seneca, Stark, Washington, and Wayne. Institutes were held in them in March and April. Proposals were issued in the summer to hold an institute the succeeding autumn in any county where teachers and friends of education would co-operate with the committee. These proposals were accepted by the following counties, and institutes were held in them in the autumn: Ashtabula, Champaign, Huron, Medina, Miami, Montgomery, Portage, Sandusky, Seneca, and Washington. The number in attendance at these spring and autumn institutes was, in the aggregate, about fifteen hundred. The sessions were one week in length.

In January, 1848, the executive committee also issued proposals "for a course of lectures to teachers, on subjects immediately connected with their qualifications and duties, and the improvement of schools, to continue nine weeks, and be given in any county of the State where the friends of education would offer the most liberal inducements to the committee for the course." The offer from Huron county, pledging nearly five hundred dollars and the use of a suitable building, was deemed the most liberal, and the course was given at Norwalk in that county. Those employed to deliver the course, were M. F. Cowdery, Lorin Andrews, Prof. H. Mandeville, of Hamilton College, N. Y., Prof. St. John of Western Reserve College, Horace Benton, M. D. Leggett, I. J. Allen, J. Hurty, J. B. Howard, G. W. Winchester, and T. W. Harvey. Evening lectures were delivered by some of these gentlemen, and by others interested in the success of the enterprise. About one hundred and twenty persons attended the course. A similar course was given in Akron during the months of September and October. The class numbered about sixty. The exercises of both of these sessions were of unusual interest, and elicited expressions of approval from the citizens of the counties in which the courses of lectures were given, from those in attendance as students, and from the press.

The institutes held in 1845 and 1846 were sustained by the voluntary contributions of teachers and friends of public schools. The General Assembly of the State passed an act to encourage institutes, February 8, 1847. This act was applicable only to the counties of Ashtabula, Cuyahoga, Delaware, Erie, Geauga, Lake, Lorain, Medina, Portage, Summit, and Trumbull. By its provisions, the county commissioners of these counties were authorized, but not required, to appropriate for their encouragement "the annual avails or any part thereof" of the funds created by the investment of the excess over five per cent. of the interest received on each county's share of the United States surplus revenue fund, distributed to the several states in 1837. The amount appropriated was to be "paid over to and expended by the county examiners of the proper county, the one-half thereof, at least, to the payment of suitable persons as instructors and lecturers to such association, and the balance to the purchase and support of a suitable common school library for the use of such association." The benefits of the institutes were to be enjoyed, without charge for tuition, by all teachers of common schools in the county, and by any person intending to become a common school teacher within twelve months of the holding of a session.

This act was amended February 24, 1848, by providing that "all the money used under the provisions" of the act amended "in purchasing libraries, shall be used in purchasing suitable common school libraries" for the common school districts in the counties that were in possession of the funds named in that act. In 1847 and 1848, institutes were held in most of the counties to which the act was applicable, but the amount of money appropriated by county commissioners for their support can not be ascertained. It could not have been very large, however, for neither common school nor teachers' libraries are known to have been sustained in the counties designated during those years.

The failure of this act to accomplish the purpose intended,

led to the passage of an amendatory act, February 16, 1849. The county commissioners of the counties named above were authorized to appropriate an amount sufficient to make up the sum of one hundred dollars, whenever, for any cause, the avails of the funds designated in the act should be less than that sum. The appropriation was to be made from "any moneys in the county treasury, not otherwise appropriated." In case there should not be any moneys at the disposal of the commissioners, they were authorized to levy a tax for the purpose named. No part of the money appropriated could be paid over to the county examiners legally, except upon the petition of at least forty practical teachers, who should declare their intention to attend the institutes in their respective counties, and who were residents of the county in which the application was made. The payment and appropriation were to be approved and recommended by the board of examiners, and before any part of the appropriation could be legally paid over, a sum equal to at least one-half of the sum for which they petitioned was to be raised by the teachers.

The provisions of these acts were extended to all the counties in the State by an amendatory act passed February 24, 1849. A large number of institutes were held in 1840 and 1850. The number of teachers in attendance in 1850 was about 1500, but the attendance in 1849 can not be ascertained, as no reports were published.

An act supplementary to the acts mentioned above, was passed April 5, 1861. It provided that whenever a teachers' institute should be organized by the teachers of two or more contiguous counties, the county commissioners of each of those counties should be authorized to appropriate for its use a sum not exceeding one hundred dollars in any one year—the money appropriated to be paid over to the committee of the institute upon the petition of at least twenty practical teachers, residents of the county in which the appropriation was made. The officers of these joint institutes were required to report to the school examiners of the proper county, at the close of the session, the names of the teachers in attendance and the amount paid for the use of the institute, and to the State Commissioner of Common Schools, within thirty days thereafter, an account of the moneys received, the sources from which they were derived, how they were expended, and such other matters relating to the institute as he might require.

These acts were in force, without amendment, until 1864. In 1851, forty-one institutes were held, with an attendance of 3,251; in 1852, thirty-one, with an attendance of 2,824; in 1853, thirty-eight, with an attendance of 3,738; in 1854, forty-one, with an attendance of 2,288. The number attending in six counties was not reported in 1854. In 1855 and 1856, the State Commissioner made no report of statistics relating to institutes. The expenses of the sessions from 1845 to 1856, inclusive, are not given in any published reports. It is known, however, that during this period, institutes were sustained mainly by the voluntary contributions of teachers, the county commissioners of but few counties making any appropriations whatever for their encouragement. The following table shows the number of institutes held from 1857 to 1864 inclusive, the attendance, the expenses, and the sources from which funds for their support were derived:

YEAR.	No.	Attendance.	Expenses.	Amount received from		
				Counties.	Members.	Other sources.
1857	21	1,603	$2,099 00	$521	$1,569 00	$9 00
1858	18	1,829	2,327 00	325	1,968 00	34 00
1859	14	1,591	2,324 34	305	1,946 60	72 74
1860	19	1,294	2,444 50	500	1,856 50	87 75
1861	10	791	1,789 89	25	1,590 39	174 50
1864	22	1,689	2,253 95	......	1,783 75	470 20

In 1862 and 1863, the State Commissioner did not report institute statistics. The number of sessions held in each of these years was about twenty—the probable aggregate attendance in 1863, about one thousand. In 1864, the amount received from counties was included in that received from "other sources."

An act for the reorganization and maintenance of the common schools of the State, was passed March 14, 1853. An act amendatory thereof, passed March 4, 1864, provided that each male applicant for a certificate of qualifications to teach, should pay to the board of county examiners a fee of fifty cents, and each female applicant a fee of thirty-five cents. The moneys received were to be paid over quarterly to the county treasurer, with a statement of the number of applicants, male and female, examined. The balance which remained after paying the necessary traveling expenses of the examiners, was to be set apart as a fund for the support of teachers' institutes. No part of this fund could be legally disbursed except upon the petition of at least forty practical teachers, residents of the county, who should declare their intention to attend a session proposed to be held. The auditors and treasurers of the counties united were required to appropriate money from this fund for the support of a joint institute, upon the petition of at least thirty practical teachers. The officers of a joint institute were required to report to the State Commissioner only. This act was amended March 28, 1865. The amount to be drawn from the institute fund for the payment of the traveling expenses of county examiners in any one quarter, was limited to one-third of the amount collected and paid over by the board in that quarter, and the examination fee of female applicants for certificates was increased to fifty cents.

No essential changes were made in the laws respecting institutes from 1865 to 1873. The institute fund was sufficiently large, in most counties, to defray the necessary expenses of a session one week in length each year; but annual sessions were not held in all the counties, and they have not been held in some of them since institutes were first recognized by law as valuable aids in educational effort. In some counties, however, they were not only held annually, but were continued three or four weeks; in others, semi-annual sessions were held.

The school laws of the State were codified in 1873. The appropriations made by county commissioners had been so small—a large majority of these officials neglecting or refusing to make any appropriations whatever for institute purposes—that the law authorizing them was repealed. The new code recognized the value and importance of institute work by authorizing any public-school teacher to dismiss the school under his charge for the week during which an institute might be held, without forfeiture of wages, if at least four days of the week should be spent in attending the session. This privilege was not extended to teachers in a city district of the first-class—a district having a population of 10,000 or more—unless the consent of the board of education should be given, nor to teachers in a union or graded school, unless a majority of the teachers in the district should be in favor of such dismission. The act also provided that when no institute should be held in a county within two years, the State Commissioner might cause one to be held in such county; and he was authorized to defray the expenses of the session out of the county institute fund. The officers of an institute were required to give their bond for the faithful disbursement of the money to come into their hands, and for making a report to the State Commissioner, within thirty days after the close of the session, giving the number of teachers in attendance, the names of the instructors and lecturers, an account of the moneys received and expended, and such other information relating to the institute as might be required. The penalty for failure to report was fixed at fifty dollars, to be recovered in an action on this bond. This law is now in force.

The following table contains the statistics of institutes from 1865 to 1875 inclusive:

YEAR.	No.	Attendance.	Expenses.	Amount received from		
				Inst. Fund.	Members.	Other sources.
1865..........	26	1,652	$3,242 38	$1,241 93	$2,540 58	$343 32
1866..........	37	2,590	6,118 11	4,724 42	1,224 96	529 84
1867..........	45	3,619	8,563 86	6,031 21	2,675 86	894 25
1868..........	57	5,066	12,566 93	9,053 33	3,145 00	1,259 88
1869..........	97	6,301	10,369 33	7,191 06	2,769 66	888 40
1870..........	92	6,487	15,021 38	10,389 71	3,242 85	1,357 54
1871..........	69	7,158	14,423 78	10,127 13	2,730 34	2,051 50
1872..........	70	6,836	16,262 86	10,221 67	4,415 51	1,262 33
1873..........	65	6,340	12,590 72	9,925 97	2,248 75	764 44
1874..........	78	8,579	15,318 81	11,792 16	3,332 33	699 41
1875..........	92	10,125	18,988 79	16,097 75	2,204 49	593 05

The laws to which reference has heretofore been made, were applicable only to county teachers' institutes. Besides these, institutes organized and sustained by township and other local associations have occasionally been held in different sections of the State. These have rarely continued longer than two days—the usual practice being to limit the exercises to what may be accomplished in a single day. No statistics relating to these local institutes have been published in any official reports; but enough is known of them and their proceedings to warrant the assertion that they have been important auxiliaries to the officially recognized organizations for normal work. They have usually been conducted by prominent teachers in the locality, though quite frequently lectures on subjects of general interest, by leading educators, professors in colleges, or gentlemen of culture belonging to other professions, have formed a part of their exercises. Most generally, however, the time has been spent in discussing methods of instruction in the branches of study pursued in the schools, and in the consideration of ways and means best calculated to secure the most desirable results in the management and discipline of ungraded schools.

At the close of the fall terms of some academical institutions, a week has been devoted to addresses on educational topics, lectures on the theory and practice of teaching, and reviews of studies. The principals of these schools, assisted by their associates, have usually conducted the exercises or taken a lively interest in them—quite frequently assuming the entire responsibility of their management, neither asking nor receiving any compensation for their services. Teachers residing in the vicinity of these institutions have been invited to avail themselves of the advantages and privileges of these sessions.

CITY AND GRADED-SCHOOL INSTITUTES.

In the laws relating to county teachers' institutes, there were no special provisions for the support of institutes in cities, or for joint institutes for graded schools. The more intelligent members of city boards of education, however, were led, at an early date in the history of graded schools, to think that valuable results would follow the holding of city institutes during the first week of the school year. The first institutes of this kind were held in Cincinnati and Cleveland. At the commencement of the fall term of the public schools of Cincinnati, in 1866, all the teachers employed in them spent a week in listening to the suggestions of the superintendent and principals respecting methods of instruction and management, and the details of work required during the school year, and in such other exercises as were thought profitable. The experiment was so successful, that since 1866 the first week of the school year has been devoted by the Cincinnati teachers to work of a similar character. Eminent educators and noted teachers of special branches have been employed to assist the superintendent in giving instruction.

In 1867, the Board of Education of the city of Cleveland made arrangements to hold an institute at the commencement of the fall term of the city schools. The results were so marked and valuable, that the institute has been continued as a feature of the city school system. At first, much of the instruction was given by those who had won enviable reputations as teachers in other cities or schools; but for the past few years, the superintendent has been assisted only by those employed as teachers or principals in the schools under his charge.

Cities of smaller size than Cincinnati and Cleveland have held city institutes, usually, if not always, during the first week of the school year. It is believed that no generous, well-informed patron has objected to this disposition of the time that would otherwise have been spent in practical school work, although the wages of teachers have been paid for the week spent in the institute, and the expenses of each sesssion have been defrayed from city school funds.

In the spring of 1870, the North-eastern Ohio Teachers' Association recommended a course of study for adoption by the boards of education of the cities and towns represented in the Association. This course was the matured result of careful deliberation, and the recommendation for its adoption was received with favor. Boards of education soon modified their courses of study—in no instance, perhaps, adopting the course recommended as a whole, but making such slight changes in it as seemed desirable—so that throughout north-eastern Ohio the grading of the schools and the courses of study pursued in them were essentially the same. It seemed very desirable that the teachers in the different grades should know what they were expected to accomplish each term, and that they should be instructed in the use of methods best calculated to produce the most satisfactory results. An arrangement was therefore made by the Association to hold a union graded-school institute in Cleveland during the last week of the summer vacation in 1870 and the first week of the coming school year. At the commencement of the session, the teachers were divided into classes—four of these composed of teachers in primary and grammar school grades, and four of teachers in high schools. The work of each grade was thoroughly and systematically presented, much attention being given to the elucidation of methods. The expenses were borne by the boards of education interested. A detailed report of this institute was published in the report of the State Commissioner of Common Schools for the year 1870.

The success of these attempts to provide a substitute for systematic normal instruction for teachers in graded schools, occasioned the insertion of two important sections in the school code of 1873. Section 118 provides that the board of education of any city district of the first class may make provision for holding annually an institute, to continue not less than four days, for the improvement of the teachers under its control. The expenses are to be paid out of the city institute fund or other city school funds. The institute fund is created by requiring each applicant for a certificate of qualifications to teach in the schools of the city to pay a fee of fifty cents. Section 119 provides that, "whenever a teachers' association, formed for the professional improvement of the teachers of several adjacent counties, shall organize a teachers' institute for the specific purpose of providing for the professional instruction of the teachers of the graded schools in those counties, any and all boards of education of city districts of the first and second class, village districts, and special districts within said counties, shall have power to contribute to such institutes from the institute and other funds under their control, and to permit the teachers employed by them to attend the same for one week without forfeiture of wages." The Cleveland experiment has not been repeated; but it is to be hoped that it will be repeated, in the near future, in various sections of the State.

REMARKS.

The most active and enthusiastic workers in teachers' institutes have felt from the first the needs of some legislation by which the value and efficiency of these educational helps may be increased, and the sphere of their usefulness enlarged. The impossibility of securing the services of experienced instructors and lecturers has, in many instances, prevented the holding of sessions at times convenient for teachers, and occasionally the exercises have not been of such a character as to be of much benefit to teachers in ungraded schools. The State Commissioner has frequently not been able to attend even one-half of the institutes held during his term of office—many of them being held simultaneously, and those succeeding each other being located at points widely separated. Their exercises have not been thoroughly classified and systematized, and all attempts to secure uniformity of method in their conduct have been futile. Quite frequently, valuable time has been consumed in arranging a programme or in the discussion of irrelevant matters.

Various plans have been suggested to remedy these defects. In 1864, the State Commissioner was requested by the State Teachers' Association, at the annual meeting, to select one or more men, thoroughly competent to conduct institutes, who should devote themselves to the work of their organization and management. In his report to the General Assembly, the Commissioner stated that he could not find any competent person who was willing to undertake the work and depend wholly upon institutes for support. He therefore recommended that an appropriation be made to aid in supporting a corps of institute instructors. It was thought that $3,000, in connection with the sum available from the institute fund, would keep three able and efficient educators constantly in the field. The appropriation was not made. The recommendation was repeated in the report for 1865, and in several subsequent reports; but an institute corps has not yet been appointed, neither has the General Assembly ever made any direct appropriation to encourage this the only agency employed in the State, under the sanction of law, for the professional training of teachers.

CHAPTER VIII.

SCHOOL SUPERVISION.

This subject will be treated under the following heads:

1. State Supervision.
2. County Supervision.
3. City and Town Supervision.*

STATE SUPERVISION.

It may justly be said, that in the year 1837 common school education in the United States took a new departure. In that year, there entered upon the discharge of the important duties of superintendent of education in two states, two remarkable men. On the 31st of March, Samuel Lewis was elected by the legislature, Superintendent of Common Schools for Ohio, an office created four days before; and on the 29th of June following, Horace Mann was elected Secretary of the Massachusetts Board of Education. Though Massachusetts may rightly claim for herself the larger part of the honors of her great son, it has been the happy fortune of Ohio to possess exclusively as her own the fame and good works of Samuel Lewis, and to divide with her sister state the glory of Horace Mann's great fame.

---

*Although "Township Supervision" has been authorized ever since the passage of the law of 1853, if not longer, it has not been thought necessary to enter upon any history of it in a sketch so brief as this, and with so few facts in possession. It will be sufficient to say, in a note, that township boards have still the same authority to employ a superintendent of schools that the boards of cities and towns possess. This authority has, however, been exercised only to a very limited extent, but, where it has, so far as results have been reported, they have been, in almost every case, highly favorable to the success of the scheme.

Both men, although of diverse characteristics, had extraordinary qualifications for the work upon which they were about to enter. Both possessed an untiring energy, and both were prompted by an intense enthusiasm in the cause of the education of the whole people. Though the qualities of their minds were so different, they were both powerful and persuasive speakers. Mr. Mann had every advantage in the way of education and general culture, and these advantages he improved with the happiest results. His spirit was fiery, and he was filled with an unquailing, aggressive courage. His eloquence possessed the highest attributes of oratorical style, and he put into it all the best qualities of his heart and mind. He did not so much seek to convince by his logic, as to stimulate to noble deeds by constantly bearing aloft a standard of true manhood. No wrong could so securely intrench itself as to withstand the vehement tide of his indignant denunciation, and his scorn for mean thinking and doing was withering. He showed Massachusetts, the earliest home of the American common school, how miserably inadequate were the notions of her people as to the true scope of an education that should equal the exigencies of American citizenship. He showed that education, to be of any great worth, must include more than reading, writing, arithmetic, and geography; that it must transcend all mere text-book lore, and have a moral side to it, incomparably more important than the intellectual.

Samuel Lewis enjoyed none of the educational advantages of his eminent co-laborer, his school training having ended before he was ten years old. Otherwise, he was possessed of an excellent capital with which to begin life—a healthy mind of great original power and a thoroughly sound moral nature. He was essentially a man of the people, self-made and well-made. He was a born orator, naturally possessing those traits of mind which enable a speaker to convince and move the people. If the true standard of eloquence is what it accomplishes, then he might well have taken his place among orators of the highest rank. Less impassioned than Mann, he was not less earnest; less vehement, he was not less courageous; possessing less beauty and elevation of literary style, he was not less convincing and persuasive—nay, his very simplicity was inwrought with a wondrous power, and was far more effective with the people among whom he labored, than would have been the most finished rhetoric. In addition to these great qualities, his keenness of practical insight has seldom been surpassed.

Before his election to the superintendency, Mr. Lewis had been well known for the valuable work he had done in the cause of education in various directions. He had made several addresses before the Western College of Teachers, which were characterized by their practical features. He was also instrumental, as the trusted friend of William Woodward, of Cincinnati, in obtaining from him, for the benefit of poor youth, that large bequest upon which Woodward College was founded, and which is now a part of the consolidated fund used for the support of the Cincinnati High Schools. In all his educational enterprises, Mr. Lewis had the hearty sympathy and active co-operation of Nathan Guilford, the author of the school law of 1825, and to whose zeal Ohio is so much indebted for the wise and stable foundation of her common school system. But it was Alfred Kelly, a man eminent as a legislator, and of the very highest capacity in business affairs, who first introduced into the General Assembly a resolution instructing the committee on common schools to inquire into the expediency of creating the office of Superintendent of Common Schools.

The duties of the State Superintendent seem not to have been fixed by statute when Mr. Lewis first entered upon the discharge of the duties of the office, but, by the law of 1838, they were defined as follows:

"1. To collect and report annually to the Legislature, information upon the common schools of the State, especially the whole number of children and their attendance at school; the number, quality, and duration of schools; the qualification of teachers, and the amount paid for their wages; the number of school-houses and the expenditure therefor; the sources and condition of school funds; and whatever else he might suppose the public interest required.

"2. To ascertain and report the condition and value of all the school lands in the State, with the amount of the different school funds due to each township from lands or interest; and to secure the immediate location of school lands as authorized by an act of Congress passed May 20, 1826, entitled "an act to appropriate lands for the support of schools in certain townships and fractional townships not before provided for."

"3. To furnish suitable forms to school officers and teachers for all returns and registers required by law, and to deliver, on the 15th of December annually, to the Auditor of the State, an enumeration of all the white children between the age of four and twenty-one years, to serve as the basis of the apportionment of school funds according to law.

"4. To take an account of all funds and property given in any way for the support of education, and report the same annually to the Legislature; and for this purpose, to exercise all needful rights of visitation, and to summon the interposition of the prosecuting attorneys of the counties.

"5. To publish bi-monthly during the year 1838–9, an official school journal, called the "Ohio Common School Director.'" *

He made his first official report to the legislature, in January, 1838. In this report he gives an account of his labors, and sets forth his views on the whole subject of common school education. His work was severe enough. Almost all his journeying was done on horseback, most of it over bad roads and through a sparsely settled country. After averaging twenty-six miles per day of travel, he spent, as he tells us in one of his letters, three or four hours a day in conversation on school matters, and frequently spoke, in addition to all this, at night. Much of his work, too, was done with the drawback of impaired health. Everywhere, as he

*Taylor's Ohio School System, page 188.

says, men agreed with him, applauded his speeches, but did nothing. The first year of his superintendency he traveled more than 1,500 miles, and visited three hundred schools and forty county seats. Much time and zeal were also devoted to the organization of associations of teachers.

In reading over his reports, one is surprised at the breadth and comprehensiveness of the views entertained by this pioneer in western education. Nothing seemed to escape his attention; and almost all the plans for the improvement of common schools, since advocated, were distinctly enunciated by him.

Mr. Lewis's sympathies were always with the poor, and he heartily enlisted in the scheme of establishing a system of schools which should give their children a fair chance in life with the children of the rich. He was utterly opposed to the idea of having one kind of education for those favored by fortune and another kind for those who earn their bread by the sweat of the brow. He labored not only to make the schools entirely free, but to make them good enough for all. "For," said he, "a school not good enough for the rich will never excite much interest with the poor. They will receive its benefits, if at all, with jealousy; and the effect will be to build still higher the wall that separates the sympathies of different classes of society."

Like Horace Mann, Mr. Lewis placed high among the functions of the common school the duty of instructing youth in sound principles of Christian morality. He seemed, too, to have little faith in the final success of the schools, unless teaching was made a profession.

He advocated such an education for women "as would be adapted to their sphere in life, and be likely to elevate their views, refine their tastes, and cultivate that delicacy of sentiment and propriety of conduct, which the good of the country, no less than their own happiness requires." He recommended the appointment of county superintendents to look after school property, to visit all the districts, examine teachers, and settle controversies. He recognized, also, the value of libraries as instrumentalities for educating the people, and recommended the establishment of a free library in every township, the State giving a certain amount on condition that the township should raise an equal sum. He pointed out, too, the advantages of union graded schools for towns and cities, years before anything of the kind had been attempted in the State outside of Cincinnati; and township high schools were one of his favorite measures for promoting educational progress.

His eye seemed to cover the whole field. He was not satisfied to restrict his attention to the organization of a school system, and the furnishing of the necessary means for carrying it into operation. Methods of instruction did not escape his animadversion. He condemned most forcibly that exclusive reliance on the memory, to the neglect of the cultivation of the reasoning powers, then almost universal with teachers in all classes of schools.

Finally, Mr. Lewis still further exhibited the breadth and comprehension of his educational views by his advocacy of a State University and a State Normal School.

Though the energy, the eloquence, and the rare good sense of Mr. Lewis were not wasted on the people, but were the good seed which have germinated into what is best in our school system, they failed to move the average legislator of his time, either into enthusiasm or liberality. He could not conquer those three formidable foes of progress, avarice, ignorance, and the small politician. He labored still harder, if possible, the second year than the first, but the opposition to the school law of 1838 (chiefly the work of his own hands), and to the superintendency, was growing, though a resolution, introduced into the legislature in this year of his administration to abolish his office, failed.

In his third annual report, December 13, 1839, the Superintendent, though he had been elected for five years, announced his determination to retire from all official connection with the schools. He had gone into the office on a salary of $500, which was increased by the law of 1838 to $1,200. It took his whole salary, as he informs us, to pay his expenses, leaving him nothing for his labor, for which, indeed, nothing was expected. After Mr. Lewis's retirement there was much wrangling over the question of continuing the office, in both the Senate and the House, which finally ended, March 23, 1840, in merging it with that of Secretary of State.

Mr. Lewis left the office with high honor. By his investigations of the management of school lands, he had saved enough money to the State to pay his salary many times over—indeed, his friends claimed that $60,000 had been thus secured. The number of schools during his three years of service had risen from 4,336 to 7,295; the number of scholars from 150,402 to 254,612; the amount paid for tuition from $317,730 to $701,091; and the cost of school-houses from $61,890 to $206,445.

Immediately on Mr. Lewis's retirement from office, the interest in common schools began to abate. The Secretaries of State who followed him, and upon whom the duties of superintendent devolved, were generally able men, and manifested a large interest in the people's schools. But it could not be expected that they could, with their other duties pressing upon them, do much more than to urge upon the legislature such measures as would carry out Mr. Lewis's great designs.

Secretary Trevitt advocated the establishment of normal schools; and Secretary Sloane recommended, for the purpose of forming a nucleus for a free library in each township of the State, the purchase of the "School Library," a work of 35 volumes published under the auspices of the Board of Education of Massachusetts. But the interval of 1839 to

1845 was a gloomy one for the schools, their decline during this period being fearfully rapid. In the election, in 1844, of Samuel Galloway to the office of Secretary, the State secured the services of a man of immense activity and enthusiasm. He fully realized the importance of that part of of his duties involved in the superintendence of the common schools. He thus speaks of the condition of those schools in his first annual report, January 15, 1845 :

"No other interest of the State has been so fearfully neglected; and any other visited with such chilling indifference, would have hopelessly perished. The common school system was started under favorable auspices, and enjoyed, during the earlier stages of its infancy, the kind protection of 'nursing fathers and nursing mothers,' but, for a a few years past, it has been doomed to an orphanage—gradually deepening in the bitterness of its destitution. Contemned by many, neglected by all, and actively patronized by but few, it must sink into insignificance, unless it is speedily quickened by the impulses of a new life, and be enabled to manifest its proper value and power, in the utility and splendor of its achievements."

Secretary Galloway, "recognizing the need of an educational revival, determined to employ all the legitimate agencies of his office in its accomplishment. He was ably seconded by influential men in various parts of the State, and was most creditably successful. He conducted a widespread correspondence, attended educational meetings, delivered public addresses, sent circulars to county auditors and other local school officers, and reported to the legislature for 1845 a more prosperous condition of the public schools than had been exhibited in any previous year, excepting 1839."*

Throughout the whole of his six years of the secretaryship, he remained the active and earnest friend of the schools, not sparing himself in his efforts to bring them up to a higher standard of efficiency. That these labors were productive of great results, is within the knowledge of all

*Taylor's Ohio School System, p. 356.

acquainted with the school history of the period. Educators caught the infection of his fiery zeal, and educational activity manifested itself throughout the State, and in various ways.

It was, however, deeply impressed upon the teachers of Ohio that the best results of the school system were not to be reached until that system should have a man at its head who should devote his time and energies exclusively to its interests. To this end, they urged upon the legislature, time and again, the restoration of the office of superintendent; and were ably supported in their efforts by the several Secretaries of State. After years of waiting, they abandoned all hope of legislative aid, and determined themselves to take up the burden the State should have borne. The State Teachers' Association in December, 1850, resolved to put an agent in the field to remedy, as far as might be, the dereliction of the State. In Lorin Andrews, then superintendent of the schools of Massillon, the Association found a man with the earnest missionary spirit, the clear head, unfaltering courage, and sympathetic power to move the people, necessary to make the enterprise a success. Mr. Andrews entered upon his work at once, directing his labors chiefly to the extension of the union graded school system, and the establishment and conduct of teachers' institutes; in both of which interprises he was eminently successful. After three years' service, he resigned his position, and was succeeded by Dr. A. D. Lord of Columbus, who added the duties of state agent of the Association to those of editor of the Journal of Education. Dr. Lord filled the place acceptably for one year. The salaries of both these gentlemen—which were quite liberal for the times—were paid by a tax imposed upon the teachers by themselves.

It is not deemed necessary to advert with special emphasis to the act passed the 22nd of March, 1850, for the creation of a State Board of Public Instruction. This act provided for a board, to consist of five members, to hold their offices for one, two, three, four, and five years respectively—one to be styled the State Superintendent of Common Schools, to act as chairman of the board, reside and keep his office at the seat of government, and perform the usual duties of such an officer; the others to be styled District Superintendents, and one in each year to act as State Superintendent by rotation. This was one of the wisest acts ever adopted by the General Assembly in the way of school legislation, but it was passed so late in the session that no appointments were made, as prescribed by the act, and for that reason it never went into operation. If the appointments had been made, and the law executed in a wise and liberal spirit, it is not too much to say the Ohio school system would have stood among the foremost of the country.

The school law of 1853 renewed the office of State Superintendent of Schools, under the title of State School Commissioner, and Mr. H. H. Barney of Cincinnati, was elected to the office in the fall of the same year.

Mr. Barney was largely occupied, during his administration, in executive work, and in explaining for the benefit of school officers the meaning of the new law and the best methods of executing it, giving special consideration to those features of the law which differed from those of preceding acts. Of these, district school libraries were the most important, and gave most care. The distribution of good books over the whole State is an object of importance as an educational agency second only to the schools themselves. That district school libraries did much good can not be questioned; but had the law provided for township libraries instead, as recommended by Samuel Lewis, there can be but little doubt that the results would have been far more satisfactory, and the permanency of the law have been secured. No adequate provision was made under the law for taking care of the books, and the few that came to the rural sub-districts one year, were scattered and gone by the time the next year's supply came to hand. This arose from the difficulty of finding a suitable place in each sub-district for a library, and a qualified person to take charge of it. In addition to this, many of the books were never called for at the office of the county auditors, and others remained unused in the hands of the township clerks. The fate of this feature of the law, with all these defects and difficulties hanging about it, notwithstanding its excellent design, was preordained. Mr. Barney decided, at an early period in his administration, that the books for cities, might be collected into one library, instead of being scattered among the several districts. Boards acting on this wise decision, then formed collections of books, that have been the foundation for those noble institutions in cities, called public libraries, and which are doing so much for the culture of the people.

Not long after Mr. Barney had entered upon the duties of his office, decided hostility began to exhibit itself in the legislature against many of the most valuable features of the new law, the commissionership among them. He was indefatigable in his efforts to prevent the passage of any amendment that would embarrass the successful working of the act. In these efforts, with the aid of educators, and the petitions of the people from all parts of the State that the law should be left untouched, he was completely successful.

By the time Mr. Barney had fairly established himself in his new position, he had so far secured the confidence of educators in his ability and prudence, that the agent of the State Teachers' Association was withdrawn from the field, as being no longer necessary to the interests of the schools.

Rev. Anson Smyth, the successor of Mr. Barney (1856–62), devoted much time and attention to the selection of books for the school libraries (a very delicate task, requiring much judgment and literary culture), and to their distribution. But, notwithstanding his endeavors in this direction, the legislature, after suspending the law providing a tax for library purposes, and then restoring it for a year, finally repealed it altogether. He advocated normal schools, and pressed the importance of teachers' institutes upon the attention of educators. But, while believing one of the greatest defects of our educational system to be the want of a more thorough supervision of the schools, and that the election of county superintendents would be the most practical way of supplying this want, he had doubts whether the difficulties of securing competent persons to fill the office and of keeping the selection out of party politics, were not altogether insurmountable.

During his term of office Commissioner Smyth entered into a correspondence with leading educators and other prominent citizens throughout the country, inquiring as to their views on the propriety and feasibility of connecting military instruction with the public school system. A majority of the correspondents seemed favorable to the undertaking. Without expressing a decided opinion of his own, the Commissioner was inclined to favor the giving of such instruction in the schools of the cities and large towns. But, except in a few schools, nothing was attempted, or, if attempted, persevered in for any considerable time.

Mr. Smyth favored restricting pupils to a much more limited number of studies than was then imposed on them in most schools; and in the last year of his term, he attempted by correspondence to ascertain the opinions of educators on the subject. As was to have been anticipated, their answers disclosed a wide diversity of views. The discussion was one of great interest, involving as it did to a very large extent the whole philosophy of education; but the movement resulted in no important modification of courses of study anywhere.

Mr. C. W. H. Cathcart, of Dayton, who was elected State Commissioner in 1862, resigned his office after occupying it nine months, and made no report of his work. Governor Tod appointed Mr. E. E. White of Columbus, to fill the unexpired term. Mr. White entered upon the discharge of his duties November 11, 1863, at a time when the schools were greatly affected by the war then raging. A large number of teachers had been drawn by patriotic impulses from their school-rooms to the field, and their places had necessarily to be filled by teachers of less ability and experience. The levies, too, for school purposes for the year 1863, in consequence of the generally disturbed condition of the public mind, had been made very low, and the poorer districts were much hampered for want of funds. The new Commissioner at once set to work to restore the schools, as far as practicable, to their former prosperous condition. He showed in his first annual report, that while the youth of school age had increased but 14 per cent. in the decade from 1853 to 1863, the number of scholars enrolled, the amount paid to teachers, the number of schools, and the value of school-houses had more than doubled, which, as he rightly concluded, showed the growing efficiency and popularity of the school system.

One act of legislation, secured by Mr. White, has exerted a very important influence on the schools of the State. It is the one which makes provision for a reliable institute fund. This is done by requiring each candidate for a teacher's certificate to pay for institute use a fee of fifty cents for the privilege of an examination. This fund has enabled the teachers of the several counties to engage for their improvement in their profession, for a short time each year, the services of some one or more of the most eminent educators of the country.

Another valuable act of legislation secured through his influence, was the creation of the State Board of Examiners, with the power to issue life certificates to teachers of eminent attainments and success in their vocation—an important step towards making teaching a profession.

In his second annual report made to the Governor, December 17, 1864, the Commissioner urged, with great force, the supreme importance of a thorough supervision of school work, stating that one-half of the great outlay for schools was "turned in unskillful hands into ashes instead of blessings." His conclusion, after a thorough discussion of the subject, was that the most feasible and efficient plan for such supervision for country schools is that of county superintendents. He also discussed the true object of the "land grant" by Congress, "donating lands to the several colleges for the benefit of agriculture and the mechanic arts," and came to the conclusion that the design of the grant was to secure for the students of the colleges founded on it "a scheme of instruction sufficiently wide and extensive to fill the full measure of a 'liberal' as well as a professional education, but that the former should be subordinated to the latter." He thought, also, that a normal department for the training of teachers would be a legitimate department for an industrial college; "for in what other way," he remarks, "can the practical education of the industrial classes be better promoted than by making the instruction of our common schools more practical?" He deemed the time especially favorable for the establishment in the State of one or more normal schools or normal departments of high order.

In accordance with a joint resolution, passed by the General Assembly March 13, 1865, Mr. White presented an able report the following winter on the subject of "the best results of normal schools in this country, and so far as practicable, in other countries, and the best plan of organizing one or more efficient normal schools in this State." This report was the closing work of his administration.

Mr. White's successor was Mr. John A. Norris, of Harrison

county. Mr. Norris was one of the many teachers who had proved themselves patriotic and gallant soldiers. He entered upon the discharge of his duties in February, 1866, served three years and was re-elected for a second term, but resigned June 25, 1869, and was succeeded by Mr. W. D. Henkle, who was appointed by Gov. Hayes to fill the vacancy. As Mr. Norris's labors as Commissioner were chiefly directed to the establishment of county supervision, his administration will be treated of under that head.

Mr. Henkle largely devoted himself to the work of preparing a codified school bill—a very laborious and important work. He did not succeed in getting this bill through the legislature, but it is substantially the same as the law of 1873. Mr. Henkle also continued the recommendation of his predecessors in favor of county supervision and normal schools, but without securing any legislation upon either. He resigned his office shortly before the close of his term, and was succeeded by Mr. T. W. Harvey, who had just been elected Commissioner by the people.

Commissioner Harvey recommended to the General Assembly, in his first annual report, "the organization and appointment of a Board of Institute Managers, consisting of not less than four experienced, practical teachers, whose sole business shall be the organization and management of district and county institutes." The district institutes which he recommended were to be co-extensive with the judicial districts of the State, and were to hold an annual session of not less than six weeks. The best teachers were to assist this board in conducting their exercises. The Commissioner believed that these district institutes would be attended by the most intelligent teachers of the district, who would go thence as educational missionaries. Neither of these excellent recommendations received any attention from the General Assembly.

Mr. Harvey also advocated in his second report (1872) the

introduction of drawing into the public schools, as a branch of instruction essential to the skillful mechanic. He said: "Our native artisans have a right to complain of the indifference of our legislators and school officials to their interests, when they see workmen trained in foreign countries occupying the best places in our workshops and factories, and our public buildings planned by foreign architects and erected under their supervision."

During the third year of Mr. Harvey's administration was passed the codified school bill, which had long been in preparation, and which is known as the act of 1873. Though this bill did not embrace many features not in the law of 1853 and its amendments, it did much to simplify and render more certain the administration of school affairs. That provision, however, which divorced boards of education in city districts of the first class from all connection with the municipal legislature of such cities, must be regarded as one having an important bearing on the management of schools.

It will be seen from this very condensed history of the work of state supervision in Ohio, what the duties of State School Commissioner are, and how broad and all-embracing the labors of the men who have held the office have been. By their printed discussions, by their addresses to the people in so many localities, by their services in teachers' institutes, by their influence on legislative action, and by their aid in unifying and directing the thought and energies of the vast body of educators of the State, they have been a great power in forming and building up the common school system. In the more restricted sense of the term, they can scarcely be called superintendents at all. They have occupied more the position of a general-in-chief, who surveys the whole field, watches the varying tide of the conflict, and directs his forces, whether for attack or defense, to the points where they are most needed. Thus far their forces have all been volunteers, over whom they possessed none but a moral authority, but volunteers who have never failed to respond with alacrity to any call that has been made upon them.

In the capacity of the judge who explains and applies the law, their services have been hardly less valuable than in the particulars above mentioned. By their labors in this direction, confusion has been superseded by order, and an ignorant, narrow management of school affairs, by one comparatively intelligent and liberal.

COUNTY SUPERVISION.

As has already been stated, county supervision was recommended by Samuel Lewis in his first report, made to the legislature in 1838, and this recommendation has received the hearty approval of all his successors in office, with perhaps a single exception. It has also been recommended by Secretaries of State in their school reports, and by Governors in their annual messages, but as yet the legislature has failed to take any action in the matter, if we may except the legislation of February, 1847, which authorized county commissioners to create the separate office of superintendent of common schools within their jurisdiction. In the event of the establishment of that office, the clerks of the school districts in the county were constituted a body of electors, and might select said superintendent, whose duties were to be as follows: "To act as *ex-officio* chairman of the board of school examiners, his signature being made necessary to the validity of every certificate; to renew, at his discretion, the certificates of teachers who had been personally examined by the board, and with the concurrence of one of said board of school examiners, to annul the certificate of any teacher who might prove incompetent in respect to learning, ability to teach, or moral character; to visit and examine all the schools in the county, and keep a full record of such visits and examinations; to meet and address the people in the several school districts and townships on the subject of education; to encourage the formation of township and county educational societies, and teachers' associations; and to transmit to the State Superintendent at Columbus an abstract of his transactions, and a statistical report similar to that required from the county auditor. His compensation was at the option of the county commissioners."*

The law was at first local, but its provisions were soon afterwards extended to the whole State. Only three counties—Ashtabula, Clermont, and Sandusky†—are known to have established the office, although it is quite possible that one or two others may have attempted a trial of the scheme. The best results from the experiment were reported from these counties.

After the failure of this law, educators continued to petition and teachers' associations to memorialize the legislature in behalf of a measure which they deemed of vital importance to the school system. In the winter of 1858, Senator Canfield, of Medina county, a warm friend of educational progress, introduced into the Senate a bill providing for county superintendents, and prescribing the duties of the office. Under this bill, the superintendents were to be appointed by three county officers, and their salary to be fixed by the county commissioners. The bill, after being referred, was not reported back to the Senate, and, as a consequence went over to the following winter's session. Possibly it might have been passed, had not the State Teachers' Association, to which body the bill, at the special request of its mover, had been referred for discussion at its meeting at Delaware, in the summer of 1858, expressed a preference for district

* Taylor's Ohio School System, p. 197.

† Mr. Taylor says Ashtabula was the only county, but in this statement, notwithstanding his general accuracy, he is certainly at fault.

superintendents, through a report presented by Mr. John Lynch. The Association very effectually blocked the way of any action by the legislature by adopting the following preamble and resolution:

"WHEREAS, At the request of Senator Canfield, the bill for the appointment of county superintendents, presented by him to the Senate during the last session of the legislature, has been considered by this Association, and in the opinion thereof, it is not expedient at this time that said bill should become a law; therefore,

Resovled, That a committee of three, empowered to represent this Association, be appointed by the chair to confer with the committee of the legislature on the question involved."

The three members appointed on the committee were the three who had expressed most decided dissent to the bill, and, of course, nothing came of their conference with the committee of the legislature, if such a conference was ever held. The bill had its faults, but if it had been adopted, it is probable that its defects would soon have been corrected, and we should have had in successful operation a measure for which the friends of education unavailingly continued to struggle for the subsequent eighteen years.

On the accession of Mr. Norris to the office of State Commissioner, in 1866, he at once bent his energies to the work of securing legislation in favor of county supervision. In his first annual report, he discussed the subject in a very thorough manner, quoting the views of his predecessors in office in support of his position. He also fortified that position by citing the favorable opinions of other educators from every part of the country.

At the meeting of the State Teachers' Association, held at Zanesville, July, 1866, the subjects of normal schools and county superintendency were discussed very fully, without a dissenting voice as to the importance of both measures. At a subsequent meeting of school superintendents, held at Columbus, during the same year, that body decided in favor of concentrating educational effort and influence to secure county supervision first; for it was claimed by those who preferred this measure that its workings would tend, in the very nature of things, to open up the way for the establishment of normal schools. The Commissioner, therefore, was assured of the aid and sympathy of the great body of teachers of the State. Mr. Norris, like his predecessors in office, deprecated the introduction of partizan politics into any school measure; and this, too, when the party which had elected him was largely in the ascendant. His words were:

"No true friend of our common schools, or wise conservator of social tranquillity, would, for one moment, consent to the adoption of any measure that would entangle school interests with party contests. The interests of our schools are paramount to the interests in ordinary party issues. School men have no right, therefore, to endanger these interests by becoming propagandists of party dogmas."

To avoid the introduction of party politics in the selection of county superintendents, he presented the following plan* for their election:

"Let the county superintendent in each county be chosen by a convention composed of the chairman or president of the several boards of education interested, two-thirds of all such officers being necessary to form a quorum for the transaction of business, and a majority of such quorum being necessary to a choice; and let such superintendent be removable for immorality, inefficiency, or gross neglect of duty, by a two-thirds vote of all the chairmen named. Furthermore, as is the case with other teachers or superfntendents of schools, let no candidate for the position be eligible unless he is able to obtain a certificate of qualifications for the discharge of the duties of his office from some competent and impartial board of examiners."

The board of examiners afterward designated in the bill framed by Mr. Norris, was the State Board of Examiners. In case of failure to obtain such a certificate, or in case of a vacancy in the office, the State School Commissioner was required to call a meeting of the presidents of boards of

*This plan is substantially the same as the one recommended by Commissioner White in 1864.

education to elect another person to act as superintendent. In case the presidents of boards of education should fail or refuse to elect a county superintendent, the State Commissioner was to appoint, the appointee to hold the office until the succeeding annual election. In counties having less than six thousand youth of school age, the superintendent was to receive an annual salary of $1,200; and in counties having more than six thousand youth of school age, he was to receive $100 additional for each one thousand enumerated youth above six thousand, until the salary should reach $2,000, which was to be the maximum.

The bill was introduced into the House of Representatives, January 26, 1867. The final vote was taken April 12, of the same year, with the following result: Yeas 48—nays 38, lacking four votes of a constitutional majority. The Commissioner and other friends of the measure did not yet relinquish the hope of securing favorable legislation, and during the summer of 1867, made strenuous efforts in that direction, but without avail.

Commissioner Norris manifested great anxiety that an advanced position should be taken in regard to teachers' institutes. He fully realized the difficulty of obtaining competent instructors to labor in the field. So unwilling was he to await the uncertainties and delays of legislation, that he appeared before the State Teachers' Association at its Dayton meeting in 1868, and earnestly asked the teachers there assembled to assist him to place in the field, if possible, four able institute instructors. This he thought could be done without much expense to them, as the institute fund provided for by law would pay the larger part of the salaries of that number of instructors. He said the educational work of the State had never been so well done as when performed by the teachers themselves through their state agent, and that if the spirit that supported without aid this agent for so long a period, were again revived, a new face would be put upon our educational prospects. The proposition met with much substantial favor in the way of funds pledged to carry it out, and Mr William Mitchell was soon placed in the field as one of the proposed instructors, but after a few weeks resigned to take again the superintendency of the Columbus schools.

Since Mr. Norris retired from the office of superintendent, nothing has been done in the legislature for county supervision until the incumbency of the present Commissioner. Since Mr. Smart's accession to the office in January, 1875, he has made that the objective point of his labors, and, but a few weeks since, a bill was introduced into the Senate through the committee on common schools, to create the office of county superintendent, with powers additional to those provided for by the bill of Commissioner Norris, that will contribute to make the office much more efficient for good, and go far to give Ohio the best school system possessed by any of the States. There is hope among educators and other friends of public education that the bill may become a law.

CITY AND TOWN SUPERVISION.

Of all the influences operating for the improvement of the schools of this country, none have been so powerful and far-reaching as that exercised by the superintendents of the schools of cities and towns.

European educators have rightly set a high estimate on inspection and supervision in a state school system, and it was this feature of the Prussian schools which, as long ago as 1833, struck Cousin, the distinguished French philosopher, most favorably. Yet the old world method, until quite recently, differed in a very marked manner from ours. There, these inspectors and superintendents were usually clergymen, and not teachers, either by education or practice. Many of them were undoubtedly earnest and able men, but from the standpoint of the educator, not qualified for the details of the work they were called upon to undertake. In this country and the Canadas, the tendency has been, from the beginning, to place supervision and inspection more and more in the hands of experts—of those who, by experience, have an intimate knowledge of the details of school-room work. The clergyman, as such, has never, except in New England, and that at an early day, entered as a factor into the management of the public schools of the United States; but the importance of having a large class of scholarly men warmly interested in the education of the people, and eagerly watching over the welfare of their schools, ready to help in matters pertaining to their improvement, and to defend from attacks of both secret and open foes, is not to be lightly valued. Such a class would be a powerful auxiliary in giving the schools the confidence of the people, and in preventing their falling into the hands of small politicians. But to have that class whose knowledge of educational matters can at best be but theoretical and general, constantly interfering with the details of the work of professional teachers, would give widely different results. It is not, however, to be inferred that we have anywhere in this country arrived at that point where school management is entirely in the hands of professional educators. The schools under the laws of Ohio are placed under the absolute control of the boards of education established by those laws. These boards everywhere in Ohio are elected by popular vote. Superintendents of schools are elected by these boards, and are endowed with such an amount of authority as the boards choose to delegate to them. The practice differs widely in this respect—some boards making their superintendents almost absolute in all matters pertaining to the instruction and management of their schools, whilst others confer little or no authority, leaving the superintendent with scarcely any influence, except such a moral influence as may result from weight of character. The theory of this class of school authorities is, that the board itself should do a large share of the supervision and inspection of its schools, through its own committees. But this class grows constantly smaller, and, as has been already stated, the tendency is to place supervision and inspection more and more entirely in the hands of professional teachers.

Since the enactment of the Akron law, in 1847, the increase in the number and influence of superintendents of schools has been rapid and constant. Under that and subsequent laws has grown up a great body of professional educators, whose zeal for their own personal improvement, for progress in methods of instruction and school management, and in the work of giving their State a high educational standing, has known no abatement from the time Lorin Andrews entered upon his noble work until now.

The spread of city and town supervision was the natural result of the growth of the graded school system. When several schools of different grades were united as an aggregate whole, there was at once felt the necessity of a unifying and directing head. Unless there was such a head, it was easily to be seen that much effort on the part of the teachers would be misdirected or entirely thrown away. In addition, an experienced hand was needed to work up the details of school organization, and prepare a systematic course of study suited to the new order of things. New teachers were constantly coming into the schools, entirely inexperienced in their work, and often of very limited acquirements. These needed to be assisted and instructed. Thus the superintendent came to do something of the work of a normal school. But the strongest and most experienced teachers had to be so directed that their efforts might count most in producing that general result, which should grow out of the harmonious labors of many different hands and brains. Not independent but united effort was now wanted. The experience and thought of one directing mind could alone furnish this. By such a scheme of supervision, the wisdom and experience of the head of a system of schools becomes the possession, in a large measure, of every teacher connected with those schools. By it, also, sluggish or indifferent teachers are urged to greater exertion, timid ones encouraged, and all stimulated to do their best work.

"Men will work better when they know that their faithfulness will be commended. A cooper makes better barrels when he knows that they must pass a rigid inspection. The wood seller gives more accurate measure in a city where he expects rigid measurement, than he does in a town where no such test is applied. The soldier or subordinate officer fights more bravely under the eye of his general, because he expects that his heroism will be commended or rewarded, and his cowardice condemned or punished. So, too, teachers in those graded schools in which there is a rigid inspection of their labors, teach better than they would in schools where no such inspection is expected."*

The duties of the superintendent have not been confined to the management of schools alone. He is often the financial adviser of his board of education; and hence, as a rule, ought to be a clear-headed man of business. He is still more frequently the architect who plans new school buildings, being careful to see that they are supplied with proper provisions for heating, ventilation, and light. He also recommends the furniture which he deems best suited to the comfort and health of pupils, and selects the reference books and apparatus necessary in the several grades of schools. †

One of the duties of the superintendent, as an inspector of the schools under his charge, is to ascertain the standing and progress of the pupils of the several grades and classes. This is done by means of oral and written examinations.

* W. D. Henkle, in Report on County Supervision, made to the State Teachers' Association, in 1864.

† See Supt. Stevenson's Report of Columbus schools, 1872.

Whilst it is undeniable that the former have their value—largely in the way of arousing in pupils an increased interest in their studies—the latter are chiefly relied on in making grade transfers, as altogether the fairest and most reliable standard of ability and scholarship. The number of written examinations had during the year varies considerably in our State. Some superintendents—chiefly in the smaller towns—make it a point to examine each grade of their schools, in all the studies pursued by the grade, as often as once a month. Others are content with quarterly examinations, whilst in one or two cities semi-annual examinations only are held. The general examinations of the superintendent are often supplemented by more special examinations conducted by the teachers themselves. Perhaps no scheme could have been devised that would have contributed so much to a well-defined and solid scholarship, as has the scheme of written examinations. They are not only, when properly applied, a measure of what the pupil knows and can do, but they measure in a large degree the character and efficiency of the teachers' work, helping both towards a solution of the question of self-knowledge.

As has been intimated, the "Akron law," passed February 8, 1847, at first restricted to Akron and Dayton, but by amendments adopted in 1848 and 1849, made general for all cities, towns, and villages that might choose to avail themselves of its provisions, was the foundation of our graded school system. It is true that Cincinnati, Cleveland, and Columbus had previous to that time organized their schools on a graded plan—Cincinnati as early as 1829, Columbus in 1845, and Cleveland in 1848. This grading was, however, until a much later date, very imperfect. Notwithstanding these individual exceptions, the fact remains that the general impulse for the organization of graded schools was derived from the Akron law.

It is not within the design of this sketch to enter into

any detailed history of supervision in the several cities and towns of the State. Those seeking such information will find it in the several local histories prepared for this centennial year.

Columbus claims to have had in the person of Dr. A. D. Lord, so long one of the leading educators of the State, the first superintendent ever elected in Ohio. He was elected May 15, 1847, and served continuously till 1854. M. D. Leggett, who has since won an honorable name as an educator and a soldier, was elected superintendent of the Akron schools in the same year of Dr. Lord's election to the Columbus schools. Lorin Andrews was elected superintendent of the Massillon schools in 1848. Cleveland's first superintendent was Andrew Freese, a man long bearing a prominent part in educational affairs, elected in 1853. In 1848, the eminent educator, M. F. Cowdery, was elected superintendent of the schools of Sandusky, and remained at their head for the long period of twenty-two years. Although the school system of Cincinnati was by many years the oldest in the State, and she had already acquired an honorable fame throughout the country for her superiority in educational facilities, yet she had no superintendent until 1850, when Nathan Guilford, so honorably known for his valuable services to education as a legislator, was elected under a special law passed March 23, 1850. This election took place under the plan of a popular vote—a plan never adopted in any other town of the State. Mr. Guilford served two years, and was succeeded by Dr. Merrell, who resigned before the close of the year. The popular-vote mode of election was abolished by the law of 1853, the first general act making specific provision for the office of city and town superintendent. The first superintendent for Cincinnati under this law was A. J. Rickoff, who, by his display of organizing and general executive power, at once placed himself in the front rank of educators. Under his administration was introduced that thorough grading of schools which has been productive of such excellent results, and has been followed more or less closely by all the cities and towns of the State. He was also the first to make a general use of written examinations for ascertaining the comparative value of the work done in the several schools of an educational system.

In the meantime, a work of organization was being carried out in Cleveland, Columbus, Sandusky, and other towns, by the able men who were directing their educational forces. Lancaster had elected John S. Whitwell superintendent in 1849; Circleville, John Lynch, in 1852, and Zanesville, Geo. W. Batchelder, in the same year; Steubenville, Thomas F. McGrew, in 1853, and Fremont, in the same year, H. E. Clarke; Hamilton, Alexander Bartlett, in 1854; and Piqua, A. G. Chambers, in 1856. About 1851, W. N. Edwards was elected superintendent of the schools of Troy, and in this office he spent the remaining years of his valuable life.

Toledo and Dayton were the last of the large towns of the State to elect superintendents. The former chose the Rev. Anson Smyth to the office in 1854; and the latter, in 1855, James Campbell, then principal of the high school, with the provision that he should continue to devote half his time to high-school work. In 1858, this restriction was removed, and Mr. Campbell's whole time, so long as he remained in office, was given to the duties of that office. The history of supervision in Dayton has been peculiar. In no other considerable town of the State, so far as we are acquainted, with the single exception of Zanesville, has the office of superintendent been abolished after having been once created. In Dayton, this has been virtually done twice. After Mr. Campbell's resignation, in 1859, the office, though not formally abolished, remained vacant until 1856, when Mr. Caleb Parker, a member of the board of education, was elected to the position. Mr. Parker held the place for two years, and declined a re-appointment. The office was again vacant until 1871, since which time it has been regularly filled.

At first, in none but the larger cities, such as Cincinnati and Cleveland, was the whole time of the superintendent given to supervision. Indeed, in some of the smaller towns, but very little of it was thus directed—not more than an hour or two each day at most—the remainder being given to instruction in the high school department of the schools. But as the value of supervision became more manifest to school authorities, more and more of the superintendent's time was set apart for the special duties of his position. The practice, however, still prevails in the smaller towns for the superintendent to devote some part of his time to the work of teaching classes, the amount being determined by the number of pupils in the schools and by other exigencies. In some cities, as Cleveland, Columbus, and Dayton, one or more assistant superintendents, under the name of supervising principals, came to be employed to aid the general superintendent in his work. At an early period of Mr. Rickoff's administration in Cincinnati, the principals of schools were relieved of the charge of a room of pupils, and were put at supervisory work, under such a rule that they were required, in all except some of the smaller schools, to give their whole time to it. In Dayton, at the present time, the principals give a part of their time to supervision, the rest being devoted to the instruction of the highest class in the school.

Nothing could more plainly exhibit the low estate of the school system, when town and city supervision first began to obtain a foothold in the State, than the meagre salaries paid superintendents. The first salary paid Mr. Leggett, at Akron, was $500; that paid to Mr. Guilford, at Cincinnati, $700; and $800 was about the outside limit paid anywhere.

In conclusion, it may be said that not alone is the superintendent felt in the power he exerts in the organization, inspection, and supervision of the schools under his charge, or in the influence he wields over their teachers and pupils, but "wherever there is a superintendent who is active, efficient, and wise, there is a more appreciative public sentiment, and a higher standard of excellence." Such a superintendent not only helps to form the character of his pupils, but he is to some extent the educator of the town in which he labors. If he be a man of large attainments and lofty character, his influence will tend to promote a higher ideal of living throughout society.

CHAPTER IX.

TEACHERS' ASSOCIATIONS.

The present liberal school system of Ohio is largely due to conventions and associations held in the interest of education. These agencies have enlarged the views of teachers, enlightened public sentiment, and indicated and secured legislative action. They have also done much to improve school instruction and management.

A history of these agencies is, therefore, an important part of the history of educational effort and progress in the State, and the writer much regrets that he has neither time nor space for more than a brief account of the more important of them.

WESTERN LITERARY INSTITUTE AND BOARD OF EDUCATION.

In 1829, some twenty teachers in Cincinnati met and organized a society, with the above title. Its objects, as stated, were to promote harmony, co-operation, and the diffusion of knowledge among its members, and to discuss subjects conducive to the advantage of education generally. Elijah Slack was elected president, Milo G. Williams, corresponding secretary, John L. Talbot, recording secretary, and Albert Picket, president of the board of control. In addition to these officers, the active members of the society included Alexander Kimmont, Caleb Kemper, Nathaniel Halley, C. B. McKee, Stephen Wheeler, Thomas J. Mathews, David L. Talbot, and C. Davenport.

Meetings were held monthly, with a good attendance, and the more important duties of the school-room were freely and fully discussed. At the anniversary meeting held in June, 1831, Rev. C. B. McKee gave an address advocating the co-operation of parents and all other citizens in the education of the young, and Rev. R. H. Bishop, D. D., presented the advantages of the common school system, and advocated the grading of schools and the employing of well qualified teachers. The proceedings of this meeting were published in a neat pamphlet.

At the meeting held in 1831, steps were taken which resulted in the organization of

THE COLLEGE OF TEACHERS.

At the meeting referred to, Milo G. Williams offered a resolution proposing a correspondence with prominent teachers in the West and South to obtain their views on the question of calling a convention of the friends of education, at some point to be determined by the correspondence. The resolution was adopted and Mr. Williams, as corresponding secretary, conducted the correspondence. The measure was heartily approved by those addressed, and Cincinnati was designated as the place of meeting. Arrangements were made and the convention called. It opened October 3, 1832, and continued in session four days.

On the first day of the session, John L. Talbot moved the appointment of a committee to take into consideration the expediency of forming a western society of teachers, and, if approved, to prepare and report a constitution for its government. The committee was composed of M. Butler and H. Bascom, of Kentucky, M. A. H. Niles and M. M. Bingham, of Indiana, and Albert Picket and Milo G. Williams, of Ohio.

The next day the committee reported in favor of forming

24

a permanent society and submitted the draft of a constitution, which, with slight alterations, was adopted. It declared the object of the society to be "to promote, by all laudable means, the diffusion of knowledge in regard to education, and especially by aiming at the elevation of instructors who shall have adopted instruction as their regular profession." Thomas J. Matthews was elected president, Milo G. Williams, corresponding secretary, David L. Talbot, recording secretary, and Timothy Hammond, treasurer, and "the Western Literary Institute and College of Professional Teachers" was thus organized.

The society held annual meetings in Cincinnati until 1845. The session opened on Monday and continued through the week, and the largest churches in the city were required to accommodate the audiences. It was attended by the leading teachers and friends of education in the Mississippi Valley, but it was chiefly directed by Albert Picket, Alexander Kinmont, Milo G. Williams, W. H. McGuffey, Samuel Lewis, Dr. Joseph Ray, Nathan Guilford, Prof. Calvin E. Stowe, and other Ohio members.

The College of Teachers contributed largely to the advancement of education in Ohio, and the West generally. In the fourteen years of its existence over three hundred addresses and reports were made before it, discussing education in all its phases and grades. The seven volumes of "Transactions" published contain an amount of educational experience and information not found in the same compass in any early publications.

It also instituted important measures and agencies for the improvement of schools. As early as 1833 it recommended the organization of teachers' associations, and it early contributed to the development of what is now known as the teachers' institute. It advocated the grading of schools and the importance of supervision, especially urging the creation of the office of State Superintendent of Public Instruction. In 1835, it secured the passage of a resolution by the General Assembly of Ohio, appropriating $500 to enable Prof. Calvin E. Stowe, of Lane Seminary, Cincinnati, who was about to visit Europe, to make an examination of the elementary school systems of Prussia and other European nations. Prof. Stowe submitted the results of his observations and enquiries in an able report, which exerted a wide and beneficent influence on American schools.

At the annual meeting in 1835, a resolution was adopted recommending that meetings of teachers and other friends of education be held at the seat of government of the several states during the sittings of the legislatures. This action resulted in the holding of conventions in Ohio, as shown hereafter, and in other states, and important legislation was secured.

The College of Teachers suspended in 1845,* but the cause is not known to the writer.

STATE CONVENTIONS.

In pursuance of the resolution of the College of Teachers, above referred to, the Ohio section of the directory, after consultation with prominent teachers, called a meeting, to be held in Columbus, January 13, 1836. *This was the first State Convention held in Ohio in the interest of public education.* Governor Robert Lucas was made president, and Milo G. Williams, secretary. Among those who were present and took part in the proceedings were Wm. H. McGuffey, of Oxford; M. P. Jewett, of Marietta; Samuel Lewis, E. D. Mansfield, and Calvin E. Stowe, of Cincinnati; Wm. Sparrow, of Gambier; John H. James, of Urbana; H. O. Sheldon, of Newark; James Hoge, William Preston, H. N. Hubbell, and Wm. M.

*It has been stated that the suspension occured in 1847, but the writer finds no record of a meeting in 1846 or 1847.

Awl, of Columbus; Charles Sawyer, of Granville; Robert C. Schenck, of Dayton; and John B. Wheaton, of London. The members of both branches of the General Assembly were invited to attend the meetings and take part in the deliberations.

A committee, with E. D. Mansfield as chairman, was appointed to report on the defects in the school laws of Ohio, and the legislation required to remedy them. The committee reported the existence of three kinds of defects, viz: 1. Too low a standard of education, as shown by the low qualifications required of teachers. 2. The want of responsibility between the agents of instruction, boards of examiners, and legislative power. 3. The want of general supervision, as shown by the absence of any officer who has charge of the department of instruction. The report closed with resolutions recommending: 1. That the qualifications of teachers should include at least English grammar, geography, and the art of teaching. 2. The creation of the office of State Superintendent of Public Instruction. 3. The requiring of county examiners to inspect officially all the district schools of their respective counties, at least once a year, and to report their condition to the State Superintendent. 4. The establishment of public district libraries. 5. The appointment of one or more commissioners by the Governor to collect statistical information relating to schools. The resolutions were adopted unanimously, and a memorial embodying their recommendations was signed by the officers and presented to the General Assembly.

On the first day of the convention Samuel Lewis delivered an address on common schools, reviewing the past and present condition of the schools of the State, the laws regulating them, and their financial resources and expenditures. The following evening Prof. Stowe read a portion of his report on the Prussian system of public instruction.

The entire proceedings of the convention were laid before the General Assembly by the Governor, accompanied by a special message, and, by a joint resolution, the journal and addresses were ordered to be printed in pamphlet form and circulated among teachers throughout the State. The committees on schools and the members of the convention had conferences, and, before the close of the session of the General Assembly, a law was passed creating the office of State Superintendent of Common Schools, and Samuel Lewis was appointed to the office.

It was thought by many in attendance that the ends sought by the convention could be better attained by an organization independent of the Ohio directory, yet connected with the College of Teachers. A constitution was framed and adopted, officers were elected, and the "Ohio State Society for the Promotion of Public Instruction" was thus organized.

The society failed to hold its first annual meeting, in 1836, and so the Ohio directory of the College of Teachers announced another convention to be held in Columbus, December 19, 1837. The call was accompanied by an earnest appeal to teachers and other citizens, and there was a large attendance from the different sections of the State.

The sessions were presided over in turn by Ex-Governor Vance, Ex-Governor Morrow, Judge McLean, and Rev. Dr. Hoge. Milo G. Williams was made secretary. Addresses were delivered by Prof. Stowe, Hon. Wm. Johnson, Wm. Slocomb, and Dr. Macenly. Rev. Dr. Hoge gave an address on the education of the blind and the deaf and dumb. Superintendent Hubbell, of the Deaf and Dumb Institution, illustrated his methods of teaching, and Superintendent Penniman explained the methods employed in the education of the blind.

Nathaniel Wright, Esq., introduced the following resolution, which was adopted:

"*Resolved*, That we hail the efforts which are now being made by despotic governments for the moral and intellectual elevation of the great masses of the people, as a new era in the history of the world, and that their example should stimulate us to redoubled exertions to establish a system of common schools so efficient that all our children may be brought permanently within its influence."

The third convention, under the Ohio directory, convened in Columbus, December 26, 1838, and continued in session four days. It had a larger attendance than either of the previous ones. Hon. William Shannon was chosen president, and J. M. Stevenson and H. A. Moore, secretaries.

Milo G. Williams read a report on the great diversity of text-books used in the schools of the State; Dr. W. H. McGuffey delivered a lecture on the influence of common school education, and Prof. Stowe read an able report on the establishing of a State Normal School at Columbus. Mr. Williams followed with a report recommending the establishment of a normal school in each congressional district. The reports on school-books and normal schools were fully discussed, and resolutions were adopted declaring a state uniformity of text-books impracticable, and urging, as important to the full success of the common school system, "the establishment of a Teachers' Seminary at the seat of government, and at such other places as may be necessary." Messrs. McGuffey, Smith, and Preston were appointed a committee to memorialize the General Assembly on the creation of a board of public instruction and the founding of a teachers' seminary.

The subject of vocal music was introduced by a communication from Mrs. Mary C. Webster, and after a spirited discussion, a resolution was adopted hailing the introduction of vocal music into primary and higher schools as a "promising era in the history of education," and recommending its introduction into common schools, academies, and higher institutions of learning. Mr. Smith made a report on the conducting of district schools in the West, which was published with the proceedings.

At the closing meeting of the session, the following resolution was ably supported by Hon. Wm. Johnson and Prof. Stowe and adopted by the convention:

"*Resolved*, That a well-regulated and efficient system of free common schools is the sheet-anchor of republican liberty, and that without it we can have no just ground of hope for the permanence of our institutions."

A resolution was also adopted strongly approving of the manner in which Superintendant Lewis had discharged his duties.

The proceedings of the convention, including several reports, were published.

Messrs. Williams and Jenkins were appointed a committee to fix the time and make arrangements for the next convention, but the writer has found no evidence that it was held. Early in 1829 resolutions were offered in the General Assembly recommending that the office of State Superintendent be abolished. The resolutions failed, but Mr. Lewis resigned his office at the close of the year, his health being impaired by severe labor, and a law was passed making the Secretary of State *ex-officio* school superintendent. It is believed that the unfavorable spirit of the General Assembly of 1839–40, so much discouraged the friends of education that no convention was called.

The period from 1840 to 1845 was marked by a declining interest in schools. In 1844, Samuel Galloway became Secretary of State. He entered with zeal upon the work of school improvement, and greatly assisted in producing the educational revival which began in 1845. He made seven reports, the first being the fullest and ablest which had appeared for five years.

In 1845, 1846, and 1847, many teachers' institutes were held in the State, the first being held in Sandusky in September, 1845. These institutes filled the place of educational conventions, and important measures for the improvement of the schools were advocated and approved. A deep and active interest in popular education was thus awakened in many counties.

OHIO TEACHERS' ASSOCIATION.

After the failure of the Ohio State Society, organized in 1835, the question of forming a state association of teachers was frequently discussed by the more active teachers in the State. In the December number of the Ohio School Journal, 1846, the editor, Dr. A. D. Lord, suggested and earnestly advocated the forming of a state common school society. This suggestion was renewed in the November number, 1847, and the hope expressed that such a society would be organized within a year.

At teachers' institutes held in Ashland, Chardon, and Akron, in October and November, 1847, M. F. Cowdery, of Lake county, Lorin Andrews, of Ashland county, A. D. Lord, of Franklin county, W. Bowen, of Stark county, Josiah Hurty, of Richland county, T. W. Harvey, of Geauga county, A. H. Bailey, of Ashtabula county, M. D. Leggett, of Summit county, and J. Sloan, of Knox county, were appointed a committee to take into consideration the propriety of forming a State Teachers' Association and to fix upon the time and place for organizing the same.

A majority of this committee met in Akron and issued a call for a convention to be held in Akron, Summit county, on the evening of December 30, 1847, and during the day of the 31st, for the purpose of organizing a *State Teachers' Association.*

The original call, published in the "Free School Clarion," was as follows:

TO TEACHERS IN OHIO.—At the Teachers' Institutes held in Ashland, Ashland Co., Chardon, Geauga Co., and Akron, Summit Co., in October and November, 1847, M. F. Cowdery, of Lake Co., L. Andrews, of Ashland Co., A. D. Lord, of Franklin Co., W. Bowen, of Stark Co.,

Josiah Hurty, of Richland Co., T. W. Harvey, of Geauga Co., A. H. Bailey, of Ashtabula Co., M. D. Leggett, of Summit Co., and J. Sloan, of Knox Co., were appointed a committee to take into consideration the propriety of forming a State Teachers' Association, and to fix upon the time and place of organizing the same.

The undersigned, a majority of said committee, assembled at Akron, and have resolved that it is expedient to hold a Convention at Akron, Summit Co., on the evening of the 30th, and during the day of the 31st of December next, for the purpose of organizing a *State Teachers' Association.*

It is hoped that Teachers in Ohio, feeling an interest in their profession, and the improvement of the Schools of our State, will be present and assist in the organization of the Association, and afterwards in promoting its interests.

There will be an address before the Convention on the evening of the 30th of December.

Educational and political papers in Ohio are requested to insert the above notice.

M. F. Cowdery,	W. Bowen,
Josiah Hurty,	T. W. Harvey,
L. Andrews,	M. D. Leggett.

In accordance with the above call, delegates representing eleven counties, assembled in Akron on the 30th of December, 1847, and organized the Ohio State Teachers' Association. The delegates included M. F. Cowdery, T. W. Harvey, Lorin Andrews, M. D. Leggett, Josiah Hurty, W. Bowen, A. K. Smith, J. R. Doig, Arvine Wales, P. Dawley, and perhaps others.

M. F. Cowdery was elected chairman, and T. W. Harvey, secretary, and a constitution was adopted.

The permanent organization of the Association was completed by the election of the following officers by ballot, to serve for the ensuing year :

President—Samuel Galloway, of Franklin.

Vice Presidents—P. Dawley, of Stark ; A. A. Smith, of Ashtabula ; A. Freese, of Cuyahoga ; R. R. Sloan, of Knox ; E. E. Barney, of Montgomery ; L. Tenney, of Washington ; J. B. Howard, of Muskingum ; A. D. Lord, of Franklin ; J. R. Doig, of Wayne ; P. S. Semmes, of Hamilton ; C. C. Giles, of Warren; Milo G. Williams, of Clarke; S. Blakeslee, of Williams; B. Rouse, of Lucas; J. Hall, of Huron; H. G. Blake, of Medina; A. Gilbert, of Columbiana; Mr. Bennett, of Miami; Wm. Finley, of Ross; E. S. Stanton, of Jefferson.

Recording Secretary—T. W. Harvey, of Geauga.

Corresponding Secretary—M. D. Leggett, of Summit.

Treasurer—William Bowen, of Stark.

Executive Committee—M. F. Cowdery, of Lake; Lorin Andrews, of Ashland; J. Nichols, of Lake; J. Hurty, of Richland; F. W. Tappan, of Portage; H. K. Smith, of Summit.

Resolutions were passed (1) requesting the recording secretary to keep a record of the names of all the teachers in the State that expect to continue in the business of teaching for three years and upwards; (2) requesting all teachers in Ohio qualified to take charge of *union schools* (graded), and wishing employment, to furnish their names, with references, to the corresponding secretary; and (3) petitioning the legislature so to amend the school laws of Ohio as to require each school district to raise annually, by taxation, an amount equal to the amount received from the state funds, for the payment of competent teachers.

M. F. Cowdery, L. Andrews, and M. D. Leggett were appointed a committee to prepare an address expressive of the views of the convention. The address submitted opened with an expression of the conviction that the office of teacher is second in importance to no other, and that teachers should turn to it "with a pure satisfaction and a deep and abiding reverence." Teachers were reminded that the future of their profession and its rank in society are in their keeping. Attention was called to teachers' associations, then existing in many counties, as an important means for the elevation of teaching, and the State Teachers' Association, just organized, was earnestly commended to the approval and support of teachers in all parts of the State. One of the first duties proposed for the Association was, to prepare the public mind for wise and liberal provisions for the improvement of schools, and to create a demand for such legislative provisions as should be most needed. Space is taken for one paragraph of the address:

"We propose, therefore, as speedily as possible, to examine and discuss, respectfully and courteously, yet vigilantly and independently, all measures and principles of interest to teachers and schools, aside from local considerations and private interests. To sustain and defend what is excellent in our schools or school system, will be our highest pleasure. To prepare the way for introducing improvements when they are needed, will be our next duty. This, it seems to us, is the safest method of conducting our reform, and the one most likely to save all wise legislation from opposition or subversion by prejudice, and from the influence of political partisanship."

The address closed with an earnest invitation to all teachers and friends of education in Ohio to co-operate in the movement, with the promise of "the high satisfaction of soon beholding our beloved State taking as high rank in all the means for promoting virtue and true nobleness as she now holds in all other elements of greatness and prosperity."

Early in January, 1848, the executive committee assigned some thirty different subjects to as many committees, with a request that written reports should be presented at the future meetings of the Association. A large number of these committees complied with the request, and their reports were put on file. A full list of the topics and committees was published in the Ohio School Journal for February, 1848. The committees on text-books were assigned the easy(?) task of securing, as far as possible, all the text-books on the subjects assigned them, and "comparing the works, article with article, subject with subject, state explicitly in their reports in what respects each work is meritorious and deficient." It may be instructive to add that these committees have not yet submitted their reports!

In the same month, conditional arrangements were made for holding, under the auspices of the Association, teachers' institutes in some forty counties in the eastern and southeastern parts of the State. Nineteen counties accepted the conditions and institutes were held, nine in the spring and ten in the autumn.

A circular letter was issued January 21, 1848, announcing a course of lectures to teachers on fourteen specified subjects, to be given between the 14th day of June and the 16th day of August, in any county making the best proposition to the executive committee, for furnishing building, apparatus, board, and accomodations for 300 students. Huron county made the best proposition and secured the State Normal Class. About one hundred and twenty persons attended the course. A similar course was given in Akron in the autumn to about sixty persons.

The executive committee also issued an address to county school examiners, reminding them of the responsibility of their position and asking for a united effort to elevate the schools. Special attention was called to the facilities afforded by teachers' institutes, and the co-operation of examiners was solicited. The necessity of complying with the provisions of the law relating to the examination of teachers was urged, and the method, adopted in Lake county, of requiring *written* answers in several branches, was strongly commended.

It is thus seen that the Ohio Teachers' Association had its origin in an earnest spirit of reform, and that it entered hopefully and zealously upon the great work of concentrating the influence of teachers and all other friends of public education in a united effort to give Ohio an efficient and comprehensive system of schools. The work mapped out and undertaken by the executive committee was without precedent.

The first regular meeting of the Association was held in Dayton, June 1st and 2d, 1848. The time was unfavorable, the academies and colleges, and many public schools being in session, and the attendance was not large. The president, Hon. Samuel Galloway, being absent, Dr. A. D. Lord, of Columbus, one of the vice presidents, occupied the chair.

Reports were read on "School Examinations and the Best Mode of Conducting Them," by A. E. Stevens, of Dayton; on "Physiology and the Laws of Health," by Dr. A. D. Lord; on "Linear Drawing," by J. B. Howard, of Muskingum county; and on "Civil Polity," by Josiah Hurty, of Mansfield. H. H. Barney, of Cincinnati, delivered an address on the "Influence of Education on Our Free Institutions."

Resolutions were adopted declaring that, "examinations should be conducted orally, or by printed questions, or by both"; that the members of the Association would use their influence to have a teachers' institute held in every county; that every child should be taught the general principles of civil government; that the office of State Superintendent of Common Schools should be created "with a salary sufficiently liberal to command the best talent in the country;" that it is the imperative duty of the State to make provision for the education of teachers by establishing normal schools. It was decided to procure signatures to memorials to the General Assembly on the subjects embraced in the last two resolutions. Resolutions were also passed providing for detailed accounts, by the delegates to the Association, of the condition of the schools in their respective counties; and commending the Ohio School Journal, edited by Dr. A. D. Lord.

The first annual meeting of the Association was held in Columbus, Dec. 28th and 29th, 1848, the president, Hon. Samuel Galloway, in the chair. The executive committee presented a report of its proceedings, including those relating to teachers' institutes, to courses of lectures for teachers, to the examination of teachers, and to the grading of schools in towns. The subject of union schools had been presented in all the counties visited by the persons employed to conduct teachers' institutes, and, as a result, several towns had adopted the graded system and others were making arrangements to do so. The committee reported a growing public sentiment in favor of all practical improvements of the school system, and presented a hopeful view of the future.

The following questions were discussed at some length, but the action of the Association upon them is not stated in the secretary's minutes:

"Is it for the interest of common schools that provision be made by the State for the education of teachers?"

"Would the interests of common schools be promoted by the appointment of State and County Superintendents of schools?"

"What plan of organization is best suited to the wants of the incorporated towns and cities of the State?"

Messrs. A. D. Lord, S. S. Rickley, and H. H. Barney were appointed a committee to prepare a report on the advantages to be derived from union schools, and on the best mode of conducting them. The report was prepared at once and published in the annual report of the State Superintendent of Schools (Secretary of State), and in the Ohio School Journal (Vol. IV, No. 4.)

The principal officers elected for the ensuing year were Hon. Samuel Galloway, President; P. Dawley, of Stark, 1st Vice President; S. S. Rickley, of Columbus, Recording Secretary; W. P. Kerr, of Granville, Corresponding Secretary; L. G. Parker, of Urbana, Treasurer; and A. D. Lord, Chairman of the Executive Committee.

Arrangements were early made for holding the second semi-annual meeting in Springfield, July 3d and 4th, 1849, but the alarm occasioned by the expected prevalence of cholera, caused a postponement of the meeting, and subsequently its omission.

The second annual meeting was held in Columbus, December 26th and 27th, 1849, the president, Hon. Samuel Galloway, in the chair. The president delivered an introductory address on "The Importance of Universal Education, and the Paramount Importance of Correct Moral

Instruction, based upon the Bible." By a vote of the Association, Mr. Galloway was requested to publish the address in the appendix of his annual report as Superintendent of Schools. At the evening session, Prof. S. H. Smith, of Starling Medical College, gave an address on the "Animal Kingdom." Reports were made by Wm. N. Edwards, of Troy, on "Moral Instruction;" by A. Freese, of Cleveland, on "Mental Arithmetic;" by Amos Gilbert, of Columbiana county, on "Phonography;" by W. G. Darley, of Trumbull county, on "Geography and Map Drawing;" by A. D. Wright, of Perrysburg, on "Primary Teaching;" and by G. R. Hand, of Cincinnati, on the "Analysis of English Words."

Resolutions were passed petitioning the legislature so to amend the school law as to fix the minimum school age at five years; asserting the importance of elementary instruction, and of employing the most talented and successful teachers in primary schools; and recommending to teachers and school committees the propriety of testing, by actual experiment, the value of the phonetic system.

Mr. Lorin Andrews presented a series of resolutions recommending the appointment of a State Board of Public Instruction, consisting of five members, each to serve four years as "District Superintendent," and one year (the fifth) as State Superintendent of Common Schools, at a salary of $1,000 a year, to be paid from funds arising from the examination fees paid by teachers. The sixth resolution required each applicant for examination to pay a fee of one dollar, and the seventh required the State Superintendent to edit an educational paper to be sent free to the holders of certificates valid in any county of the State one year.

The resolutions were referred to Messrs. H. H. Barney, Lorin Andrews, M. G. Williams, A. J. Rickoff, A. D. Lord, and the president, who, the next day, reported them to the Association for adoption. The first six resolutions were discussed one by one, and adopted. The consideration of the seventh and eighth resolutions was postponed to the afternoon session, and the official minutes contain no further reference to them.

The adoption of the resolutions relating to supervision was followed by the appointment of Messrs. A. D. Lord, M. G. Williams, and H. H. Barney, as a committee to prepare a memorial to the legislature, praying for the enactment of a law securing a general supervision of the schools of the State. The committee discharged the duty assigned, and an act providing for a State Board of Public Instruction was passed March 22, 1850, but the legislature adjourned without appointing the board.

Messrs. M. F. Cowdery, J. M. Howe, and A. J. Buel were appointed a committee to prepare an address to the teachers of Ohio relative to the action of the Association.

Messrs. H. H. Barney, L. Andrews, A. D. Lord, M. F. Cowdery, M. G. Williams, M. D. Leggett, E. E. Barney, A. E. Stevens, A. H. Bailey, E. D. Kingsley, Samuel Galloway, and A. D. Wright were appointed delegates to the National Educational Convention, to be held in Philadelphia the next August.

Hon. Samuel Galloway was elected President for the ensuing year; P. Dawley, of Stark, 1st Vice President; E. D. Kingsley, of Columbus, Recording Secretary; I. W. Andrews, of Marietta, Corresponding Secretary; John Ogden, of Columbus, Treasurer; and A. D. Lord, of Columbus, Chairman of the Executive Committee.

In its annual report for 1849, the executive committee declare that the passage of the "Act for the better organization of the public schools in cities, towns, etc.," drafted by Hon. S. T. Worcester, constitutes "an important era in the school legislation of our State."

The semi-annual meeting was held in Springfield, July 3d and 4th, 1850. The president being absent, Milo G. Williams, one of the vice presidents, was called to the chair.

Addresses were delivered by Rev. D. Shepardson of Cincinnati, on "The Genius of Our Government and the Prosperity of Our Republic, as Incentives to the Teacher," and by Prof. J. C. Zachos, of Cincinnati, on the "Philosophy of Education."

Reports were read by A. A. Smith, of Ashtabula county, on "Normal Schools," and by Josiah Hurty on "The Importance to Teachers of a Knowledge of other Branches than those they are required to teach." A report on "Elementary Instruction," by the venerable Albert Picket, Sen., was read by M. G. Williams. Mr. Picket received a vote of thanks for his able report.

The discussions were chiefly devoted to Mr. Smith's report on normal schools, and to the subject of supervision. Resolutions were passed, declaring that "the best interests of the common schools of Ohio require that provision be made in the constitution of the State for the establishment of one or more normal schools;" and recommending "that provision be made in the constitution, to be formed for this State, for the election of a State Superintendent of Schools by the people, and such a number of district and county superintendents, as may from time to time be deemed necessary."

Resolutions were also passed approving of "the practice of having female teachers give instruction in teachers' institutes;" hailing with pleasure the appearance of the "Ohio Teacher," and recommending it to the patronage of the profession and the public; recommending the publication of articles on education in newspapers; requesting clergymen in the State to deliver to their congregations a lecture on the subject of education, in October; declaring that the principle that common school education should forever be made *free* to every child in the State, should be incorporated in the constitution; and instructing the executive committee to prepare a series of tracts on important educational topics.

Considerable time was profitably devoted to the hearing of five-minute reports on the condition of schools in the several counties represented. Reports were presented from twenty-six counties.

Messrs. A. D. Lord, A. H. Bailey, H. H. Barney, D. Shepardson, T. Rainey, M. F. Cowdery, Wm. Travis, I. J. Allen, Joseph Ray, and E. L. Curry were appointed delegates to the Free School Convention, to be held in Syracuse, N. Y., July 10th, 1850.

The third annual meeting was held in Columbus, December 25th and 26th, 1850, the president in the chair. Thirty-five counties were represented by about one hundred and fifty delegates.

The annual address of the president discussed the present condition of education, errors in teaching, and the objects to be aimed at by the Association. Hon. Ira Mayhew, of Michigan, gave an address on the "Aims and Means of Popular Education."

Considerable time was devoted to the discussion of a series of resolutions presented by the business committee, Dr. A. D. Lord, chairman. The first resolution deemed it to be the imperative duty of the legislature to provide for a thorough revision of the school laws of the State. The second urged the importance of an early appointment of the members of the State Board of Education, created by the act of March 22. The third requested the legislature to appoint no man a member of the board "who is not well-known as an experienced and successful teacher."

The first and second resolutions were adopted, but the third was so amended as to recommend the appointment of no man "who has not given an earnest of his efficiency and success as a zealous and enlightened educator." The resolution, as amended, was adopted.

It was announced that the trustees of Miami University had established a normal school in connection with that institution, and President Anderson stated that the scholars in the normal school would be admitted to the lectures on different branches delivered to the regular classes. This announcement was received with much satisfaction. A resolution was introduced by Mr. Stearns, declaring that the interests of education in Ohio demand the establishment of a State Normal School. The resolution was opposed by several on the ground that such a school would cripple many of the colleges in the State which had organized normal departments! This objection was fully answered, but the resolution was laid on the table—the first unfavorable vote on the normal school question given by the Association.

The business committee reported a series of resolutions, referring to the dissensions in the State of New York on the free school question, and declaring that the organic law of the State should guarantee a free and adequate education to all its youth, and that education can not become universal unless it be made free. The resolutions were adopted.

A resolution was also adopted, after discussion, recommending to teachers the reading of a portion of the Holy Scriptures in their schools.

M. F. Cowdery was elected president on the first ballot by four majority, but declined serving, and Isaac Sams, of Hillsboro, was elected on the second ballot. Dr. Joseph Ray was elected first vice president; John Lynch, of Ashland, recording secretary; P. Dawley, of Massillon, corresponding secretary; John Ogden, treasurer; and Lorin Andrews, chairman of the executive committee.

Messrs. A. D. Lord, M. D. Leggett, and Josiah Hurty were appointed a committee to prepare and publish, in pamphlet form, the history and the proceedings of the Ohio State Teachers' Association, with a list of its members and also of its officers.*

* An edition of 1,000 copies was printed, a part being covered and the remainder reserved for future use. The writer has seen but one copy of this pamphlet—a copy kindly sent him by Mr. Cowdery.

The year 1851 is a memorable one in the history of the Ohio Teachers' Association. The Constitutional Convention, which met in Columbus in 1850, re-assembled in March, 1851, and there was a wide spread expectation that the new constitution would contain wise and liberal provisions relating to education. Later in the year it was generally believed that the first General Assembly under the constitution would enact an efficient and progressive school law. These expectations aroused a hopeful and earnest spirit and caused unusual activity among the friends of public education.

Early in the year, Lorin Andrews, the recently elected chairman of the executive committee, was induced to resign his position as principal of the Massillon Union School and become a "Common School Missionary," without any assurance of pecuniary reward, except the small and uncertain compensation afforded by teachers' institutes. Early in February, he issued a circular calling for assistance in the institutes to be held in the spring, and at once entered on a thorough canvass of the State as the Agent of the Association. Forty-one institutes were held in the year, and in about one-half of these Mr. Andrews was the principal instructor.

The semi-annual meeting of the Association was held in Cleveland, July 2d and 3d, 1851.* There was a good attendance and the proceedings were characterized by great earnestness. The labors of Mr. Andrews as State Agent, were cordially approved and a resolution to sustain him pecuniarily was unanimously adopted. By this act the teachers of Ohio pledged themselves to do what the State had repeatedly refused to do, and for three years they kept their pledge, contributing from their small salaries the means required to keep an agent in the field. This action of Ohio teachers

*It is believed that the official minutes of this meeting of the Association have never been published.

was without precedent, and it has never been successfully imitated by the teachers of any other state.

The Association passed resolutions declaring that boys and girls ought to sit in the same school-rooms; that phonotypy should be used as a means of teaching reading; and that the legislature ought to establish one or more houses of reformation for juvenile offenders. It is believed that the adoption of the last resolution was the beginning of the public movement which resulted in the establishment of the Ohio Reform School for Boys.

At this meeting a committee was appointed, with Lorin Andrews as chairman, to consider the propriety of establishing an educational paper as the organ of the Association.

Endorsed and sustained by the Association, and encouraged by a hearty reception by the people, Mr. Andrews devoted himself with renewed energy to his self-denying labor, with most promising results.

The fourth annual meeting of the Association was held in Columbus, Dec. 31, 1851, and Jan. 1, 1852, President Sams in the chair. The large attendance attested the value of the General Agent's efforts in awakening a general interest in educational progress.

On motion of M. F. Cowdery, Mr. Andrews was employed to act as General Agent for the ensuing year, and a committee was appointed to obtain contributions to meet the deficiency in his salary for the past ten months. The amount required was promptly raised.

Mr. Andrews, as chairman of the committee appointed at the semi-annual meeting, submitted a report, recommending that a "a paper be published monthly, in octavo form, each number to contain thirty-two pages, at one dollar a year, and that all the teachers of the State be requested to act as agents and correspondents."

The report was discussed at length and adopted, and the entire management of the proposed paper was entrusted to the executive committee. Messrs. A. D. Lord, J. K. Kidd, Chas. Rogers, D. Huffman, D. Parsons, W. B. Fairchilds, and G. W. Batchelder were appointed a committee to solicit subscriptions and pledges for its support. The next day the committee reported pledges for 1,200 copies.

The executive committe decided to call the new paper THE OHIO JOURNAL OF EDUCATION, and Messrs. A. D. Lord, H. H. Barney, J. C. Zachos, M. F. Cowdery, I. W. Andrews, and Andrew Freese were appointed editors. The first number was issued in January, 1852, and its publication by the Association was continued eight years.

A resolution was adopted requesting the legislature to provide for district school libraries. Messrs. H. H. Barney, George Willey, and Isaac Sams were appointed a committee to prepare a petition to the legislature praying for the appointment of an adequate number of superintendents of common schools. Persons circulating this petition for signatures, were requested to forward the same to Lorin Andrews, to be by him laid before the legislature.

Messrs. Samuel Galloway, A. D. Lord and M. F. Cowdery were appointed a committee to petition the legislature for an appropriation for the support of the Agent of the Association for the coming year.

Addresses were delivered at this meeting by Prof. Joseph Ray on "The Qualifications of Teachers;" by George Willey, Esq., of Cleveland, on "Education;" and by Wm. D. Swan, of Boston, on "The Teacher's Profession." Reports were read by A. H. Bailey on "District School Libraries," and by Prof. I. W. Andrews, of Marietta College, on "The Relations of Schools and Colleges."

The chairman of the executive committee, Mr. Andrews, submitted an elaborate report, which, by request, was published by the Secretary of State in his annual report as Superintendent of Schools. It was also published in the first number of the new organ of the Association, in connection with the proceedings of the meeting.

Rev. W. C. Anderson, D. D., of Oxford, was elected president for the ensuing year; G. R. Hand, first vice president; Chas. Rogers, recording secretary; F. Hollenbeck, corresponding secretary; John Ogden, treasurer; and Lorin Andrews, chairman of the executive committee.

The semi-annual meeting held in Sandusky July 7th and 8th, was attended by three hundred delegates, representing forty-three counties.

The school bill, reported by the Senate committee, was discussed at length, and the legislature was urged to take favorable action upon it. Messrs. L. Andrews, Willey, Wright, Batchelder, and Kingsley were appointed a committee to confer with the Senate committee and others.

Mr. Cowdery, of the finance committee, reported a plan for raising funds, in addition to those already pledged, to sustain the Agent. The plan was adopted and a reserve fund of $602 was pledged.

Mr. Andrews, of the executive committee, submitted an encouraging report respecting the *Ohio Journal of Education*, and the importance of a vigorous effort to increase its circulation was urged by several speakers.

Addresses were delivered at this meeting by Prof. J. H. Fairchild, of Oberlin, on "The Joint Education of the Sexes;" and Dr. A. D. Lord read a report on "The Smithsonian Institution."

Delegates were appointed to the American Institute of Instruction, the American Association for the Advancement of Education, and the New York State Teachers' Association.

The fifth annual meeting was held in Columbus, Dec. 29th and 30th, 1852, President Anderson in the chair.

The opening address by M. F. Cowdery reviewed the recent educational history of the State, and made a stirring appeal to the members of the Association to meet the high responsibilities resting upon them.

The executive committee gave the cheering results of the efforts of the year just closing. The *Journal of Education* had been a financial success, the receipts exceeding the expenditures by over $200. The resident editor, Dr. A. D. Lord, was paid $150 for his services. Eight hundred new subscribers were pledged.

The number of institutes held in the year was thirty-one, ten less than in 1851. This decrease was attributed to the increase in the number of graded schools, and the difficulty of securing competent institute instructors. The committee recommended that application be made to the legislature so to amend the laws that institutes could receive pecuniary aid from the State, and that the Association employ at least four institute instructors to assist the General Agent.

The report also contained a valuable table giving statistics of forty-five union or graded schools in Ohio. Only five of these schools were organized previous to 1848.

The afternoon of the first day was devoted to a discussion of the school bill then pending in the Senate. Resolutions were passed specially approving of the provisions relating to the state tax, the office of State Superintendent of Schools, township boards of education, and school libraries. A committee was appointed to confer with the Senate committee on schools.

Lorin Andrews was employed as Agent for the ensuing year, at a salary of $1,500. Dr. Joseph Ray, of Cincinnati, was elected president; D. F. DeWolf, of Norwalk, recording secretary; J. Hurty, of Lebanon, corresponding secretary; J. C. Pearson, of Columbus, treasurer; Lorin Andrews, chairman of the executive committee; and M. F. Cowdery, chairman of the finance committee.

The semi-annual meeting in Dayton, July 6th and 7th, 1853, was large and enthusiastic. The new school law embodied most of the important measures advocated by the

Association, and there was much rejoicing over its enactment. Over five hundred teachers commended the law "to the hearty good will of the people, and the earnest co-operation of the friends of education."

Mr. Cowdery, of the finance committee, reported that $410 was due the Agent. A call for pledges of money was made at the next session and the needed $410 was raised.

Prof. I. W. Andrews, of Marietta College, presented resolutions setting forth the qualifications of Lorin Andrews, and most earnestly recommending him to the people of Ohio as a fit person for State Commissioner of Common Schools. The resolutions were unanimously adopted, and a committee of seven was appointed to prepare an address to the people of the State.

The annual meeting, held in Columbus, Dec. 28th and 29th, was one of great interest. The opening address was delivered by Rev. Dr. Thompson, President of the Ohio Wesleyan University, and the annual address by Hon. Horace Mann, of Massachusetts. Reports were read by S. N. Sanford, of Cleveland, on "Natural Science;" by Mr. Smith, of Toledo, on "Moral Instruction;" and by John Hancock, of Cincinnati, on "The Position and Duties of Teachers."

The annual report of the executive committee showed an increase in the number of institutes held, and a considerable increase in the number of graded schools, the number then in the State being estimated at about one hundred. The report strongly advocated the establishment of a State Normal School, and closed with an earnest appeal to teachers to stand by the school law.

Mr. Andrews's election to the presidency of Kenyon College caused his retirement from the position of Agent, and Dr. A. D. Lord was elected his successor. He resigned his position as superintendent of the Columbus schools, and soon "took the field."

The rules, requiring the election to be by ballot, were suspended, and Lorin Andrews was elected president of the Association for the ensuing year by acclamation. John Hancock was elected recording secretary; H. Anderson, corresponding secretary; D. C. Pearson, treasurer; A. D. Lord, chairman of the executive committee; and M. F. Cowdery, chairman of the finance committee.

It has seemed advisable to sketch the proceedings of the Association the first six years of its history, with sufficient fullness to indicate their aim, scope, and spirit. A want of space forbids even a brief summary of the proceedings of the meetings held since 1853, and the fact that the official reports of all these meetings, with the more important papers and addresses, have been published in the "Journal of Education," and its successor, the ""Educational Monthly," makes such a summary unnecessary. A brief statement of the more important facts in this later history must suffice.

The Association continued to hold two meetings a year until 1858, when the semi-annual meeting was discontinued and the time of the annual meeting changed to July. The average attendance for twenty years past has been over five hundred, and some meetings have been attended by nearly a thousand teachers.

In 1863 the Association was divided into two sections, but after a trial of the plan for two years, it was abandoned. The Ohio Superintendents' Association met for several years the day before the Teachers' Association and at the same place, but in 1874 it was merged in the Ohio Teachers' Association, and has since been conducted as a section. In December, 1857, the Association was incorporated, with the title of "The Ohio Teachers' Association."

The meetings of the Association have been, almost without exception, harmonious and spirited, and, for many years, there has been little or no canvassing in the election of officers. In no instance in the knowledge of the writer, has the honor of the presidency been conferred on a known aspirant for the position. The nominating committee has reported the names of persons deemed competent to fill the offices designated, and worthy of the confidence and honor of the Association, and the nominations thus made have been approved by the Association without division.

The great measures of school progress advocated by the Association in the first years of its history, were teachers' institutes, normal schools, school supervision (state and local), graded schools, and school libraries. When it held its sixth annual meeting, all of these measures, the second excepted, were more or less satisfactorily embodied in school legislation. All efforts to secure the establishment of state normal schools had failed. In his final report as chairman of the executive committee, in 1853, Lorin Andrews made one more stirring appeal on this subject, and, at the semi-annual meeting in 1854, Dr. A. D. Lord, Mr. Andrews's successor as Agent and as chairman of the executive committee, submitted a report recommending the establishment of a normal school *under the auspices of the Association.* The proposition was earnestly advocated by Mr. Cowdery, Prof. I. W. Andrews, Lorin Andrews, and others, and the executive committee was instructed to report at the next annual meeting a definite plan for the establishment of a normal school, including the raising of funds for such a purpose.

At the next annual meeting, President Lorin Andrews read a letter from Cyrus McNeely, offering to transfer to the Association the house and grounds of his school in Hopedale, valued at $10,000, for the purposes of a normal school. The proposition was referred to the executive committee. At the semi-annual meeting, held in Cleveland in July, 1855, Mr. McNeely's proposition was accepted, with the thanks of the Association for the munificent gift, and a committee of eleven was appointed to take possession of the property. There were many present at this meeting who doubted the ability of the Association to sustain such an institution, but the enthusiasm and confidence of such leaders as Lorin Andrews, M. F. Cowdery, and Dr. Lord, carried the Association. An effort was at once made to raise an endowment fund, and thousands of dollars were pledged by the more zealous friends of the enterprise. The school was conducted under the auspices of the Association for several years, and then passed under private control. The present connection of the school with the Association is nominal. In 1858, the Association petitioned the General Assembly to make the school a state institution, but the bill was defeated.

At the annual meeting in 1855, Prof. Alfred Holbrook presented a report from a committee, containing a petition to the legislature, asking that the state be divided into four normal school districts, and that an annual appropriation of $5,000 be made by the State to one normal school in each district, on condition that such school be established by members of the Association, with property valued at not less than $15,000. The report was discussed at length, and adopted. This discussion disclosed the fact that several members of the Association doubted the value of normal schools, and a committee was appointed to inquire into "the causes of the failure of normal schools in this and other States."

The "Ohio Journal of Education" was published by the Association eight years. The first four volumes were edited by Dr. A. D. Lord; the fifth by Rev. Anson Smyth; the sixth by John D. Caldwell; and the seventh and eighth by Wm. T. Coggeshall. Dr. Lord received a small compensation ($150 to $200) as resident editor of the first three volumes, and his salary as editor of the fourth volume and State Agent was fixed at $1,800; Mr. Smyth was paid $1,500 for services as editor and State Agent; and Mr. Caldwell's salary as editor was fixed at $1,500. The receipts of the first five volumes exceeded the expenses, not including a portion of the editor's salary as State Agent, but the sixth volume closed with a deficit of several hundred dollars, besides the editor's salary for the year. The propriety of disposing of the Journal, and thus relieving the Association, was urged at the annual meeting in 1857. The proposition of Messrs. Follett, Foster & Co., to publish the seventh and eighth volumes, assuming all financial responsibility, and paying the Association forty per cent of the net profits, was accepted by the executive committee. At the annual meeting in 1859, the executive committee was authorized to provide for the future publication of the Journal, and it was decided to commit its management to private enterprise. It was transferred to F. W. Hurtt and Anson Smyth, who changed the name to the "Ohio Educational Monthly." In 1861, the magazine passed into the hands of E. E. White, and in 1875 it was sold to W. D. Henkle, the present publisher. It is still recognized as the organ of the Association.

It is seen from the foregoing, that the financial enterprises, early undertaken by the Association, proved a heavy burden. The salary of the State Agent the first three years was largely met by the voluntary donations of a few generous teachers, some of whom gave full ten per cent of their income to sustain the Association. At the annual meeting in 1855, over forty members pledged the payment of one and one-half per cent of their salaries. But these noble sacrifices were not adequate to meet the demands upon the treasury. In 1857, the indebtedness of the Association on the Journal's account was $482, exclusive of the editor's salary for the year. In 1858, the trustees of the McNeely Normal School reported debts amounting to $1,000 to $1,200. This indebtedness was fortunately reduced by the sale of volumes of the Journal. The editions for the first six years were considerably in excess of the circulation, and the Association was thus left in possession of several hundred copies of each volume. Dr. Lord had received sets of the first five volumes in part payment for his services in 1854, and, in 1858, two hundred sets of the first three volumes were sold to the State Commissioner for school libraries, thus reducing the debt about $400.

At the annual meeting in 1859, action was taken by the Association, which resulted in the transfer of both the Journal of Education and the McNeely Normal School to private control. The executive committee assumed the payment of the portion of the debt incurred for instruction ($225 due Miss Cowles), and the trustees settled all other claims, in part from the proceeds of pledges. Mr. Caldwell generously deducted $900 from his claim against the Association for services as editor. Other claims were reduced, and the remaining indebtedness was paid from the proceeds of sales of the second three volumes of the Journal, and from membership fees. At the annual meeting in 1862, the executive committee had the pleasure of reporting the Association free of debt, *with ten cents in the treasury*. Since 1862 the receipts of the Association have exceeded its expenses, including the cost of publishing full reports of the proceedings of most of the meetings.

The proceedings of the Association for the past fifteen years have been largely devoted to the consideration of questions relating to school organization, instruction, and management, special attention having been given to classification and grading, courses of study, and methods of teaching. Vigorous efforts have also been made to secure legislation for the improvement of the school system. The most important of the measures urged since 1865, are teachers' institutes, normal schools, county supervision, the township system, and professional certificates. The discussions on these subjects, from year to year, show great unanimity of sentiment among the teachers of Ohio respecting the legislation needed to give greater efficiency to the school system. The necessity of normal schools and county supervision has been repeatedly affirmed by the Association.

The Ohio Teachers' Association has a history of which every friend of education may justly be proud. No other body of teachers has ever undertaken such enterprises for the advancement of education, and it is believed that no other has exerted a stronger or more salutary influence.

The following table gives the principal officers in each year of the Association:

DATE.	PRESIDENT.	RECORDING SECRETARY.	TREASURER.	CHAIRMAN EXECUTIVE COM.
1848......	Samuel Galloway....	T. W. Harvey........	Wm. Bowen	M. F. Cowdery.
1849......	" ...	S. S. Rickly..........	L. G. Parker.........	Asa D. Lord.
1850......	" ...	E. D. Kingsley......	John Ogden	"
1851......	Isaac Sams	John Lynch...........	"	Lorin Andrews.
1852......	W. C. Anderson.....	Charles Rogers	"	"
1853......	Joseph Ray............	D. F. De Wolf	D. C. Pearson	"
1854......	Lorin Andrews......	John Hancock........	"	Asa D. Lord.
1855......	Andrew J. Rickoff..	William Mitchell....	"	"
1856......	Anson Smyth........	M. D. Parker........	"	John Hancock.
1857......	I. W. Andrews......	W. C. Catlin	"	"
1858–59..	M. F. Cowdery......	S. M. Barber and George L. Mills......	J. J. Janney.........	John Lynch.
1860......	John Hancock	R. W. Stevenson ...	Alex. Duncan	E. E. White.
1861......	A. D. Lord............	J. H. Reed	"	"
1862......	Wm. N. Edwards ..	Edwin Regal	Chas. S. Royce........	"
1863......	E. E. White...........	Samuel A. Butts ...	"	Wm. Mitchell.
1864......	Charles S. Royce ...	Wm. E. Crosby......	Daniel Hough........	"
1865......	T. W. Harvey.........	H. J. Caldwell	"	"
1866......	Eli T. Tappan........	W. H. Venable......	J. F. Reinmund.....	A. J. Rickoff.
1867......	Wm. Mitchell........	S. A. Norton..........	R. W. Stevenson ...	"
1868......	W. D. Henkle........	W. Jones	Allen Armstrong...	M. F. Cowdery.
1869......	Lyman Harding.....	Geo. W. Woollard..	Geo. M. Walker.....	W. D. Henkle.
1870......	R. W. Stevenson.....	B. O. M. De Beck..	"	"
1871......	A. C. Deuel	J. F. Lukens.........	T. C. Mendenhall ..	"
1872	Geo. S. Ormsby	L. S. Thompson.....	A. B. Johnson........	"
1873......	U. T. Curran.........	"	"	G. A. Carnahan.
1874......	D. F. De Wolf	J. M. Clemens	L. S. Thompson	"
1875......	A. B. Johnson........	G. N. Carruthers...	"	Samuel Findley.
1876......	Samuel Findley.....	W. W. Ross...........	M. C. Stevens........	H. M. Parker.

NOTE.—M. F. Cowdery was Chairman of the Finance Committee from 1853 to 1858 inclusive.

OTHER STATE ASSOCIATIONS.

A convention of Ohio colleges was held previous to 1855, but no permanent society was formed until 1867, when a constitution was adopted and officers elected. The first meetings were held in connection with the Association, but for several years past they have been held at another time and place, and with increasing interest and success. The society is called the Association of Ohio Colleges.

The Ohio Association for the Promotion of Female Education was organized in Sandusky. in July, 1852. For several years the meetings were held the day before or the day after the meetings of the Ohio Teachers' Association. Rev. P. B. Wilbur, of Cincinnati, Rev. S. Findley of Chillicothe, S. N. Sanford, of Granville, Dr. A. D. Lord, of Columbus, and E. Hosmer, of Cleveland, were among the active members.

LOCAL ASSOCIATIONS.

As early as 1857, the teachers of north-western Ohio organized an association with the title of the "North-western Ohio Educational Association." Several successful meetings were held. The Association was revived in 1859, and large and interesting meetings held.

Similar associations have been formed in the north-western, eastern, central, and south-western sections of the State. The most successful of these is the North-eastern Ohio Teachers' Association, which has sustained its meetings since 1869. It has published its proceedings in a large and handsome centennial volume. The Central Ohio Teachers' Association has held one or more successful meetings each year since 1870.

County teachers' associations have been held in Ohio since 1850, and a few may have been organized earlier. Several counties have sustained monthly meetings. These associations have usually had their origin in the teachers' institutes. Township associations have also been organized in a few counties.

CHAPTER X.

EDUCATION IN THE PENAL, REFORMATORY, AND BENEVOLENT INSTITUTIONS.

Those who are under the care or guardianship of the public institutions of the State, are composed of three classes: the infirm, the criminal, and the unprotected. In the first class are the lunatic, the idiotic, the blind, and the deaf and dumb; in the second are all the subjects of criminal or police laws; and in the third we may properly place the orphans and the paupers. All of them taken together make what is defined as the *dependent class*. In every community, even where the highest Christian civilization prevails, this is a large class, and, on the principles of humanity and justice, it must be provided for.

In 1838, the Commissioner of State Statistics, E. D. Mansfield, reported the whole number of the dependent class in Ohio to be 34,497. Since that time the number has increased, and the census of 1870, with the annual reports of the Secretary of State, and of the benevolent institutions, enables us to make a more accurate statement. Several new institutions, such as the Boys' and Orphans' Homes and the Reform Farm for Boys have also been established. Using this material, we find that the dependent class in Ohio is composed of about 58,800 persons, as follows:

Lunatics	2,600
Idiotic or Imbecile	2,000
Deaf and Dumb	1,350
Blind	1,030
Prisoners confined in jails	6,000

Prisoners in the Penitentiary	1,200
In Asylums, Houses of Refuge, Homes, etc,	2,000
In Work-houses	700
In State Reformatories and Homes	1,400
In County Infirmaries	5,000
In City Infirmaries	600
Out-door poor partially supported by the cities	20,000
Persons arrested, tried, and convicted for statute and police offenses	15,000

The last two classes all cost the State something, but are a floating and temporary population. Nevertheless, as the same numbers return each year with a gradual increase, they become, in fact, a permanent body partially charged upon the State. Putting these aside, however, there are remaining no less than 23,880 persons who are under the permanent care of the State. For all this vast body there are no hopes for any restoration to a healthy moral or physical life, except in what is generally known as *education*. If the defects of nature are to be supplied, as in the case of the deaf and dumb, or infirmness helped, as in the case of the idiotic, or the conscience quickened, as in the case of the criminal, it is always by some kind of education, either moral, intellectual, or physical, that the cure or the reform is accomplished. It becomes then, a question of great importance whether to all or to which of these classes, and in what modes, education can be applied.

In examining the various forms of infirmity, want, or crime, lunacy seems to be the only one to which education, as commonly understood, cannot minister. "Who can minister to a mind diseased." And yet, a certain form of education is applied even to lunatics. This is the education of discipline and of amusement. The effects of discipline, even on lunatics, may be known by the fact that in an asylum of 150 inmates, 140 came down to evening prayers, notwithstanding their evident nervous agitation. This discipline was a large part of the Greek education. So far as this point goes, Ohio is not excelled by any State in the Union in regard to the care extended to this unfortunate class of the infirm. There are no less than five great Lunatic Asylums in the State, two of which are now building. When all are completed, there will be room, care, and comfort for all of this class.

Leaving this class out of view, there are still 21,280 of the idiotic, deaf and dumb, blind, criminals, prisoners, paupers, and orphans, who are the proper subjects of education. The next question is, "How far has the State provided for them, and what measures, either of instruction or appropriation, has the State taken?"

Here we may note four divisions of the great dependent class, to which education may be applied in different ways, viz: 1. The infirm class, whose defects may be either helped or cured by education. Such are the idiotic, the blind, and the deaf and dumb. 2. The youth, who may be either assisted, reformed, or supported, according to their several cases. Such are juvenile offenders and orphans. 3. The permanent resident inmates in Infirmaries, Widows' Homes, and Hospitals. Many of these are ignorant. 4. The adult criminal class, several thousands of whom are constantly in prison. These make a dangerous class of community, and it is a well ascertained fact that a very large proportion of these are ignorant also, although such crimes as forgery, or swindling, etc., require some education to make the criminal an adept. It is here that our system of laws and means for reformation fail more than in anything else. Some persons, beyond doubt, have criminal instincts, but the great body of criminals are the victims of a vicious state of society.

Before we note the state of education in our penal, benevolent, and reformatory institutions, we will state the order in which these institutions have been created. It is as follows:

Ohio Penitentiary, established in	1815
Ohio Institution for the Deaf and Dumb, in	1829
Ohio Institution for the Blind, in	1837
Ohio Lunatic Asylum, in	1838
Ohio Asylum for the Idiotic, in	1857
Ohio Reform Farm School for Boys, in	1858
Ohio Girls' Industrial School, in	1869
Ohio Soldiers' and Sailors' Orphans' Home, in	1871
Cincinnati House of Refuge, in	1851
Cleveland Industrial School, in	1857
Cincinnati Work-house, in	1869
Cleveland Work-house, in	1870
Cleveland House of Refuge, in	1871
Cincinnati Orphan Asylum, in	1850

These dates are valuable as showing that these institutions grow up and increase with the progress of Christian civilization. Only one of the whole number was known to the greatest and most civilized of heathen nations.

INSTITUTION FOR THE BLIND.

This institution is located in Columbus. It has three departments of instruction—one of common literature and knowledge, one of music, and one of useful arts. Many of the pupils have been thoroughly educated. In addition to the elementary branches, history, rhetoric, natural philosophy, algebra, geometry, analytical geometry, differential and integral calculus, mental science, and Latin have been taught successfully. In the music department, the success has been extraordinary. It has been equally great in the work department. The kinds of work in which the blind can engage are necessarily limited in number, but, fortunately, they are remunerative. In the last year, there were taught broom-making, cane-seating, sewing, machine-sewing, bead-work, knitting, and accounts. An inquiry among the pupils who have gone out from the institution, shows that they have been quite successful in earning a livelihood.

Broom-makers have averaged $243.41 per annum, and those engaged in mercantile pursuits, $764.28. Thirteen teachers are employed, three of whom are teachers of music, and four of domestic work. It is to be regretted that more of the unfortunate blind do not avail themselves of the advantages furnished by this institution.

For three years from the commencement of the institution, A. W. Penniman was in charge of the school. In 1840, Wm. Chapin was appointed superintendent and held the office for six years, followed by Mr. Penniman as acting superintendent for two years. George McMillen held the office from 1848 to 1852; R. E. Harte from 1852 to 1856; A. D. Lord from 1856 to 1868; and G. L. Smead from 1868 to the present time. Mr. Penniman, the first teacher, had been trained in the New England Institution for the Blind, under the care of the late Dr. Samuel G. Howe. Dr. Lord, before he entered the institution, had taken a very active and useful part in advancing popular education in Ohio. He was called away to take charge of the New York State Institution for the Blind at Batavia, N. Y. Mr. G. L. Smead had been a successful teacher under Dr. Lord for several years, and became his worthy successor. The institution has never been more prosperous and useful than at the present time.

INSTITUTION FOR THE DEAF AND DUMB.

This institution is located at Columbus. It is a kind of graded school, in which the pupils are advanced in studies as far as its means permit. There is a primary, a grammar, and an academic department. The course of study embraces the branches usually pursued in the public schools, including Latin, and requires ten years for its completion. Twenty-four teachers are employed, who have an average of seventeen pupils each. The admission is free, and the yearly period of instruction is forty weeks. The vacation of twelve weeks is spent by the pupils at their homes.

The first principal of the institution was N. H. Hubbell, who laid the foundations of its success wisely, and labored with great skill and energy for many years. He was succeeded by J. Addison Carey, who died within a year after his appointment. Rev. Collins Stone, followed Mr. Carey, and remained for eleven years, administering the affairs of the institution with rare ability and success. He resigned to take charge of a similar institution at Hartford, Conn. He was succeeded by Mr. George L. Weed, who remained for three years, rendering valuable service. His successor, the present superintendent, is Gilbert O. Fay. The ten years during which Mr. Fay has been in charge, have been years of great prosperity. The institution has been exceedingly fortunate in its superintendents and teachers.

ASYLUM FOR IDIOTIC AND IMBECILE YOUTH.

This institution is, in its very nature, a school—one which takes the feeble-minded children and endeavors to educate them to some degree of usefulness. This is done with marked success. In the school, as in other schools, the elements of knowledge are taught, and a much larger number acquire them than is generally supposed. Of the whole number under instruction in 1875, two hundred and fifty-three had been taught to read and write. It has been ascertained that one-third of the inmates can be so trained as to be able to support themselves. The habits of the remainder can be greatly improved, and the burden of their care reduced by proper physical and mental training. This is a result far beyond public expectation at the time the institution was founded.

The institution is under the general supervision of three trustees appointed by the State. The first superintendent was R. J. Patterson, M. D., who held the office from 1857 to 1860. He was succeeded by G. A. Doren, M. D., the present superintendent. Under Dr. Doren's charge the institution has greatly prospered. The fine buildings of the asylum are located on beautiful grounds in the western suburbs of Columbus.

REFORM FARM FOR BOYS.

This institution is located on the Hocking hills, south of Lancaster, Fairfield county, and occupies twelve hundred acres of land. Its object is the education and reformation of juvenile delinquents. With the exception of a class of "incorrigibles," who, being found incapable of restraint or reform at home, are admitted by the courts to the Farm, all the inmates have been guilty of minor offenses against the law. It is the first reformatory in the United States founded upon the plan of a family. There are no walls, cells, or bars of iron to restrain the pupils, and it is probably the only place in the country where young criminals are treated on purely Christian principles. The experience of eighteen years has fully justified the experiment.

In the conduct of the school, it is assumed that the young offender whose heart is not yet hardened, may, by kindness and instruction, be led to adopt a better life. This kindness is shown in such a practical form, that its reality and its object cannot be doubted. The pupil is made to see that the Farm is a home, made for his reformation and improvement. He is conducted to a "family building"—one of nine—where he is received by an "elder brother," who is henceforth to be his friend and counselor. This elder brother may himself have been a pupil in the school; at any rate, he understands the temptations and needs of young criminals. He is the head of a "family," and it is his duty, by acts of kindness, to lead those under his charge to think better of the world, and to begin a new life. The result of this treatment is most satisfactory. Of 704 inmates, in 1875, but 30 attempted to escape. Many of those who run away, return voluntarily.

The managers of the institution have adopted methods of discipline and instruction which are impossible in any public school. The inmates are awakened at dawn, and employ half of the day in labor and half in school, except an hour of rest or play on the grounds, where there is nothing to tempt or annoy them. On Sunday, there is public worship and Sunday school, in the exercises of which the boys show both interest and aptitude.

Instruction is given in labor, in the branches usually pursued in schools, and in religion. Each of the "elder brothers" engages more or less in all kinds of instruction. There are five female teachers, six superintendents of workshops, and a gardener. The boys are employed in cultivating the farm, in fruit raising, and in the making of boots and shoes, chairs, clothing, and other articles. For this work, they are divided into classes and properly trained. The school instruction proper is done as systematically and thoroughly as in the best of the public schools. The boys are in school about five hours each day.

Of the boys admitted to the Reform School, nine-tenths are between the ages of ten and sixteen; more than one-half of them have been convicted of some form of theft or robbery, and three-fourths have been found guilty of crimes of some kind; two-thirds of them have lost either one or both parents, and one-third of the whole number can neither read nor write. Of the 2,270 who have been inmates since the establishment of the institution, 1,700 have gone out to meet the realities of life. Most of these have maintained their integrity, and become useful members of society. Among them may be found employes on railroads, mechanics, farmers, clerks in business houses, and teachers.

The Reform School took its rise from an appointment by the Legislature of Hon. Charles Remelin, Hon. J. A. Foote, and J. D. Ladd, Esq., as commissioners to visit the reform schools and houses of refuge of the country, and report a plan for something of the kind for Ohio. The investigation extended to Europe, where Mr. Remelin examined similar institutions in England, France, and Germany. As the result of their investigations, the "family system" was recommended. The plan was accepted by the legislature, and the same commissioners were authorized to organize the institution. Mr. Remelin was appointed "Acting Commissioner," and had a personal supervision of the school. He resigned in 1859, when Geo. E. Howe, Esq., was appointed as his successor. Mr. Howe is still at the head of the institution. He has been ably and wisely aided by Mrs. F. M. Howe, whose personal influence over the boys has been very great, and whom they regard with filial love. To the personal devotion of Mr. and Mrs. Howe to the work, and to their peculiar sagacity and wisdom in wielding the moral force by which the school is chiefly ruled, the remarkable success and prosperity of the Reform Farm School is mainly due. They have ever had the sympathy and co-operation of the commissioners, who have been remarkably devoted to the interests of the school. James D. Ladd, Esq., served as commissioner for nine years, Hon. J. A. Foote for eighteen years, and Rev. B. W. Chidlaw has held the position for the last ten years.

GIRLS' INDUSTRIAL HOME.

The Girls' Industrial Home is located at White Sulphur Springs, Delaware county. Like other reformatory institutions, it is emphatically a school. The inmates are expected to devote half of each day to study and recitation. Instruction is given in reading, writing, spelling, arithmetic, English grammar, geography, history, algebra, and natural philosophy. In addition to school instruction, the girls are taught needle-work, house-work, etc. They are grouped in families of thirty girls each. Each family is under the care of an assistant matron, a teacher, and a housekeeper.

The institution has but one superintendent, John Nichols, M.D. Mrs. Mary E. Nichols is the matron. Both are doing an excellent work, in instructing and reforming the girls under their care.

SOLDIERS' AND SAILORS' ORPHANS' HOME.

This institution is located near Xenia, Greene county, on a farm of 275 acres. It may be said to be a continuation of the institution previously established in the same place by the "Grand Army of the Ohio." The "family plan" has been adopted, and the children are distributed in twenty cottages or family buildings. The graded plan is followed in the school department. There are eleven grades or departments, including the high school. The schools are under the general supervision of the superintendent of the Home, but are conducted by a principal and ten female assistants. In addition to the schools there is an industrial department, in which are taught blacksmithing, tinning, tailoring, shoemaking, printing, dressmaking, and other industries.

L. D. Griswold was the first superintendent. In 1874, A. E. Jenner, M. D., was appointed to the superintendency. He was succeeded by W. P. Kerr, in October of the same year. The Home is now under the superintendency of Capt. W. L. Shaw.

THE OHIO PENITENTIARY.

The Ohio Penitentiary is located in Columbus, on the left bank of the Scioto. Its management is becoming one of the most important objects of care to the State—the more so, since no great progress has been made in reforming criminals, notwithstanding the existence of prison-discipline societies, and the trial of theoretic schemes to reclaim the lawless. Education, as a means of reformation, seems to be almost wholly neglected in the penal institutions of the country. As the great mass of criminals are very ignorant, it may fairly be presumed that education and moral culture are potent means to be used in their reformation.

The educational advantages of the Penitentiary are limited to (1) its discipline; (2) to some opportunities for reading and occasional instruction; (3) to the Sunday school.

The discipline of the institution is admirable, and accomplishes much, especially in physical training. The early rising, the simple food, and the regular work, all minister to the health of the body, but, unfortunately, do little towards increasing knowledge or improving the morals of the convicts. The institution is, however, a far better one with this discipline than without it.

The library contains 2,500 volumes, principally standard novels, histories, school readers, magazines, and Bibles. The prisoners are allowed to subscribe for papers, if they pay for them from their private funds, and are permitted to receive any reputable papers sent to them by their friends. They work from 6 A. M. to 6 P. M., in the summer, and from 7:30 A. M. to 4:30 P. M., in winter. After supper, they are permitted to read until 9 P. M. This gives an average of three hours each day for reading. Some of the prisoners improve the opportunity, and become quite intelligent.

In order to secure religious instruction the Penitentiary has a chaplain. The prayer meeting on Sunday morning is attended by about 400 convicts, and the Sunday school has an attendance of nearly 900. Members of the Young Men's Christian Association and citizens of Columbus are teachers in this school. The chapel services at 9 A. M. on Sunday are attended by nearly all the convicts.

These are unquestionably advantages far superior to those afforded in any penal institutions of this kind a few years ago. The main object of the State, however, aside from that of punishment and confinement, has been to make the work of the convicts available for their support. In this, success has been attained. The net earnings of the convicts in 1875, as appears from the report of that year, exceeded the expenses of the institution by $33,636.88. It remains for the experience of the future to determine, whether a portion of the time devoted to work would not be spent more usefully in intellectual and moral culture.

CINCINNATI HOUSE OF REFUGE.

The Cincinnati House of Refuge is similar to the Reform School. The school is systematically organized on the principle of work and study united—all the labor being done in workshops. Five schools hold two daily sessions, one hour in the morning, and two hours in the evening. The inmates are mostly from twelve to sixteen years of age, and very few of them have received any education. The main difficulty in the management of the institution arises from the fact that a large percentage of the pupils are discharged too soon. Nevertheless, many have remained long enough to be essentially benefitted. The superintendent says: "The Refuge is in all particulars an industrial school. Every effort is here made to teach the children to read, and to write, and to work, and to train them to habits of industry and perseverance, hoping thus to make them useful citizens." This object is in a large degree accomplished.

Religious services are held every Saturday afternoon, conducted by ministers and laymen of every denomination.

CLEVELAND HOUSE OF REFUGE.

In Cleveland the House of Refuge is a part of the Work-house, and is called the "House of Refuge and Correction." The Refuge department is, however, entirely separate, and is conducted in its general plan much the same as that in Cincinnati. It is a school, uniting work and study. The children go to school at 7 A. M., and remain until 10½ A. M., and then work until noon. At 6½ P. M. they go to school again until 8 P. M. This gives five hours of study, and nearly an equal amount of work.

The school is also supplied with books and magazines, partly by friends and partly by the board of education. It is soon to be separated from the Work-house.

Religious services are conducted regularly every Sabbath by ministers of the city and young men of the Christian Association.

CINCINNATI WORK-HOUSE.

The work-house system is now so important and essential a part of city police, that some notice may be taken of it here, though its connection with education is slight. The Cincinnati Work-house is on the same general plan with the Ohio Penitentiary, except that the period of confinement in the Penitentiary is long, while that in the Work-house is short. The average period of confinement is only forty days. This is so short a time, and there is so much uncertainty about it, that a regular school cannot be kept up. The main reliance is on systematic work. As in the case of institutions already mentioned, this work does something in the way of discipline; yet the experience of the work-house system is that inebriates and thieves are little benefited by it. Something is done to divert their minds. There are religious services every Sabbath; there are also regular musical exercises and some amateur singing. The great difficulty with such an institution is, that its inmates are mostly the incorrigible. The young and improvable are sent to the House of Refuge.

CLEVELAND WORK-HOUSE.

This institution is quite similar to that of Cincinnati. Its main object is work for the short term prisoners, for whom no permanent provision can be made, and to make their work available. They have religious instruction on Sundays, conducted by clergymen of different denominations in rotation. The Work-house of Cleveland has a respectable library, principally given by the board of education. How completely a work-house congregation is composed of the incorrigible, may be learned by the following extract from the annual report of the directors:

"Nearly three-fourths of the adults who are sent to the Cleveland Work-house are sent for intoxication, or for crimes committed under the influence of intoxicating beverages. Of the entire number sent, about one-third can neither read nor write, while the remaining two-thirds, with few exceptions, have but a very indifferent common school education. All is done that reasonably can be, while they are in prison, to effect their reformation; but, as a general rule, very few of them go out permanently reformed. Experience has shown that it is morally impossible to correct the vicious appetites, and still more vicious principles of hardened criminals, within the short period of thirty or sixty days, which is the usual term of sentence."

INDUSTRIAL SCHOOL OF CLEVELAND.

This school is a purely benevolent enterprise, and is mainly dependent on the charity of the public. Its object is to provide for and restrain vagrant and destitute youth of the city, by educating them to become good and useful citizens. It is not only a benevolent enterprise, but an efficient police measure in restraining and preventing beggary and crime. In fine, it is on the same plane with the House of Refuge, except that it is an individual and not a public charity. There is a principal school and two branches. The course of instruction requires the children to devote half the day to study, and the other half to work, such as domestic service, horticulture, or agriculture. They are also instructed in sound morality, cleanly habits, and respectful manners. No sectarian doctrines are taught, but the tendency of the institution is to teach the virtues, to save from vice, and to lead the youth to an honorable and useful life. Such has been the result with many, who, having been trained in this school, have reached positions of honor and trust, and now frankly acknowledge that they are indebted to this school for their success in life.

ORPHAN ASYLUMS AND WOMEN'S HOMES.

There are three orphan asylums in Cincinnati, which have been in operation for many years, and probably contain an average aggregate of 400 children. There is a Children's Aid Society in this city, and another in Cleveland. There are also a Widow's Home. a Home for the Friendless, and a Boarding House for Women out of Employment, maintained by the Women's Christian Association. There are similar institutions, doubtless, in Cleveland and other cities, but we have no means of ascertaining their statistics.

All the orphan asylums have schools, either independent or connected with the public schools. The Cincinnati Orphan Asylum sends its children to a public school near the institute. All of them, likewise, have religious services on Sunday. Each of the orphan asylums may, therefore, be considered as a school since education receives attention. When of proper age, the orphans are placed in respectable families.

This department of public charity, although managed by very different hands, and often under difficulties, is very well attended to in Ohio, and this class of unfortunate youth receive both care and instruction.

The Widows' Home and the Home for the Friendless are of a character which render a school both unnecessary and impossible—the former being comprised wholly of the aged, and the latter of temporary inmates.

COUNTY INFIRMARIES.

There is a county infirmary in each of the counties of Ohio. These contain, in the aggregate, about 6,000 persons.

This is only one-fifth of what may be called the dependent poor. The remainder consists of what is called "out-door poor," all of whom, however, receive some public support. In all the infirmaries there are children and youth capable of instruction, and the State has wisely provided that boards of education may sustain schools for their instruction. How far this is done, we cannot tell; but it is done in some of them, and may be in all if the directors consent.

SUMMARY OF RESULTS.

Having now reviewed, and given the results of education and reform in the penal, reformatory, and benevolent institutions of the State, it may be useful to present the whole, as far as possible, in a tabular form, that we may see what has been done.

The following table gives the whole number of inmates received, and the present number in each of the institutions named:

	Number received.	Number present.
Asylum for the Blind	868	158
Asylum for the Deaf and Dumb	1,522	488
Asylum for Idiotic and Imbecile Children	1,100	423
Reform Farm School for Boys	2,270	504
Girls' Industrial Home	299	182
Soldiers' and Sailors' Orphans' Home	900	600
Ohio Penitentiary	11,063	1,191
Cincinnati House of Refuge	3,482	267
Cleveland House of Refuge	350	127
Cincinnati Work-house	18,072	421
Cleveland Work-house	4,000	243
Industrial School (Cleveland)	5,000	300
Orphan Asylums, and "Homes"	2,000	600
Infirmaries	....	6,000
Totals	50,926	11,504

This leaves out of view all the jails and lunatic asylums, and it includes the Penitentiary and the work-houses, in which there is really no school education. Let us take then, what may properly be called the educational part of these institutions, and consider the result. Of these, eleven classes are enumerated above, giving this result: whole number received, 17,791; present number in institutions, 3,649.

Some of the institutions enumerated are of a recent date, and therefore present but a small number of inmates, but these are among the most promising. In all except the Penitentiary, schools are regularly sustained.

There are two remarks to be made upon this statement of facts, without which a complete knowledge will not be had. First, several institutions are omitted, from the want of information, which could not be had in time. There are, for example, in Toledo, Zanesville, and probably other places, orphan asylums and special institutes, generally founded by private beneficence, which provide for portions of the dependent class. There are Children's Aid Societies, which directly or indirectly aim both to help and to educate destitute children. Secondly, there are other provisions of law for the education of the poor and destitute, the effect of which cannot be exactly ascertained. For example, there is a provision of law, already mentioned, that boards of education may provide schools for youths in infirmaries. It is impossible to say how far this law has been executed, but from the poor condition of many of the infirmaries, there is reason to believe that it has not been very effective. Again, there is a law which enables the counties to provide homes for the poor and neglected youth, and also that any two or three counties may unite for such an object. This has been carried into effect in a few counties, and is likely to prove a most beneficent provision. In fact, it enables each county to do for itself what the State has done in its "Homes." Washington county has such a home for its poor children, which has been a great success, and is a model school of its kind.

From this review and statement, it is evident that the State of Ohio, or some of its communities, has provided in various forms and in abundant measure for all the dependent class. It has provided education for all the youth, whether of the criminal or the unprotected class. Its schools for reformation are not exceeded by any in the world. These are the best results of Christian wisdom, civilization, and progress. In all this, the people of Ohio rejoice, and present these results as an offering of first fruits from the first State of the North-west.

CHAPTER XI.

BIOGRAPHICAL SKETCHES.

It has been a matter of some delicacy to decide who of the prominent educational men of Ohio, ought to appear in the list of those whose biographical sketches should be included in this volume. It would not do to draw the line between the living and the dead. To include all the able and deserving men now actively engaged in the promotion of education, would require a space beyond the limits of a single chapter. It will be observed that none of the State Commissioners of Common Schools appear in the list. It has not been the intention to include persons whose educational labors, although deserving of a grateful remembrance, have been confined to particular localities. The only exceptions that have been made, are Robert Steele, Esq., of Dayton, and Rufus King, of Cincinnati, whose long educational services and great prominence make it eminently proper that brief sketches should be allotted to them.

It is to be regretted that a full sketch cannot be given of Nathan Guilford, of Cincinnati. Efforts were made to secure the necessary personal facts, but without success. The few facts given are such as the writer happens to have at hand. The law of February 21, 1849, was adopted in so many towns of Ohio by special vote, that it is fitting that a sketch of its author, the Hon. Samuel T. Worcester, should be given. The Hon. Harvey Rice's connection with the school law of 1853 makes a sketch of his life also deserving a place with those who have promoted education in the State.

It is a source of regret that these sketches do not include Alexander Kinmont, Horace Mann, Andrew Freese, and many others. Mr. Mann, however, was more prominently connected with education in Massachusetts than in Ohio, although he is held in grateful remembrance by many young men and teachers in the State in which he passed the last years of his active and useful life. Unfortunately, the sketch given of Albert Picket lacks details.

EPHRAIM CUTLER.

Ephraim Cutler was born at Edgarton, Martha's Vineyard, Mass., April 13, 1767. He was the son of Rev. Manasseh Cutler, LL.D. He came to Ohio in 1795, and lived a few years in Ames, Athens county, and afterwards removed to Warren, Washington county, where he spent the remainder of his life. His interest in the promotion of education doubtless arose, in a measure, from the fact that his father was the author of the famous educational provision in the ordinance of 1797.

He was appointed, by the first territorial legislature, one of seven commissioners to lease all the ministerial and school sections in each township of the Ohio Company's lands. This was the first effort made by legislative authority to promote common school education in Ohio. In 1802, he was a member of the Constitutional Convention, and secured the adoption of the provision which imposes upon the General Assembly the obligation forever to "encourage schools and the means of instruction."

After nearly twenty years' retirement from active political life, he was elected in 1819, a member of the General Assembly. As chairman of a special committee of the House of Representatives, he prepared a bill providing for the division of townships into school districts, for the building of school-houses by money raised by levies upon the taxable property of the districts, and for the partial payment of teachers from the public funds. This bill passed the House by a vote of 40 to 20, but the General Assembly adjourned before the Senate acted upon it.

In 1823, Mr. Cutler was elected Senator. He was a member of the school committee, and chairman of the committee on revenue. In his efforts to secure the passage of a school bill he was ably supported by Nathan Guilford. This bill passed the Senate, January 26, 1825, by a vote of 28 to 8, and the House, February 1, by a vote of 48 to 24. At this day, when our common school system is universally popular, the intense earnestness with which Mr. Cutler followed up his favorite measure, cannot be properly appreciated. The imperfect law of 1825 cost far more labor than the subsequent acts based upon and supported by an advanced public sentiment.

In addition to his legislative labors, he was, in 1823, appointed one of seven commissioners, "to report a system of education adapted to common schools," and also to collect information as to the condition and value of school lands. In June, 1822, three commissioners met at Columbus and organized their board by making Mr. Caleb Atwater chairman. At this meeting, the following counties were allotted to Mr. Cutler for the purpose of preparing educational statistics: Scioto, Pike, Jackson, Lawrence, Gallia, Meigs, Athens, Hocking, Morgan, Monroe, and Washington. As appears from letters of Mr. Atwater to Mr. Cutler, the commissioners spent nearly three months in their investigations, and reported to the next legislature.

As a private citizen Mr. Cutler was an active and earnest supporter of schools and all other means of instruction. The first school ever taught in his own neighborhood, near Marietta, was accommodated by the use of a room in his own house. It was taught by the late Gen. John Brown, of Athens, Ohio. When residing in Ames, Athens county, he induced a younger brother, a graduate of Harvard, to teach a school, a part of his house being used as a school-room. He was active in forming a local library—*the first public library in the West*—obtained largely by proceeds of the sale of furs, and often called the "coon-skin library." The influence of the good schools he helped to establish, and of this library upon the little community was very great. Mr. Cutler died on the 8th of July, 1853, in the eighty-seventh year of his age.

NATHAN GUILFORD.

The House of Representatives of the General Assembly of Ohio, in the winter of 1821–2, appointed a committee on schools and school lands. This committee, of which Caleb Atwater was chairman, urged in their report the necessity of liberal popular education, and recommended the appointment of seven commissioners to devise and report upon a common-school system. The committee's report was accepted in January, 1822, and Gov. Allen Trimble appointed Caleb Atwater, the Rev. John Collins, the Rev. James Hoge, Nathan Guilford, Ephraim Cutler, Josiah Barber, and James M. Bell, as the seven commissioners. They published three pamphlets to awaken public interest, and recommended a system of public schools based upon that of New York. Mr. Guilford declined to co-operate with the commissioners, because he thought that the plans recommended were inadequate to meet the needs of the State. He published a letter on free education, in which he urged a general county *ad valorem* tax. This letter was published by the General Assembly of 1823–4, with the report of the commissioners. The Assembly, however, was not wise enough to risk advanced school legislation. An appeal to the people resulted in the election of a set of wiser men, among whom was Nathan Guilford, elected as Senator from Cincinnati. Ephraim Cutler was Mr. Guilford's coadjutor in urging forward the work of education. Mr. Guilford was made chairman of a joint committee on school legislation. He made an able report, and with it presented a bill, which required a tax of one-half a mill on the dollar to be levied for school purposes by the county commissioners, made township clerks and county auditors school officers, and provided for school examiners. The bill passed the Senate without amendment, by a vote of 28 to 8, and the House by a vote of 46 to 24.

Mr. Guilford was elected superintendent of the public schools of Cincinnati in 1850, a law establishing such an office having been passed by the General Assembly of 1849–50. He served two or three years. In his report of 1852, in reference to immigrants to this country he said:

> "We must EDUCATE THEM ALL! Universal suffrage and universal intelligence must go together. The State must provide the means of a good education freely to all. She must plant and liberally support PUBLIC SCHOOLS in every neighborhood, where the rising generations of all classes, without distinction of sex, rank, or nativity, may freely receive such mental and moral training as shall enable every individual to comprehend the genius of the institutions under which he lives; clearly to understand his rights and duties; to form judicious opinions of the measures of administration; to distinguish the true from the counterfeit; to despise the demagogue, and to honor the true patriot.
>
> "The children of our foreign population must, through the influence of these institutions, become *Americanized*, by mingling in early life with our native youth, learning in the same schools obedience, order, self-control, and virtuous habits; imbibing the principles of American republicanism, and becoming familiar with our language and history."

In the same report he entered his protest against the memoriter system of recitation which had recently been adopted in the Central High School.

ALBERT PICKET.

All that is here given in reference to Albert Picket, is gathered from incidental references to him in educational periodicals. The labors of such a pioneer deserve a minute description, but unfortunately the materials for it are not at hand.

He began in New York City, in January, 1811, a periodical called the "Juvenile Monitor, or Educational Magazine." It is believed to be the first periodical of the kind published in the United States. It did not enter upon the second volume. In February, 1818, he, with J. W. Picket, started in the same city the "Academician" which was equally short-lived. The connection of Albert and J. W. Picket with educational periodicals in Ohio is referred to in the next chapter.

Through the exertions of Albert Picket and Alex. Kinmont, in 1829, there was organized in Cincinnati, the Western Academic Institute and Board of Education, from which originated the famous Western Literary Institute and College of Professional Teachers, before which, in 1834, he delivered the opening address, on the objects of the Institute. He afterwards delivered addresses and reports as follows: in 1835, on "Education;" in 1836, on "Parents, Teachers, and Schools;" in 1837, on the "Formation of Character in Individuals;" in 1838, on "Reforms in Education;" in 1839, on the "Qualifications of Teachers;" and, in 1841, on the "Want of Education." When in Cincinnati, he was principal of the Cincinnati Female Seminary. He afterwards became a resident of Delaware, Ohio, and in July, 1850, at the meeting of the Ohio Teachers' Association, in Springfield, there was presented by Mr. Williams a report prepared by Mr. Picket, on "Teaching Reading."

The following is found in the *Ohio School Journal*, of September, 1848, edited in Columbus, Ohio, by Dr. Lord (Vol. III., p. 138):

"Albert Picket, Sen., for many years Principal of the Manhattan School in this city, one of the most efficient and enterprising teachers of our country, is still living at Delaware, in Ohio. This gentleman, now in his 79th year, taught half a century, and was always twenty years in advance of the majority of the profession. He always acted well his part, and he is still quickening and comforting those who labor for the cause of education.—*Teachers' Advocate* (N. Y.).

"We rejoice to meet, from the scene of his former toils, this just tribute to a veteran teacher. It has been our privilege, in addition to occasional correspondence, to enjoy the privilege of several cheering interviews with 'Father Pickett,' as he is affectionately and reverently styled here in Ohio, and, last autumn, to labor with him for a week in the instruction of a class of some hundred teachers.

"It is matter of gratitude that he is permitted to spend the evening of his days so quietly and pleasantly in the family of a beloved and affectionate son. But, as he looks back upon his life, what unutterable emotions and what varied recollections must throng the echoing chambers of his soul! 'He taught for half a century!' and during that time laid his forming hand, as it were, upon some thousands of opening minds. In each and all of these minds, he awakened emotions, kindled aspirations, developed energies, and into all instilled principles, to which, but for him they might forever have been strangers. And these minds still live! They are not of the perishable material upon which the architect, the painter, or the sculptor lavishes his labor and skill. The emotions awakened continue to thrill them; the aspirations kindled, to elevate them; the energies developed, to propel them; and the principles instilled, to guide them onward through time and through eternity. Many of those on whom his forming influence was exerted, and to whom his instructions were imparted, are now filling important and responsible stations in life, and are in turn exerting a controlling influence in the formation of those who are to succeed them upon the stage; others have passed from earth, but, whether in this or the unseen world, they still live, and the impressions made, and the influences exerted upon them, have done their work toward forming the characters they now possess, and which they will be likely to retain while canvas shall moulder and granite and marble crumble to dust. But perhaps one of the most interesting reflections which arise in the mind of the faithful teacher, on a review of his labors, is, that among all his pupils he has not a single enemy. Let others wear laurels and receive the plaudits of mankind, but give me the retrospect of the famous teacher."

JOHN L. TALBOT.

John L. Talbot was born October 20, 1800, near Winchester, Frederick county, Va. With his parents he emigrated in 1806 to the Redstone settlement, in Washington county,

Pa., where he resided till 1816, when he removed to Mt. Pleasant, Jefferson county, O. In 1819, he descended the Ohio river on a raft and took up his permanent abode in Cincinnati.

During his residence in Pennsylvania he usually attended school one quarter each year. His time in school was devoted mainly to spelling and arithmetic, in which he excelled. In Cincinnati he served a short apprenticeship to the carpenter's and joiner's trade, attending a night school taught by Cornelius King. At this school he went through Walsh's Arithmetic and studied trigonometry, surveying, and navigation. Subsequently he was employed as an assistant in the school.

In 1822, after having manufactured his furniture, he opened a school of his own, which was largely attended. He gave instruction to many youths, who in after years occupied prominent positions.

In 1823, he assisted in organizing a society for the improvement and elevation of teaching as a profession, and in 1828 in founding the Ohio Mechanics' Institute. About the same time he took part in the establishment of the Academy of Fine Arts and the Academy of Natural Sciences. In all these organizations Mr. Talbot was an active member, serving as secretary, treasurer, or actuary. From 1829 to 1845, he was an active member of the Academic Institute, afterwards the Western Literary Institute and College of Professional Teachers.

Mr. Talbot was the author of an arithmetic, which the writer remembers as the first he studied after Warren Colburn's. He is not able to state in what year the book was first published. A revised, enlarged, and improved edition appeared in 1841. It was again copyrighted in 1845, with the title, "The Western Practical Arithmetic." The copyright of this book having passed out of Mr. Talbot's hands, in 1843 he copyrighted a new arithmetic called "The

Scholar's Guide to the Science of Numbers." Mr. Talbot still resides in Cincinnati, Ohio, having long since retired from the work of teaching.

MILO G. WILLIAMS.

Milo G. Williams was born in Cincinnati, April 10, 1804. His parents were natives of New Jersey. His father, Jacob Williams, came west in 1795, and settled in Cincinnati. In 1814, he retired from business, and removed to the country. His farm formed what is now a part of the city known as Camp Washington. He died in Cincinnati, in 1840.

Mr. Williams commenced his pedagogical career in 1820, and ended it in 1870, including the period of 50 years. His early education was limited to the merest elements of learning. His first essay as a teacher was in the charge of the village school in which he had occasionally been a pupil. In this humble school, he recognized the beginning of a deep interest in the education of the young, the necessity of a practical education among all classes of our citizens; and here also he was led to the knowledge of his deficiencies, and the necessity of his own improvement before he could become a succcssful instructor.

In his nineteenth year, Mr. Williams opened a private school in Cincinnati. Pupils came in gradually, and at the opening of the second year he needed more room. In a few years, he went to other rooms where he could have assistant teachers. He graded his classes and organized four departments. The study of constitutional law was successfully introduced into this school.

In 1833, Mr. Williams accepted the general supervision of a manual labor institution, established at Dayton. The question of connecting manual labor with literary institutions had been before the people for several years, and some of the best educators regarded it with favor. But the experience of a few years showed that the system was not well adapted to the wants of our country, and could not be employed successfully.

The Dayton school was closed at the end of the second year, and Mr. Williams accepted the situation as principal of the Springfield High School, then about to go into operation under the management of a board of trustees. The several departments were placed under able teachers, and it continued under this organization till 1840, when the property passsed into the hands of the conference of the Methodist Episcopal Church.

About this time the friends of the New Jerusalem Church (Swedenborgian) were completing their arrangements for opening a school in Cincinnati, in connection with the church, and Mr. Williams was made the principal. A year or two after, he was made a professor in Cincinnati College, then under the presidency of Dr. Biggs, and in 1844 he returned to Dayton to re-organize the Dayton Academy.

A meeting of gentlemen from different parts of Ohio was held in Urbana in the autumn of 1849, and it was agreed to found at Urbana an institution of learning in the interest of the New Jerusalem Church. A charter was obtained from the Ohio General Assembly, with university powers. The organization of the board of directors was completed in 1850. Mr. Williams was appointed the president, and to him was assigned the chair of science. He continued as the acting president of the faculty until 1870.

Mr. Williams, from 1829 to 1852, was actively engaged in promoting the cause of education. In 1829 he assisted in organizing "The Western Literary Institute and Board of Education," which afterwards became, through his persistent effort, "The Western Literary Institute and College of Professional Teachers." He was for ten years corresponding secretary of this association and took an active part in all its proceedings. He was prominent in the series of educational conventions, held in Columbus, beginning in 1836. In the convention of 1838 he made a report on the diversity of text-books, in which he opposed state uniformity, and a report on normal schools, in which he recommended the establishment of one in each Congressional district. He was an active member of the State Teachers' Association until 1852, when his duties at the Urbana University made regular attendance impracticable. Mr. Williams still resides in Urbana.

SAMUEL LEWIS.

It is fitting that the name of Samuel Lewis should occupy a leading place in the brief notices designed to commemorate the life and labors of the early educators of Ohio. Among the first in point of time, he was also pre-eminently so in the eloquence, the persistency, and the rare disinterestedness with which, for the greater part of an active life, he advocated the right of the poor and ignorant to the benefits of a common school education. He was the first to make himself thoroughly and personally acquainted with the inefficiency of the school laws, the ignorance of teachers, the wretched hovels in which the youth of the rural districts were herded together for two or three months in the year, the waste and dishonesty in the management of the school fund, arising from the sale of public lands; all these, and kindred abuses, encountered in him a stern foe.

He was born in Massachusetts, March 17, 1799, but Ohio, in whose interests his strength was poured out, proudly claims him as her own. His parents were poor, and "strong necessity, supreme 'mong sons of men," was the nurse of his youth, and may be said to have aocompanied him through life. His father, the captain of a small coasting vessel, having lost what little property he possessed, determined to try his fortune in what was then considered the far west. In 1813, the entire family, consisting of father, mother, and nine children, left their home by the sea, and began their journey westward. For the father and sons, this meant traversing the entire distance as far as Pittsburgh on foot. There a flat-boat was purchased, on which they floated down the river as far as Cincinnati. There the work of his life began. At fifteen, he is working on a farm at seven dollars a month, his wages going to his father. Then having learned a trade, he pays his father fifty dollars a year for his time—a strong proof that parental authority asserted itself in those days.

Working, studying, laboring with head and hand at whatever was honorable, sustaining and improving, at the age of twenty he resolved to study law. The industry and self-denial with which he prosecuted his studies, remind one forcibly of the same qualities, as evinced in the life of Horace Greeley.

In 1824, he was licensed as a local preacher in the Methodist Church, of which he had been an earnest and consistent member from the age of ten years. His powers as an orator were now often exerted in behalf of temperance and popular education. His interest and labors in the latter cause at this period still survive in the two high schools of Cincinnati. A trustee of both, he may almost be said to have called the Woodward school into existence by his advice, made influential by his personal friendship for the founder.

The active, intelligent teachers of the State, who knew what must be done, how deep and broad the foundations must be laid, on which should rise the superstructure that was to gather within its sheltering walls the future youth, were not long in ascertaining that in Samuel Lewis all their wants would be met. In 1837, he was elected State Superintendent by the legislature. The limits of this sketch will not permit an extended account of the herculean tasks he performed in his new sphere. The whole State was to be awakened to the necessities of the hour. There was no network of railways connecting distant counties; the circuit rider's mode of locomotion was then the only practicable one. In his crusade against ignorance, he rivalled in enthusiasm a medieval knight. The first year he traveled over fifteen hundred miles, chiefly on horseback, quickening school officers, parents, and teachers, and collecting and arranging facts to be embodied in his first report to the General Assembly. In that report, he seems to have been gifted with a rare prescience. It gave shape and consistency to the school law passed at that session, and many of its suggestions have stood the test of time, and are to-day in active operation. For the first year his salary was five hundred dollars. The Superintendent's salary was then fixed at twelve hundred dollars. The law also made him editor of a monthly journal, to be published at the expense of the State. This journal, the "Common School Director," he edited for one year, in addition to his other labors. It was then discontinued, no provision having been made for its future support.

Mr. Lewis's labors as Superintendent ceased in 1839, when he resigned his office, his health having been greatly impaired by the hardships incident to his work.

It can not be denied that he had met with much opposition. No revealer of abuses or apostle of a new gospel escapes. The large-hearted measures, recommended by him, had awakened a spirit of parsimony which succeeded in repealing some of the provisions of the law of 1837. But the work had been too well done to be overthrown by the malice of the few, and the cause of popular education had received an impetus which it has never lost.

The temperance and the anti-slavery causes both received a large share of Mr. Lewis's attention in the latter years of his life. He was frequently a candidate of the Liberty party for various state offices, and his stirring, winning eloquence still lives in the memory of many. Exhausting work for his fellow-men had worn him out before his time, and in 1854 death came to him not unexpectedly. He died as he had lived, happy, hopeful, and fearless.

CALVIN E. STOWE.

Many unacquainted with the early educational history of our State, will wonder to see the name of C. E. Stowe, whom they have always associated with the East, in the list of her public school benefactors. To the pioneers in the great work no explanation will be necessary; they will remember him as an able champion in the early days of the battle with ignorance.

Calvin E. Stowe, or as he is popularly known, Professor Stowe, was born at Natick, Mass., in 1802. His early history is that of many New England boys—very limited means, very strong thirst for knowledge, and a will which ultimately attained the goal of his ambition, a college education. He graduated at Bowdoin College, Maine, in 1824. After having graduated from Andover in theology, and filled the chair of professor of languages in Dartmouth, he accepted, in 1833, the professorship of Biblical Literature in Lane Theological Seminary. Here his connection with our subject begins. He recognized at once the great need of the West—common schools—and he set himself to work to advance their cause, in common with Samuel Lewis, Dr. McGuffey, and other public spirited citizens. He visited Europe in 1836, on business connected with the Seminary, bearing with him also an official appointment by the legislature to examine into the system and management of European schools, particularly those of Prussia.

On his return, in 1837, he submitted his noted "Report on Elementary Education in Europe." A copy was sent to every school district in the State, and it was republished and largely circulated by the legislatures in other states.

In it, thoroughness, freedom from routine and from slavish subservience to a text-book, were particularly enjoined upon teachers. Upon the necessity of training or normal schools, he delivered an able address in 1838, before the State Educational Convention, in Columbus, at which Gov. Shannon presided. Of the Western College of Teachers, he was an active member, contributing from time to time valuable papers on the subjects which came up for discussion. In 1850, he returned to Andover, Mass., where the greater part of his life has since been spent. He still lives, having passed the psalmist's limit of three score years and ten.

DR. WM. H. M'GUFFEY.

The history of school books exhibits in a marked degree the uncertainty of popular favor. "The Eclectic Series of Readers," so well known throughout the length and breadth of the land, has been a rare exception. The author, Dr. Wm. H. M'Guffey, was born in 1800, in Trumbull county, Ohio. Unaided, he succeeded by unremitting toil, mental and physical, in preparing for college, and graduated at Washington College, Pa., in 1825. His life henceforth was devoted to the profession of teaching. He was soon appointed professor of ancient languages in Miami University, where he remained until 1836, when he was called to the presidency of Cincinnati College. He remained in that position three years, and then accepted a similar one in the Ohio University. During all these years, he was active in the cause of popular education, then beginning to be widely discussed, and rendered efficient aid in teachers' conventions both by pen and presence. He was a ready, fluent speaker, using no manuscript, and impressing himself upon his audience both by voice and eye.

In 1845, he accepted a professorship in the University of Virginia, which he held until his death in 1873.

SAMUEL GALLOWAY.

The State Teachers' Association of Ohio was founded in 1847. Samuel Galloway, the subject of this brief sketch, was the first president. He was born in Gettysburgh, Pa., in 1811. He removed to Ohio in early youth, and graduated at Miami University, at the age of twenty-two. For several years he engaged successfully in teaching, until failing health induced him to change his employment, and, having studied law, he was admitted to the bar in 1842. He shortly afterward removed to Columbus, where he resided until his death in 1873.

His election as Secretary of State made him *ex-officio* State Superintendent of Common Schools, and brought him into direct association with the leading educators throughout the State. The cause of popular education undoubtedly owes much to his efforts. His reports to the legislature, embodying many valuable suggestions, did much to call public attention to the subject, and prepare the way for the legislation which soon followed. It is gratifying to note, that though Mr. Galloway's special sphere was mainly that of lawyer and politician, he did not remain unmindful of other claims. His wit, his learning, and his eloquence were freely used in behalf of all measures tending to the improvement of humanity.

DR. ASA DEARBORN LORD.

There are few who have served their country in the training of its youth, more deserving of its love and gratitude, than Dr. Asa D. Lord. He was born in Madrid, St. Lawrence county, New York, June 17, 1816. His early youth was passed on a farm. From his mother, who had herself been a most successful teacher, he is said to have inherited his love of study. In 1839, he accepted the position of principal of the Western Reserve Teachers' Seminary, at Kirtland, Ohio, which he held for eight years. Here his zeal, his energy, his professional enthusiasm, his interest in all who strove for something better than they had yet known, were signally displayed. He made the seminary a center to which the youth of both sexes crowded from the adjoining counties. Many of these have since occupied useful and honorable positions as teachers, cherishing with the warmest gratitude the memory of him who first kindled in their young hearts a love for the teacher's calling. Here, in 1843, was held what was in substance the first Teachers' Institute in the State.

From Kirtland, Dr. Lord removed to Columbus. Here he inaugurated the first graded school in the State. He had had the system under consideration for some time, and had become satisfied that it offered the best advantages to the children of towns and villages. For his services as superintendent and as principal of the high school, he received the first year a salary of $600, of which $100 was contributed by a public spirited citizen.

Dr. Lord's services as editor of the "Ohio School Journal," the "School Friend," the "Public School Advocate," and "Ohio Journal of Education" are referred to in the next chapter.

For one year, his connection with the schools of Columbus was suspended, while he acted as agent of the State Teachers' Association, which he had been active in establishing.

He had, while at Kirtland, taken his degree in medicine. He now added to his other labors a course of systematic theology, and, in 1863, was licensed to preach by the Presbytery of Franklin. Those who knew him well assert that he never intended to practice either calling exclusively. He strove to make himself thoroughly acquainted with the wants of both soul and body, that he might the better administer to those committed to his care. He made the Institution for the Blind, at Columbus, to which he was appointed in 1856, an honor and a blessing to the State. He taught its pupils valuable lessons in work-shop and school-room, and thus won to his views legislators of widely different politics, who voted liberally for the erection of a building in which his plans could be successfully carried out. Fully aware of the extent and results of his labors, he saw that the work which he had set for himself was well-nigh done, yet he resolutely accepted in 1868 a call to a similar institution, in Batavia, N. Y.—a call to harder work and diminished salary. Here he pursued the same course until his death, in 1874.

DR. JOSEPH RAY.

The name of Dr. Joseph Ray is held in grateful remembrance by many for his works on algebra and arithmetic, which robbed mathematics of its terror for the young beginner. He was born in Ohio county, Va., in November, 1807, and evinced from early youth great fondness for study, and an earnestness of purpose which supported him under many discouragements. He entered Washington College, Pa., supporting himself by teaching at intervals, but left without taking a degree.

Turning his attention to medicine, he graduated from the Ohio Medical College, Cincinnati, but in October of the same year entered upon the profession of teacher, and adhered to it through life. Henceforward, his history as teacher is bound up with that of Woodward College, afterwards Woodward High School, first as professor and afterwards as president, which office he held at the time of his death, in April, 1856.

In all these years, Dr. Ray was prominently identified with the leading teachers of the State and the great cause which they had at heart. He was rarely absent from the meetings of the State Teachers' Association, and in 1852 was elected its president.

LORIN ANDREWS.

Lorin Andrews was born in Ashland county, O., on the 1st of April, 1819. His boyhood was spent in labor upon his father's farm. When eighteen years of age, he entered the grammar school at Gambier, and afterwards Kenyon College. The strong religious element in his character, which manifested itself in his future life, was here first awakened under the teaching and personal influence of Bishop McIlvaine. In 1840, he engaged as an assistant in an academy at Ashland. He afterwards taught for a time at Mansfield; but returned and took charge of the Ashland Academy, at the same time pursuing the study of law. In 1847, he was admitted to the bar, and the same year was called to the superintendency of the public schools of Massillon.

Mr. Andrews was active in the organization of the State Teachers' Association in 1847. He acted as its agent in 1851–2–3, was recommended as the choice of the Association for the office of State Commissioner of Common Schools, in 1853, and was elected its president the same year. He was elected President of Kenyon College in 1853, and held the office until his death.

When the call for volunteers was made in 1861, he was the first man to respond. He recruited a company in Knox county, and soon after was appointed Colonel of the 4th Regiment of Ohio Infantry, and detailed to service in Western Virginia. His regiment soon became noted for its discipline and efficiency. In the midst of his duties he was attacked by camp fever, of which he died at Gambier, on the 18th of September, 1861, universally beloved and deeply lamented.

MARCELLUS F. COWDERY.

M. F. Cowdery was born in Pawlett, Rutland county, Vt., in 1815. He spent his early life in western New York. After an attendance for several years at a district school, he entered the academy at Wyoming, New York, and subsequently that at Canandaigua, one of the eight institutions that received legislative aid for the education of teachers. In 1836, Mr. Cowdery began the work of teaching in Ohio, and taught in district and private schools until 1841, when he became connected with the Western Reserve Teachers' Seminary, of which Dr. Lord was then principal. Here he met with many who had taught in the public schools, or were preparing to teach, and his attention was thus turned to consider the defects in the common school system. From 1845 and onward, Mr. Cowdery labored faithfully in the interests of the schools of the State, attending nearly all the earlier institutes, meeting with others at Akron, in 1847, to organize the State Teachers' Association, instructing in the normal class at Norwalk, and every where laboring by word and work, to infuse into others the same interest and diligence which he himself felt and exhibited. In November, 1848, he commenced his labors in Sandusky, and, excepting one interval of about seven months in 1863-4, continued in the superintendency until July, 1870.

Few have been associated with Mr. Cowdery, either as teachers or pupils, without acquiring something of the earnest, conscientious spirit he brought to his work, and of his desire for the physical, moral, and intellectual well being of those intrusted to his care—in a word, for their education in its broadest signification. His well known collection of "Moral Lessons" illustrates the spirit of the man.

ISAAC SAMS.

Isaac Sams was born in Bath, England, November 12, 1788. He first taught in England in 1813, but in 1818, having become fascinated by Morris Birbeck's account of the United States, he came to Maryland and established a boarding school, which he conducted for seventeen years, with eminent success. In 1835, he removed to Brooklyn, N. Y., in order to extend the field of his exertions. His school soon became very popular. His health utterly failing, he was compelled, in a short time, to retire to an estate which he had purchased near Hillsborough, Ohio.

After ten years spent in farming, his health being restored, he took charge of the Hillsborough Academy, and conducted it for six years. He then turned his attention to the establishment of a union school in Hillsborough. In this school he taught mathematics for one year, and for three years acted as superintendent.

In 1838, he was appointed a member of the board of school examiners of Highland county, which position he held for many years. In 1851, he was elected president of the State Teachers' Association. He continued teaching until 1862. He still resides in Hillsborough, at the advanced age of eighty-seven.

WILLIAM NORRIS EDWARDS.

Mr. Edwards was born in Pittsfield, Mass., July 4, 1812. and graduated at Williams College. The writer became acquainted with him about a quarter of a century ago, when he conducted a private academy in Dayton, Ohio. In 1852, he became superintendent of the public schools of Troy, Ohio, and continued to serve the people there acceptably until his sudden death, August 3, 1867. He had a strong hold upon the confidence and affection of the people of Troy. His funeral was largely attended, many of the business houses being closed, and private residences draped in mourning. Those who for many years met Mr. Edwards in the meetings of the State Teachers' Association, learned to appreciate his worth. He was elected president of the Association in 1861, but did not preside at the next meeting, being detained at home by illness. Mr. Edwards was a man of great culture, and his deliberation before he acted or recommended action made him a safe counselor. He will long be remembered with gratitude by the pupils trained under his guidance, and with the highest respect by his fellow teachers.

SAMUEL T. WORCESTER.

Samuel T. Worcester was born in Hollis, N. H., August 30, 1804. He entered Harvard College in 1826, and graduated in 1830, in the class of which Charles Sumner was a member. After leaving college he taught a little more than a year at Weymouth, Mass., and afterwards, for nearly a year, conducted a private academy at Cambridge. He then began to study law at Hollis, and continued the study at the Harvard Law School. In the spring of 1834 he removed to Norwalk, Ohio, where, after residing the legal time, one year, he was admitted to the bar, in 1835.

Mr. Worcester remained a citizen of Norwalk until 1867, when he returned to New England to engage in the settlement of the estate of his deceased brother, Joseph E. Worcester, the lexicographer.

During his residence in Norwalk, he took an active interest in the efforts to improve the condition of the schools in that place and vicinity. In consequence of his known desire to have the school laws of the State made more efficient he was elected Senator in 1848. Upon the meeting of the General Assembly in December of that year, he was appointed chairman of the Senate committee on common schools. He drafted the bill, which afterwards became a law, February 22, 1849, and which was not repealed until the passage of the codified school law of May 1, 1873. This bill was an improvement upon the Akron law of 1847 in relieving boards of education from any dependence upon the action of town or city councils. The bill passed the Senate without amendment and without opposition. It also passed the House without amendment and without serious opposition, although some of the members had a doubt as to the constitutional right of the voters of a town or city to tax the people for the support of education. The next winter Mr. Worcester reported some amendments to this law, and also to the Akron law, to enable cities and towns that had adopted the latter to adopt the law of 1849.

HARVEY RICE.

The school law passed by the General Assembly March 1, 1853, was chiefly prepared by the Hon. Harvey Rice, of Cleveland, a member of the Ohio Senate, and chairman of the committee on common schools. Mr. Rice was born in Massachusetts, June 11, 1800, and graduated at Williams College. He came to Ohio in 1824, and settled in Cleveland. For a short time he engaged in teaching while preparing for the practice of the law, upon which he soon entered. Mr. Rice's abilities and worth were soon recognized by his fellow townsmen, who manifested their appreciation by electing him to various important offices in the county, and to a seat in the lower house of the General Assembly.

In 1851, Mr. Rice was elected to the Senate. The session which followed was a very important one. Ohio had outgrown her old constitution, and this was the first meeting of her legislature under the provisions of the new. It was evident to all who had watched the growing educational needs of the State, that the school system needed a thorough revision. Since the passage of the act of 1838, the population of the State had more than doubled, and its resources had increased in a still greater ratio. Mr. Rice addressed himself to the work of procuring the passage of an act for the reorganization of the common schools, and providing for their supervision. The bill passed the Senate with but two negative votes. He had previously taken a prominent part in the passage of an act providing for the establishment of two asylums for lunatics, and he now advocated the establishment of a State Reform School, at that time a novel idea. A few years saw it in successful operation.

Mr. Rice still lives in Cleveland. He has lived to see the State of his adoption enjoy the fruit of his labors, to see her, in his own words, "lead the column in the cause of popular education and human rights." His active life as a politician and public spirited citizen has not prevented the cultivation of his taste for literature. He is well known as a graceful writer, both in prose and verse. A volume of his poems has been published.

ROBERT W. STEELE.

Robert W. Steele, for more than thirty years a member of the board of education of Dayton, is the son of one of the earliest pioneers of that city. His father was a man of considerable prominence in the early history of that part of the State, and took a deep interest in popular education long before the establishment of the public school system. His public spirit in this and kindred matters seems to have been largely inherited by his son, the subject of the present sketch, who was born in Dayton in 1819. Mr. Steele still resides in the city of his birth, whose growth and interest he has watched with untiring care. He prepared for college at the Dayton Academy, and graduated from the Miami University in 1840. In 1842, he began his long connection with the public schools, by acting as a member and clerk of the board of managers, then appointed by the city council. For twelve years he served as president of the board, permanently retiring in 1875.

RUFUS KING.

Rufus King, of Cincinnati, bears an honored name. His grandfather was an eminent patriot and statesman of Revolutionary times. His father, Edward King, came to Ohio at an early day, established himself as a lawyer at Chillicothe, and rose to eminence in his profession. His son, Rufus, was born in 1817. He graduated at Harvard University, and has, for many years, been a leading lawyer of Cincinnati. For fifteen years Mr. King was a member of the board of education of that city, and for twelve of these years its president. He took an active part in re-organizing the public schools, and his labors have contributed largely to their increased usefulness. The high schools of the city are governed by a separate board, and of this board Mr. King was also a member for many years.

In 1853, Mr. King urged upon the Hon. H. H. Barney, State Commissioner of Common Schools, the importance of consolidating the public school libraries in cities. Mr. Barney decided that this could be done, and thus the way was prepared for the formation of a great central library in Cincinnati. Mr. King is now president of the board of trustees of the Cincinnati University, which has under its care the McMicken fund, the Schools of Art and Design, and the Cincinnati Observatory.

CHAPTER XII.

EDUCATIONAL PERIODICALS.

Educational periodicals have done much to promote the cause of education in Ohio, although the earlier ones were short-lived. Of some of them the writer knows nothing more than the fact of their publication.

The first annual meeting of the Western Academic Institute and Board of Education, also considered the first anniversary of the College of Professional Teachers, was held June 20th, 1831. The institute appointed a committee to conduct a periodical to be called "The Academic Pioneer," the first number of which appeared in July, and contained the proceedings and addresses of the meeting the preceding month. The periodical was not continued, for want of patronage. A second number appeared in December, 1832, which contained the proceedings of the second annual meeting.

There is a record that there appeared in 1834, at Oxford, a periodical called "The Schoolmaster and Academic Journal." No additional facts in reference to it are at hand.

"The Common School Advocate," was begun in Cincinnati in 1837, and discontinued in 1841.

"The Universal Educator" was started in January, 1837, in Cincinnati, but it is not known how long it was continued.

"The Western Academician," edited by John W. Picket, was started in March, 1837, and adopted as the organ of the College of Professional Teachers. It was continued but one year.

The "Ohio Common School Director," under the editorship of the Hon. Samuel Lewis, State Superintendent of Common Schools, appeared in May, 1837. It was published under the authority of the General Assembly. At the close of the session of 1837–8, no appropriations being made for its support, it was discontinued.

"The Pestalozzian" was started at Akron in April, 1838, by E. L. Sawtell and H. K. Smith. The last number was published the same year.

"The Educational Disseminator" was started in Cincinnati in July, 1838, by S. Picket, Sr., and J. W. Picket, M. D. It was soon discontinued.

"The Ohio School Journal," the first number of which is dated at Kirtland, July 1, 1846, was edited by Asa D. Lord. This journal marks an era in Ohio educational journalism. At the time of the starting of this journal, there were but four other school journals published in the United States—one in Boston, one in Providence, one in Albany, and one in Syracuse. Four or five more were started within the next three months. The first volume, consisting of only six numbers, was published at Kirtland. The subsequent volumes were published at Columbus. Its publication as a separate journal ceased in December, 1849.

"The School Friend," was started in Cincinnati, in October, 1846, by W. B. Smith & Co., publishers of the Eclectic School Books. In 1848, Mr. Hazen White was announced as the editor. In January, 1850, the "Ohio School Journal" was united with the "School Friend," under the title, "The School Friend and Ohio School Journal." It was published in Cincinnati. Its editorial department was under the management of Dr. Asa D. Lord, superintendent of the Columbus public schools, H. H. Barney, principal of the Cincinnati Central High School, and Cyrus Knowlton. The last number of this journal was issued in September, 1851, without any announcement of discontinuance.

The "Free School Clarion" was started in Massillon in Nov., 1846, by Dr. W. Bowen. In 1848, it passed into the hands of Lorin Andrews, superintendent of the schools at Massillon, and M. D. Leggett, superintendent of the schools at Akron. Under Dr. Bowen's management, it reached a circulation of 700. It was discontinued in 1849 or 1850.

The "Western School Journal," a monthly devoted to the cause of education in the Mississippi Valley, was started in Cincinnati in March, 1847, by W. H. Moore & Co. Like the "School Friend," it was at first sent free to teachers, but with No. 7, of the second volume, October, 1848, the price was fixed at 50 cents per annum. It was discontinued in 1849.

"The Ohio Teacher," edited by Thos. Rainey, author of an arithmetical work on cancellation, called "The Abacus," was begun in May, 1850, and was published at Columbus and Cincinnati. With the fourth number Cleveland was added to the places of publication. It is not known when the last number was issued.

The "American Educationist and Western School Journal" was started in Cleveland, in Jan., 1852, with B. K. Maltby aseditor. It is not known how many numbers were issued. It was discontinued the same year.

"The Ohio Journal of Education" began its existence in Columbus in January, 1852, under the auspices of the Ohio State Teachers' Association, with the following named editors: A. D. Lord, Columbus; M. F. Cowdery, Sandusky; H. H. Barney, Cincinnati; I. W. Andrews, Marietta; J. C. Zachos, Dayton; Andrew Freese, Cleveland. Dr. Lord acted as the chief editor. The Journal was printed on better paper than any of its predecessors, and its general typographical execution was excellent. In 1853, C. Knowlton, of Cincinnati, and S. N. Sanford, of Granville, appear in the list of editors, instead of H. H. Barney. In 1854 and 1855, Joseph Ray, of Cincinnati, and A. Holbrook, of Marlboro, appear in the list instead of Messrs. Zachos and Knowlton. With the February number, of 1856, the Rev. Anson Smyth, superintendent of the Toledo public schools, became editor of the Journal, by a vote of the executive committee of the State Teachers' Association. John Ogden, of Hopedale, E. E. White, of Cleveland, and Alphonso Wood, of College Hill, succeeded S. N. Sanford, Andrew Freese, and Joseph Ray as associate editors.

In February, 1857, Mr. Smyth, having been elected State Commissioner of Common Schools, was succeeded by John D. Caldwell, of Cincinnati. In the list of associate editors, Wm. S. Palmer, of Cleveland, W. H. Young, of Athens, and Wm. N. Edwards, of Troy, succeeded Messrs. Holbrook, Ogden, and Wood.

In Jan., 1858, Wm. Turner Coggeshall, State Librarian, became, by appointment, editor of the Journal, and continued as such for two years. The Association had contracted with Follett, Foster & Co., to publish the Journal, relieving it from all pecuniary liability. No associate editors were appointed.

The "Ohio Journal of Education" appeared under a new name in 1860, it having become the property of F. W. Hurtt & Co. The following was the title page of 1860: "The Ohio Educational Monthly, (successor to the Ohio Journal of Education.) A Journal of School and Home Education. Old Series, Vol. IX. New Series, Vol. I. Official Organ of the Ohio State Teachers' Association, Columbus. Edited and Published by F. W. Hurtt & Co., 1860."

In May, 1861, E. E. White & Co., that is, E. E. White and the Hon. Anson Smyth, succeeded F. W. Hurtt & Co., as editors and proprietors of the Monthly. Mr. Smyth remained associated with Mr. White until February, 1863, when he retired from the office of State Commissioner, after having served two terms, or six years.

Mr. White continued to edit the Monthly until September, 1875, when he transferred it to its present editor and proprietor, W. D. Henkle, who changed the place of publication to Salem. Under Mr. White's editorship the Monthly acquired a national reputation. In October, 1870, he began "The National Teacher," which was an edition of the "Ohio Educational Monthly," for circulation outside of Ohio. In January, 1876, the two were united by the present editor under the name "The Ohio Educational Monthly and National Teacher."

In February, 1865, after Mr. White had been acting as State School Commissioner about a year, Aug. T. Jenkins became publisher of the Monthly. Mr. White retained the editorship, with John Hancock, of Cincinnati, M. F. Cowdery, of Sandusky, T. W. Harvey, of Painesville, and T. E. Suliot, of Kent, associate editors. Mr. White resumed the publication in January, 1866.

In November, 1854, a mathematical department was started in the "Ohio Journal of Education," under the editorship of Dr. Joseph Ray. His name appeared last at the head of this department in the June issue of 1855. After the death of Dr. Ray, F. W. Hurtt, who was then his assistant in the Woodward High School, edited this department until he was succeeded, in February, 1857, by Prof. W. H. Young, of Ohio University. This department was discontinued in 1858 and 1859, but was resumed in March, 1860, in the "Ohio Educational Monthly," and in April, 1860, W. D. Henkle, of Lebanon, became the editor, and continued the editorship until May, 1861. At that time the department was discontinued and has not since been resumed.

The "Journal of Progress, in Education, Social and Political Economy, and the Useful Arts," was begun in Cincinnati, January 1, 1860, with Elias Longley as publisher and general editor. John Hancock, of Cincinnati, edited the the educational department. A portion of the periodical was printed in phonotypy.

A mathematical department, under the editorship of W. D. Henkle, was begun January 1, 1861. In consequence of the pecuniary effect of the war on the publishing interest, the "Journal of Progress" closed its career with the issue of August, 1861. In September an extra of four pages was issued announcing that the subscription list had been transferred to the "Ohio Educational Monthly."

The "News and Educator" was published in Cincinnati in 1864-5-6. Richard Nelson and John Hancock were announced as editors, and Nelson & Co., as publishers. In January, 1867, the name of this periodical was changed to that of "The Educational Times: An American Monthly Magazine of Literature and Education." Mr. Hancock edited the first number, and introduced it with his valedictory. It was published for the proprietors by R. W. Carroll & Co. The writer does not know how long it was continued. It doubtless died a peaceful death, not for lack of editorial ability, but for want of adequate pecuniary support.

"The National Normal" was started in Cincinnati in October, 1868. In October, 1869, R. H. Holbrook was announced as editor, and Sarah Porter as assistant. The names of the editors had not previously been given. It was published in Cincinnati, at first by Josiah Holbrook and afterwards by George E. Stevens & Co., until October, 1874, when the subscription list was transferred to the "National Teacher."

"The Normal School Visitor," edited and published by J. Fraise Richard, at Fostoria, was begun in January, 1875, and after nine months was transferred to J. J. Frazier, of the same place, who continued it under the name of the "Common School Visitor."

"Educational Notes and Queries," edited and published by W. D. Henkle, in Salem, was started in 1875. Before the close of the year it had secured subscribers in thirty-five states and territories.

In this sketch of educational periodicals it has not been found practicable to include the many college and school periodicals which have been published from time to time in the State, such as the "Public School Advocate and High School Magazine," Columbus, 1851; "The Pantagraph," Xenia, 1870; "The Educational Advance," begun at Ada, in April, 1873; "The Wittenberger," "The Denison Collegian," "The College Mirror," "The Oberlin Review," "The Otterbein Dial," "The College Olio," "The Philomathean Argus," "The Mute's Chronicle," "The Literary Advance," "The Normal," and "The School and Home."

APPENDIX.

STATISTICAL TABLES.

TABLE I.—SHOWING THE REPORTED NUMBER OF SCHOOLS IN THE STATE, FROM 1837 TO 1875.

DATE.	No. of counties.	No. of counties reported.	Number of schools.				
			High.	Common.	Ger.-Eng.	Colored.	Total.
1837	75	62	....	....	....	....	4.336
1838	76	54	....	....	....	....	4,030
1839	76	65	....	....	....	....	7,295
1840	79	14	....	....	....	....	....
1841	79	45	....	....	....	....	3,181
1842	79	53	....	....	....	....	3,627
1843	79	45	....	....	....	....	4,284
1844	79	45	....	....	....	....	3,321
1845	81	52	....	....	....	....	5,385
1846	83	55	....	....	....	....	4,332
1847	83	56	....	....	....	....	4,882
1848	85	57	....	....	....	....	5,062
1849	89	80	....	....	....	....	11,075
1850	87	79	....	....	....	....	12,279
1851	88	81	....	....	....	....	12,664
1852	88	70	....	....	....	....	9,916
1853	88	70	....	....	....	....	5,894
1854	88	77	57	10,451	16	48	10,572
1855	88	81	91	12,012	55	88	12,246
1856	88	85	97	11,076	58	88	11,319
1857	88	87	113	12,078	55	93	12,339
1858	88	88	139	12,224	110	129	12,602
1859	88	87	151	11,338	53	131	11,673
1860	88	88	161	13,192	72	159	13,584
1861	88	88	167	13,479	85	168	13,899
1862	88	87	144	14,728	108	172	15,152
1863	88	88	175	14,233	86	167	14,661
1864	88	88	149	11,661	39	145	11,994
1865	88	88	143	11,419	37	143	11,742
1866	88	88	141	11,413	35	157	11,746
1867	88	88	151	11,373	33	182	11,739
1868	88	88	155	11,405	34	189	11,783
1869	88	88	198	11,257	55	204	11,714
1870	88	88	383	13,568	....	....	*13,951
1871	88	88	310	13,876	....	....	14,186
1872	88	88	363	13,838	....	....	14,201
1873	88	88	350	14,193	....	....	14,543
1874	88	88	412	14,356	....	....	14,768
1875	88	88	450	14,418	....	....	14,868

* In this year and in subsequent years, the common schools of the State are classified as primary and high schools.

TABLE II.—SHOWING THE ENUMERATION AND ENROLLMENT, FROM 1837 TO 1875.

DATE.	ENUMERATION.*			ENROLLMENT.		
	Boys.	Girls.	Total.	Boys.	Girls.	Total.
1837 ...	....	....	468,812	76,975	69,465	146,440
1838 ...	....	....	588,590	57,539	51,467	109,006
1839 ...	....	....	....	....	....	254,612
1840 ...	....	....	618,746	....	....	....
1841 ...	....	....	....	76,047	61,823	137,870
1842 ...	....	....	....	5,544	3,967	9,511
1843 ...	....	....	....	24,239	20,503	44,742
1844 ...	....	....	....	25,698	23,172	48,870
1845 ...	....	....	712,152	10,794	8,520	19,314
1846 ...	....	....	728,638	19,834	15,029	34,863
1847 ...	....	....	754,193	33,232	30,626	63,858
1848 ...	....	....	....	50,211	44,419	94,630
1849 ...	....	....	796,109	213,738	153,870	367,608
1850 ...	....	....	810,163	236,827	184,906	421,733
1851 ...	....	....	828,853	238,571	207,426	445,997
1852 ...	....	....	838,669	240,152	197,560	437,712
1853 ...	....	....	811,957	....	....	....
1854 ...	....	....	816,408	191,956	166,461	358,417
1855 ...	422,067	398,557	820,624	294,888	257,051	551,939
1856 ...	416,339	393,827	810,166	299,226	262,089	561,315
1857 ...	424,065	413,972	838,037	320,386	282,961	603,347
1858 ...	431,745	411,482	843,227	328,625	283,095	611,720
1859 ...	444,468	421,446	865,914	322,253	277,781	600,034
1860 ...	457,708	435,136	892,844	363,598	321,579	685,177
1861 ...	467,007	445,953	912,960	381,153	336,573	717,726
1862 ...	471,287	449,603	920,890	378,522	346,147	724,669
1863 ...	464,974	454,900	919,874	383,770	366,643	750,413
1864 ...	474,061	464,911	938,972	353,541	341,379	694,920
1865 ...	476,214	468,638	944,852	359,121	343,431	602,552
1866 ...	494,809	479,494	974,303	381,452	347,538	728,990
1867 ...	506,484	488,766	995,250	368,841	335,926	704,767
1868 ...	519,619	499,573	1,019,192	383,760	348,012	731,772
1869 ...	525,605	503,272	1,028,877	388,979	351,403	740,382
1870 ...	530,509	511,171	1,041,680	380,655	344,241	724,896
1871 ...	539,511	518,537	1,058,048	383,722	348,400	732,122
1872 ...	546,051	526,223	1,073,274	370,719	338,081	708,800
1873 ...	506,506	485,202	991,708	368,890	335,128	704,018
1874 ...	505,001	480,946	985,947	371,204	336,739	707,943
1875 ...	522,418	495,308	1,017,726	375,436	336,693	712,129

*Until 1853 the school age was 4-21. From 1853 until the passage of the new school law, in 1873, the school age was 5-21. The present school law makes 6-21 the legal school age. Since the passage of the act of 1873 the enumeration has been taken under oath.

TABLE III.—SHOWING THE DAILY ATTENDANCE, THE NUMBER OF WEEKS THE SCHOOLS WERE IN SESSION, AND THE NUMBER AND COST OF SCHOOL-HOUSES BUILT, FROM 1837 TO 1875.

DATE.	Daily attendance.			Average number weeks common schools were in session.	Number of school-houses built.	Cost of school-houses built.
	Boys.	Girls.	Total.			
1837 ...	....	....	....	20.44	4,378	$513,973
1838 ...	40,179	33,126	73,305	16.64	393	65,732
1839 ...	....	....	....	16.00	735	148,959
1840 ...	....	....	....	....	....	....
1841 ...	29,593	21,921	51,514	13.32	123	21,722
1842 ...	36,213	25,217	61,430	13.48	153	25,831
1843 ...	44,226	30,581	74,807	12.48	125	14,930
1844 ...	33,518	22,999	56,517	13.40	115	17,217
1845 ...	49,166	35,310	84,476	12.64	194	42,127
1846 ...	43,714	35,036	78,750	14.16	164	27,325
1847 ...	44,257	34,606	78,863	22.24	175	35,866
1848 ...	50,442	40,254	90,696	12.44	153	39,727
1849 ...	173,240	145,316	318,556	14.56	158	36,443
1850 ...	190,891	146,984	337,875	14.04	248	64,823
1851 ...	203,487	159,760	363,247	17.72	300	109,304
1852 ...	144,982	121,285	266,267	10.40	171	61,837
1853 ...	....	....	....	....	....	....
1854 ...	150,529	126,667	277,196	23.92	770	346,944
1855 ...	170,545	145,306	315,851	22.50	740	438,602
1856 ...	171,877	150,766	322,643	24.60	627	374,547
1857 ...	187,951	162,912	350,867	24.60	570	293,040
1858 ...	189,037	163,108	352,145	25.40	589	391,305
1859 ...	188,182	162,217	350,399	25.20	475	282,443
1860 ...	215,620	189,972	405,592	24.80	446	341,273
1861 ...	225,902	199,181	425,083	25.20	454	435,368
1862 ...	224,451	208,891	433,342	24.60	373	243,433
1863 ...	223,802	216,924	440,726	24.40	229	186,808
1864 ...	199,447	196,809	396,256	25.15	227	186,304
1865 ...	197,941	193,608	391,549	25.78	237	227,213
1866 ...	215,231	199,911	415,142	27.29	292	274,505
1867 ...	205,908	191,578	397,486	27.33	549	955,792
1868 ...	214,312	196,409	410,721	27.81	635	1,178,561
1869 ...	227,054	207,811	434,865	30.19	664	1,874,118
1870 ...	232,858	213,289	446,147	31.16	645	1,391,597
1871 ...	223,470	208,982	432,452	33.00	578	1,025,077
1872 ...	210,818	197,720	408,538	30.92	566	893,422
1873 ...	210,551	197,366	407,917	27.97	542	1,008,786
1874 ...	221,522	208,108	429,630	29.00	579	1,164,104
1875 ...	225,431	209,918	435,349	28.00	544	1,010,786

TABLE IV.—Showing the Number of Teachers Employed in the Common and High Schools, from 1837 to 1875.

Date.	High.		Common.		Totals.		Grand total.
	Male.	Female.	Male.	Female.	Male.	Female.	
1837	....	....	....	....	4,757	3,205	7,962
1838	....	....	....	....	2,677	1,728	4,403
1839	....	....	....	....	....	....	7,288
1840	....	....	....	....	....	....	....
1841	....	....	....	....	1,746	1,400	3,146
1842	....	....	....	....	5,409	1,461	6,870
1843	....	....	....	....	2,693	1,573	4,266
1844	....	....	....	....	2,210	1,179	3,389
1845	....	....	....	....	3,224	2,095	5,319
1846	....	....	....	....	2,581	1,988	4,569
1847	....	....	....	....	2,829	2,577	5,406
1848	....	....	....	....	2,799	2,412	5,211
1849	....	....	....	....	8,005	4,374	12,379
1850	....	....	....	....	7,924	5,168	13,092
1851	....	....	....	....	8,350	5,706	14,056
1852	....	....	....	....	7,272	5,292	12,564
1853	....	....	....	....	....	....	....
1854	....	....	....	....	7,540	6,476	14,016
1855	115	81	11,087	9,893	11,202	9,974	21,176
1856	102	78	9,347	8,286	9,449	8,364	17,813
1857	120	83	9,997	8,494	10,117	8,577	18,694
1858	170	93	10,371	9,420	10,541	9,513	20,054
1859	157	106	10,164	9,931	10,321	9,037	19,358
1860	189	130	10,596	9,563	10,785	9,693	20,478
1861	187	115	10,776	10,054	10,963	10,169	21,132
1862	179	90	10,194	10,661	10,373	10,751	21,124
1863	183	113	8,429	12,339	8,612	12,452	21,064
1864	180	132	7,652	12,694	7,832	12,826	20,658
1865	140	87	6,516	13,585	6,656	13,672	20,328
1866	192	102	7,595	13,345	7,787	13,447	21,234
1867	188	153	8,160	13,067	8,348	13,220	21,568
1868	174	132	8,680	12,606	8,854	12,738	21,592
1869	188	147	8,983	12,308	9,171	12,455	21,626
1870	261	181	9,141	12,255	9,402	12,436	21,838
1871	310	190	9,253	12,354	9,563	12,544	22,107
1872	300	188	9,418	12,155	9,718	12,343	22,061
1873	305	193	9,484	11,917	9,787	12,110	21,899
1874	355	356	9,556	12,108	9,911	12,464	22,375
1875	427	214	9,759	12,092	10,186	12,306	22,492

TABLE V.—Showing the Average Monthly Salaries of Teachers, and the Whole Amount Paid Teachers, from 1837 to 1875.

Date.	Average monthly salary of teachers.				Amount paid teachers.		
	High.		Common.				
	Male.	Female.	Male.	Female.	Male.	Female.	Total.
1837...	....	....	....	....	....	....	$286,757
1838...	....	....	....	....	$154,284	$46,272	200,556
1839...	....	....	....	....	....	....	392,091
1840...	....	....	....	....	....	....	....
1841...	....	....	....	....	94,627	29,809	124,436
1842...	....	....	....	....	301,200	30,460	331,660
1843...	....	....	....	....	144,631	31,890	176,521
1844...	....	....	....	....	112,220	24,482	136,702
1845...	....	....	....	....	158 792	45,616	204,408
1846...	....	....	....	....	138,237	55,504	193,741
1847...	....	....	....	....	160,102	62,736	222,838
1848...	....	....	....	....	141,967	44,814	186,781
1849...	....	....	....	....	435,807	113,302	549,109
1850...	....	....	....	....	493,691	138,428	632,119
1851...	....	....	....	....	510,503	175,590	686,093
1852...	....	....	....	....	599,187	172,958	772,145
1853...	....	....	....	....	....	....	....
1854...	$58 00	$28 50	$23 00	$13 00	565,026	289,276	854,302
1855...	61 35	30 60	25 02	14 20	923,280	469,941	1,393,221
1856...	57 30	30 63	26 70	15 63	1,023,212	531,195	1,554,407
1857...	61 10	33 34	27 71	16 22	1,181,819	598,157	1,779,976
1858...	61 81	32 82	27 89	12 95	1,304,038	691,737	1,995,775
1859...	66 52	33 85	27 82	16 29	1,270,573	670,983	1,941,556
1860...	62 27	34 00	27 81	16 25	1,317,694	728,367	2,046,061
1861...	61 12	34 08	27 81	16 05	1,320,260	753,544	2,073,804
1862...	58 34	34 04	26 35	15 32	1,155,903	744,975	1,900,878
1863...	60 08	31 91	25 73	15 41	1,011,855	869,013	1,880,868
1864...	62 87	34 81	28 25	17 95	1,956,920	130,960	*2,087,880
1865...	73 31	41 97	36 25	21 55	2,361,730	139,781	2,501,511
1866...	80 12	46 52	37 51	23 05	2,719,137	142,469	2,861,606
1867...	87 10	43 97	38 52	23 80	3,018,079	177,149	3,195,228
1868...	92 41	49 97	39 86	24 75	3,178,537	209,364	3,387,901
1869...	92 28	48 62	40 47	26 03	3,440,762	231,143	3,671,905
1870...	91 11	55 57	38 70	27 89	3,642,456	264,811	3,907,267
1871...	91 84	58 00	41 28	26 07	3,790,222	317,573	4,107,795
1872...	80 15	55 86	41 64	28 79	3,898,156	321,407	4,219,563
1873...	82 99	56 12	40 61	29 45	3,950,610	355,192	4,305,802
1874...	82 19	59 00	41 82	29 32	4,206,398	408,101	4,614,499
1875...	72 00	57 00	47 00	31 00	4,138,371	469,592	4,787,963

*In this year and in subsequent years, instead of "Male" and "Female," read "Primary" and "High." Thus, for the year 1864, Primary, $1,956,920; High, $130,960; Total, $2,087,880.

www.ingramcontent.com/pod-product-compliance
Lightning Source LLC
LaVergne TN
LVHW021130110826
845150LV00005B/981

* 9 7 8 1 4 2 5 5 5 0 2 1 9 *